Prime Times

Second Edition

Prime Times

A Handbook for Excellence in Infant and Toddler Care

Jim Greenman

Anne Stonehouse

Gigi Schweikert

Redleaf Press®
www.redleafpress.org
800-423-8309

Published by Redleaf Press
10 Yorkton Court
St. Paul, MN 55117
www.redleafpress.org

Second edition 2008

Cover design by Mayfly Design
Cover photographs by Michael Fein
Interior typeset in Mercury and designed by Cathy Spengler
Printed in the United States of America
15 14 13 12 11 10 09 08   2 3 4 5 6 7 8 9

Photo Credits: Jim Greenman, pages 33, 84, 89, 94, 124, 182, 248, 261, 263, 270, 280, 284, 297, 305, 308; KidsFIRST, pages 52, 70, 250, 256, 272, 278; Michael Fein, pages 7, 8, 9, 21, 28, 32, 38, 41, 42, 47, 61, 67, 79, 98, 99, 133, 149, 150, 153, 156, 169, 195, 218, 245, 254, 274, 276, 280, 300, 315, 316; Steve Wewerka, page 119

The brain graphics on page 44 are from "Positron emission tomography study of human brain functional development" by Harry T. Chugani, MD, et al, in *Annals of Neurology* 22, no. 4 (October 1987), 487–97. © by Harry T. Chugani. Reprinted with permission from Harry T. Chugani.

The principal dimensions of an organized work environment on pages 141–42 are from *A Great Place to Work: Improving Conditions for Staff in Young Children's Programs* by Paula Jorde Bloom (Washington, DC: National Association for the Education of Young Children), 4. © 1997 by Paula Jorde Bloom. Reprinted with permission from Paula Jorde Bloom.

The principles listed on pages 158–59 are from *Infants, Toddlers, and Caregivers* by Janet Gonzalez-Mena and Diane Widmeyer Eyer (New York: McGraw-Hill, 1992), 9–24. © 1992 by the McGraw Hill Companies. Reprinted with permission from McGraw-Hill.

The poem "let's take a nap" on page 171 is from *Spin a Soft Black Song* by Nikki Giovanni, illustrated by George Martins (New York: Farrar, Straus and Giroux 1971, 1985). © 1971, 1985 by Nikki Giovanni. Reprinted with permission from Hill and Wang, a division of Farrar, Straus and Giroux.

High/Scope's key experiences on pages 262–66 are from "The Infant and Toddler Key Experiences— Anecdotal Examples" by Jackie Post in *Supporting Young Learners 2: Ideas for Child Care Providers and Teachers,* edited by Nancy Brickman (Ypsilanti, MI: High/Scope Press, 1996), 239–244. © 1996 by High/Scope Educational Research Foundation. Reprinted with permission from the High/Scope Educational Research Foundation.

Library of Congress Cataloging-in-Publication Data

Greenman, James T., 1949–
    Prime times : a handbook for excellence in infant and toddler programs / Jim Greenman, Anne Stonehouse, Gigi Schweikert. — 2nd ed.
        p. cm.
    Includes bibliographical references and index.
    ISBN 978-1-929610-90-7 (alk. paper)
    1. Child care—Handbooks, manuals, etc. 2. Infants—Care—Handbooks, manuals, etc.
    3. Toddlers—Care—Handbooks, manuals, etc. 4. Child care services—Management—
    Handbooks, manuals, etc. I. Stonehouse, Anne. II. Stonehouse, Anne. III. Schweikert, Gigi, 1962– IV. Title.
    HQ778.6.G74 2007
    362.71'2—dc22

                                                                        2007030772

Printed on acid-free paper

Prime Times

About the Authors

Jim Greenman

Jim Greenman is senior vice president of education and program development at Bright Horizons Family Solutions and chairman of the board of the Bright Horizons Foundation for Children. He has over thirty years of experience as an early childhood teacher, administrator, researcher, program and facility designer, college professor, and consultant. His experiences range from working with Fortune 100 companies to working with inner city and university child care, Head Start, family child care, and public school programs. He also teaches an annual institute on child care design at the Harvard Graduate School of Design.

Mr. Greenman speaks widely and has written numerous articles for magazines and journals. His books include *Caring Spaces, Learning Places: Children's Environments That Work; What Happened to MY World? Helping Children Cope with Natural Disaster and Catastrophe; Places for Childhoods: Making Quality Happen in the Real World;* and *What Happened to the World? Helping Children Cope in Turbulent Times;* and his videos include *Great Places for Childhood: Children's Environments That Work* and *Best for My Baby: Low Income Families and the Struggle to Do the Right Thing.*

Anne Stonehouse

Anne Stonehouse has worked as an author, academic, professional development speaker, and consultant in Australia and overseas for over thirty years. She has worked at the Centre for Community Child Health at the Royal Children's Hospital in Melbourne, Monash University, and the Northern Territory University.

Two of her most recent publications are *Making Links: A Collaborative Approach to Planning and Practice in Early Childhood Services* (2004, with Janet Gonzalez Mena) and *Dimensions: Excellence in Many Ways,* published in 2004 by the National Family Day Care Council.

Her significant consultancies include codeveloping *Shared Visions for Outside School Hours Care,* a resource on planning and practice for care outside of school hours widely used in Victoria and other Australian states; developing a family day care quality assurance system for the National Family Day Care Council in Australia; and working with the Office of Childcare in New South Wales to produce a curriculum framework for all services for children birth to school age.

Gigi Schweikert

Gigi Schweikert is the mother of four and an author and speaker on parenting and early childhood education. Her latest books include *There's a Perfect Little Angel in Every Child, Holding the World by the Hand,* and *I'm a Good Mother: Affirmations for the Not-So-Perfect Mom.* She contributes to periodicals and journals in the early childhood and parenting fields including *Children and Families, efamily News, Child Care Information Exchange,* and *Northwest Baby & Child.*

Gigi has over twenty years of experience in early childhood. She directed the United Nations Early Childhood Program in New York City and helped develop the Johnson & Johnson System of Family Centers. She hosted the television show *Today's Family* and is a frequent speaker known for her humor and down-to-earth parenting and teaching tips.

Acknowledgments

Bits and pieces of this book were published previously in the *Child Care Information Exchange* and in Jim Greenman's book *Caring Spaces Learning Places: Children's Environments That Work,* published by Exchange Press. We greatly appreciate the generous permission to use the material and acknowledge the support, encouragement, and friendship over the years of Bonnie and Roger Neugebauer, publishers of *Child Care Information Exchange* and Exchange Press, who have enriched all our lives and careers. Material in this book was also published originally in or adapted from Anne Stonehouse's book *A Good Beginning for Babies* (with Henry Ricciuti, NAEYC, 1975).

Janet Gonzalez-Mena has been an ongoing inspiration and source of wisdom. Her books have influenced our thinking, and we appreciate her generosity in allowing us to use her material.

A good portion of this handbook was originally developed for programs operated by Bright Horizons Family Solutions over the past twenty-five years. Bob Lurie, Marlene Weinstein, Susan Brenner, Jackie Legg, Lynne Meservey, Linda Whitehead, Margy Conley, and many others have been a source of ideas and support and contributed to original versions of material adapted here. The support of Mary Ann Tocio has been essential to completing this updated edition.

Prime Times reflects the practical wisdom of hundreds and hundreds of teachers and directors in the United States, Australia, the United Kingdom, and Ireland.

Photographs have come from a number of sources, including dozens of centers, and we owe a debt of gratitude to Bright Horizons for permission to use many photographs of its centers, children, and families. Margy Conley and the staff at Kids-FIRST@Wachovia in Philadelphia contributed numerous photographs—thanks also to the children and families of this wonderful program. Michael Fein's great photographs at the Cisco Family Connection, Universal Child Care Center, Discoveries Learning Center, and South Bay Children's Center helped make the book come alive, and we are also grateful to the children and families in those programs.

We would also like to note more than anyone our respective children—Jim's Anne and Emma; Anne's Daniel and Eric; and Gigi's Ashley, Genevieve, Marielle, and William. Our children have taught us about the joys and challenges of young children. They have always been and continue to be constant reminders of two things: when it comes to doing the right thing by children, it is a lot easier to talk, teach, and write about it than to do it, and sensitivity and sensibility come more from reading children than from reading books.

And of course we greatly appreciate the support and hard work of the staff at Redleaf Press.

Introduction: Excellence Is Complicated and Hard Won

Our experience with infant and toddler care spans eight countries, four continents, nearly every state, four territories, and a combined total of over eighty-five years—small programs, large programs, rich programs, and poor programs; programs in homes, church-based centers (above and below ground), centers both in ramshackle and multimillion-dollar state-of-the-art (a grossly overused term) buildings. We have worked with programs sponsored by universities, nonprofit agencies, government agencies, employers, unions, large for-profit companies, family child care, and mom-and-pop centers. We have been teachers, directors, consultants, trainers, and last but certainly not least, parents in child care settings. We have learned from hundreds of dedicated professionals, parents, infants, and toddlers about what works and what doesn't. All of our experience has led to one truth:

Excellence is complicated and very hard won!

Prime Times: A Handbook for Excellence in Infant and Toddler Care is intended as a general handbook for programs serving children under the age of three, and as a text for students intending to work with infants and toddlers in child care. We have tried to include enough material to help program developers and directors set up and manage programs and at the same time retain a focus on teachers as the users of the information. The material also is designed to be a useful resource for trainers and others supporting infant and toddler programs. While the basic approach and much of the information applies to family child care, a form of care we strongly endorse, the major focus is center-based care, which requires serious consideration of how to create the kind of intimate, informal, "homey," noninstitutional care that comes naturally in family child care. On the other hand, many of the ideas about organizational systems and environments included in the book will be directly relevant to family child care, particularly the type that involves family or nonfamily helpers and dedicated playrooms.

About Our Language

An explanation of the terms used in this book also serves as an introduction to some of the important issues concerning child care for very young children.

Language is a tricky business in child care, in part because of general perceptions about the relative values of caring and providing education. In a just world, *care* would be recognized as the all-encompassing term and given considerable status; *education* would be understood as one critical component of care. That is not how our world operates. Today, at least in the United States, one derives status and legitimacy primarily as an educator, more specifically as a teacher. Many centers feel driven to identify as schools. However, quality child care does not look like school, and staff do not behave like our preconceived notions of teachers. So where does that leave us in terms of nomenclature?

We prefer the term *center* to *school*, and *homebase* to *classroom*. *School* is a narrower, more institutional, and more deceptive term than the all-purpose term *center*. We prefer the term *homebase* to *classroom* because it better describes what a child care room should be: a homelike place and a base for children's daily activities. A base connotes that it is just that—a starting place for children's daily experience of life, not merely the room in which they spend their time. We have tried to avoid the homebase/classroom issue by using the word *homebase* when the term *room* did not seem to work.

We have long preferred *caregiver* to *teacher* as a generic term for those who work directly ("on the floor") with young children. But after much thought and not a little anguish, despite our preference, we no longer use the term *caregiver*. Instead we use *teacher* or *staff*. Like it or not, in America, *teacher* is the only term that gives staff the recognition they deserve as educators. The common practice of using *caregivers* for staff serving children under age three and then using *teachers* when older children are involved does a disservice to infant and toddler staff, so we use *teacher* throughout. We will make an exception to this rule and retain the term *caregiver* when referring to the primary caregiver for a child. *Note:* we believe that family child care providers are equally worthy as educators, and when we do not specifically use the term *provider,* the term *teacher* applies to them as well.

We also struggled with the terms *baby* and *toddler*. In our hypothetical ideal world (that is, the one in which care is valued and *caregivers* is the accurate term for adults working with all young children under the age of five), the term *baby* would apply to children up to two years old, and the act of toddling would not cost children their status as babies, as it does in today's headlong rush to grow up. However, recognizing that the term *baby* has become virtually synonymous with *infant,* we generally use it the same way. We use the term *toddler* to describe older babies, from about a year old to around two-and-a-half years old. The most transitional period, age two-and-a-half years to age three, is the age at which children may find themselves in toddlers, twos, or preschool groups. We think of them as twos, an age that of course overlaps with that of older toddlers.

As to the issue of gender, we have bowed to reality and used the feminine for teacher and director (fully understanding that there are males in those roles), and we have alternated between male and female when referring to individual children.

About the Book

This book is fueled by a number of convictions about how quality care for infants and toddlers actually happens.

The Importance of a Good Organization

Excellence does not happen simply because of good people. It happens when good people are hired and then provided with the organizational supports necessary to do their jobs: a decent environment, good working conditions and compensation, and a program culture that respects and develops people and values active intelligence. As centers grow larger, organizational quality assumes an even greater importance.

Good care is always the product of both sensitivity and thought—active, think-on-your-feet intelligence. Juggling the needs of individual children and families with the individual and collective needs of caregivers is complicated. There are endless trade-offs that have to be made and hourly balancing acts—everything from weighing the value of exuberant exploration against safety concerns to balancing staff-child ratios, parent fees, and teacher salaries. Leading, managing, and caregiving involve active brains as well as welcoming laps, good minds as well as good hearts.

Quality is always a balancing act. We have laid out a vision of what we consider the principles and practices that lead to excellence, and at the same time we have made it clear that there is rarely if ever a single right way to do things in the real world. We have tried to include the *why* of policies and practices, not just the *what* and the *how*. It is invariably true that those who develop and implement programs have to shape and twist practices to fit their circumstances.

Prime Times

Is it odd to think of babies and toddlers being in the prime of their lives? Not when prime means fundamental, important, and primary. The first years are when our lives are launched: the people we will become are developed then, and our sense of self, security, and what the world has to offer are shaped. These years are truly prime.

We use the term *prime times* to signify the critical importance of care and one-to-one interaction during the child's life in the program. Caring times are prime times, when the child's primal human needs for food, sleep, disposal of bodily waste, bathing, clothing, nurturing, and learning from others are addressed. These times occupy a large part of both the child's and the teacher's day in care. With a relaxed pace and gentle one-to-one contact between teacher and child that is full of language, interactions, and real give-and-take, these are prime times for developing a strong sense of personal worth and power, language, and a basic trust that the world is a good place. If the child is actively involved, respected as a person, and has personal needs met, these can be prime times for developing a sense of autonomy. And when a teacher or provider and child intimately share a moment of delight, these are prime times for discovering the joy of being human.

Rushing through diaper changing, dressing, consoling a distressed child, or sharing a child's concern in order to get back to teaching or managing children is exactly the opposite of what should happen. Those are the times to draw out, talk, listen, touch, respond, and reassure. The often-heard complaint of some staff—"All we do is care for the kids. We never get to the curriculum"—fails to recognize that those caring times are the prime teaching times: the times that the child learns through responsive care, "I am somebody, I am important."

The Importance of an Environmentally Based Program: A Literal World at Their Fingertips (and Toes, Lips, and Minds!)

We believe strongly that while the most important ingredient in good care for babies and toddlers is the quality of the staff who work with the children, what often separates high-quality programs from other programs with similar staff-child ratios, group size, and staff qualifications is not the staff but the overall environment that supports them and promotes good care and learning. A good environment works for the staff and children by supporting competence and a sense of belonging and by furthering the program's goals and objectives.

Our book emphasizes an approach built on the learning environment rather than an activity-oriented curriculum. We call this a *world at their fingertips*. The educational program does not happen *in* the environment; rather, the environment *is* the curriculum.

An all-day program has many hours into which learning experiences can be built. An environment set up to allow children to explore independently, to discover and play, also allows the staff to focus on prime times. A rich, responsive learning environment set up to engage children with valuable learning experiences allows each child to have the full human presence of a teacher to encourage and share the delight of discovery.

Neither infants nor toddlers benefit from large-group learning. Three or four is a large group for an infant or a toddler. They can enjoy each other and learn from each other better in very small-group environments. An environmentally based program allows individual play, play in pairs, and small-group play to occur simultaneously and minimizes the times when all children are doing the same thing or spending time as part of a crowd.

An environmentally based program assumes that children learn from the entire experience the day provides. The ways that time and space are structured, the routines, the furnishings, the equipment and materials, and all the ways adults and children behave teach young children what the world is like, how it works, what they are capable of, and their place in that world. Much of the staff's planning revolves around how to build learning into the environment. What furnishings provide learning (for example, a couch that also serves as a walking rail)? What equipment creates a sensory or reaching and kicking activity center? While some adult-initiated and -led activities such as a simple cooking experience or sensory play with fingerpaints may take place, the program should not be activity based; that is, structured around activity times or groups. Music may take place anytime, as may some large-motor experiences. Activities take place individually and in small groups within an environment rich with built-in learning.

The Importance of the Family-Staff Partnership

Only when families and staff work in partnership is high quality possible, because the family's experience of child care is as important as their children's direct experience. Good quality inherently includes parents feeling satisfied, competent, and in control of their children's care. Unlike school, child care serves families and recognizes both the similarities and the differences in needs, concerns, and values that each family brings to the program. There are no such things as good centers, good homes, or good staff that dictate the right way to parents or that exclude parents from influencing their children's care. Excellence is a true partnership of mutual respect and sharing of power that results in individualized care based on parental values and concerns.

Using the Book

This book is designed as a handbook for the training of students, center staff, and leaders, and as a guide for program development. It offers a logical sequence for going through the material, and also functions as a reference that can sit on a shelf in a center and answer questions about practice as needed. This handbook offers four parts, plus numerous supplements on a CD-ROM:

- Part 1: The Context of Good Care: Good Organizations for Infant and Toddler Care
- Part 2: Organizing the Program
- Part 3: Quality Care and Learning
- Part 4: Staying Good: Evaluation and Quality Control
- A CD-ROM offers practical forms, handouts, checklists, assessments, and additional training exercises to supplement the training and implementation of the principles and practices covered in this book

Part 1 explores the real world of child care that every program operates in—a world in which child care is not completely understood and is undervalued. Chapter 1 is appropriate for caregivers as well as administrators, because both need a broad perspective on the range of program alternatives. Quality comes in different packages, with a number of thorny issues and few easy or absolute answers; it is important for everyone to comprehend the complexity of child care in order to avoid simplistic views. Teachers should understand and respect the issues directors face just as directors should understand and respect the difficulties confronted every day by teachers. We have witnessed many instances when narrow thinking has created divisions, such as when individuals refuse to respect the challenges faced by people in other roles. Excellence is an outgrowth of team effort.

In part 1 we also examine how centers work, the characteristics of good organizations, and, in chapter 3, what high-quality care for infants, toddlers, and their families really looks like.

Part 2 begins with two chapters on understanding infants and toddlers—what to expect and what is most important to keep in mind about their development and needs for care. This part addresses the structure of a high-quality program, how children are grouped, and how time and space are structured to achieve the personalized care, individualized education, and relaxed, happy days characteristic of quality care. Also included are chapters that explore how programs partner with families and create a good place for staff.

Part 3 describes the what, why, and how of good programming, and the policies and practices that lead to a high-quality experience for young children. Chapter 11 describes in detail what good care is. Chapter 12 analyzes caring routines. Chapter 13 addresses the critically important issue of how to ensure the health and safety of every child. Chapter 14 looks at socialization and guidance, and chapter 15 considers adult-child interactions—the caregiver as teacher. Chapter 16 looks at curriculum and learning in terms of what experiences are important. Chapters 17 and 18 focus on the indoor and outdoor learning environment that a quality program provides for babies and toddlers. Chapter 19 provides a process for planning the learning experience.

Chapter 20 recognizes that "good enough never is," and that quality depends on monitoring, evaluation, and change. Chapter 20 also discusses useful tools for program evaluation, and the importance of accreditation and standards.

The CD-ROM provides supplemental forms, handouts, notes to parents and staff, assessments, and training exercises in order to promote efforts toward quality. And while this supplementary material offers practical and convenient ideas and information, it is just that—additional information. It is by no means an exhaustive source of all that is necessary to make high-quality infant and toddler care a reality. The additional material is intended for practical use and to inspire programs to create their own useful tools.

A Final Word

Group care for infants and toddlers, particularly toddlers, is inherently challenging, however favorable the human and material resources available to a program. A handbook is more a guide than a script; it needs to be used wisely and adapted to the particulars of each setting. We all still have a lot to learn about how to make quality care happen.

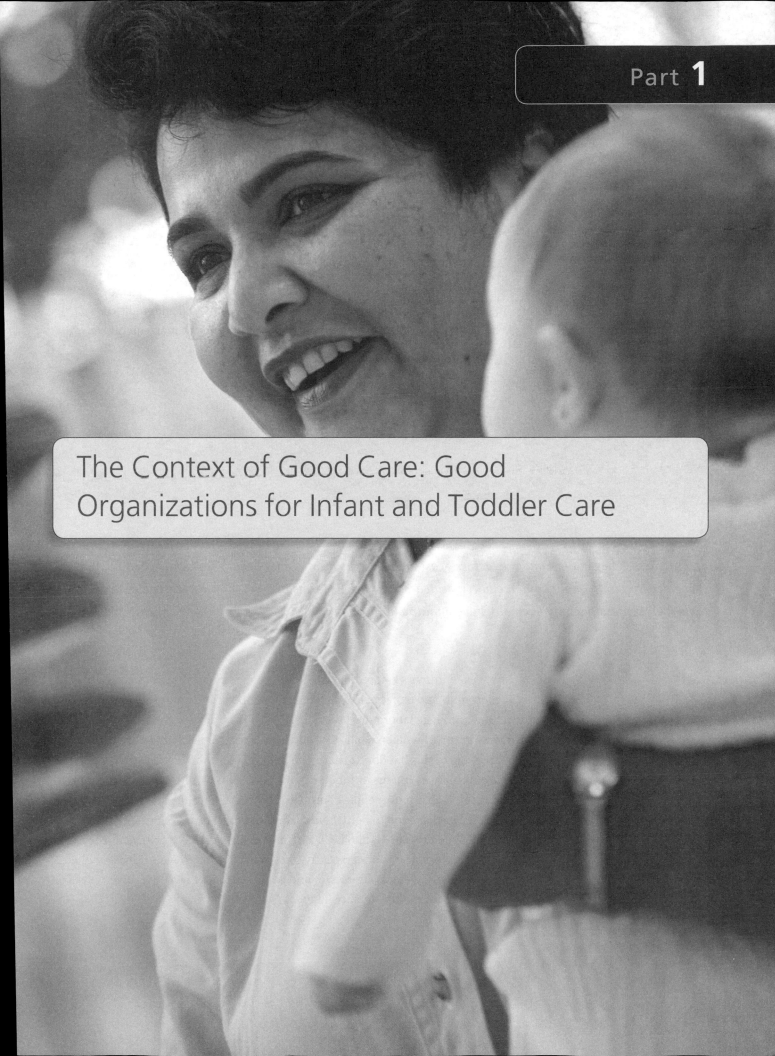

Part 1

The Context of Good Care: Good
Organizations for Infant and Toddler Care

Chapter 1

Child Care in the Real World

Excellence *Teachers have a realistic perspective on the world of early care and education for infants and toddlers. They understand the factors—cost, quality, and affordability—that shape child care and they recognize that both quality and mediocrity can assume various forms in different settings. Their knowledge fuels their professional involvement and commitment to quality.*

Who cares for infants and toddlers? People come to programs from a variety of backgrounds and experiences, ranging from child rearing and babysitting to student teaching in college laboratory programs. Walk into good programs, and you will find a diverse group of women of all ages, and even a few men. Chances are that they and many readers of this handbook share one point of common history: they were not enrolled in child care as infants or toddlers (of course, you wouldn't remember anyway!). The result is that most people coming to child care have neither life experience nor professional background to help them place child care issues in perspective and understand what quality care is and isn't. But such a perspective is critical, for teachers as well as directors. Without perspective, we are apt to narrow our ideas of what does and doesn't work, what matters a lot and what matters only a little. This leaves us with fewer options for making quality happen.

Before getting to the nuts and bolts of good care for infants and toddlers, it is useful to tour the real world of child care providers, centers, and homes, and to look at the issues that child care programs face.

Infant-Toddler Care in Centers Is Now Mainstream

While not every family uses group early care and education today, nearly every sort of parent and family is now found at centers, as well as at family child care homes: rich, poor, professional, single parents, extended families, rural, urban, and from all cultures. That is a big change from the past, when child care existed on the margins of society, mostly as a social service for families labeled *broken* or for children termed *disadvantaged,* or as a cottage industry of largely unregulated homes and small mom-and-pop centers for low- and moderate-income families.

Today, infants and toddlers are in centers to stay, and the world of child care centers has changed in many ways to encompass a wide range of programs. Centers range from the small programs to large centers of up to 300 children or more. Centers are sponsored by a wide range of employers, including Fortune 500 companies such as Johnson & Johnson, Toyota, and Citibank; professional firms or small businesses; universities and institutions, such as the United Nations, the FBI, the Pentagon, the World Bank, and the International Monetary Fund; and sports organizations such as the Professional Golf Association. Television and movie studios, the professional golf tours, and nearly every other kind of employer provide child care for working families, many operated by companies like Bright Horizons Family Solutions. Small, owner-operated centers predominate, and some have expanded into local or regional chains of centers.

Large child care companies such as Kinder Care, Knowledge Learning, and Children's World have come together as Knowledge Learning Corporation, with over 2,200 centers. Regional companies are growing as well. While some nonprofit, community-based centers have gone out of business, many have expanded.

What is likely to happen in the twenty-first century to the world of infant and toddler care? It's probable that the number of parents using group care will continue to grow, and if current trends are an indication, more and more parents will choose centers over homes. Barring major changes in economic conditions or sociopolitical thinking, the current mixture of large and small, for-profit and nonprofit, public and private programs will continue. Employer-sponsored care will grow slowly but steadily. Sadly, quality is likely to remain uneven unless high-quality standards are adopted nationally and public financial support increases.

A Note about Family Child Care

Regulated and nonregulated family child care—that is, care in the home of a non-relative—still accounts for much of the child care available for infants and toddlers in the United States. Family child care provides some of the best and worst care available. At their best, family child care homes are wonderful places for young children: the small scale, informality, and richness of the home environment allow for personalized care, experiential active learning, and enduring relationships between providers who love what they do and children and families—the next best thing to a good family and home environment. Family child care homes are undervalued as learning environments for young children. A good home can offer a rich variety of experiences and sensorimotor learning—different textures, sounds, sights, lighting, props, and furniture to crawl on, over, under, around, and in. When children are involved in the life of the home—cooking, cleaning, shopping, doing laundry—as well as in planned experiences, opportunities for language and other developmentally appropriate experiences abound. However, homes that try to mimic center care without taking advantage of home life and that restrict children largely to a playroom often offer care that is marginal at best.

At their worst, family child care homes are dispiriting places subject to little outside scrutiny or regulation. They may not offer infants and toddlers more than confinement and the hypnotic stimulation of the television. When home-based caregivers are untrained, uninterested, motivated primarily by money or obligation to family or friends, homes offer little to children.

The Wrong Question: Is Child Care Good for Infants and Toddlers?

Research on child care is reported frequently in the media. These studies, sometimes indiscriminately grouped together, focus on a recurring question: "Is child care bad for kids?" The coverage is often reported in a sensational way that causes parents to agonize over whether to use child care. For many parents already prone to bouts of child care guilt ("Should I stay home with my child?"), the media's sensationalization of research only makes it worse. Granted, sometimes there might be a positive story— "Does child care make children smarter?"—but these stories also distort the issue, as if the goal of child care is to improve children.

Research is is not designed to produce a headline verdict on child care, which is part of the fabric of society and is here to stay, but rather to uncover the factors that have significant effects on outcomes in children. Research may identify questions and issues, but it seldom offers much specific wisdom for parents. Child care decisions are interwoven with the many decisions parents need to make about child rearing, career, income, and family life. The realistic question for parents is rarely quite as simple as "Should I stay home?"

There is no question that group out-of-home care in centers and homes will have some effects on an individual child's social growth and behavior—some positive, some negative. The same is true, of course, of care at home from a parent, or in other care arrangements. As with all parenting choices, there are pluses and minuses to group life, pluses and minuses to the alternatives.

No study has really effectively controlled for quality beyond the more easily measurable factors of ratio, group size, and staff qualifications. Child development research does not offer much specific information to guide child care practitioners.

After all the research is taken into account, it is probably safe to say that the best arrangement for a child under three is to be at home with an engaged parent who is eager to stay home, when a family can afford to make that choice. There is also little question that the worst arrangement is a usually a group setting of low quality. The debate about outcomes chiefly concerns options that lie between these two extremes. Most research evidence points to the conclusion that high-quality child care by a nanny, a family child care provider, a child care center, or a relative has no lasting negative developmental consequences and may have some positive effects on the child. Mediocre or low-quality child care certainly has some negative quality-of-life effects (as does low-quality care within a family) and may negatively affect a child's development, but those effects need more study. The real lesson of research is that quality matters for the well-being of both children and families. A child care program could be good for a child and or it could be bad. The question for parents is not whether to use child care but rather what variables are important and how to identify and find good child care. Infant and toddler care is here to stay, and research can help support the need for greater investment in high-quality early care and education. The question for society is how to make child care good for all children and families. When fewer than 8 percent of centers in the United States are accredited by the National Association for the Education of Young Children (NAEYC), that is a profound and essential question.

The High Cost of Quality

There is a reason why quality child care is a scarce commodity. The most fundamental factor that shapes the quality of infant and toddler care is obvious: care is very expensive, and that is true even of stripped-down, bare-bones, not very good care. Providing care for infants and toddlers is always going to be costly because it is labor-intensive: programs need good staff-child ratios to provide quality care (1 to 3 or 1 to 4 for infants, 1 to 4 or 1 to 5 for toddlers under age two, 1 to 5 or 1 to 6 for two-years-olds). Because continuity of caregivers is as important as good ratios, using volunteers, student interns, or other short-term staff to keep the staffing cost down is a good idea only to supplement and not to replace regular staff. Using an assortment of people short-term creates huge problems if it is not done well.

> ### The Cost of Ratios
>
> To understand why infant and toddler care will almost always be expensive, consider this: an elementary school classroom usually has one teacher per 20 to 35 students. The cost—salary and benefits—of that teacher and classroom is spread across those students. Now think about early care and education. A preschool classroom usually has 2 teachers for 16–24 children, a toddler room has 2 teachers for 8–10 children, and an infant room has 2 teachers for 6–8 children. The infant teacher's cost is usually the same as a toddler or preschool teacher's cost, but it is paid for by the tuitions of only 6–8 children, fewer than the tuition paid for toddlers or preschoolers.

High personnel costs and the need to keep parents' fees down usually lead to tight budgets. Center fees are also subject to a downward pressure in most communities because other child care options for infants and toddlers (in-home care by friends and relatives and family child care) are undervalued and usually cost quite a bit less. Tight program budgets lead to low salaries, at or close to minimum staff-child ratios, and limited spending on furnishings and equipment.

> **Quality?**
>
>   **Minimum staffing**
> \+ **Minimum salaries**
> \+ **Minimum space**
> \+ **Minimum societal support**
> ─────────────────
> = **What kind of quality?**

Caregivers and families experience the results: regulations that represent relatively minimal standards. Regulations, which are supposed to be floors below which no service is allowed to go, lest children be harmed, unfortunately serve as ceilings that many programs struggle to achieve. The expectation seems to be that quality will somehow emerge from minimal staffing, minimal salaries, minimal space, and minimal support. Of course, it usually does not.

There are good, mediocre, and downright bad programs under every sort of sponsorship, in every kind of setting, in the for-profit, nonprofit, and public sectors. The availability of quality is really a market-niche issue: it grows out of the ability of parents to pay, the availability of funding from public and private sources beyond parent tuition, the available talent pool, professional and public notions of quality, prevailing practices, and parents' expectations.

There are even fewer people available with knowledge and expertise on the practice of group care for infants and toddlers than with knowledge of preschool programming. Unfortunately, the view that the care and education of infants is less intellectually challenging still prevails. As will become clear throughout this handbook, infant and toddler care is not only inherently expensive, it is also conceptually and operationally complex. Even good funding is no guarantee of quality. Good staff, educated in infant and toddler care and participating in ongoing training, increase the probability of quality programs.

Sketches from the Real World

People who visit many programs are likely to make a number of discoveries:

Quality comes in many different shapes and sizes, and so does its dismal cousin, mediocrity. Both are seen in large and small programs, new facilities and church basements, those with college-trained staff and experienced staff with vocational training, for-profit and nonprofit programs. Some programs look good to a visitor and feel bad to a baby or parent. Some programs may not look so wonderful but are great for a toddler or parent.

Mediocrity is a lot more common than quality. Most programs are victims of the minimums—in funding, wages, facility, ratios, and training. For the most part, the people involved—aides, directors, family child care providers, trainers, and support services—make terrific efforts. But in a sense they are often asked to construct child care shantytowns, creating good places for babies using underpaid staff, spaces and materials that are cobbled together, and all the energy, love, and commitment they can muster.

Following are some composite sketches of what one is likely to encounter in the real world of child care.

See Supplement: *An Insider's Guide to Quality Child Care*

Nelson's Family Child Care

Karen Nelson has been taking care of five or six children for the last eighteen years; in fact, she has two children of former children she cared for. She usually has two or three children under the age of three. Her own children are grown and help out occasionally. Karen's child care children are swept up into the life of her home. Their cooking, cleaning, running errands, and helping Karen's husband Jerry with projects add richness to the planned experiences, toys, and games that Karen provides. Karen's training over the years through the local resource and referral agency has led her to make a conscious effort to build language, math, and self-help skills into the children's participation in home life.

Preschool children have jobs, and school-age children help with the youngest children. Clearly, each child is treated like an individual family member, and infants and toddlers are on individualized schedules. The multiage setting allows infants and toddlers opportunities to interact with older children much of the time. Karen always has a waiting list for children under two.

Karen is considering expanding into becoming a group family home care. With a full-time assistant, she can be licensed to serve twelve children. If she lived in a neighboring state, she would need to be licensed as a center. She is planning to convert a porch into a three-season space available to children when her program expands.

The Y Children's Center

The Y Center recently expanded and is licensed for 110 children, plus thirty school-age children when school is out. While it has been renovated, the wear and tear

---

"How Can You Make Money Off Children?"

That question is asked in outrage by some advocates, and in curiosity by entrepreneurs. The United States has a market economy. Unlike schools, but like health care, child care has always depended on a mixed system: for-profit, nonprofit, and public child care. While the number of ideologues is diminishing, a small number of critics still believe that for-profit child care is inherently wrong; others believe that nonprofits and public child care offer unfair competition.

Is there a moral issue here? Perhaps for a few, but the more important issues are quality care for children and families and good employment for caregivers. Providing low-quality services, exploiting staff, and gouging consumers to increase profits or surplus are indefensible—whomever the sponsor, for-profit or nonprofit. The practices of some nonprofit agencies can mirror that of some for-profits, with high overhead and indirect costs accessed to fund other departments, replacing profit. The for-profit sector has brought growth and child care alternatives to many communities because of its access to capital through venture capital, family investment, and profits plowed back into the business. Competition has resulted in a stronger focus on customer service and a variety of service offerings in the for-profit sector. Whether you believe there should be a national child care system or a completely market-driven system, it is important to judge child care providers by their practices and outcomes, not their business models.

shows. But the rooms are ample and most have exterior windows. Most of the staff have been there for years (pay scales are high for the area), are well trained, and have degrees or certifications. Funding from the United Way and the county supports the center. While quality has fluctuated over the past fifteen years, the program is in good shape and has been reaccredited many times by NAEYC. The Y is doing a capital campaign to renovate or construct a new building.

The infants and toddlers are in rooms with experienced staff, and the atmosphere is both quietly nurturing and active. Children are crawling over and under various pieces of equipment, sloshing at a water table, and preparing for a walk. Parents and children are greeted warmly.

The center has a mission to serve low-income and single-parent families, but because of cuts in subsidy funding for poor families, more of the families are middle class. Parent support and education are built into the program budget.

Barbara's Babes

Barbara's Babes takes only children under age three and is licensed for twenty-eight children. Barbara owns and runs the center, which is adjacent to her house. Open for ten years, the center has a good reputation: "Barbara cares about kids and families." She has core staff who have been with her since opening, although turnover is a problem with her assistant positions. Staff-child ratios are better than state minimums, and Barbara's constant presence helps alleviate problems. The center is very expensive because there are no older children to offset the cost, but Barbara has an affluent clientele.

Children in Barbara's program get a lot of loving in a good learning environment, and there are ample supplies of toys and materials, some designed by Barbara. Parents are enthusiastic, and many rely on Barbara as their advisor on a range of child-rearing questions.

Barbara is unabashedly entrepreneurial and has opened up a second center for preschool children. Active in the local child care community, although occasionally at odds with the nonprofits, Barbara is something of a model of the successful small businessperson in child care. She understands that her market niche is upper-income child care. She knows what her customers want and provides it for them.

Kidz World

The Oak Park Kidz World is part of a local chain of ten centers, with more being added. At first glance, the center is appealing, with a homelike sloped roof, lots of windows, and a fenced yard with swings and a climber. The center is licensed for 150 children in a compact building of fewer than 10,000 square feet. Inside, it is crowded and noisy, and the voluminous amount of artwork on the walls of the brightly colored, narrow corridors combines with harsh florescent lighting and gleaming tile floors to make you feel as if you are walking through a kaleidoscope. Each room is filled with children and two staff, some of whom look very young, some of whom seem overwhelmed. Ratios are at state minimums, and sometimes less at the beginning and end of the day. Salaries are low and staff turnover is high.

The infant room has lots of toys, rocking chairs, high chairs, and cribs. Babies seem to be held and soothed more than stimulated. Older babies are often discouraged from motor exploration. Schedules are only partially individualized, and all children seem to be on the same schedule by the age of nine or ten months.

The toddler room is chaotic and hard for visitors to endure: fourteen toddlers and two staff try very hard to do activities mostly suited to the older two-year-olds in the group. Biting and general distress seem to be common. Neither staff nor children seem relaxed or happy.

For the most part, parents are happy with the center, except for staff turnover and the times when biting reaches epidemic levels. The moderate fees are a big attraction when compared to the higher fees of the Y Children's Center and Barbara's Babes.

A couple of miles away, the same company has a center that feels quite different. A new building has slightly more room and better lighting, giving it a homier feel. The young, enthusiastic director has managed to motivate the staff despite the low salaries. She has provided some training for staff on developmentally appropriate care, and the center is hoping to try for some form of accreditation in the future.

Corporate Kids Development Center

The Corporate Kids Development Center serves around 250 children and is housed in a new, 14,000-square-foot, self-proclaimed state-of-the-art building designed for child care. Using security badges, parents enter with their children. The building is new and impressive, but the spaces are still tight. There is a lot of natural light, wide corridors, and bathrooms in each room; support space (offices and a staff lounge/workroom); a full kitchen; and a large playground. There are two infant rooms, three toddler rooms, and two rooms for two-year-olds in a separate wing. The center also has six rooms for preschoolers and schoolagers. Staff love the building, except for one thing that is all too reminiscent of the less-advantaged programs they came from: small homebases and cramped storage. New buildings are, per square foot, expensive to build, and once support space is added, something has to go. Often it is homebase space or storage. There is some multipurpose space available to reduce the number of children in each room. Staff-child ratios are above state minimums, but group sizes are fairly small. Salaries are slightly less than at the Y, and benefits are fairly limited. Staff have breaks, some training, and limited planning time, but turnover is still fairly high.

The program is formal, institutional, fairly academic, and very well received by parents looking for a "good school." The children seem happy.

New Generations Early Care and Education Center

New Generation is an employer-sponsored center, similar to Corporate Kids, and is run by a national company. It is large, with over 250 children in a new building of 22,000 square feet. The feel of the center is that of a thriving community of learning

"We are not just day care, we are educational!"

"We are not just day care!" is a refrain used by many homes and centers as well as by Head Start, nursery schools, and schools to enhance their image or to set themselves apart from their competition. The seven centers described here go to considerable lengths to assure parents that they are indeed schools or early education centers. They also aim to make it clear, either by insinuation or open criticism, that family child care and many other centers offer little more than custodial care.

But is there such a thing as *just* day care? No. All child care is educational: children learn something in every setting, whether we acknowledge it or not, and that learning has implications for future learning. Is it all good education? No—in fact, some is actually quite awful. Many centers and homes are not adequately funded to provide good early education. Others may suffer from lack of understanding or ambition. Poor, underfunded learning environments provide poor educational experiences and, most often, poor care as well.

The program name or sponsor is no sure indicator of educational value. Good and bad care and education take place in programs calling themselves schools, child development centers, day care or child care homes, academies, nursery schools, Head Start, learning centers, and Montessori programs.

While most programs run from the term *day care* because of the negative connotation ("We don't take care of days," sniff the experts), it is a term that accurately reflects the critical distinction between programs in their complexity and purpose: all-day or part-day. That said, most programs would be advised to recognize that using the term *day care* puts them at a perceptual disadvantage when marketing.

and caring, and the scale feels much smaller. The feeling of community has been created by the design of the building, which offers community gathering places and ample space for display and documentation, and by the practices and culture of the operating company, which empower staff. The space is efficiently designed and staff-friendly; it offers adequate storage, natural light, and decent-sized rooms. The rooms are arranged in family groupings (infant, toddler, twos, preschoolers) with shared family rooms. The playground has a natural feel to it, with trees and shrubs.

Thanks to the sponsor, the salaries are above market rate and the child care company providing the program is known for its good benefits, working conditions, and an organizational quality that supports directors and teachers. Staff morale is high, and parents love the center. The program is accredited by NAEYC.

Park Methodist

Park Methodist Center was established for children from low-income families, and almost all Park Methodist's families receive a subsidy to attend. The director is constantly searching for new support to supplement unpredictable state funding. Although the center is housed in a church, its rooms are a good size and have been renovated. The core staff have worked in the center for five to ten years and live in the community. Staff-child ratios are at state minimums. Furnishings and equipment are barely adequate, and there is no playground area suitable for infants and toddlers.

The children seem to be prized by their teachers, although infants are more likely to be held than encouraged to actively explore. Young toddlers are treated much like the infants, and older toddlers much like the threes. There is quite a bit of correction and redirection.

Parents and staff are from the same community and often have relationships outside of child care.

This is both a source of support and a problem, because little that goes on at home or in the center is a secret for long.

Williams Child Care

In a low- and moderate-income neighborhood, Williams Child Care is making a heroic effort to survive after two years. It has a capacity for sixty children, and struggles to keep tuitions down and staff salaries above minimum wage. A mom-and-pop, for-profit center (profit in name only), it has husband-and-wife owners who work hard to provide safe, caring, decent-quality care. The rooms are small and the program is only marginally appropriate for toddlers' and preschoolers' development. The infant room has a great feel to it because of Miss Amelia, who clearly adopts each baby and family. Because state subsidies have been cut and the reimbursement rate is low (75 percent of the market rate), enrollment is a huge issue: the center needs preschoolers. How long Mr. and Mrs. Williams can keep the center afloat is unclear.

It Takes All Kinds

These centers and home are sketches of commonly found kinds of centers. They serve different clientele and thrive or struggle because of different circumstances. Some are favored by support beyond parents' tuition, by affluent families, or by dedicated staff, while others are not. The children and families in all would benefit from more societal support.

Cost, Quality, and Affordability

Obviously there is a direct relationship between cost, quality, and affordability. Usually only centers with affluent populations who can afford high fees can offer high-quality care without additional sources of support beyond parents' tuitions. That support is usually the public, an employer, the United Way, a church, staff that stay despite minimal wages, or the unpaid labor of love that goes into a mom-and-pop center. It is also usual for the preschool rate to subsidize the infant and toddler rates, because it is difficult to charge the true cost of caring for infants and toddlers. At New Generations and the Y centers, the actual cost of care is high, which shows in the quality of their programs. It is less so at the Corporate Kids Development Center. At all three centers, parents pay high fees, though less than the highest market rate, and the rates are supplemented further by tuition assistance for moderate-income families. Barbara's Babes costs the most. Oak Park Kidz World and Williams Child Care have moderate fees, and their programs' struggles with untrained staff and turnover are reflected in their low fees. Nelson's Family Child Care is less costly and certainly the best value, but only a small, select group of families hear about the home and actually get in. Park Methodist's rates are on par with Kidz World, but it has few private-pay families; most receive public subsidy.

Individualized Care and Special Needs

Individualized care is a critical quality outcome for infants and toddlers (and parents). Recognizing, appreciating, and addressing differences is essential and will be stressed throughout this book. Children are all special, with special needs that change as they participate in a child care program. Whether special needs are the result of a sleepless night, illness, separation problems, growth spurts, an injury, culture shock, individual differences in temperament and physiology, or a more serious and permanent condition, the result is the same: *the program needs to fit the child,* not the reverse!

Staff in many programs may encounter infants and toddlers with special needs that lie beyond the range of what is typical developmentally for the child's age: children with physical, emotional, cognitive, or family needs that require even more individualized attention. Because infants and toddlers are so new to the world and are in the first stages of development, their special needs may not be suspected or identified prior to coming to child care.

Staff have to understand that these children belong in child care because of family need, because it's good for society not to isolate and segregate children with differing abilities, and because it's the law. The Americans with Disabilities Act (ADA) entitles people with disabilities to have equal access to public services and public accommodations. Working parents of children with disabilities have the same need for child care that other parents do. Under ADA, programs have the responsibility to make reasonable accommodations to serve children and parents with disabilities. What is reasonable is in part determined by program resources, but programs may have to provide extra training, make changes in the facility, or alter program operations, including adjusting staff-child ratios.

Providing good child care to children with special needs is not the same as providing therapeutic or remedial services. The goals are the same as for any other child: high-quality care and education that fit each child's individual needs. While some centers may be able to provide specialists who offer special therapeutic or developmental services, all programs should partner with parents to identify resources that allow the child access to services beyond child care.

"That's Not Quality!"

"I thought this center believed in quality, and you are changing that," said the veteran teacher to the new director, after hearing of the proposal to change the staff-infant ratio from 1 to 3 to 1 to 4, a change suggested to cope with a budget crisis and to avoid falling further behind on staff salaries. "How can you do this to us?" she complained, refusing to listen to the director's explanation that the recent, extensive facility renovation may have boosted quality significantly enough to more than compensate for the ratio change.

"That's not quality!" is a charge sometimes hurled whenever a change is suggested. In the real world, quality is an outcome and a moving target, not a simple set of program characteristics. How many programs have the funding for great ratios, salaries, facilities, and other supports, unless they serve the very affluent or manage to acquire exceptional funding? One program element— as important as ratios—is not a cast-in-stone, quality determinant. To calm down the teacher and moderate her feelings somewhat, the director ended up taking her to visit two similar NAEYC-accredited programs with 1 to 4 ratios, as well as some less supportive facilities.

Mainstreaming children with special needs (integrating them into regular programs) certainly makes sense for all the children in the program. The children with special needs will learn more by being around other children and are more likely to be seen and to see themselves as full human beings with different abilities. Typically developing children benefit as well by being exposed to all sorts of children and by taking part in a program that recognizes and adapts to the special needs of all children.

When serving children with special needs, keep in mind that they will thrive in the least restrictive environment—that is, in an environment that allows them to have experiences much like those available for typically developing children.

Of course, not all programs have the resources and expertise to serve all children with special needs. What is important is that child care professionals understand and accept that it is normal, expected, and right to serve children and families with a range of needs.

A Final Word: Quality Child Care Requires Financial Support

It is not unusual for some issues about quality to be discussed as if they bear little relationship to funding: building better facilities; adopting practices such as the best ratios, group sizes, or staffing patterns; continuity-of-care practices such as "looping" (having teachers stay with children for the first two or three years in the program, and then starting with a new group of babies). But all these items compete for funding with each other as well as with improving salaries and benefits and lowering parents' fees. The above-described centers with the greatest number of challenges to high quality were mostly struggling with a lack of funding rather than with a lack of motivation to be good or with a lack of knowledge.

Improving child care at a societal level will require more financial support from somewhere, probably from everywhere: the public, employers, foundations, and parents. Issues regarding the form of care (home or center), sponsorship of care (private, public, employers), for-profit or nonprofit, program ideology, and even training have far less significance than the need for better funding. But funding will probably never be optimal, and all programs have the responsibility to maximize the resources they have. High quality in the real world, as opposed to quality described on a page in a book or in the college classroom, is complicated and hard won.

exercises

1. Visit three centers or homes that represent the types of programs sketched in this chapter. Look for and record differences in philosophy and approach.

2. Ask the administrator of the center or home how they are able to stay in business financially, if there is any support beyond parents' fees, what are the biggest challenges the program faces, and what is the center's competition? Record the answers.

3. Interview three or four early education professionals and ask them what they see as the differences (if any) between centers calling themselves "day care centers" or "child development centers," and "nursery schools" or "preschools." What's the basis for their name choice? Are their answers based on operational differences, labels, or bias? Record the results.

4. Look through the Yellow Pages (paper or online) under "child care" and "preschool" to get an idea of the child care marketplace in your area. Call or visit the local child care resource and referral agency (CCR&R) and ask for a description of the child care opportunities available to families. How does the CCR&R determine the "child care/education" distinction? Record your observations and the responses

Chapter 2

Understanding How Child Care Centers Work: The Center as an Organization

excellence *The program maximizes both material and human resources by developing an organization and creating a culture that can provide consistently high-quality care for all children and families and is viewed by staff as a great place to work.*

How many times have you heard or thought that good care for young children all boils down to good people? This is certainly true for care in the child's home, fairly true in family child care, but only partly true in center-based care. Many things have to be carefully thought through and organized before "good people" can lead to good care for an infant or toddler.

Most members of the general public have a simple conceptual model of good child care.

Is It Really This Simple?

Good people (aka women?)

+ **Toys and books**

+ **Adequate space (aboveground, windows preferred but not essential)**

= **Good child care**

No!

Good people are vital to quality, but so much more is involved.

Some people might elaborate this simple model slightly: *enough* means good staff-child ratios and group sizes; *good people* means trained, well-paid people; *toys* are educational materials; and *space* should be better than minimal. But even with these elaborations, the simple model is far too simple, at least for centers serving more than twenty children.

The Key Elements of an Organization

What children and parents experience over time in a center is a reflection of organizational quality, not just the quality of the individual people. People come and go, but the framework they work within continues. This framework is more than the building and equipment; it includes all the resources, systems, policies, routines, and cultures of the center—"the way we do things here." Organizational quality ensures that good people are hired, stay, grow on the job, and receive the support to perform well. It also ensures that children (and parents) are well cared for and that everyone involved feels like a member of a community.

Making Quality Happen: Organizational Dimensions

Human Resources	Impact through	Physical Resources	Impact through
People	Hiring	Facility	Design
• Talents	Orientation	Equipment	Budget
• Motivation	Training	Outdoor environment	Selection
• Continuity	Recognition	Community resources	Policies
	Reward		Culture
	Supervision		
	Culture		

Organization & Systems	Impact through	Organizational Culture	Impact through
Organization and distribution of:	Policies	"The way we do things here"	Training
• People	Training	Shared beliefs and values	Communication
• Physical resources	Supervision	• Stories, symbols, rituals	Leadership
• Authority	Communication	• Norms and expectations	Supervision
• Ideas	Structures	Behavior norms	
• Recognition		• Taboos	
• Information		• Shared feelings and attitudes	

Human Resources

Those good people—where do they all come from? What is the talent pool that the center draws from? Why do staff stay at the center? How do they become good or get better at caring for young children?

Good child care for infants and toddlers is built around good people performing well and staying. The talent pool—the population eligible and available to draw employees from—varies from center to center and depends on the demographics of the area, the center's requirements for the job, and the desirability of the center as a workplace. It changes with the state of the economy and the competition for talent. When a center is having trouble finding good people, what is considered "good" may have to be reconsidered—perhaps the definition is too narrow. Are there good teachers for infants and toddlers out there who simply lack credentials? Are there older people, and/or people from a variety of cultural or other kinds of backgrounds? Is your center a good place to work if you are relatively old or young, male, or from a particular cultural background? Is it a good place to work if you have a disability but are still able to do a good job?

Physical Resources

Infant and toddler care happens in a place filled with furnishings and equipment. Are the furnishings and equipment adequate and in good repair? Is the space a good place to be a young child and to be with a young child—suited for reasonable group sizes, offering good acoustics, supporting convenient care and learning? What are the surroundings like? Are there resources to be tapped—sidewalks, parks, libraries? Are there negative elements to be screened out and avoided—toxic land, smells, sounds, unsavory people, or harmful animals or pests?

Organizational Structures and Systems

Distribution of human resources. Resources have to be distributed. How are people distributed throughout the center? Are there noncontact staff who take care of management, cleaning, cooking, and all those other jobs that have to be done in addition to being with children? Beyond adequate ratios and staffing requirements, what about staff expertise and talent: are knowledge and talent spread evenly? Are staff placed so that they can capitalize on their expertise and strengths? The distribution of knowledge, authority, responsibility, and information involves choices that may lead to greater or lesser quality. Does a teacher's skill at curriculum or organization go beyond her own group of infants and toddlers? Are program and homebase decisions made by isolated individuals, a small team, or everyone involved, or are they often not made at all but merely assumed because of fear of conflict, simple inertia, or unquestioning acceptance of past practices?

Distribution of physical resources. The distribution of physical resources obviously involves choices that have implications for quality. What determines the use of particular spaces and equipment: decisions made long ago and not revisited, staff seniority or the force of assertive personalities, or interpersonal relationships or staff politics? It is not uncommon to discover that staff who have been there the longest have the most resources, and that the use of multipurpose space depends on the relationships between caregivers.

Information flow. Information always flows. However, without systems, communication may be intermittent and may follow lines of happenstance or friendship, leading to confusion, misunderstanding, ill will, gossip, and missed opportunities.

Organizational Culture

"That's just the way we do things here." Good centers, like all good organizations, have cultures that shape how their members think, feel, and behave. Just like the culture we are born into, the established organizations we join come with worlds of shared beliefs and values, behavioral norms, and attitudes.

You can go to two programs and see very similar people, yet one program feels relaxed and fun-loving, accepting and creative, if a bit chaotic at times, while the other seems efficient and businesslike, formal and industrious, and sometimes rather regimented.

One program may have a drive for reflection and excellence, while another is staffed by people who are satisfied just doing what they have always done. Programs also vary greatly in the way people treat each other: relations may be respectful and caring or the opposite, formal or informal, collegial and supportive or distant, communicating the message that staff are on their own. There may be tolerance of an in-crowd or friendship cliques that exclude others.

Some programs have no real culture and little sense of overall program. Individual teachers set the tone in their rooms. One room feels very different from another and changes as staff change. Or the overall tone is set by the director and changes when the director changes. Culture creation is a major part of developing a new center or of changing a center, and acculturation of new staff (as well as parents and children) is a key task in maintaining quality.

At Child's Garden, the staff have worked hard for over twenty years to establish a consistent culture. Reading through the parent handbook, looking at signs on the wall, observing in each classroom, sitting in on meetings, and reading newsletters, visitors discover that everyone who works there buys into the same basic ideas: messy, active play is essential, and teachers need to listen to children. Teachers throughout the center work together, use each other's good ideas, and look for ways to inject fun and humor into the day. Children are treated with respect. Unfortunately, however, parents are at best junior partners. All staff believe that the parents' role is to support the program, not to offer advice or guidance that might diverge from what the staff believe is the truth. The hiring and socialization of new staff reinforce the program culture. A new director hopes to change the aspect of that culture that marginalizes parents, but understands doing so will take time.

> ### Room to Roam Culture
>
> At Babyland Child Care, Mary and Alicia have a fairly low tolerance for noise and bursts of movement, and their toddler room reflects that. They usually do what they have been doing for the past ten years. They are friendly with other staff and parents but seek little input into their practices. Anne and Melina's room couldn't be more different. Toddlers are all over—stretching, climbing, jumping, hauling—and the teachers are always seeking out new ideas, critical reactions, and suggestions for improvements. After a succession of directors, there is no strong program culture at Babyland, and each room reflects the staff currently responsible for it.

Creating Culture Culture is created through shared expectations, stories, rituals, and common language. There is lots more to creating a common culture than shared language, but shared language is important, particularly language that describes a vision of excellence and "our way of doing things." A common definition of a term like *primary caregiver* or a shared understanding of a metaphor such as *messy little scientist* helps to acculturate new members into a community of caring. Common sayings such as "We are all in this together: building quality for every child, every day" and "It's not either-or, it's both and more" represent both an approach and an attitude. Shared stories and examples become part of the common wisdom. What kind of stories? Stories of heroic effort on behalf of a child or family: staying late, extra phone calls, or bringing in resources; stories of overcoming failure and of successful change—stories that reflect staff behaving at their best as defined by the program mission and values.

Common ideas, attitudes, and shared expectations are promoted in written materials, displays, and the way people are encouraged or allowed to talk. Posted notices and spoken language that tend to be stern—for example, "Parents must sign in" rather than "Please sign in," or "No running" instead of "Please walk"—say a lot about the culture.

Some Dimensions of Organizational Culture

Formality
Procedures
Communication
Use of written documentation
Humor and whimsy
Appearance

Work Ethic
Achievement-oriented
Fast / Slow pace
Career / Job orientation

Thinking or Doing
Analyze-question / Just do
Problem solving / Just do
Why not try? / Why change?

Maintain Status Quo or Innovation
Seek and welcome new ideas / Hold on to tradition
Constructive conflict / Avoid conflict
Make waves / Smooth waters
Improvement-driven
Risk-taking

Authority and Power
Empower / Control others
Top down / Bottom up
Mutual Trust / Mistrust
Grow people

Staff Relations
Professional
Collegial / Individual
Team / Hierarchical
Respect / Trust

Relations with Parents
Individuals
Us / Them, or Partners / Allies
Defensive / Open
Formal / Informal
Client / Customer-friendly / Nuisance

Relations with Children
People / "Cute Pets"
Teaching Focus / Learning Focus
Control Behavior / Empower
Individual / Group focus
Value action / Value quiet or passivity

Reactions to the Outside
Open to ideas / Closed to ideas
Open to people / Closed to people
Open to community resources / Closed to community resources

See Supplement: *What's Your Organizational Culture Like?*

Becoming Good

The goal of a child care center or any organization is organizational quality: resources, culture, and systems that maximize the use of the talent and resources available. Creative program directors use all three dimensions to achieve quality outcomes, using strengths in one dimension to overcome weaknesses in another.

"I Thought It Would Always Be Fun!"

Alison worked at the Oak Ridge Center for five years before moving to another highly respected program, the Front Street Center, for a slightly better salary and benefits. A year later, she went back to the original program, despite its lower compensation, because of the differences in program cultures. Her comment:

It was a good program at Front Street, and I liked most of the staff, but it just wasn't much fun. It's hard to describe. At the new center, we were more formal with each other, less spontaneous, not as loose. I felt that I couldn't be as goofy as I normally am with the children or as free conversationally with the parents. Staff worked well together, but in a much more businesslike way. It wasn't bad, everyone was nice, and the kids were great; it just wasn't as much fun. We never even had a "pajama day"!

The difference in the culture of the two programs was real enough to send Alison back to her previous job. Other staff at Front Street liked the culture and formality. They felt that it was a truly professional place without being stuffy (although Alison would disagree: "It was certainly a little stuffy," she said). The program had a sense of decorum and seriousness of purpose that led parents to take staff seriously.

To an outsider, the differences were pretty subtle and hard to identify. To Alison, they were real enough to make a difference.

For example, most child care programs have trouble maintaining quality over the course of a ten- to twelve-hour day. Often quality deteriorates in the afternoon. Why? Is it because the children (and staff) are worn out and are anticipating the arrival of parents by late afternoon? Because most of the senior staff often work the early shift? Because the morning is simply considered more important? Maybe it's because that's just the way it always has been since the days of nursery schools. What to do? This problem can be attacked in a number of ways, some of which have higher costs, others of which may inspire staff resistance.

Two of these ways involve adding, upgrading, or redistributing human resources.

- The most costly solution would be to improve adult-child ratios or to hire more qualified staff for the late-afternoon shift.
- Talent and authority can be distributed differently. The afternoon can be made the clear responsibility of the lead teacher as supervisor and planner, holding her accountable whether or not she works those hours.
- Resources can be distributed differently. Staff can be rescheduled for a better balance of expertise in the late afternoon, or physical resources can be reconsidered, perhaps by trading toys between rooms.
- Physical resources can be improved. Special, very attractive equipment that increases the likelihood that children will be stimulated can be purchased just for late-afternoon use, a less-expensive solution than increased staffing alternatives.
- Cultural change may be necessary. The afternoon hours need to be established in people's minds as learning and caring times that are just as valuable as the traditional nursery-school learning times of 9:30 to 11:30 AM.

Because there are different routes to quality, nearly every exercise in program design or problem solving benefits from using a multidimensional approach. For example, increased softness can result from some combination of environmental change (adding soft furniture or removing hard plastic furniture) and changes in practice (more use of laps and carriers that put babies against the chests of staff). Staff-child ratios, room size, quality of facility and equipment, staff expertise, leadership, and organizational systems are interactive factors. Budgets rarely permit having what we want in all those areas. By strategically using resources, particularly funding, quality can be maximized.

A Final Word: Staying Good

Quality is most easily maintained when good staff are hired and stay. This usually happens when the center is a good place to work relative to other child care programs in the area, and when employees feel valued and fulfilled by the work. A good place to work is the product of a supportive facility, thoughtful and respectful organizational systems, and a culture based on care and respect of children, families, and staff.

How does a center stay good if good people leave? Obviously, by hiring good people to replace them. Less obviously, by making sure that much of what was brought to the center by those good people who left—their ideas, visions, attitudes—stays with the center. In a quality organization, a number of things happen:

- Information, ideas, and know-how are not permitted to reside only in people's heads, lost to the program when they leave.
- The ideas are put into accepted practices across the center: handbooks, posters and charts, videos, prop boxes, and scrapbooks. Good systems, routines, and practices are institutionalized so that they become part of center life and don't vanish because of the whims of individuals: for example, the diapering procedure, parent notes, staff appreciation days, and collaborative planning of the playground.
- Active intelligence is prized. Issues are brought up, old ideas reconsidered, and new expertise, ideas, and ways of doing things are sought to avoid the dark side of institutionalization: stagnation and mindlessness.

Program cultures grow out of conscious efforts to take those good things that are occurring and build them into the life of the program. That culture shapes the next generation of program employees.

Exercises

1. Characterize the organizational culture of two or more centers in terms of
   - respect for children, families, and employees
   - authority
   - status quo / Innovation
   - openness
   - staff collegiality
   - drive for improvement.

2. Identify a way to better distribute the talent and expertise that exist in an identified center.

3. Approach your homebase as a substitute might. What expectations are clear? What practices or routines might seem confusing or illogical?

Chapter 3

Foundations of Quality: Visions, Goals, Characteristics, and Fundamental Assumptions

εxcellence *A clear vision of quality that highlights outcomes in terms of the experiences of everyone involved actively guides the program: children, families, and staff. This vision, understood and embraced by all staff and parents, actively guides program practice and is reflected in ten characteristics of high-quality child care:*

1. *A great place to live*
2. *A place of beauty*
3. *A place that promotes strong families*
4. *A community of caring*
5. *A place for learning together*

6. *A safe, nurturing, creative environment designed for exploration and learning*
7. *A place to raise competent, responsible, and compassionate children*

8. *A place in and of the wider world*
9. *A great place to work*
10. *A place for childhood.*

High-quality early care and education begin with a vision of the outcomes to be experienced by all involved, based on principles, values, and articulation of the key goals and operating assumptions that guide the program in all its complexity. The vision of quality extends beyond a concern for good care, education, health, and safety to the children's total development, including the relationship between children and their families and the quality of life during each child's one and only early childhood. The vision acknowledges the fact that children and families exist within discrete as well as overlapping cultures, that cultures differ, and that all cultures deserve respect.

The curriculum or program encompasses the total experience of the children in care, not just the relatively small portion of the day when they may be engaged in so-called educational activities.

There is another important fact to keep in mind: child care can't be good for children without being good for families and staff. Warm, supportive, and respectful relationships between adults, between adults and children, and between the children themselves lie at the heart of good care for children. A good center pays attention to all the human needs.

See Supplement: *A Vision of Quality: Charlie and Emma's Very, Very Good Day at the Bright Horizons Family Center*

Twenty-first Century Child Care: What Kind of Place?

A great place to live: *a noninstitutional, welcoming place to be for the large amount of time that a child spends at the center.*

Eating, drinking, sleeping, separating and reuniting with loved ones, growing, changing, learning, falling in and out of love, getting knocked down and picking oneself up, despairing deeply and being filled with joy: in short, *living is what children do in child care.* Depending on what we offer them, they may be living fully or not, living well or not. *Noninstitutional* means a relaxed rather than a school-like atmosphere with flexible use of space and time, minimal waiting, and few occasions when everyone has to do the same thing at the same time. Children need a variety of places to spend time, places with different feels because of their varying light, texture, smell, and enclosure, places that allow different kinds of movement.

If we create good places to live, those environments encourage competence, comfort, and acceptance of each individual—their culture, quirks, needs, and dispositions. Home is where people take you as you are: the colicky infant or the toddler with boundless energy, the easy-to-startle child, the shy child, the child struggling with self control.

A place of beauty: *a sensoryscape of taste and sensibility that encourages an appreciation of life and what the world has to offer.*

We work and feel better in beautiful places. What is beautiful? Beauty, of course, is in the eye of the beholder—and culture and upbringing certainly play a huge role. It is a matter of taste. If every program aspires to create a place of beauty, the end results will be different and perhaps idiosyncratic but all efforts will likely reduce the psychedelic kaleidoscope that consists of every wall and window covered with a riot of color and information (however valuable); too-lush rainforests of materials hanging from the ceiling; proliferations of cute commercial images, permanent murals, and cheesy décor.

When the beholder is an infant or toddler who experiences the world through senses more than through thinking, beauty is much more than visual. Beauty flows from the entire sensory experience. A child's environment is a *sensoryscape:* an aromascape, a soundscape, a colorscape, a texturescape, and a lightscape—a world to be experienced through the skin, the fingers, and the taste buds.

A place that promotes strong families: *a place that supports the rights and responsibilities of parents and the development and well-being of families.*

Child care is foremost a service to families who need assistance in caring for their children. It is easy to believe in families and to want to respect and support them. But practicing what we preach is much, much harder. Families come in all shapes and sizes, with cultures, beliefs, and values that are not always aligned with our own, or their ways may conflict with what we believe to be reasonable. One size does not fit all, and the way families live their lives may well be at odds with efforts to maintain our policies and practices. Good centers try hard to align center practices with family preferences: true partnerships with families require responsiveness to individual and collective parental needs, requests, and concerns about the care and education of their children. Alignment is a key concept. It recognizes that accommodation must come both from the program and from the families, and it is more than simply convincing families that our practices are correct, acquiescing, or trying to be all things to all people. Responsiveness and alignment create good business and empower families. Program hours, services, and policies reflect the needs of families, including acknowledging that siblings need time together. Parents are encouraged to contribute, make suggestions, and have influence over their children's care.

Operating a place for families means welcoming them by accounting for their presence in the size and scale of the space in a setting. It means allowing for multiage sibling interaction, both indoors and outdoors. A place that empowers families has the capacity for display and documentation that keeps families engaged, as well as spaces for confidential discussions and meetings.

A community of caring: *a place that encourages individualized, personalized care and long-term, warm, meaningful relationships between adults and children who know and trust each other.*

Does the environment support individualized care, relationships, and community—or does it assume "standard operating procedures" that divide people up by the narrowest of ranges and keep them apart, separated by classroom, age, and role? In a community, people know each other and have a sense of belonging—there are no strangers. Community flows out of an organization that values and sustains relationships throughout the organization. An environment can connect and bring people together with gathering places and transparency that allows glimpses from place to place. It can also be designed to allow moments for being alone or with another when respite from the group is needed and to support relationships that last over time.

Community can soften the impact of staff turnover, particularly turnover of primary staff. It is hard to calibrate the developmental damage when children are cared for by a succession of relative strangers, however kind and skilled—perhaps very nice people who blink in and out of the children's lives as they progress through the center. The experience must be similar to being an adult and experiencing the difference between a love life within a committed relationship and a series of short-term affairs. However exciting, the loss is enormous; missing is the intimacy and the deep knowledge of each other. We know that young children spend an enormous amount of energy coping with unfamiliarity and change, that exploration and learning are built on a foundation of security, and that emotional and moral intelligence grow from a foundation of early trust and guidance. Whether loss is made visible by children in distress or kept invisible because the lost potential is not tangible, the damage done by impersonal care, shallow relationships, and the lack of community is real.

A place for learning together: *a warm, secure place that encourages ample, sensitive adult-child interactions, huge amounts of language and intellectual stimulation, great conversations, and many moments of undivided attention.*

Perhaps the quickest and most fundamental evaluation of a child care setting comes from observing the quantity and quality of conversations—responsive interactions that are both verbal and nonverbal. Are adults listening to children, provoking the ideas of children, and offering one of their most precious gifts—undivided attention and full human presence? Can such exchanges occur with ratios and group sizes in the real world and with all the daily demands of care? They can take place only in environments that support staff and that are well designed and prepared for independent use by children. And what characterizes an environment designed for conversation? Good acoustics and places that lend themselves to conversation: rocking chairs, couches, benches under a tree, and infant carriers for young infants that put them right there to experience all the murmurs and reassuring words of the adult.

A safe, nurturing, creative environment designed for exploration and learning: *a safe place of high expectations that engages and challenges the mind and body of every child and prepares them for success in school and life.*

Are both challenge *and* safety possible for infants and toddlers, who need to live exuberantly and explore with their bodies and senses, who punctuate their discoveries with noise and movement? Yes, if they are given enough room to grow, planned environments, and the freedom to test their limits. Every program has to define what constitutes harm. Regrettably, the range of what constitutes a safe and healthy environment and what kinds of exploration and challenge are reasonable for young children is narrowing. The word *challenge* applied to infant-toddler programs raises many concerns at the same time that it creates a sense of opportunity.

If children are not allowed to stumble and fall, how will they learn to pick themselves up? If children in care are not allowed physical challenges and the inevitable normal bumps, bruises, and scratches of childhood, we will smooth out their childhoods and rob them of their luster. If indoor and outdoor environments are not rich with the stuff of exploration and expectations, the materials that infant and toddler research tells us their bodies and senses need, our low expectations will surely diminish their vision of themselves and stunt their development.

If there is continuous monitoring of the physical environment, equipment, materials, and caregiving practices to ensure the health, safety, and appropriate supervision of children, accidents will be minimized.

A place to raise competent, responsible, and compassionate children: *a place that encourages the development of responsibility, compassion, and community.*

Institutions typically are not great breeding grounds for competence, independence, responsibility, compassion, and community. Child care centers need to be designed so that all of their inhabitants can be together, work together, depend on each other, become competent, and take responsibility for daily life and growth. An environment designed for competent staff and children can expect all the inhabitants (toddlers on up—infants have only the responsibility to be themselves!) to work together and contribute to daily life—for example, by helping to set up and take down activities and to clean up.

A place in and of the wider world: *a place connected to the natural world, the larger community, and the world beyond.*

Good child care develops good people from a vision of a good society and world to live in. It is important that policies, practices, and curriculum promote a nonsexist, nonbiased approach that understands, values, and respects other cultures, individual differences, the physical environment, and preservation of the natural world.

It also means getting children out into the world: a challenge because the twenty-four-hour world of sensational news and increasing alienation from the natural world has created the perception in America that our world is a terribly perilous place for children. Because potential harm is often thought to lurk within every stranger and every strange situation, there is more of a tendency to stay behind fences and within the confines of our own communities. Adding to the limits and confinement is the institutional concern about liability; the idea of accidents is being replaced by the notion that there must be liability somewhere, if not downright malevolence.

But children raised in well-meaning bubbles, disconnected from the world outside the fence or the windows of the center or the car, are effectively crippled and will be more vulnerable as they grow up. And childhood is the time when human beings are supposed to fall in love with the world and its complicated delights and mysteries. Do we really want children to know more about tigers or migrating humpback whales on television than the crow, the worm, and the willow outside their windows? Do we want them to develop their ideas about people at work and about community life from sensational police dramas rather than from walks in their neighborhood? Most children can easily distinguish between fast-food icons such as the golden arches and Taco Bell, but not between sparrows and chickadees or elms and maples.

A great place to work: *a place that supports active intelligence, competence, growth, collegiality, and the demanding, complex emotional requirements of addressing the needs of children, families, community, and staff.*

Staff need to feel secure, valued, and respected as professionals who have difficult jobs that involve both thinking and doing. In a great place to work, teamwork and collegiality are valued and supported. Communication mechanisms are in place for program planning, evaluating, and problem solving; mechanisms also exist for regular staff input on policies and procedures. Individual strengths and needs are acknowledged, respected, and addressed. Roles and responsibilities are clearly articulated, and supportive supervision and professional development experiences are provided.

What do you have if you fail to provide office space, resource rooms, a staff lounge or workroom, adequate storage, places to meet or have confidential meetings, and the means to support adult communication? You have a place that assumes adult mindlessness, a simple place for simple tasks and simple people: mechanical routines, no collegiality, no creativity, and no intellectual life or sense of a past. Only the heroic efforts of talented and committed people can overcome the preordained mediocrity, workplace despair, and burnout likely to follow when we cheat on the required spaces for active intelligence.

A place for childhood: *a great place to be a child for the one childhood each child will have.*

Every child deserves a childhood, a time of magic and wonder, of safety and security in which to discover what life has to offer. The center should be a warm, soft, aesthetically pleasing, homelike place with the right mix of freedom and restraint, exuberance and serenity, and an abundance of warmth and laughter. Children are not entirely fenced off from the world of people and nature or regimented into routines and activities based on group or institutional requirements.

When everything comes together—when we get it right and it truly is a wonderful place to be a child for the up to 12,000 hours a child may spend in child care, and it is a great place for staff to want to make being with children their career—a place in and of the world—we have created a place for a childhood.

See Supplement: *Are You a Place for a Childhood?*

Fundamental Assumptions for a Quality Infant and Toddler Child Care Program

Where does the vision of quality for infants and toddlers come from? In the evolution of society, infant and toddler group care programs are fairly new as social forms compared to schools and preschools. Because many of us come to them with more experience with preschoolers and older children, we often don't know quite what infant and toddler groups should be like—perhaps sort of homey schools with classrooms, cots, and baby toys? Five assumptions underlie the goals of a good-quality infant-toddler program and bring into focus the critical distinctions that distinguish child care from other early education programs.

Basic assumption 1: Good homes are good models for infant and toddler group care.
The most useful concept is that the best group care setting for a young child's development is one that approximates a good home environment. Keeping this in mind is particularly important in light of continued pressure to provide early

education in its narrowest sense. Unfortunately and mistakenly, education is equated with school, and homes are undervalued. A good home is wonderfully educational, a great place for infants and toddlers to learn nearly all they need to know. And good homes come in many cultural and socioeconomic varieties.

Of course, there are considerable differences between an in-home experience in a child's own family and a group care experience. But it is worth reminding ourselves what a good experience growing up in one's own family is like—the activities and experiences offered as well as the physical and human environments. The good home is a rich, multisensory environment with different places to be and lots of opportunity for exploration, discovery, and movement. There are usually variously textured furniture to climb on, low tables to cruise around, and small spaces in which to create a place of your own. Housekeeping chores such as preparing and serving food, setting the table, going shopping, helping with younger children, cleaning up, and folding linen provide experiences in language, math, and science and create a sense of belonging through participation in meaningful work. These same tasks can be incorporated into the daily experience of the children at the center with the same result: a sense of belonging and community.

Basic assumption 2: Learning and care are inseparable, and both occur nonstop during the day. Unfortunately, in many early childhood settings, learning and care are often considered as separate. Learning, or at least the most valuable learning, is seen mostly as flowing from teaching and as occuring during circle, "project," or "work" time, and not during free time or playtime. (The period from 9:30 to 11:30 AM is often deemed the best time to learn, largely because of tradition.) In good child care, as in a good home, there are no such separations—all interactions and explorations in the environment count. The interactions during diapering or mealtime, late-afternoon play, and cuddling to ease the pain of the latest bump are all learning times worthy of careful reflection, evaluation, and planning.

Basic assumption 3: Infants and toddlers are very different from older children. Children under age two and a half or three are sensorimotor beings without most of the developmental skills needed for large-group living. Most of their learning involves movement and direct sensory experience. Group care is not a necessary developmental experience for babies; it is instead a necessity for modern families. But children under age three can thrive, perhaps in spite of group care, when a center or family child care home has successfully individualized care and learning and has broken down the negative institutional effects of group care.

Basic assumption 4: Child care settings are not schools but places to live and learn. Child care settings are places where adults and children live together for seven to ten hours a day, forty-five to fifty weeks a year, for a number of years. Are they also educational places? Of course—absolutely! But formal education is only one part of learning. Education is not the same thing as schooling, and teaching is not the same thing as learning. With schooling, we associate teaching, instruction, and socialization focused on adapting to the requirements of group life. Child care settings for young children are primarily places for learning, discovering, and mentoring, not for instruction.

Basic assumption 5: The experience of parents is as important as the experience of children. Quality includes parents who feel satisfied, competent as parents, and in control of their children's care. Unlike schools, child care programs serve entire families and recognize both the similarities and differences in needs, concerns, and values that each family brings to the program. There is no such thing as good centers or good teachers that dictate the "right way" to parents or that exclude parents from influence over their children's care.

Achieving the Vision of Twenty-First-Century Quality: Eight Key Concepts of Program Quality

There is no single model for program excellence that embodies the ten characteristics of quality mentioned above. Good-quality programs reflect differences in program services, children and families, communities, culture, local practice, sites, budgets, and talents and creativity of staff. However there are eight key concepts that can provide a framework to help define what programs of excellence for infants and toddlers often have in common:

- high expectations for every child
- prime times: the importance of adult-child interactions
- planned child-choice learning environments
- emergent curriculum
- developmentally appropriate instruction
- making learning visible through documentation and display
- full partnerships with parents
- twenty-first-century technology.

High Expectations for Every Child

All children deserve the gift of high expectations from others: an optimistic and determined view that they can develop their abilities to the fullest. The program's responsibility is to recognize children's individual strengths and challenges, their culture, and their families' desires and values, and work with families to help their children succeed in school and life. High expectations require program goals and objectives, knowledge of development, and knowing children through observation and communication with family.

"What About My Values?"

Staff in a program may not always agree on the right way to go about the ins and outs of good care; neither do families. After all, we don't always agree as parents or as citizens. The more diversity in staff backgrounds, the wider the range of beliefs and values. Whether boys and girls should be treated differently, the value of competition, how much children should be allowed to assert themselves, and how independent children are encouraged to be are just a few of the areas where differences are likely to occur.

It should be okay for staff to be different and to believe different things. The same is true for parents. There are few "right ways" or truths that are independent of culture. However, it is also important that a program have a clearly articulated point of view and goals and practices that all staff understand, accept, and practice (even if they would choose to do it differently if they were in charge). Acceptance means agreeing to follow program guidelines for behavior and practice, including those areas where individuals may have to adapt their own caregiving practices to meet center standards.

Prime times: the importance of adult-child interactions

Children are in the prime of their lives. Early childhood is when our lives are launched, the people we will become are developed, and our sense of self, security, and what the world has to offer are shaped. The term *prime times* signifies the critical importance of nurturing care and one-to-one interactions in the child's life in the program—those moments when the child experiences the full human presence of another human being (adult or child) or is thoroughly engaged in a learning moment. Prime times occur when the key elements of emotional intelligence are developed.

Caring times that are responsive, nurturing, and appropriate to each child, viewed within the context of family and culture, are *prime times,* and they are to be valued and prized. The essential sense of trust and security for children (and parents) is built on care given when the child needs it and in ways that are comfortable for the child. Each prime time is filled with language and is not rushed in order to move on to less valuable activity time. These are prime times for developing a strong sense of human dignity, personal worth, power, language, and a basic trust in the world as a good place. If the child is actively involved and respected as a responsible, capable person while having personal needs met, these are prime times for developing a sense of personal responsibility. When the child and staff are engaged in learning together, sharing moments of struggle or success, these are prime times for becoming a capable and confident learner, eager to meet challenges. And when a teacher and child share a moment of delight, this is a prime time for discovering the joy of being human and a member of a community: the child learns "I am somebody. I am important."

Note: Prime times also apply to families—those one-to-one interactions that validate and empower families and establish the partnership between parents and staff. Staff who serve as advocates for the child and family, as monitors of quality, and as vehicles for parental influence are the best guardians of prime times.

Planned Child-Choice Learning Environments

Well-planned learning centers allow for child choice, self-directed, active learning through play and supportive interactions, individualized caring schedules, and relaxed caregiving: these are the heart of program excellence. All children are not the same, and each child deserves a full range of developmentally appropriate experiences, free of stereotypes or limits based on race, sex, and ethnicity. Throughout the day, children have opportunities to make self-directed and guided choices and to participate in small groups and projects. Children are guided to critical learning experiences that form the building blocks of healthy development. Changes to the learning environment, activities, and projects reflect children's own emerging interests and individual goals. Indoor and outdoor learning centers offer guided experiences that encompass all the skills and understandings necessary for optimal development.

Emergent Curriculum

Emergent curriculum means curriculum planning that arises from staff experience with individual children in the group. The curriculum, in other words, emerges from the children themselves: teachers plan learning experiences based on observations of the children's interests, skills, and understandings rather than from a set plan of teacher-derived assumptions or themes for "typical" children. A planned learning environment establishes the foundation for learning throughout the day. Emergent curriculum encompasses planned activities, projects, and adaptations to the learning centers, as well as guided interactions between teachers and children. Teachers guide the children's experience with the help of parents, developing projects and planning activities that correspond with children's developmental characteristics. A project for an infant or toddler might include a collection of experiences that provokes the child's drive to explore and discover: perhaps different sounds or textures or objects.

Developmentally Appropriate Instruction

As children grow, they need some instruction from adults, in the sense of deliberate teaching of expected skills and behavior (for example, being gentle with others, using a spoon, waiting your turn). They also need adults to understand their capabilities and needs, including hands- and minds-on experiences so that they can acquire the knowledge and expertise eventually expected of them. *Developmentally appropriate* essentially means that we take into account what we expect children to know and how we expect them to learn and behave, based on our knowledge of individual children and child development (including cultural variations). There is no clear formula for what is developmentally appropriate for a child; it is always a process of observation, analysis, and dialogue with parents.

Making Learning Visible through Documentation and Display

Observing, documenting, and displaying the efforts of individual children and the group are essential for optimal learning and for assuring parents that credible educational experiences are being offered. Careful planning of a learning environment results in activities, projects, and documentation that clearly reflect a program's educational intent. Parents and teachers should together track the discoveries and the accomplishments of each child, using child-observation instruments and child portfolios.

Full Partnerships with Parents

The partnership with parents extends to parents the right and responsibility to be involved and influential in all aspects of their child's experience at the center, including curriculum. The partnership is established from the family's first contact with the program. Parents are welcomed as experts on their children and as partners in setting goals, planning, and evaluating care and curriculum so that these correspond with their child's emerging interests, needs, and strengths. Opportunities for one-to-one interactions and conversation with families are valued as prime times.

Twenty-First-Century Technology

In the twenty-first century, the world is brought to our fingertips electronically—through data transmission from terminals, television screens, and printers. Staff should have access to such technologies (for example, computers and digital cameras) as everyday tools for communicating with families and each other, and for their own professional development.

Setting Goals for All Concerned

Each of these items is part of a broad vision of high quality as well as an individual element in creating quality. Overarching them should be program goals: for children and their parents, these are the statement of what really matters to the program—reference points that allow them to assess whether policies or practices are achieving what we hope to achieve. What would nearly all parents like to see nurtured in their young children?

Goals for Children

- a sense of belonging to the family and the family's culture, with primary attachments to parents and other family members
- the capacity to trust people, to feel secure when away from home and with people other than family members. Security implies that children can trust that their parents will return when they go away and can trust the people in whose care they have been placed by the parents.
- enjoyment of other people, sensitivity to people's feelings, acceptance of diversity, the beginnings of a caring and respectful approach to interacting effectively with others
- a positive sense of themselves as important people who are cared about, who are able to control their own behavior to some extent, and who have an effect on the social and physical world (mastery)
- the ability to comprehend language and other forms of communication, to give and seek information, to ask questions, to convey needs, wants, and feelings, and to communicate in ways that can be understood by others
- the ability to solve simple problems, and the beginning of an understanding of how the world works
- competence in using the body and hands
- development of autonomy and independence—the ability to think and act with pleasure and competence.

Goals for Families

- acknowledgment from the program that families are the most important people in their child's life
- a sense of control over and involvement in the child's care, even when families are not present
- a sense of competence and confidence that families can navigate the complex waters of modern parenthood.

Goals for Staff

- a feeling of recognition from the program that they are important and valued
- a sense of competence and confidence that they can nurture and guide children and partner with families

- recognition in program practices that quality is an outgrowth of observation, reflection, program planning, and continual professional growth.

The Logic of an Environmentally Based Program

While the most important ingredient in good care for infants and toddlers is the quality of the staff who work with the children, what separates high-quality programs from others (assuming staff-child ratios, group size, and staff qualifications are relatively equal) is often not the staff but the overall quality of the environment. A good environment works for the staff and the children and helps to further their goals. Here are some of the assumptions behind environmentally based programming:

- The environment is set up to allow the child to explore, discover, and play independently. This also allows the staff to focus on prime times, those moments of one-to-one care and learning that lie at the heart of healthy development. Rushing through diaper changing, dressing, or consoling a child in distress in order to get back to teaching or managing children is the opposite of what should happen. Those are the times to draw out, talk, listen, touch, and reassure. So too is the time when a baby makes an important new discovery: Alex discovers his hand or Marie explores consonant sounds. A rich, responsive learning environment set up to engage Alex's and Marie's friends with valuable learning experiences allows Alex and Marie to have the full human presence of a caregiver to encourage and share the delight of their discoveries.
- Neither infants nor toddlers benefit much from large groups. Three is a large group for a baby. An environmentally based program allows individual play, pair play, and small-group play to occur simultaneously, and minimizes the times when all children are doing the same thing or spending time as part of a crowd.
- An all-day program has many hours in which to build learning experiences. There is no need to rush experiences and no point in concentrating them into a limited part of the day. An environmentally based program assumes that children learn from all the experiences that the day provides. The way time and space are structured, the routines, the furnishings, the equipment and materials, and all the ways adults and children behave teach young children what the world is like, how it works, what they are capable of, and what their place is in it.

A good environment is planned to support all the care and learning we would like to see occur. Much of the planning revolves around how to build learning into the environment. What furnishings by their nature help children learn? What equipment creates a sensory or reaching and kicking activity center? While some adult-initiated and -led activities such as a simple cooking experience or sensory play with fingerpaints may take place, the program should not be activity based; that is, structured around activity times or groups. Music may take place anytime, as may some large-motor experiences. Activities take place individually and in small groups within an environment rich with built-in learning. In other words, it is not that the program happens in the environment; rather, the program is the environment.

A Final Word: Quality Comes from a Comprehensive Vision

Each program needs its own vision of quality, which is incorporated into each child's day, into the daily interchange between parents and staff, and into the way partici- pants feel about themselves and each other as they go about the business of living and working in the world of child care. Everything about the center should be considered in light of this vision of quality: how it looks and sounds and what it expects from its members.

See Supplements: *A Continuum of Quality: Infant/Toddler Program Continuums* and *Four Levels of Infant/Toddler Programming*

Exercises

1. List the ways infants and toddlers benefit developmentally from their environment, interactions, and activities in daily life in a good home.

2. Take an existing program and consider the question, "What kind of place is this?" Take two of the characteristics in this chapter and describe how the program reflects them.

3. Apply the Key Concepts for Quality to your program. What characteristics in your program support or contradict the key concepts?

4. Choose one of the eight key concepts and add new practices to the list of existing program practices that might enhance quality.

Part 2

Organizing the Program

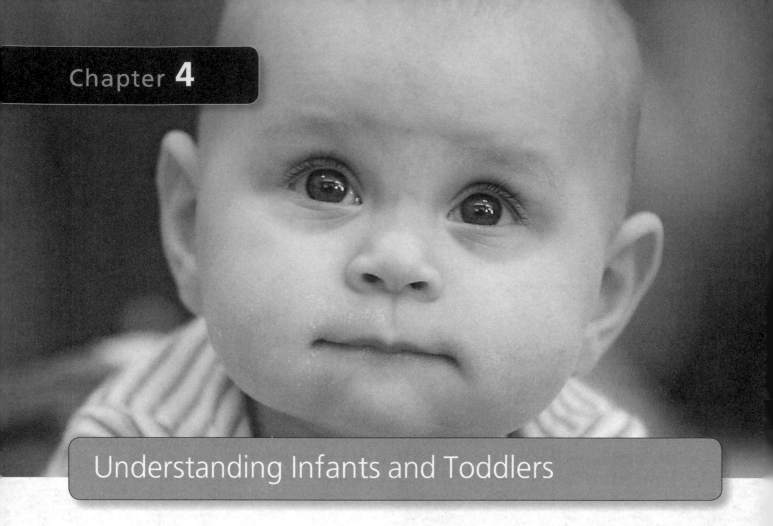

Chapter 4

Understanding Infants and Toddlers

ɛxcellence *Caring and learning are based on knowledge of and enthusiastic appreciation for*

- *The importance of the first three years of life in laying the foundations for future development and learning*
- *The developmental characteristics of infants and toddlers*
- *The culture and the unique characteristics of each child*
- *Partnership with and respect for the child's family and culture*
- *The need for children to have lots of hands-on, minds-on experiences.*

High-quality infant and toddler care programs value children for who they are and what they can do right now, not just for what they will be able to do in the future or what they are in the process of becoming—a preschooler or a kindergartner. Infants and toddlers are truly appreciated for their strengths rather than their needs and vulnerabilities, are accepted for their most challenging characteristics, and are always viewed in a positive way.

Understanding Infant and Toddler Development

Babies are not like us.
—Jean Jacques Rousseau

Newborns ride on intermingling waves of sight, sound, touch, taste, and especially smell. . . . His world smells to him much as our world smells to you, but he does not perceive odors coming through his nose alone. He hears odors, and sees odors, and feels them too. His world is a melee of pungent aromas—and pungent sounds, and bitter-smelling sounds, and sweet-smelling sights, and sour-smelling pressures against the skin. If we could visit the newborn's world, we would think ourselves inside a hallucinogenic perfumery.

—Daphne and Charles Maurer (*The World of the Newborn*, 1988, 51)

Babies are not only not like us, they are not much like each other or even like themselves from day to day, especially considering the phenomenal changes in all facets of development that occur in the first two and a half years of life.

What do babies know and when do they know it? is the bedrock question for everyone who studies child development. What is inborn (*nature*) versus what is learned from experience (*nurture*)? Everyone agrees that both nature and nurture help determine the people we become; the relative influence of each and when or how one or the other dominates is the subject of a debate that goes back to ancient times.

Looking into a Baby's Brain

The first three years of life determine the basic architecture of the brain, the foundations for emotional and moral intelligence, and often the architecture of the child's family relationships (Shore 1997; Goleman 1995; Coles 1998). Research on brain development, widely reported in newspapers and in special issues of *Time* and *Newsweek,* was summarized by Rima Shore in *Rethinking the Brain: New Insights into Early Development* (1997). Using Positron Emission Transmography (PET) that captures brain activity on film, along with other research techniques such as tests that measured a baby's physiological responses through saliva testing and pupil reflexes, scientists could literally peer inside a baby's brain and help unlock the emotional complexity of the infant experience. This research has established a new understanding of how the human and social environments influence a baby's genetic material and developmental processes to contribute to brain growth, allow the baby to acquire language, and build the foundation that permanently affects some developmental outcomes.

Babies are busy "wiring" their brains. They are born with all the brain cells (neurons) they need, but they are not "intelligent" as we understand that term; that is, they perceive but don't think the way we do because they can't retain images or symbols in their minds. Babies construct intelligence through experience, welding sparsely connected neurons into densely interconnected pathways with billions of interconnections (synapses). This weave of connections constitutes intelligence. With experience and growth, the architecture of the brain is established. Shore (1997, 21) explains this process:

The synapses that have been strengthened by virtue of repeated experience tend to become permanent; the synapses that were not used often enough in the early years tend to be eliminated. In this way the experiences—positive and negative— that young children have in the first years of life influence how their brains will be wired as adults.

What does the research say about the first three years of life? These years are extraordinarily important for cognitive and emotional development and for language acquisition. Infant and toddler brains are working very hard taking in everything.

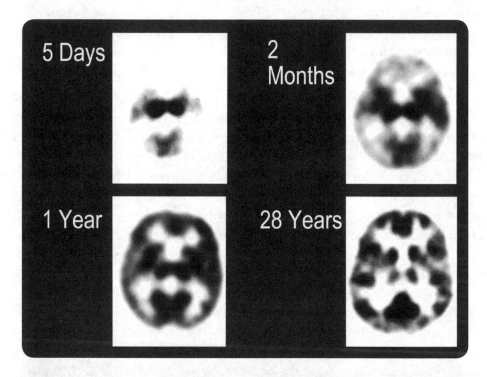

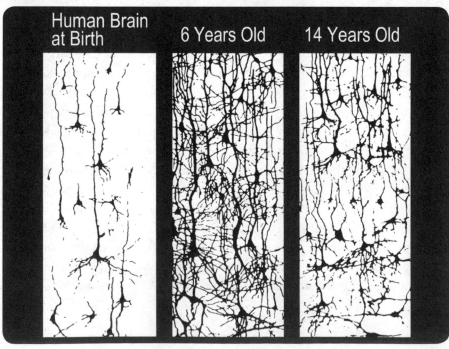

By age three, a young child's brain is working twice as hard as an adult brain. What research boils down to for our purposes is that babies need environmental settings in which they receive nurturing, responsive care from someone who knows them well and who provides an environment rich in responsive language interactions along with a safe world to explore.

Children as Sensorimotor Scientists: Piaget's Four Stages

Swiss psychologist Jean Piaget has had a huge influence on how we think about child development. He asserted that children construct their own knowledge through interactions with people and objects. Children's thinking develops in four stages. In each stage, their way of constructing knowledge is different.

Piaget called the stage that begins at birth the *sensorimotor stage,* which lasts for the first eighteen months to two years. During this period, children investigate the world and learn how it works through moving and using all their senses. Piaget saw children as inhabiting a world that begins with only a few categories: "things I suck and everything else" is only a slight oversimplification. Over time, the infant's world becomes a familiar place, with recognizable people, sights, sounds, smells, and textures. During this sensorimotor stage, children also learn about object permanence: the powerful understanding that something is the same when viewed from any angle and that it still exists when it's out of sight. Object permanence explains why peeka-boo and hiding games are endlessly fascinating to babies. During the first two years, children learn how to navigate the world better and better, coordinating hands and feet, mind and body. They also develop a physical, but not a mental, understanding of up and down, over and under, and other spatial concepts. In addition, they begin to understand cause and effect—that is, that actions can cause reactions. At this stage, young children are also are learning how to use tools.

Preoperational thinking, the next stage, usually begins around age two and lasts until around age seven. During this period, children's thinking incorporates language and mental images. They can imagine and remember more clearly, and they develop a sense of time, of order, and of place. Separation becomes easier because they can visualize the people they love even when those people are absent. Of course, that same capacity allows them to become fixated on a person's absence, and as they develop they begin to worry about abandonment. Toddlers in the preoperational period are capable of lots of make-believe and acting out. Toddlers are usually egocentric: the world revolves around them, they cause what happens around them, and they believe things happen because of them—which is why toddlers when hungry may sit down at the table. They are thinking, "Isn't that why the food comes?"

At around age seven, children enter the stage of *concrete operational thinking,* during which they begin to reason like adults and are on their way to abstract thinking, although their logic is tied to the world they can see and act on. The final stage, *formal operations,* usually begins around age eleven. During this stage, children become increasingly capable of abstract reasoning.

Beyond Piaget

While much of what Piaget hypothesized is still widely accepted, there is considerable evidence that the process of development is less staged and much more of a social and

The Scientist in the Crib

The analysis of the child as scientist is beautifully portrayed in *The Scientist in the Crib: Minds, Brains and How Children Learn* (Gopnik, Melzoff, and Kuhl, 1999). Written with charm and humor by three scientists, the book discusses how young children learn and what they need in order to thrive. It also offers insights into the joys of caregiving. While we may lament our adult loss of a childlike view of the world or perhaps be unaware that we ever lost it, if we have the opportunity and are willing, we can participate in seeing the world through the eyes of a child by being around and interacting with very young children.

We participate simply by watching children. Think of some completely ordinary, boring, everyday walk, the couple of blocks to the 7-Eleven store. Taking that same walk with a two-year-old is like going to get a quart of milk with William Blake. The mundane street becomes a sort of circus. There are gates; gates that open one way and not another and that will swing back and forth if you push them just the right way. There are small walls you can walk on very carefully. There are several lids with fascinatingly regular patterns, and scraps of brightly colored pizza delivery flyers. There are intriguing strangers to examine carefully from behind a protective parental leg. There is a veritable zoo of creatures, from tiny pill bugs and earthworms to the enormous excitement, or terror, of a real barking dog. The trip to the 7-Eleven becomes a hundred times more interesting, even though, of course, it does take ten times as long. Watching children awakens our own continuing capacities for wonder and knowledge (211).

emotional process than he envisioned. There is also a growing view that much more inborn capacity that is not preconstructed exists than Piaget maintained.

Lev Vygotsky A contemporary of Piaget whose work came to light decades later, Vygotsky believed that social interaction was a critical factor in development. While Piaget emphasized children's interactions with objects, Vygotsky recognized that children's interactions with adults and more knowledgeable peers were also essential to cognitive learning. Children at all ages learn from questions, conversations, directions, and assistance; they model the strategies they observe others using.

Vygotsky's *zone of proximal development* is the hypothetical, dynamic region in which optimal development takes place. It is the distance between what a child can accomplish during independent problem solving and what the child can accomplish with the help of an adult or more competent member of the culture. *Scaffolding* is a useful metaphor for describing optimal teaching and learning interactions. Children construct themselves through active interaction. The social environment is the *scaffold* that allows them to move forward and build new competencies. The quality of the scaffold, the social environment that supports children—their family, teachers, friends, and older children—greatly influences their development.

Stanley Greenspan A clinical psychologist who has studied children for over thirty years, Greenspan views emotional development as intertwined with cognitive and social development. He believes that children need strong, supportive, trusting relationships with significant adults in order to develop emotionally, socially, and cognitively. He hypothesizes six milestones of emotional development from birth to age four (Greenspan and Greenspan 1985, 4–6):

Self-regulation and interest in the world. In the early weeks of life, babies confront two simultaneous challenges: to feel regulated and calm and to use all their senses to take an interest in the world. Suddenly, after nine months in the darkness and relative quiet of the womb, they are plunged into a new world. The ability to organize these sensations—to feel tranquil in spite of them and to reach actively for them—is the first milestone.

Falling in love. The second milestone is taking a highly specialized interest in the human world. Once the relaxed and interested three- or four-month-old discovers the incomparable attractions of the world, you can observe their enraptured smiles and eager joyfulness as they gaze excitedly at your face, feel your rhythmical movement, hear your soft voice, and even, in their uncoordinated way, explore your face.

Developing intentional two-way communication. At this stage, at around three months, love alone is not enough and babies want dialogue and conversation, expecting adults to respond to their unique signals. It is now a cause-and-effect world.

Emergence of an organized sense of self and a problem-solving ability. By ten or twelve months, Johnny knows his readiness for the fourth stage of development by taking his emotional dialogue with the world one step further and learning to connect small units of feeling and social behavior into large, complicated, orchestrated patterns. He understands things like "the cookie is in the cupboard," asserts things such as "I *neeeed* that cookie," uses his newly emerging skills (going to the cupboard and pointing), and can problem solve (using his charm to convince his parents).

Creating emotional ideas. Children can now imagine, dream, pretend, and use play to make sense of the world and to explore their feelings. As Greenspan says, "Johnny learns to go from understanding how objects function to being able to create these objects in his own mind's eye." (1985, 5)

Emotional thinking. Children in the sixth phase expand their world of ideas into the emotional realm of pleasure and dependency, curiosity, assertiveness and anger, self-discipline or setting their own limits, even empathy and love. In this phase, the world becomes a more logical place, and children begin to be able to distinguish between reality and fantasy, "my reality" and "the reality of others."

Elizabeth Spelke and the Harvard Laboratory for Developmental Studies

Elizabeth Spelke and her colleagues at her Harvard Laboratory for Developmental Studies have produced a body of research that convincingly challenges both William James's famous observation that the world of an infant is a "blooming, buzzing confusion" and Piaget's view that babies are born with sensory capacity but lack knowledge. "Nowadays every psychology student is taught that Piaget and James were wrong," cognitive and evolutionary scientist Steven Pinker wrote in *Time* in 2001. "From the earliest months, in fact, children interpret the world as a real and predictable place. . . . This new understanding is largely the legacy of Harvard psychologist Elizabeth Spelke" (cited in Talbot 2006, 93). Spelke's research showed that not all knowledge is constructed the way Piaget envisioned. Babies possess innate capacities at birth—a stock of concepts about space, objects, motion, unity, persistence, identity, and number— that create an orderly world. Spelke notes:

[I]nfants are world class learners and can be trusted to select, more or less to create on their own, experiences that will enhance learning. From an early age, they attend to novel objects and events. They are also highly predisposed to learn by observing and interacting with other people. (Talbot 2006, 93)

Spelke's research does not imply that Baby Einstein–type enrichments and pushing babies to learn more is warranted. She warns:

There seems to be a common assumption, in thinking about children's development, that earlier is better, so the reasoning goes, if it is good for a four-year-old to understand counting, it would be even better if a two-year-old could be induced to understand counting. There is no evidence to support this assumption and some reason to be skeptical of it. Two-year-olds are already engaged in the task of mastering much of the encyclopedic knowledge about objects, events, places, and people that we adults take for granted. Diverting them from this task by introducing other tasks, like learning to read or work with numbers, seems useless at best and possibly harmful. (Talbot 2006, 93)

A Child's Job

A child's job is to learn all about the world and fully develop into the very best person that he or she can be.
—Jim Greenman

Trying to integrate the ideas of Piaget, Vygotsky, Erik Erikson, Spelke, Greenspan, and other influential scientists is not easy. Child development is complicated. There are many research studies and thick textbooks that cover every aspect of child development. It can be useful to try to boil all this information down to the basics. Doing so helps us articulate the fundamentals of development to parents and staff, which in turn explains the logic of why good programs do things the way they do. Think about children as being born with a job to do. *Their job is to learn about the world and to develop into the very best people that they can be.* Children are fully equipped and driven to pursue that job. They are filled with possibilities. From birth, they are marvelous learners, immediately investigating the sights, sounds, and feel of the world. They are born to be competent little scientists, driven to move, to experiment, to know. They also are programmed to connect with and learn from the people around them, and they need people who prize them. Children are in a state of constant learning long before an infant's first steps and first words; long before toddler's first real social play and first sentences; long before the plunges into reading, writing, sports, and a complicated social life that mark children's development in preschool and early school-age years—long before they are given the label *students*. As they move through childhood, they are exploring all their own bodily powers and what the world is made of: sensations, people, things, relationships, and the elements and forces of the natural world.

A Child's Job Description

Make sense **of the world.** To newborn babies, the world probably is not yet differentiated clearly by sight, sound, touch, smell, and taste. They experience these, but all these sensations blend together and flow into the nervous system as waves of sensation. Immediately after birth, the task of separating out and sorting through sensations begins, and babies are very good at it. This process continues all through childhood; senses become refined, and children learn to make more subtle distinctions. Maturing senses become sharpened by experiences, and the world becomes a finely woven fabric of color, size, shape, texture, taste, and much more.

Learn to communicate *fully*. Babies are wonderful communicators and engage adults with cries and smiles. They are wired to grab people's attention, and people are wired to seek it out and to respond to it. Toddlers make huge leaps in facial expressions, sounds, body language, and, ultimately, words. From the point at which children use words, communication explodes to a more expansive use of physical expression, oral language, written language, and the other ways that children and adults learn to communicate their thoughts and feelings.

Discover and develop *all* bodily powers. Babies begin to hold their heads up, discover their hands, grasp, creep around the room, and develop the cognitive capacity for sophisticated language and symbolic thought. These first infant initiatives begin the process that years later results in all the wonderful things minds and bodies can do: running, playing sports, writing, using tools, making things, singing and dancing, and much more.

Understand how *everything* works. Curiosity is a powerful human trait, and young children are born with a drive to discover—they are bursting with *whys* and *hows*. Babies touch, taste, poke, suck, pick up, and drop things. Toddlers do all that plus throw things, climb up and down, go over, under, and around—actions that are really experiments in gravity, spatial relationships, and physics. They love to turn things on and off and combine unusual objects: "What's that cookie doing in the DVD player?" Older children construct and even tear apart places and things that they have created—communities built with toys, blocks, dolls, and props.

Development Is Not a Race

When did you take your first step? Were you a biter or the hapless victim of a biter? When did you start using words? And just for the record, when were you toilet trained?

Early childhood is a time when parents and caregivers watch development closely, caring intensely about many things. Unfortunately, often these things have no developmental significance. There is no future developmental advantage and rarely any significance in early achievement of most milestones. As parents, we cringe when our little Jason's same-age cousin is saying "Mom," "Da Da," and "Pass the cookies" while Jason is happily smiling and only infrequently producing nonsense words. Or when Martina down the street is out for a stroll while our Alice only creeps along. But Jason may become the orator and Alice the track star, because *earlier is not better.*

Normal development assumes many different forms and proceeds at a pace appropriate to each child. Albert Einstein hardly said a word before three, and Mohammed Ali began walking at fourteen months. Yes, we should look for signs of developmental delays that possibly signify physiological problems. But alertness does not have to create a climate of comparison, competition, and worry.

Deeply Connect with People. A sense of safety and security; enthusiasm and desire to please; development as family members, friends, members of a culture, and citizens of a community and the world—all these flow from children's innate drive to form deep relationships. Babies' sounds and gestures attract adults with their smiles and murmurs, and their cries cause concern—these are part of the bonding process. As children mature, they develop empathy and the ability both to give and to receive love, support, and affection. They become friends, helpers, and citizens.

When Children Do Their Jobs Much of what gets children trouble occurs when they are doing their jobs in ways that may drive adults crazy or may result in harm to other people, things, or themselves. Development is not trouble- or pain-free—there will be mishaps, bumps, bruises, social strife, and heartache. Exploring a new world and testing new powers are not always easy.

- Pushing or biting are actually the beginnings of social science, as is the later statement, "You are not my friend."
- Poking the baby, climbing on the table, throwing the ball through the window, jumping on the bed, or screaming as loud as possible is part of the "Look what I can do" drive.
- Dropping the spoon, opening the forbidden door, or stuffing the DVD player with a toy is an example of "What will happen?" or "How does the world work?"

A Final Word: You Can Never Know Too Much

Part of being a great teacher is knowing what you don't know and seeking to learn more. The more you know about development and the greater your awareness of developmental milestones, the more rewarding working with babies and toddlers will be. So much is happening in the first three years. Watching it happen and supporting it can be great fun. Some of the more subtle milestones, such as transferring an object from one hand to the other, make a big difference in babies' efforts to learn about the world. Celebrate these milestones when they happen and think about their implications not only for children's learning but also for what they need in the environment and from you to support that learning and exploration.

Exercises

1. Match specific behaviors of the children you work with to items in "A Child's Job Description."

2. Choose two infants or toddlers whom you know well and who are developing typically and are the same age. Compare and contrast what large and small milestones they have reached.

3. Write down when you achieved developmental milestones in early childhood, and ask your colleagues when they achieved the same milestones. How do the two match up in terms of strengths and talents as adults?

References

Coles, R. 1998. *The Moral Intelligence of Children: How to Raise a Moral Child.* New York: Plume.

Goleman, D. 1995. *Emotional Intelligence.* New York: Bantam.

Gopnick, A., A. Metzoff, and P. Kuhl. 1999. *The Scientist in the Crib: What Early Learning Tells Us about the Mind.* New York: Perennial.

Greenspan, S., and N. Greenspan. 1985. *First Feelings: Milestones in the Emotional Development of Your Baby and Child.* New York: Viking.

Maurer, D., and C. Maurer. 1988. *The World of the Newborn.* New York: Basic Books.

Piaget, J. 1974. *To Understand Is to Invent.* New York: Viking.

Shore, R. 1997. *Rethinking the Brain: New Insights into Early Development.* New York: Families and Work Institute.

Talbot, M. 2006. "The Baby Lab." *New Yorker,* September 4.

Chapter 5

The First Two Years of Life: What Do Infants and Toddlers Need Most?

εxcellence *Planning, provisioning, and interactions are based on thoughtful awareness of and deep respect for*

- *individual differences—the unique qualities and style of each child*
- *variations in typical development*
- *the child's family and culture.*

What Really Matters in Caring for Very Young Children?

A sense of basic trust. The first year of life is when children need to acquire what psychologist Erik Erikson called *basic trust* (1950)—a feeling of safety and security that the world and oneself are all right. Basic trust comes from caring people: responsive, predictable, nurturing care from familiar others whom one loves and to whom one is deeply attached. Without this sense, the world is far too scary a place to cope with and learn about. All self-esteem and all courage to accept challenges are founded on developing a profound, basic trust.

Bruno Bettelheim suggested that in a group setting, security derives from the feeling that we can safely relax, that we need not worry (1969, 63). In order to "safely relax," a child needs to feel "at home." In the words of a hypothetical young child,

This is my place. I know these people. They know me and they like me, despite my crying and diarrhea and difficulty going to sleep. I can count on them to take care of me, to respond to me. I can be me here, with all my own quirks, and still be accepted. I will be safe here, and I can step out and explore this strange and mysterious world.

What makes a feeling of being at home is that sense of predictability, familiarity, acceptance, and safety. A feeling of being at home is being with people you know and care about, and who care about you as well.

Ample opportunities to explore the world of things and people. Young children need a safe world where, as Jerome Bruner has written, they are "encouraged to venture, rewarded for [their] own acts, and sustained against distraction or premature interferences in carrying them out" (1973, 8). Children need a world rich in opportunities to see, hear, feel, touch, and move, to undertake all the actions listed earlier. They need a setting in which they will feel the world at their fingertips— a world that is there to explore and enjoy.

Ample opportunities to move. Obviously movement is essential to development. Even very young babies need lots of floor time, including tummy time (time on their stomachs) to develop all their muscles Although infants should always be put down to sleep on their backs, tummy time strengthens neck muscles and is important in helping to prevent Sudden Infant Death Syndrome (SIDS). An easy reminder is "back to sleep and front to play."

In the best programs, nearly all the child's waking time would be spent either in physical contact with an adult or on the floor, or even on the grass. In some programs, children spend too much time of little value in bouncy chairs, high chairs, buggies, or propped up by boppies or pillows. Infants need to develop all their muscles; in time, the neck, stomach, arm, and leg muscles are all in use. Moving around is essential to learning; it gives babies different perspectives and vantage points, which they need in order to move from an entirely egocentric view of space toward a more sophisticated sense of the relations between self, space, and other people. Older children know that objects are the same regardless of the angle or the distance from which they are observed, whether bathed by sunlight or blanketed by shadows, but an infant does not know this; for example, an infant may think that a ball that is further away from him is smaller than a same-size ball that is closer.

Ample language interactions. The first two years are critical for the development of language, and lay the foundation for conceptual thought, expressive language, and reading. The brain is being wired for language with every language interaction, every conversation. What is a conversation with an infant? It is not *"Hey, how you doing?" "Oh, I'm okay—but a little wet. How about a change?"* A conversation with an infant requires the adult to respond to smiles, frowns, sounds, spit bubbles, or gestures with words and attention. A conversation is watching and listening and responding—creating a call and response: *"Oh, what a great smile—I'm happy that you are happy!"* or *"Look at you, so serious. Are you watching the sunlight?"*

Research on cognitive development and language (Shore 1997; Hart and Risley, 1995) points increasingly to the likelihood that permanent cognitive capacity and language skills are increased through early language interactions. What is said and the words used matter less than the quantity of words and the positive interaction. Talking *at* a child is of less value than conversation. The *frequency* and *quantity* of words addressed to a baby matter in the first two years, and forever! A limited language environment will seriously affect the child's ability to think and to read.

Ample touch. A safe, secure world to explore begins with a baby's need for physical contact—lots of it: holding, snuggling, touching, rubbing, patting, hugging, and providing a body to lean on. Touch is even more important than vision for survival and healthy development. Touch reassures infants that they are safe and not alone. In a real sense, touch gives their bodies permission to grow and their minds permission to explore. Babies in institutions, otherwise well cared for, once died of "skin hunger"—that is, inadequate physical contact—and even older children can stop growing until placed in a nurturing setting (Gallagher 1993).

It is not just being held that provides trust and security and "permission to develop." For infants, one of the best things about getting picked up is not only being touched but also being moved about.

> *Because adults don't spend time being jiggled and seem none the worse for it, the regulating effects of vestibular stimulation—rhythm and movement—are hidden from adults' eyes. But like a sailor on the high seas, the fetus lives in almost constant motion. . . . Its own activity too is necessary to the formation of its nervous system, joints, bones, muscles, lungs, and other body parts. After birth, developing infants continue to need movements to mature their nervous systems* (Gallagher 1993, 124).

A sense of autonomy. Autonomy is the sense of being a separate, independent self. Infants and toddlers need to begin to feel this:

> *I'm a me, a self separate from my mom and dad and my caregivers. I can have an impact on this huge world. If I can say "No" freely, I can also say "Yes" freely. I can use my powers so that I can begin to control this body and these feelings.*

A sense of power and competence. Only when children feel a personal sense of power ("I can make things happen," "I can make a difference") and competence ("I can do things and achieve things") can they step out into the world as active learners and problem solvers, prepared to cope with what will come.

In group settings, children are more likely to feel powerless; there is little under their control. Giving children choices—the freedom to move, the chance to try things, the power to get others to respond to their physical and emotional needs—tells them that they are people who make a difference. Giving them an opportunity to do things successfully—for example, get unstuck from under a table, put on a coat, or carry a basket of bread rolls—tells them that they are capable.

Getting to Know Infants and Toddlers: What Do They Do?

In a good program, staff know enough about development to recognize the important skills infants and toddlers are acquiring as they "do the work of development." Staff recognize and delight in emerging skills and understandings when they occur and provide many opportunities for children to use them when they are ready. They know that young children only rarely need to be taught skills or to be pushed to perform. Rather, they simply need lots of opportunities, occasional help, and people who can enjoy their success and achievements with them.

Staff in good programs also guard against the natural tendency to overemphasize the dramatic milestones, such as the first step and the first word, at the expense of all the small, visible, and often invisible achievements essential to healthy development. These include such achievements as pulling up, learning to grasp, experimenting with sounds, and beginning to understand object permanence.

Infants and Toddlers Can Do Many Things

Some of the many things infants do include the following:

see	turn	
watch	roll	
look	lift head up	
inspect	sit up	
hear	transfer objects from one	
listen	hand to the other	
smell	crawl to, in, out, over	
taste	creep around, in, under	
feel	swing	
touch	rock	
mouth	coo	
eat	babble	
reach out	react to others	
reach for	imitate sounds and	
knock away	simple actions	
grasp	solicit from others	
hold	recognize people	
squeeze	and things	
pinch	experiment endlessly	
drop		
pull up		
shake		
bang		
tear		
clap together		
put in		
take out		
find		
look for		
kick		

In addition to many of the above, toddlers may also do the following:

walk in, out, up, down	take out
climb in, up, over, on top	hide
climb over, under,	discover
around, through	investigate by trial
slide	and error
swing	explore with each sense
hang	imitate familiar acts
jump	imitate adult behavior
tumble	engage in doll play
take apart	paint
put together	smear
stack	draw
pile	mix
nest	separate
set up	pour
knock over	sift
collect	splash
gather	make sounds and labels
fill	"read" symbols
dump	converse
inspect	follow directions
examine	cuddle
select	hug
sort	kiss
match	test others
order	adjust their behavior
carry	to others
transport	help to wash, eat, and
rearrange	dress themselves
put	

Toddlers Are Not Infants (or Preschoolers, Either!)

Toddlers are child care's equivalent of young adolescents—"in betweens." Leaving babyhood and approaching preschool status, they exhibit uneven behavior, often giving the appearance of more maturity than they actually possess. The result frequently is that adults expect toddlers to act maturely all the time, or at other times babying them and prevent them from testing their emerging skills. The tendency in many programs is to treat toddlers as if they were preschoolers, just smaller and less competent ones. Their "collective monologues" (talking at each other but not with each other), their frequently parallel and sometimes cooperative play, their bursts of understanding, and their sometimes remarkable willingness to cooperate and please mask the substantial differences between two-year-olds and four-year-olds.

Neither infants nor preschoolers, toddlers are increasingly mobile, autonomous, beginning to be social, verbal, thoughtful creatures with constant urges to test and experiment. They have limited language, so they still mostly use behavior to communicate. They are living contradictions: the erratic do-it-myself desire competes with their passive and completely dependent "You do it." They are prone to change their minds about what they want. These restless, mobile characters have a drive to take apart the existing order and to rearrange it—by force, if necessary—to suit the whimsical logic of their universe. They are often charming and engaging but at times determinedly defiant or out of control from frustration or anger. Toddlers are very exciting people to work with, but their stage of development brings with it many challenges and considerable frustration for both them and their teachers.

> **Anarchists with a Herd Instinct**
>
> Toddlers are anarchists with a herd instinct. They march to their own drummers and organize their world according to their own idiosyncratic logic. At any given time a toddler may cooperate good-naturedly, or may not (either cooperate *or* be goodnatured!). A group of toddlers is a group in name only. But they do swarm and herd. One minute they are each doing their own things; the next minute, seemingly every child suddenly has a need to occupy the same space.

Infants and Toddlers Are Very Eager, Competent Learners

They need less adult-directed stimulation and more respect, time, and materials for their learning. Babies need to learn and understand that they can influence the people and things in the world around them. They need to develop a sense of personal power: "I can do it," "I matter."

Education results when, in T. Berry Brazelton's words, a baby finds "the pleasure of being the cause"; of learning how to act in order to produce the results he wants, of learning about things that are the results of his own actions (Gonzalez-Mena and Eyer [1980] 1993, 45).

Infants and toddlers are sensorimotor beings. They explore the world with their developing senses and motor skills. Long before they understand a concept like *under* or *far* with their minds, their bodies are learning to move and understand the up-and-down, over-and-under physical world. Sensory exploration expands a world that once had only a few categories into a complex, meaningful place with textures, colors, sounds, weight, uses, and other qualities.

Infants and toddlers are communicators. They begin with the birth cry and continually expand their range of signals and messages, both those they use and those they understand. Until language becomes a vital tool, they use behavior—body language, gestures, and facial expressions—to tell others what they want and how they feel. In the first year of life, crying and gurgling rapidly become sophisticated sounds and gestures. Babies learn language by hearing lots of it in individual conversations and by having people around them listen and respond to their efforts to communicate.

Infants and toddlers are social beings. Their communication is directed at those they love and need, the adults who care for them, and the other large and small people with whom they share the world. It is the give-and-take of communication that connects babies to the world of other people. But they are not yet social in the sense that older children are, and therefore they are not very well suited to cope with group experiences.

Infants and toddlers are people with feelings. They may not understand all the language they hear or the motives of others, but they are very sensitive to tones and feelings expressed through oral and body language. They experience feelings of rejection, anger, jealousy, humiliation, and hurt. They, like all human beings, thrive on love, empathy, praise, and appreciation.

Infants and toddlers come with parents and families. All efforts to understand and care for children require that children be viewed within the context of their families—their beliefs, values, culture, and circumstances.

What to Expect from Infants and Toddlers

Creating a good place for infants and toddlers—a relaxed, nurturing learning environment—depends on having appropriate expectations. This means expecting infants to behave like infants and toddlers like toddlers, with all the typical variations that individuals present.

Expectations for Infants

Quality child care is based on an understanding of and appreciation for the natural behavior of children and the ways they go about the job of development. Expect babies to

- *be different from each other.* Children will differ in interests, moods, pace, ability to signal how they feel, how they learn, how they react to change, and the care they need.
- *cry to communicate.* Crying is the way infants let others know they need help. They don't cry just to annoy others.
- *desperately need caring adults.* Being allowed to remain in distress is not good for infants and is likely to lead to increased crying. It works against the feeling of basic trust and security that provide the foundation for healthy development.
- *explore.* Continuous curiosity fuels the process of learning about the world.
- *test all limits.* Babies learn how the world works by testing the reactions of people and things to their actions.

- *experiment with their bodies.* They use their growing physical powers to test the properties of people, things, and space. If they are to learn they need to crawl, walk, run, kick, step up and down, move, stack, drop and throw things, take things apart, fit themselves and things inside of other things, and climb in and over.
- *experiment with their senses.* Babies use their mouths, eyes, ears, and skin as tools for learning. They need to touch, taste, feel, look, and listen to the world. A baby's mouth and whole body are the chief tools used. For example, babies suck on everything, testing the feel of baby food or paint on their cheeks or stomachs.

Additional Expectations for Toddlers

Toddlers are sold short when they are thought of *only* as being between babies and preschoolers, as resembling old babies or immature three-year-olds. These inaccurate or incomplete understandings of toddlers result in programming that is neither interesting nor challenging or that is too sophisticated and therefore frustrating. Either way, it is easy to develop negative views of toddlers ("terrible" instead of "terrific"), defining their competence as the problem ("they are bored—they need to move up") or defining them through what they lack (for example, the skills of preschoolers). The toddler stage of development has integrity and its own particular characteristics, strengths, and needs.

Expect toddlers to

- *explode with energy.* Their new competence and curiosity often lead to sheer exuberance and bursts of energy.
- *explode with frustration.* Too few or too many choices, challenges, or obstacles and too much or too little power can be overwhelming for toddlers. Frustration comes easily when they are blocked, because internal controls and patience come slowly. They also can now imagine doing things that they cannot yet do.
- *dawdle.* Toddlers often dawdle, whether to "smell the roses," examine a curious object never noticed before (or even a familiar favorite one), assert themselves, or become lost in their vague sense of time.
- *lose control of themselves.* When the world caves in on toddlers, for whatever reason, they often desperately need reassurance, whether they are stuck in a tantrum of rage or an inconsolable pit of despair.
- *be contrary.* "No" is a declaration of independence. Toddlers refuse requests, defy, and resist control because they are learning that they can exert some control. They are learning how to be assertive. This is an important step in learning self-control.
- *change moods.* Because so much change is happening for them inside and out, it is natural for toddlers to swing from being sweet and compliant to being little tyrants, to swing from joy to rage, and to swing from being needy babies to being seemingly mature helpers and comforters of others.
- *act fearful.* As their thinking develops and they move into the world, they discover that it has scary elements.
- *act powerful.* Toddlers begin to understand that they can: cause things to happen or not happen, do things on their own, create things, go places, and elicit strong positive or negative reactions from people. When they discover these

powers, they want to use them, and it is hard for them to learn how to use them appropriately.

- *experience separation intensely at times.*
The pain of separating from parents may be present at times. The intensity varies from day to day and from hour to hour. It is likely to be strongest in the morning, at sleep times, and at the end of the day.

Alike and Different

The importance of expecting children to be different and of basing care on that expectation is so critical that it cannot be stressed enough. Infants new to the world not only do not look alike or act alike, they come to us with different parents, genders, cultures, temperaments, learning styles, physiologies, physical abilities, rates of development, special needs, and on and on. Of course, children are fellow human beings and are also alike in lots of ways, so much of teachers' behavior is based on experience with other children. But that is only the starting point of providing responsive care until the teacher comes to know the individual child.

Temperament Children are born with personalities. The work of Alexander Thomas, Stella Chess, and Herbert Birch, who were among the first to articulate the concept that basic temperaments can be identified in infants, has been hugely influential. These researchers considered temperament an inborn characteristic that predisposes individuals toward specific emotional responses. Temperament helps define the differences in infant behaviors such as crying, reacting to physical contact and strange situations, exploring, and activity level.

Thomas, Chess, and Birch identify some babies as *easy*—flexible, adaptable, approachable, and good-natured (Chess and Thomas 1987). These babies often take change or mild stress in stride. Other babies are less approachable and are slow to warm up, often reacting negatively to change or new situations. They are often

---

Toddlers' Rules of Property

A toddler's sense of self, of *I* and *me,* emerges in a group environment and a culture which private property and the acquisition of things are somewhat sacred. This makes the learning of related concepts like *mine* particularly challenging:

1. If I like it, it's mine.
2. If it's in my hand, it's mine.
3. If I can take it from you, it's mine.
4. If I had it a little while ago, it's mine.
5. If it looks just like mine, it's mine.
6. If I saw it first, it's mine.
7. If you are doing or building something and you put it down, it automatically becomes mine.
8. If it is mine, it must never appear to be yours in any way.
9. If it is broken, it's yours.
10. If it's broken, where's mine?

(Anonymous)

See Supplement: *Toddlers' Rules of Property*

Specific Personality Characteristics

Children vary on a number of temperament characteristics:

Activity level	low	high
Biological rhythms	regular	irregular
Tendency to approach or withdraw	approach	withdraw
Mood	positive	negative
Intensity of reaction	low	high
Adaptability / flexibility	low	high
Sensitivity to sensation	low	high
Persistence	low	high
Distractibility	low	high

The more children's individual temperaments are recognized and understood, the better care can be adapted to each of them.

Helping Shy Children

Anne was born shy and cautious, unlike her older sister Emma, who greeted new people like long-lost friends and who plunged into new territory with little thought. New people and situations were difficult for Anne.

From birth, Anne had trouble with novelty and changes in routine. She was usually very slow to warm up to new people and to enter new situations. Separation from her parents or her primary caregiver at child care was difficult for her; almost all transitions were hard. The slightest change in her morning routine could ruin her day.

Children like Anne, who tend to be cautious, shy, timid, anxious, slow to warm up, or fearful, are no less capable of success in life than children born with a temperament inclined to plunge into new situations or to take risks, or children who seem to take everything in stride, adapting flexibly to what life has to offer. Shyness and having difficulty with novelty are as normal as adaptability. Many children are born with this tendency. It does not mean that they won't grow up to be presidents, Olympic athletes, CEOs, lawyers, rock stars, or even talk show hosts.

Parents and teachers can play critical roles in helping children overcome shyness and fearfulness. The key for adults is not to be overly protective or solicitous, on the one hand, or to ignore it and expect the child to sink or swim, on the other. What children like Anne need is gentle coaching, acceptance, patience, encouragement, and support to help them develop in their own time the confidence and skills to master new relationships and situations.

perceived as having a "shy gene" and are sometimes seen as withdrawn or fearful, although cautious is a more accurate description. Given time, patience, and gentle coaching, they eventually adapt. The third type of temperament, seen in about 10 percent of babies—thankfully a relatively small percentage—are often described as difficult or feisty. These babies tend to be more active and restless, may experience more negative moods, have unpredictable, intense, and irritable reactions, and are hard to settle into regular routines for eating and sleeping. They react strongly to new people, situations, and change.

Temperament is not destiny The temperament people are born with is a powerful influence on the adults they may become, but it does not determine their destiny. Temperament is relatively stable but does not remain unchanged; experience shapes and refines inborn traits. Personality is shaped by continuous interaction among three factors: temperament, environment, and experience. Therefore, the care children receive will help to shape their personalities.

Children born with a disposition toward caution and shyness can develop personalities that enable them to master new social situations and overcome any fears that might hold them back; however, they may perhaps remain *mindful* and *cautious*. Difficult babies are not destined to be difficult adults, provided they receive care that adapts to their needs. Without sensitive caregiving, however, difficult babies may be at risk for developing attachment problems.

A difficult child may not be an easy child to attach to, and the child's parents will need support and understanding. In fact, supporting the parent-child relationship may be more important for the child's future than the experiences the child has while in care.

A Teacher's Job: What Do Infants and Toddlers Need Most from the Program?

More than thirty-five years ago, Mary Elizabeth Keister, in *The "Good Life" for Infants and Toddlers* (1970), eloquently described what infants and toddlers need from care: the kind of lives they lead in good homes. As with homes, good programs occur in diverse settings and diverse ways. Inevitably, however, good homes and programs provide the sort of setting that Keister describes:

- Each child is prized for being a unique individual, worthy of love and personalized care.
- Other people know the ways in which each child is different from every other child.
- Others care about how each child feels and what he or she is learning.
- Adults have discovered much about how to keep each child involved and comfortable by looking for and responding to each child's signals and interactions.

Sensitive Teachers

The relationship between the adult and the child provides the security and encouragement to venture out into the world. Consider Mary Ainsworth's description of "the sensitive mother," which applies to all people in a caregiving role—in the family, in family child care, and in child care centers:

The sensitive mother is able to see things from her baby's point of view. She is tuned in to receive her baby's signals: she interprets them correctly, and she responds appropriately. Although she nearly always gives the baby what he seems to want, when she does not she is tactful in acknowledging his communication and in offering an acceptable alternative. She makes her responses temporally contingent upon the baby's signals and communications. The sensitive mother, by definition, cannot be rejecting, interfering, or ignoring.

The insensitive mother, on the other hand, gears her interventions and initiations of interactions almost exclusively in terms of her own wishes, moods, and activities. She tends either to distort the implications of her baby's communications, interpreting them in the light of her own wishes or defenses, or not to respond to them at all. (McCall 1980, 118)

Very young children need adults who

- listen, smile, and talk with them or babble when they babble
- retrieve toys and play peekaboo, hide-and-seek, and other games
- feed them when they are hungry
- sing to them and rock them when they are tired
- hold them when they feel small or sad or want to get or give some loving
- notice and communicate pleasure over such newfound skills as creeping, climbing, holding, dropping, or adding new sounds and words
- change their position or help them discover new possibilities when they are bored
- watch for the kinds of things that turn them on, such as toys, talk, or chances to explore and mess about
- watch for when they need quiet and solitude.

Each infant and toddler needs a setting in which diapering, easing in and out of sleep, being helped with the mysteries and struggles of toilet learning, and learning to use a spoon are all considered precious prime times for one-to-one nurturing and learning. All children need their days shaped to their own temperament and pace by people who provide more encouragement than direction, and more exploration and challenge than restriction, and who provide reassurance, comfort, and limits.

Respect for Parents and Cultural Differences

Children need a setting that

- respects their parents as the most important people in their lives
- acknowledges and uses parents' expert knowledge of their own children
- values the intense caring that parents can bring to the setting
- encourages parents to recognize the important contributions they make to their children's learning and development.

Babies come with families, and families come with cultures. Sensitive teaching in practice will lead to variations, some of which derive from family and cultural backgrounds. Cultures that prize individualism, such as the Anglo-American, nurture differently than cultures that are more communal and interdependent, such as the Japanese (see Konner 1991; Gonzalez-Mena and Eyer [1980] 1993; Gonzalez-Mena 2004). Cultures vary in everything from sex roles to sounds and smells, from the personal space and distance people claim as they talk to one another to the way soothing happens and frustration is expressed. In speech and language alone, the differences are many: words, structure pronunciation, speed and cadence of speech, the ways that children and adults are addressed.

Cultures vary in what they expect of children and those who care for them—what is tolerated and what is not. While it is desirable for programs and staff to reflect the cultures of the families served, it is difficult to accomplish this and be all things to all people. If having the children's culture and language represented in the staffing of the center is not possible, at the very least the program and staff need to understand, appreciate, and respect the parents' culture and work closely as partners with the family to achieve some continuity of care. It is possible to have the program reflect the child's language through learning some of the key words that infants and toddlers hear at home. The program environment can also include familiar objects and sensations—sights, sounds, smells, and textures—and staff can learn important words and phrases in the language of the children. Respecting families in practice is discussed in chapter 7.

Respect for Teachers

Infants and toddlers also need a setting in which the people who care for them are respected as important people who use their minds and bodies to do the very difficult job of providing personalized care and relaxed, happy days to children in groups. Respecting staff in practice is discussed in chapter 9.

Infants and Toddlers with Special Needs

Of course, all children have special needs. But many programs will have young children whose conditions require consideration beyond that required for the average child: developmental delays, disabilities, chronic illnesses, or family situations that put them at some risk. Moreover, staff will often be concerned that particular children may have serious undiagnosed special needs that might benefit from early diagnosis.

This handbook takes the view that in a good program, each child is always viewed as special—that is, as worthy of individual consideration and program adaptation. Further, an inclusive program will benefit all children by reinforcing the conviction that children are individuals. Any child may have a special need at one time or another, caused by lack of sleep, developmental spurts, or situational stress. Because of this, programs can never be "one size fits all" or mechanically follow daily routines. Children with any sort of special need require care that responds to their strengths and is shaped by the cues they provide. Caring for children with any kind of special need requires teachers to respond with more time, patience, tolerance, and willingness to learn about these children. The learning activities that help infants and toddlers with disabilities or special needs to maximize their development differ little or not at all from those used by other children. However, these children may need some additional support or adaptation, and adaptations to the environment may be necessary for those children with physical or sensory impairments in order to help them achieve autonomy and successful experiences.

Intervention

Some special needs become apparent in utero, at birth, or during routine infant screening and exams. Many, however, do not become evident until the child's behavior offers clues to a particular problem. The result is that symptoms may first come up when a child is under the program's care. The dilemma for staff is that while their concern may turn out to be false, to not act on it would be irresponsible, given the importance of early intervention.

The first consideration in addressing the issue of infants and toddlers with special needs is understanding that the possibility or reality that something may be seriously wrong with their child will be an emotional earthquake for parents. It will strike at the heart of their being, at their present, future, and even their past as parents, raising the question, "Is it our fault?" The child's primary caregiver often plays a key role in discovering whether or not a child is developing normally. As a result, she is likely to experience the full gamut of parents' fear, denial, hope, and anger. The critical importance of a strong partnership with parents, based on trust and mutual respect, becomes clear when the possibility of special needs arises.

All states have early intervention services to identify and support children with special needs. The federal legislation that applies to children from birth to age three is referred to as part C of the Individuals with Disabilities Education Act (IDEA). The legislation establishes state or community teams of professionals—physical and speech therapists, physicians, public health nurses, social workers, other therapists, and educators—that work with the family to create an individual family service plan (IFSP). Early care and education programs for children with special needs are usually part of the team. The IFSP may become the centerpiece for tailoring the child's experience. School districts are good sources of information about local resources.

Children at risk from social circumstances also have special needs. Child abuse, neglect, and the effects of poverty may result in developmental delays, chronic health problems, and behavioral disorders. The major difference in serving these children may be the teacher's relationship with the parents. The challenge teachers face is that the partnership with parents in at-risk homes is more difficult and more critical than with other families having special needs.

Types of Special Needs Often Present in Child Care

The more common types of special needs that providers are likely to encounter are the result of genetic (inborn) conditions, diseases, injuries, and environmental factors.

Motor delays. Often, special needs are discovered in infancy through observation of the baby's reflexes and delays in motor functioning. Any number of conditions may lead to motor delays or variations from typical motor development: visual or hearing impairments, brain damage, cerebral palsy, inadequate nutrition, chronic illness, premature birth, or birth trauma. Regular medical exams and screening are important because early intervention is essential to maximize development.

Sensory or perceptual impairments. Vision and hearing problems are often first discovered while a child is in child care. An infant with a hearing loss may not react to sounds and may be surprised by the presence of other people. Vocalizations may appear (such as the onset of babbling) but then stop, apparently because they are not as self-pleasing as they are when infants hear their own sounds and adults' responses. Parents and teachers should be aware that untreated ear infections can lead to hearing loss. Infants with visual impairments may be uninterested in objects and fail to reach, retrieve, or fail to search for objects past the time when object permanence should have developed.

It is important to remember that most sensory impairments are not total and that effective intervention builds on the child's existing capacity as well as on developing other senses.

Cognitive special needs. There are no reliable tests of infant or toddler IQ. Delays or retardation are assessed through observation and clinical testing of the child's motor behavior, reflexes, adaptive (problem-solving and predictive) responses to experiences of people and things, perceptual behavior, and language. Because the infant's or toddler's motor, sensory, and cognitive functioning are so interrelated, pinpointing the cause of the exact condition is often difficult. Cognitive retardation may be the result of genetic conditions such as Down Syndrome, prenatal experiences (malnutrition, drugs, alcohol) or brain damage (as a result of accident or disease—for example, rubella).

Chronic illness and special health needs. Children with heart monitors, acquired immune deficiency syndrom (AIDS), and chronic health concerns are mainstreamed in child care centers. In each case, the child may present a range of unique special needs.

Drug- and alcohol-affected infants and toddlers. Children exposed to drugs and alcohol in utero typically have medical and behavioral problems that vary depending on the severity of their exposure. Typically, infants are irritable and hard to calm, difficult to nurture, and require slow, deliberate interactions adapted to their cues. Swaddling, massage, and very low levels of stimulation may be necessary. Some children may be unresponsive. These are not easy children to attach to, yet that is exactly what they need. Older infants and toddlers are often likely to be easily upset, distractible, and may have difficulty adapting to new situations.

Speech and language special needs. Speech and language problems are common in preschool programs and may go undetected in infant and toddler programs. Many potential problems may be reduced by early discovery and intervention.

Communication disorders may be the result of physical, emotional, or social conditions. Nonresponsive environments may be nearly as damaging as physical impairments. Hearing problems, retardation, muscular problems, ear infections, and other illnesses may lead to problems in producing speech or processing language.

Families at risk. Many programs serve children who are at risk of abuse, neglect, or the effects of poverty. These infants and toddlers may present several health issues and usually have parents as needy as their children. The key to serving these children is careful observation and patience, access to and coordination of social service resources, and recognition that the parents deserve the same respect and support that all parents do.

A Final Word: The Teacher's Job Is Supporting Each Child

Infants and toddlers alike are wonderful human beings. A teacher's job is to support children in doing their jobs. *Each* child deserves the opportunity to do and learn what they need to do in order to thrive. If they are to eventually step out and take advantage of what the world has to offer, they need

- opportunities for practice and mastery of tasks that fit their emerging skills and understanding
- a sensorily rich, aesthetically pleasing environment filled with conversation and written language
- a place for exploration and discovery of the natural world, toys and games, interactive time with safe machines and household objects, as well as opportunities to experiment with various media
- ample opportunities to use and test their motor skills, both large and small
- people they care about and trust.

The teacher's job is to be patient and protective, but not too protective, and to encourage children's innate sense of adventure: to provide a safe yet challenging world at their fingertips. Teachers are guides who know when to step in and when to step back!

Exercises

1. Make a list of behaviors typical of children at six months, twelve months, eighteen months, twenty-four months, thirty months, and thirty-six months that are developmentally appropriate and necessary but that can be annoying to adults who are caring for them (for example, crying before sleep, exploring with their mouths, asserting "No" at difficult times). Circle those behaviors that drive *you* crazy.

2. For five minutes, observe a child from each of the above ages. Notice all the ways the child explores, copes, or masters the environment.

References

Bettelheim, B. 1969. *The Children of the Dream*. New York: Avon.

Bruner, J. S. 1973. "Organization of Early Skilled Action." *Child Development* 44:1–111.

Chess, S., and A. Thomas. 1987. *Know Your Child: An Authoritative Guide for Today's Parents*. New York: Basic Books.

Erikson, E. 1950. *Childhood and Society*. New York: Norton.

Gallagher, W. 1993. *The Power of Place*. New York: HarperCollins.

Gonzalez-Mena, J. 2004. *Diversity in Early Care and Education: Honoring Differences*. 4th ed. New York: McGraw-Hill.

Gonzalez-Mena, J., and D. Eyer. [1980] 1993. *Infancy and Caregiving*. Mountain View, CA: Mayfield.

Hart, B., and T. Risley. 1995. *Meaningful Differences in the Everyday Experience of Young American Children*. Baltimore: Paul H. Brooke.

Keister, M. E. 1970. *The "Good Life" for Infants and Toddlers*. Washington, DC: NAEYC.

Konner, M. 1991. *Childhood*. New York: Little Brown and Company.

McCall, R. 1980. *Infants*. New York: Vintage.

Shore, R. 1997. *Rethinking the Brain: New Insights into Early Development*. New York: Families and Work Institute.

Chapter 6

Grouping Infants and Toddlers

excellence *Children experience the day in small, stable groups with teachers they know and trust. The program supports attachment relationships between teachers and children, continuity of care over time, individualized care and learning, and relaxed, happy days.*

How children are grouped obviously has an enormous impact on the program. Grouping affects care, learning, feelings of staff and parents, cost, and continuity of care.

There's no consensus on the best ways to group children under the age of three. If you investigate child care in different states or countries, you will discover all sorts of grouping arrangements for children under age three. They range from separating children every six months—young infants, infants, young toddlers, toddlers—to multiage rooms for children six weeks to two or even three years old. There is no universal, fixed set of assumptions free of "it depends on other factors." Staff-child ratios, group size, room size, staffing patterns, and age range of children are interacting factors that affect both cost and quality.

Regulations and accreditation criteria set the parameters for allowable practice but rarely impose fixed options on programs. Each factor interacts with the others, and the combination limits optimal grouping. But while there are few "best ways," there are certainly choices that are undesirable, leading to low quality and high costs for families—for example, children changing primary caregivers or groups every six months.

Continuous Relationships

If there is an invisible cost to children in typical child care, it is the lack of continuous relationships between children and teachers, often the main issue in discussions of continuity of care. In *The Irreducible Needs of Children: What Every Child Must Have to Grow, Learn, and Flourish* (2000), T. Berry Brazelton and Stanley Greenspan make clear that children need to develop deep, knowing, and trusting relationships with caring adults that last over time—more than six months or a year, even two years. Parents and teachers also need to develop close relationships based on understanding and trust. No matter how wonderful, kind, smart, or experienced the staff, the relationship is not the same as a familiar, intimate, extended relationship. Staff turnover or planned moves from room to room force everyone to repeatedly start over.

There are a number of strategies to achieve more continuous relationships:

- *Mixed-age grouping:* because the age range is wide (six weeks to twenty-four months or older), children can remain in the same room with the same teacher.
- *Looping:* or assigning children to the same teacher, who progresses with the group of children as they move through the program. For instance, Valencia began with four infants, and they stayed together until the children reached thirty months, at which time Valencia looped back to a new group.
- *Pairing rooms:* for example, an infant room and a toddler room, in order to create a close environment in which infants (and families) transition between people and places that they already know well.
- *Community of Caring:* a concept that applies when, because of staff turnover, longer-term relationships with individual

continued on next page

Determining Age Groups: Who Goes with Whom?

What is the best way to determine who goes with whom? First, it is important to clarify what state regulations and NAEYC accreditation criteria allow. Because regulations change and there is usually more than one option, check what the regulations say rather than make assumptions based on your usual practice. There may be other options. For example, in some states, regulations allow a six-weeks to one-year infant group and a one-year to two-year toddler group as well as a fifteen-month to thirty-month option. Consider the program's need for flexibility. Too narrow a definition of a group (for example, young infants or one-year-olds) may result in fewer options than a wider age range when you are trying to fill an opening. Finally, of course, grouping has implications for each child's and family's experience.

The Value of Mixed-Age Grouping

Wider age groups that allow children and adults a longer time together are generally preferable, all things being equal and time and space structured accordingly. Looping—moving teachers along with children—is another option, but often harder to achieve or less desirable if there is turnover of children or staff or if there is a tight budget.

Wider age groups are so uncommon that it may seem that the practice of age-grading childhood activities—that is, marching children through experiences with children their own age—is "the right way." Isn't it common sense to organize the program into infants (six weeks to one year), toddlers (one to two years), twos, young preschool, pre-K, and so on? Many states, in fact, require it. But that pattern ignores the child's (and the family's) need for a longer-term relationship with a teacher and the undesirability of unneeded transitions. It also ignores the value for all children of open-ended materials and a variety of experiences offered by flexible teachers, with something for everyone. There is also an evolutionary logic to mixed-age groups—after all, they are the model for how children have developed throughout time. They are more natural, closer to a family model, and probably superior as learning groups.

After all, human children have never been birthed and raised in litters.

There is another positive advantage to multiage groups. In group care, staff naturally tend to minimize attention to individual differences. Unfortunately, this inclination is strongest when the age range is narrow. A wider age range results in greater awareness of children's individual differences. In addition, a narrow age range may encourage parents to compare their child with others. That children about the same age are very similar is an illusion that adults maintain to keep from being overwhelmed by the variety of differences that children present. At any age, development is not uniform across developmental areas. A twenty-four-month-old child may equal thirty-month-old child in language and perceptual development, a seventeen-month-old child in large-motor development, and a twenty-three-month-old child in small-motor and social development, yet all these children are perfectly normal. Having eight children the same age says little about the developmental range of the group; a broad developmental spectrum must still be planned for.

Centers in the United States rarely use extended-age grouping for children under three years old (in family child care, of course, it is the norm). There is rarely a span beyond a twelve- to eighteen-month range, reflecting the age-grading in school and the licensing guidelines that often make mixed-age grouping more costly. But when it is feasible, there are many advantages to giving children the opportunity to be with others older and younger than themselves:

- Greater continuity means that a child will make fewer transitions from group to group. Children (and parents) are in the group and with the staff for a longer time, and therefore are more likely to develop real relationships. Child care centers struggle with the inevitability of staff and child turnover as it is. To needlessly force a move every year or at even shorter intervals creates instability, resulting in frequent changes of staff as well as of physical environments and peers.
- Older children have the opportunity to be the most competent and to learn helping, caring, and communication skills through interacting with younger children.

Continuous Relationships, *continued*

teachers are proving difficult. It is the conscious adoption of community-building strategies to create closer relationships among all members of the center's community, both adults and children.

Every strategy needs to take into account budget, facility, talent pool, turnover of staff, turnover of children, and family preferences. The "best way" is the strategy that best fits the program and provides the best chance of continuous relationships.

What Is an Infant? What Is a Toddler?

Is fourteen-month old Celina an infant or a toddler? Depending on the country, state, or province that she happens to live in, she may be considered either. Is twenty-six-month-old Tyler still a toddler? Again, it depends on where he happens to live. In a developmental sense, Celina is obviously a toddler, and has been one since she triumphantly rose and toddled across the room at eleven months. Tyler still has the slightly ovoid shape and diaper-bound waddle of a toddler, whatever the state says. But each licensing jurisdiction defines what an infant or toddler is, if twos are a separate group and if a program can mix children over and under age one, age two, or age three. From those decisions flow the legally minimum staff-child ratios, group sizes, and other regulations. Unfortunately, they also usually define whether Celina and Tyler sleep in a crib, are allowed a morning nap, and, in some programs, are considered too old or too young for the room.

- Siblings may be able to stay together.
- Young children learn many new ideas and skills from being with older children.
- Routines may be easier to manage and individualize because of the wide range of needs and schedules. While some children are sleeping, the number of awake children is reduced.
- Staff and children avoid the tension that can come when a group is made up totally of toddlers, all of whom have trouble sharing and coping with group life.

Dealing with a wider age range happens to some extent anyway. The actual age range experienced by the children is dependent on another factor: space available in the next age group. In a center that is usually full, children often get stuck, unable to move on until a space opens up. Or they may have to move a little sooner than anticipated to take advantage of a space.

It is true that if the age range extends beyond eighteen months or so, staff must possess the knowledge and skills to provide a program appropriate for all children in the group. It can be a challenge to provide the range of materials, equipment, and experiences needed by children of diverse ages within one space. There is often a movement toward the lowest common denominator—that is, toward providing only materials and experiences that are safe and manageable for the youngest children and that therefore do not fully meet the needs of the oldest children—or alternatively,

toward the middle, which slights both older and younger children. There also may be staff members who feel uncomfortable with the younger or older children and who would not work as well in a multiage group.

Are There Advantages to Grouping Children as Close to the Same Age as Possible?

There are no real advantages to grouping children within a narrow age range. However, the success of whatever method of grouping is used depends to a considerable extent on the perceptions of staff and parents, who often prefer narrower age groups. Staff may be negative or feel stretched when dealing with a wider age range. Parents of younger children worry about whether their children will be safe and well cared for: "Won't that big lurching toddler crush my little baby?" Parents of older children fear that their children may not be challenged, may regress, or may be slowed in their development. These perceptions are important because any arrangement must have the support of parents and staff alike.

Many of the benefits of narrow age grouping are illusions based on the notion that same-age children are the same and that it is very difficult to create wonderful environments for a wider age group. It just seems easier, because you can provide the same equipment and schedule, do the same things, react the same ways, and de-emphasize the ways in which children really differ—and besides, working in this way is usually familiar. But in reality, narrow age ranges are only easier when the children are supposed to fit the program, not the reverse, and when staff are supposed to do things to and for the children, such as instruct and care for them in a mostly standardized fashion.

Family Grouping

Family grouping comes in two forms: a single room and a cluster of rooms. A few centers have been designed specifically to accommodate family groups within a room, with spaces fitted out for small groups of children, usually six weeks to two or three years old but sometimes up to five years old. Adjacent to the room are areas where the older children can be taken for activities and experiences not suitable for the younger children. The schedule includes starting and finishing the day and eating with the mixed-age group in the room, as well as providing some time for the older children with children their own age, away from the room. In a well-designed facility, this arrangement is close to ideal for children. However, a major drawback is the cost of care. Typically centers have to provide staff-child ratios for the youngest child. Generally, groups with a wide age range benefit from smaller group sizes.

Note: There are also centers with twenty to thirty children under five years old who spend a good portion of their day together in so-called *family groups*. This is a significant misnomer. Families are not of such a size, and this type of grouping places particular stress on the younger children in the group.

Family grouping also applies to organizing rooms within a larger center to create the atmosphere of a smaller center. Instead of pairing same-age rooms and organizing into wings (an infant/toddler wing, a preschool wing), an infant, toddler, and preschool room may be organized into a family group around a shared multipurpose family room. This allows different ratios and group sizes for each age group and at the same time allows longer relationships and more mixed-age interactions.

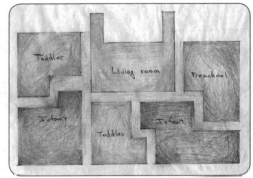

Recommendations: Flexible, Moderately Wide Age Ranges

Almost any arrangement can be made to work with thoughtful adaptation; however, maintaining a moderately wide age range in rooms is desirable and can gain the support of staff and parents. The following age ranges are recommended (assuming the approval of licensing authorities):

- Infants: six weeks to fifteen to eighteen months
- Toddlers: twelve to thirty months
- Intermediates (or twos): twenty-four to thirty-six months.

Allowances for overlap provide flexibility in new enrollments, necessary move-ups, and individual needs.

It is possible to include very young babies and younger walkers in a single group within a well-planned environment in which younger babies have some protection from older, mobile babies. The routine care of younger babies—feeding and holding, for example—does not take up so much time that teachers have little time for older babies. The relative ease and enjoyment of playing and interacting with more responsive older babies does not prevent staff from ensuring that younger babies are spending their time well.

There is a natural developmental break somewhere between twelve and eighteen months. Developmental changes during that period include an increase in language comprehension, huge developments in mobility, greater self-assertion, and increases in social interactions with other children. Another natural break occurs at around twenty-four to thirty months, when children experience a burst in language expression, increased attention span, and the ability to engage in more focused and complex play. These changes have implications for the environment, the experiences offered, and the ways adults interact with the children.

If grouping happens within relatively narrow age ranges, there are other avenues to ensure mixed-age experiences. All children benefit from being with older and younger children. Shared activities, playground time, walks, and mealtimes create opportunities for children from infancy to school-age to spend time together. But infants and toddlers do not belong in large groups, and teachers planning multiage experiences should take that into account.

Organizing for Quality: Staffing and Group Size

Everyone involved (except children, of course) needs to understand that staff-child ratios and group sizes have enormous impact on the cost, quality, and accessibility of child care. For example, if comparable quality can still be achieved with a ratio that adds one more child per teacher, the unit cost of care is reduced and the cost savings (or additional income) can go toward increasing staff compensation or reducing parents' tuition. If ratios need to be decreased to improve quality, the reverse is true. If a slightly larger group size is acceptable, it can result in fewer separate rooms needed to serve the same number of children, reduced facility cost, or more space for something else (for example, two toddler rooms of twelve rather than three rooms of eight). Or it can result in enrolling additional children, thus serving more families and generating more income for the program, which can then be applied to salaries or tuition.

Staff-Child Ratios

There is widespread professional agreement that children under two years old deserve staff-child ratios of one adult to four children or fewer. Many child care authorities believe that, ideally, groups of children six weeks to twelve months old should have no higher than a 1 to 3 staff-child ratio; children six weeks to fifteen months, no higher than a 1 to 3 or 1 to 4 ratio; children twelve to twenty-four months or older, a 1 to 4 ratio; and children eighteen to either thirty or thirty-six months, a 1 to 5 ratio.

Is quality care possible with staff-child ratios that are slightly higher? This is an important question because staff-child ratios are not only a key quality factor, they are also the key cost factor, and thus determine if care is affordable for parents as well as if more money is available for staff compensation. In a program with a stable, highly skilled, experienced staff and a well-designed, supportive facility, a 1 to 4 ratio for children under fifteen months, a 1 to 5 ratio for children fifteen months to twenty-four or thirty months, and a 1 to 6 or 1 to 7 ratio for children twenty-four to thirty-six months can result in good care. But ratios higher than 1 to 4 for infants or 1 to 5 for toddlers will rarely, if ever, produce quality care, even factoring in other, more favorable conditions.

Group Size

Group size is an important factor in its own right, independent of staff-child ratios. Generally, smaller is better. Smaller groups are likely to lead to

- more attention to individual children
- children spending time in groups of one to three children
- a more relaxing, serene environment
- less noise
- less emphasis by adults on crowd control
- less regimentation of children
- increased opportunities for staff to get to know each individual child and parent
- a manageable number of adults and children, so that young children can become familiar with and to the people around them.

It is important to note that automatically assuming that a center is better organized into rooms with very small groups is a mistake. In some circumstances, a small two-teacher group has drawbacks—it may not lead to the above outcomes or it may create other problems. Group size always interacts with other key factors: design of the facility, space per child, staffing patterns, the length of the center's day, and staff turnover.

The Number of Teachers per Group

If smaller groups are better, it may seem like a good idea to have a room of one teacher to three or four children. However, for a number of reasons, two heads are better than one, and in some circumstances a staff team of three may be the best alternative, even when it leads to a slightly larger group size. With at least two staff members in a group, one can leave the room when necessary or assist in an emergency situation that requires two adults. Infants and toddlers are charming, but they are not very good conversationalists. Having another adult to talk to and with whom to share observations, amusing moments, difficult situations, accomplishments, and frustrations is important.

A staff team of three has a number of advantages that can offset the effects of a slightly larger group size:

- It allows coverage of a ten- or eleven-hour day without having to combine rooms, shift children, or excessively use part-time staff.
- In centers with frequent staff turnover or personnel policies that include generous paid time off, staff stability is easier to maintain in three-person groups.
- In a two-staff group, the actual ratios, group size, and amount of individual attention experienced by the children may be worse than in a three-staff group. The children may always be together in one group, and while one teacher is cleaning up or caring for a child, the other is with the rest of the children. In a three-staff team, it may be possible to create routines and programming that result in more one-to-ones, with groupings of two or three children.
- Better use can be made of scarce expertise by spreading highly skilled staff across more children.

Groups with three staff are only desirable when the space is ample, staff-child ratios are optimal, and group size can be kept down: probably infant groups of three

> ### What about Continuity?
>
> Ten-month-old Jesse begins her day at 7:30 AM with Jaleel. At 8:00, she moves into her room with Beth, her primary caregiver, who has been at the center for five months. Shayna, the lead teacher, is on maternity leave, and her replacement, Steven, arrives at 9:00. Jesse stays with Steven and Beth until Beth leaves at 4:30 and is replaced by Sharrone. Jesse spends the last fifteen minutes of her day with Steven and Sharrone. In six weeks, Shayna will be back, and Steven will go to another room. That's a lot of people for Jesse to have to learn to bond with.
>
> How important is continuity of teachers? Very important, but is it important enough to override some of the concerns about larger group size or the cost of staffing the long day to minimize shuffling? This is a critical question. Groups based on two teachers are more likely to result in infants and toddlers experiencing discontinuity because of turnover of teachers than are groups based on three teachers. Children also experience discontinuity during those beginning- and/or end-of-the-day shuffles of teachers—and again, these occur more often in groups with two teachers. The effects of discontinuity on children are less visible in smaller groups than in larger ones, but they are no less real. Three-teacher groups are not *the* answer to discontinuity. But under some circumstances, they are certainly worth considering.

teachers and no more than nine to twelve babies, and toddler groups of three teachers and no more than twelve to fifteen toddlers.

Room Size and Grouping

Children need room to grow! Infants need room to crawl and creep and lurch about. Toddlers require space to climb up, over, and through; to push and pull wagons and strollers; to move around without fear of trampling their colleagues. The room needs to include items like a small couch or easy chair, rocker, soft spaces, changing areas, and equipment that can provide lots of motor and sensory experience. Regulations usually require 35 square feet per child (in addition to crib space), but that ratio should be taken as an absolute minimum. The smaller the group size, the more space per child is necessary. Two hundred and ten square feet (6 children x 35 square feet) amounts to a small, closet-sized room for two adults, six children, and visiting parents to spend a lot of time in together. The experiences desired and the furniture necessary (except the number of cribs) is the same as in a 450-square-foot room for nine children. Three hundred square feet is probably the minimum size of a room that will feel tolerable to two adults and six children.

Pairing Rooms into Modules

One solution to the dilemma of small group size leading to small rooms and a two-staff unit covering a long day is to pair two rooms into a module or suite: for example, two groups of six to eight infants or eight to ten toddlers, or one infant and one toddler group pairing up. Under this arrangement, children and parents have a sense of their own room, teachers, and module, and staff are able to function as four-person teams to cover the day.

Ideally, the module would consist of two separate physical spaces with shared areas and some shared functions—perhaps food preparation and napping (see diagram that follows). There is enough separation to provide a clear sense of two rooms and enough openness and access to encourage the staff to think of the space as a single unit, thus avoiding duplication of all learning centers and reducing the territorial instinct that comes with "owning" a room. All the staff in the module become familiar faces to the children, thus easing the anxiety of combining rooms at the beginning and end of the day. By placing the module under the supervision of one lead teacher, staff time and talents can be optimized.

Paired Homebase Modules

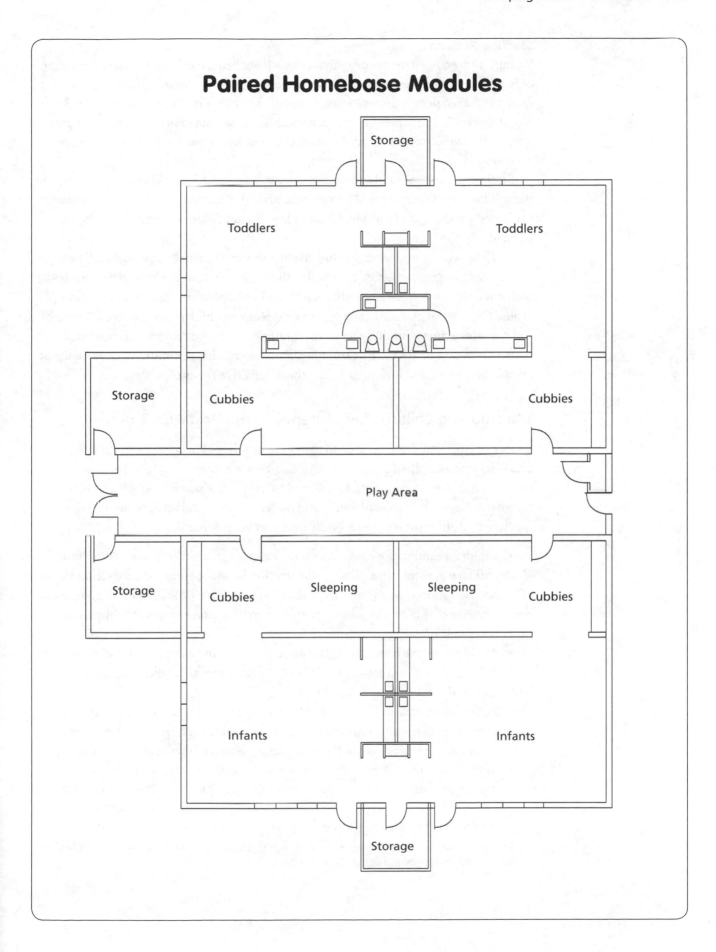

Staffing Patterns

Young children need the security that comes from being cared for by a small number of familiar adults. A center should always consider continuity over time, and limit the total number of people involved in the care of the children. Rotating staff through different groups in the center on a regular basis destroys continuity. A reliance on part-time staff or volunteers adds to the number of teachers that children must become accustomed to.

Staffing patterns should reflect actual attendance patterns and not result in gaps in the teacher-child ratio while staff await the arrival of another teacher or the departure of children at the end of the day. Breaks, planning, and meeting time should be incorporated into the plan.

Staffing every group from opening to closing may present budget difficulties, typically leading to groups being combined at the edges of the day. This can be done badly, with children sometimes being shuffled about in a haphazard fashion to maintain ratios. Thoughtful planning can prevent this. Helping children feel secure at arrival and departure times should be a priority. Staffing patterns, program practices, and room combinations should be carefully planned to minimize children's experience of unfamiliar people and locations during those sensitive times of separation.

Transitioning Children (and Parents) to the Next Age Group

Sooner or later, children move on to the next age group. For some children and parents (and some attached primary caregivers), this is a time of anxiety. For others, it is a time that has been eagerly anticipated, and there are few tearful looks back. Successful transitions depend on good planning and on recognizing and understanding the perspective of children and parents. Some things to keep in mind:

- Children cannot move up until there is a space in the next group. Sometimes children get stuck in a group while waiting for an opening, and sometimes children get moved up a little earlier than expected to take advantage of an opening. Because of this, it is important to make sure the group works for children at both ends of the age spectrum.
- Avoid giving the impression that there is something competitive about moving up—that it is like graduation or is an indication that the child has superior skills and abilities.
- Be transparent with parents of a child who stays in the same group when another younger child has moved to the next-older age group. Let parents know what the criteria are when there is a choice about who moves to a new group.
- Most children need more than a few days of visiting to feel comfortable. Preparing for transitions is an ongoing process that begins a long time before the actual move.
- When possible, move children along with a friend.

See Supplements: *A Note to Parents: How Our Feelings about Transition Can Affect Our Children* and *A Note to Parents: Moving on Up to the Twos*

Here are some things you can do to make this transition go more smoothly.

Ongoing relationships between rooms. Ideally, even in large centers there is a sense of community and a relationship between different age groups and different rooms. A child in an infant room will come to know the toddler staff and the toddler rooms through visiting, shared activities, and common space. The same is true of toddlers and preschoolers. Through the newsletter and other communications, parents will come to know about the people and aspects of life that their children will soon become part of.

A ready list. It helps to have a ready list of children. Once a child is ready to move on, whether or not space is yet available, and perhaps a few months before a move is anticipated, staff in the two rooms should make a concerted effort to begin the transition. This involves visiting, accompanied by the primary caregiver, and sharing activities and other efforts to gradually familiarize the child with the new room. At the same time, parents should be made aware of the approaching transition and be given information on the child's future homebase.

The last few weeks. When a moving date is known, the current primary caregiver and the newly assigned primary caregiver should get together and map out a plan for daily visits to the new group and to make sure that parents have all the information necessary to feel secure about the move. Each child's and parent's needs will be different.

The new group. The first week in the new room should follow the routine for the first week of any new child and family: picture on the cubby, welcome sign, first-day note to parents (see Supplement: *Sample First-Day E-mail and Photo*), and a reassuring phone call, if helpful. It is also important for many children to keep in contact with the old room. Cold-turkey transitions are not a good idea.

> ### "We Care for Infants, Not Toddlers. Get Those Old Guys Out of Here!"
>
> A common lament from infant staff: "Halima and Paul have to move up. They are bored here. At sixteen months, they are too old for the group." It is not uncommon for staff in one age group to adopt a narrow view of what the room can offer and to view the child outgrowing the room—or the opposite, being too young for the new room ("Paul isn't ready for our room") as a problem, rather than realizing that the room environment and activities are failing to keep pace with the children. For any approach to age grouping to be successful, room staff must accept responsibility to program for the educational and caring needs of every child in the group. The programming changes with the children. Two principles are fundamental:
>
> - The program has to fit the children, not the reverse.
> - No child is ever too old or too young, too slow or too advanced for the group that she is in.

A Final Word: Circumstances Change, and There May Always Be a Better Way

How children and staff are grouped lays the foundation for providing high-quality care. It is an important element in determining the best use of staff and facilities and a factor in determining the cost of care. There is no one right way to produce quality. Periodically, the grouping patterns in the center should be examined to make sure they still make sense and are the most cost-efficient way to achieve the vision of quality outlined in this volume.

Exercises

1. Develop a list of curriculum adaptations or equipment changes necessary to ensure that a room works for twelve- to -fifteen-month-olds awaiting an opening in a toddler group. How would you adapt a toddler group for younger infants?

2. Develop two staffing plans for caring for a group of infants across an eleven-hour day: a group of seven infants with a 2 to 7 staff-child ratio, and a group of ten infants with a 3 to 10 staff-child ratio.

Reference

Brazelton, T. B., and S. I. Greenspan. 2001. *The Irreducible Needs of Children: What Every Child Must Have to Grow, Learn, and Flourish.* New York: Perseus.

Chapter 7

Structuring Time and Space for Quality Care

εxcellence *Time and space are structured to accomplish the program goals of providing children with a safe and secure experience, rich with relaxed and happy days and individualized care and learning. There is a balance between familiar, predictable experience and novel, changing experience.*

Think of space and time as the framework for composing the experiences of the day. An over-compartmentalized and rigid framework will leave staff and children feeling cramped, confined, and frustrated, while one that is too loose and flexible will breed anxiety and confusion.

Structuring Time: Balancing Flexibility and Order

Planning a schedule is always a balancing act. Security flows from familiar, predictable routines. Things happen when you expect them to: a morning group gets together at 9:00, eats at noon, and goes home between 4:30 and 5:30. Yet a timetable that is too rigid drives us crazy with its monotony. And with infants and toddlers, it is the individual rhythms of eating, sleeping, and exploring that are critical. For infants, and to the extent possible for toddlers, group schedules should be built around individual schedules, not the reverse. At the same time, staff should think of the day as an organic whole, and resist the temptation to carve it up into little bits for the group, filling children's days with disruptive stops and starts.

> ### *Play* Time?
>
> Unfortunately, the term *play* has diminished in value somewhat in early care and education, now that anxious parents worry that play, even in the earliest years, is less valuable than more adult-directed experience. It is useful to remind families that play is simply the way that infants and toddlers explore, discover, and master concepts and skills. It may be necessary to strategically change the term *play time* to *exploration and discovery time.* Staff can remind parents, as Elizabeth Spelke points out (see chapter 4), that infants and toddlers are fully capable of choosing the experiences they need.

Any timetable or plan for the day is a guide to or a best guess about what will work. Adjustments are made as the children get older and their needs change. Daily adjustments to the plan are likely to be necessary for a variety of reasons. It is easy for staff to get locked into a timetable because schedules are familiar and reduce the need to think. But if a timetable becomes mindless, then the day's rhythm and its basis in the actual needs of the children can be lost.

Go Slowly, One Child at a Time

In good programs, staff slow down to children's time. To the extent possible, adults adapt to the children's pace, becoming active participants in experiences and supporting the children as they undertake activities they are developmentally ready for, instead of rushing them through experiences at an efficient adult pace. Taking the time to allow children to engage in hand washing, using the toilet, eating, dressing, and undressing as their ability and interests dictate rather than doing it for them can make the day go more smoothly and efficiently. More important, these are the prime times for each child to learn the critical things in life: "I am trusted and liked" and "I can do it."

Allowing children to experience these routines or daily living experiences one by one or in very small groups works better than trying to have the whole group participate at once. In some ways this may defy common sense, or at least common practice, for it may seem that having all children do everything together at one time is the most efficient way to get through the day. However, this strategy often results in considerable frustration for children and staff. Children end up waiting, a waste of their time and something that infants and toddlers are not very good at doing. Staff end up having to spend a lot of time and energy managing. In a good program, a number of different things are always going on simultaneously.

Children at this age need choices in play. It is not appropriate to expect all children under age two, for example, be expected to engage in table activities or to sit for a group activity. Smaller groups for singing, stories, and other activities can happen spontaneously. Besides, it is very hard work to get a group of toddlers to all sit still at the same time!

Planning the Environment

Good programs exist in all sorts of spaces: church basements, storefronts, and designed buildings. The space does not determine the program, but it certainly shapes it. As Elizabeth Prescott (1979) explained, *the environment regulates our experience:* the physical facilities, arrangement of space, and equipment available either work for you or against you, and can make good quality easier or more difficult to achieve.

Sample Schedule for Infants and Toddlers (Up to 15 to 18 Months)

Following is a schedule that includes flexibility provided by overlapping chunks of time. That is what is meant by the characteristic of *wholeness*—avoiding breaking up the child's day into small, discrete segments.

Note: For infants: sleep schedules will reflect the child's rhythm and parental consultation. Bottle feeding is individualized, based on the child's needs and parental consultation. *For toddlers:* schedules are usually shaped by the absence of a separate sleeping area, and typically include group mealtimes and naptimes; however, individualized schedules are desirable when possible.

Time	Activity
6:30–8:30	Arrival, greeting children and parents, self-directed play, bottles or early morning snack.
8:30–9:00	Family-style breakfast or morning snack for non-bottle-fed older infants and all toddlers. Brief morning group ritual for toddlers. Bottle-feeding and sleep as individual schedules dictate throughout the day.
9:00–11:15	Self-directed play in planned learning areas, indoors and out. Walks, guided-learning experiences, and, for toddlers, projects for individuals or small groups.
11:15–11:30	Cleanup, washup, and, if waiting is unavoidable, brief fingerplays or singing at table for awake, non-bottle-fed older infants and toddlers.
11:30–1:15	Lunch for non-bottle-fed infants and toddlers, staggered as morning nappers wake up.
12:30–3:00	Naptime for many older infants and most toddlers; individualized wake-up.
1:15–5:00	Self-directed play in selected learning areas for awake children. Guided learning for individuals.
2:00–3:00	For older infants and toddlers, a snack offered on an individual or small-group basis.
4:30–5:30	Self-directed play in planned learning areas, indoors and out. Walks, guided-learning activities, and, for toddlers, projects for individuals or small groups. Special materials or activities for those departing late. Late-afternoon snack for those who need it. Good-byes, conversation with parents, departure.
5:30–7:00	Extended-hours care for children whose parents require a later pickup time, with an evening snack or dinner.

A good setting for infants or toddlers is a comfortable space. It will be so well organized, divided, and equipped that

- the staff have a lot of time to be fully engaged with the children on a one-to-one basis and do not have to spend all their time setting up and packing away equipment and materials or managing children

- children experience much of their day in small groups of one to three or four children
- as they show interest, children can exercise autonomy, show initiative and self-sufficiency, and do things for themselves.

What makes the room a great place for an infant or toddler to be in? For an adult to be with a baby? Think of the room as a place for work: the work of the staff is to care for children and to create a learning environment; the work of the children is to engage in developmentally appropriate play. It is a place where both children and adults can be competent.

A Great Place *to Be* and *to Be With* a Very Young Child All Day

A great place for children, staff, and parents *to be* is

- A comfortable place where adults can be relaxed while feeding, soothing, and changing, easing children into and out of sleep, cuddling, mentoring, and nurturing young children—a place with a couch or easy chairs, cushions, and comfortable floor space; a warm, homelike space that is pleasant for staff, children, and parents.
- A place that contains different places to be and places to pause, to avoid crowding and overstimulation: semisecluded, protected from other children, small spaces, open spaces; space divided by shelving units, curtains, or pieces of fabric, behind couches or chairs, under cabinets, or on top of low cubes or furniture; spaces where a child can safely spend some time alone.
- A child-scale place, because infants and toddlers are small people; and an adult-scale place as well, because staff are not small people (relatively). The environment needs to be scaled down for children. Chairs should allow young feet to touch the floor, tables should be a comfortable height (just above waist-high when sitting), and objects or pictures on the wall should be easily visible to babies who are on the floor, walking, or being carried by adults.
- A spacious, bright, and cheerful place with low windows so that children can look out. Windows that open add needed fresh air and sensory stimulation and should be made of shatterproof (tempered) glass or fitted with other kinds of protection, such as wide ledges or screens, to prevent children from banging them with toys or climbing on them.
- A place with natural light complemented by artificial light that allows for a range of lighting conditions, in which staff avoid the tendency to overuse artificial lighting. This creates a homey lightscape, much like that of a living room. Turning off the lights allows the changes in natural light to help create a rhythm to the day.
- A place of beauty and tasteful aesthetics that reflects a concern for color, texture, light, and pattern. Avoiding primary colors on walls, floors, and permanent murals makes sense because so much of the equipment and so many play materials are likely to be brightly colored. Children's art and teachers' displays, documentation panels, mobiles, and brightly clad, moving bodies in the room add a lot of color. The challenge in creative programs is to not overstimulate by creating rooms that make children feel as if they are inside a kaleidoscope. Using

subdued, somewhat neutral colors on walls and floors (much like those used in living rooms and art galleries), helps to create a peaceful setting. Of course, crib or napping areas and bathrooms should also be aesthetically pleasant.

- A well-heated, -cooled, and -ventilated place from the floor on up. Radiant floor heat is desirable in colder climates.
- A quiet place that tolerates noise. Intrusive, unpleasant, or overwhelming noise discourages attempts by infants and toddlers to communicate, and desensitizes or puts staff on edge. Divided space, acoustical ceiling tiles, ceiling fans, carpeting, soft furnishings, limited group size, and zoning of activities reduce noise.
- A nice place for touching that includes a variety of textures, responsive materials, and lots of softness: soft furniture, water, grass, swings, rugs, pillows, fingerpaints, playdough, clay, and laps.

See Supplement: *Aesthetically Pleasing Environments for Infants and Toddlers*

> ## Sensoryscapes
>
> In *Children, Spaces, Relations: Metaproject for an Environment for Young Children* (1998), Italian architects Giulio Ceppi and Michele Zini emphasize viewing an early childhood program as a *sensoryscape*: a *colorscape, lightscape, soundscape, aromascape,* and *texturescape.* It is worthwhile for staff to ask themselves what they see, hear, smell, and feel when they use all their senses to observe their room. When the room's aesthetic is carefully assembled, avoiding chaotic or kaleidoscopic overstimulation, there is a *rich normality* of sensory richness—a harmony that encourages an appreciation of life and what the world has to offer.

A Great Place to Work

What characteristics of a place enhance the children's ability to do their job and the staff's competence in helping them accomplish that task?

A room arrangement that regulates behavior. A divided space with clear boundaries, traffic patterns, spaces of different sizes, and capacity for different functions will regulate crowding and wandering. Children will spread out if the room is arranged and activities are planned to draw their attention to different areas and if adults spread out too. Bounded and contained spaces will help control the flow of all the smaller materials and equipment pieces that may stray. Portable (movable) dividers as low as 18 inches enable areas to be changed in size, shape, number, and arrangement, yet still allow staff to keep an eye on what is going on. The alternative—big open spaces strewn with play materials—is like a mine field: unattractive, unsafe, and unworkable, and it reduces staff to the role of traffic cops.

A variety of floor coverings that are easy to clean. Carpet or area rugs, small throw rugs, and tile or linoleum. Floor surfaces help babies learn about the world: for example, they investigate the textures and discover that a ball goes a long way with a little push on a tile floor but not on carpet. They learn that crawling is easier on one type of surface than another.

An "I can do it" place that allows autonomy. For the child, equipment such as towels, sinks, clothing, as well as books and play materials placed at their level, encourage autonomy and choice. Of course, staff need adult-height sinks and storage in the room.

A place where learning is built into the environment. Sensory learning occurs during encounters with different textures, lighting, colors, temperatures, and breezes, as well as views or angles of vision: carpeting, rugs, fabric, and materials that have different feels to them or that respond differently to light; mirrors, reflective glass, and metal; open windows; lights on and off; use of fans to provide air currents. Motor learning is encouraged by furniture and equipment that allow climbing up or over, moving around, through, over, under: couches, pillows, stairs, ramps, planks and crates, small platforms, and cubes.

A place with ample, convenient, labeled storage for children and adults. Wall storage, cabinets, open and closed shelves, duffel bags, and toy boxes all have their place, as do individual cubbies or bins and hooks for the belongings and portfolios of individual children, accessible to parents and staff. Note a fundamental law of storage: the closer materials and equipment are to the point of use, the more they will be used.

A place with ample, easy-to-use communication space and equipment that is accessible to both parents and staff. This includes clipboards, chalk, and whiteboards, Post-it notes on walls, and writing implements.

A place of order. Compulsive tidiness will frustrate adults and children, but an arrangement that encourages children to focus on and distinguish the properties

of things (toys, food, materials) is important. A tasteful, organized, orderly environment can tolerate the considerable creative disorder that comes with messy play and dumping by toddlers. In a room with covered storage, attractive walls, carpets, and basic furnishings, the creative use of cardboard boxes, rags, rocks, old clothes, and other "junk" often appears inventive and enriching. In a drab room, the use of the same materials may result in a junky effect. Money spent on basic furnishings is money well spent.

A place with sufficient space. Sometimes centers assume that the youngest and smallest children need the least amount of space. Actually, infants and toddlers need as much or more space per child as older children. The reasons for this include the following:

- The space must accommodate a greater number of adults in the room.
- More furniture and large equipment (for example, couches, cribs, feeding chairs, changing counters) are required.
- These youngest children do not always cope well being in close proximity to each other.
- One of their favorite activities is moving around.

Overcrowding leads inevitably to frustration, bad tempers, and an increase in unpleasant interactions, especially biting. Thirty-five square feet of activity play space free of cribs, changing areas, and cubbies is only an adequate minimum—more space is highly desirable.

A work place for staff. An in-room teacher nook that provides counter space and the tools of the trade for planning and communicating. A telephone and computer will support teachers in their leadership role.

A Great Place for Parents

A great place for parents is a place that is welcoming and caters to their needs when they drop off and pick up their children. This includes children's cubbies, a communication space, places to sit and watch, places for purses and coats, and signage that provides essential information so that parents can function in the space and know that this is also a place for them.

Crowding and Bunching Up

When children spend much of the day close together in a group, they experience more stimulation, more distractions, more distress, more stress, more risk of harming each other, less constructive play, and less personal attention from staff. Bunching up is common in infant and toddler programs: the majority of adults and children end up close together, using only a limited amount of the available space, whatever its overall size. There are two reasons for this. First, infants often seem to stay within close proximity of their teachers. Second, adults tend to position themselves close to each other, often facing each other, and thus increase the number of children in the bunch. Layout of furniture often encourages this, because the adults draw from their experience of homelike settings when arranging the furniture. The couch and chair arrangement illustrated on the top right (arrangement 1) seems comfortably homey, but it often results in two or more adults sitting on the couch and chairs and five to ten children crowded into the adjacent tiny area—a decidedly non-homey condition.

In living rooms and lounges, furniture is used to draw adults together to socialize. In classrooms, the aim of space arrangement is often to accommodate group activities. But in settings for infants and toddlers, the opposite is the aim—namely, to separate children and spread them throughout the available space so that they will actively engage in individual exploration, thereby increasing the field of action and reducing the chance of conflict and collision (see arrangement 2 at bottome right). No good comes from infants and toddlers being kept together even in small groups.

Unfortunately, achieving this is easier said than done. First, adults' instincts are to face each other and to face the action. It feels strange to turn and focus away from centers of activity and from other adults. Second, adults amid charming but nonverbal

Arrangement 1

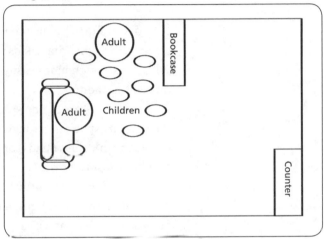

Arrangement 2

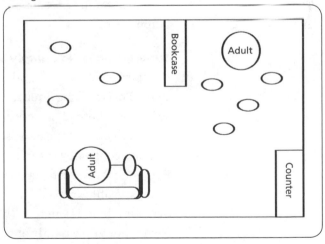

> **Get Out of the Room**
>
> *Use all your space.* Get outside! Infants' health and learning benefit from having opportunities to go outside. Use the playground, sidewalks, strollers, and carts.
>
> *Use all the inside space, including common spaces (don't forget the corridors).* Visit other parts of the center, of course, checking first for potential hazards.

crowds of small people tend to want some opportunities to talk with other equally verbal human beings.

Separate Crib Areas? Whether or not children in care will sleep and play in the same room has become a licensing issue in the United States (which is unfortunate, because the child safety issue associated with that tends to be greatly exaggerated). Ideally, with infants there is at least a separate crib *area*, if not a separate room, with lots of transparency that allows staff to easily observe sleeping children. When cribs simply border the play areas, staff often restrict the play of children who are awake, lest they disturb other children who are asleep. They also tend to try to have all children sleep at the same time. This isn't necessary. Most infants are amazingly flexible and will adjust much more easily than adults to resting or sleeping while activity is going on around them.

Whether the sleeping space is an area separated by a half wall or a separate room, it should be spacious enough so that cribs or cots are separated by 24 inches (36 inches between children's heads) or have a hard crib-side or a divider between them. Carpet will help absorb noise. If there is little ventilation, a wall-mounted or ceiling fan increases air circulation and provides some masking noise. A window treatment is necessary to regulate light. A glider chair within the space can be used by staff to help babies go to sleep and as a quiet spot for breast-feeding mothers.

Cots and mats for toddlers should be comfortable, safe, and easily cleaned and stored. Soft music is calming for some babies, so a CD player in the sleeping area is helpful.

Supervision Is Not Simply Surveillance "We need to see every child every second to supervise them." This adage sounds sensible and is typically built into state regulations. This thinking often leads to having very open spaces that lack possibilities for seclusion. "Behind" spaces are eliminated by pushing couches and storage units up against the wall, little or no separation is created between cribs and play space, and staff are constantly scanning the room, never focusing on the child in front of them. Everyone is always together: children are kept in groups unless restrained in seats or swings, visible and audible to each other at all times. In such centers, the likelihood of overstimulation is high. In these settings, accidents and incidents of infants exploring each other unpleasantly or of acting up aggressively will be high.

Good supervision is not simply a matter of teachers acting as sentries or police officers, as accident and crime stoppers. Good supervision creates a well-planned, child-proofed, safe, engaging, "yes" environment and a relaxed, orderly day. Children understand the expectations adults have for them, and staff know the children. In a wide-open environment, there are likely to be more problems because children are bunched up and likely to cause harm to each other; the only virtue is that staff can see them while this happens (unless, of course, their backs are turned or they are filling bottles or performing other necessary tasks). With low dividers, couches, and counters, and with shelving as dividers, children are only momentarily out of view, much as they are at home, and staff can supervise by sight and sound. But the reduction in stimulation and group size can greatly improve safety and security in the room.

Avoiding bunching up requires a room arrangement and daily planning that consciously draw staff and children toward the far reaches of the room, to secondary rooms, or outside—in other words, that encourage spreading out. Self-monitoring and supervision that recognize the tendency to bunch up and the need to spread out are always essential.

Accessibility and Special Needs

Infant and toddler spaces have to work for all children and adults, including those with differing motor and sensory abilities. Unfortunately, one of the keys to accessibility is square footage and ample space, and these are almost always in short supply. Pathways and turning radiuses large enough to accommodate child and adult wheelchairs or walkers are important when needed.

Accommodating children and adults with sensory impairments is largely a matter of designing access and an environment with clear sensory cues. There should not be a jumble of sight, sound, smell, and texture. Individuals with hearing or visual impairments try to maximize their other abilities. Hearing and touch take on special significance when sight is limited, as do recognizable visual cues that work with limited sight. Visual cues, touch, and vibration are important for maximizing the experience of children with hearing impairments. Landmarks and sensory markers are useful for many children with special needs. For a child who is visually impaired, the sound of the fish tank, the breeze from the fan, the eucalyptus in the science area, the dividing line between the carpet and tile, and the red-felt name tag on his cubby are important cues. For a child with a hearing impairment, good room acoustics and a relatively orderly acoustical environment (that is, not a three-ring-circus atmosphere) are important to help maximize what hearing the child possesses.

All infants and toddlers benefit from environments that are clear and manageable, but these qualities are particularly important for children with impairments or delays: clear displays and a manageable number of learning choices, clear pathways and delineation of areas, and designs that allow children to accomplish basic care tasks as independently as possible.

Learning Centers

In a program based much more on independent learning than on adult-led activities, space is planned first so that children can function relatively autonomously. An environmentally based program includes activity areas for routine activities—for example, diapering or feeding areas—and other areas for learning, called *interest areas* or *learning centers*. The term *learning centers* is used here to describe a part of the space to be used for learning purposes, recognizing that a loveseat or chair can be a learning-center site (for reading, snuggling and conversation, singing, and motor activity). In learning centers, materials are stored nearby and used to facilitate child-directed play. In a learning-center-based program, learning centers are the basic units of planning. Note the difference between a learning-center-based program and an activity-based curriculum, in whick most planning is thought of in terms of activities that are set up and put away by teachers, and organized into time blocks (for example, an activity takes place from 9:30 to 10:00).

Learning centers not only help adults organize materials and equipment in a sensible way, they also encourage children to spread out, to see possibilities for play more easily, and to play and explore more constructively and with more focus. Further, they can help parents recognize the infant and toddler rooms as educational sites.

What areas to have depends on the amount of space available, the age range of the children, and staff expertise. The small size of babies makes a number of learning centers possible even in a small space, and centers often assume a number of functions. In limited space for toddlers and twos, a wet or messy area may offer play with art and craft materials, sensory play, and projects. Quiet areas become multipurpose sites for quiet experiences. A table area becomes the site for table toys and projects (as well as lunch). With more space, areas can develop more specialized functions.

One drawback to learning centers is that when an area is defined by content—dramatic play, for example—it is easy to lose sight of the reality that dramatic play exists everywhere and in many activities. Sometimes a tendency toward inflexibility about where activities may take place can develop—for example, thinking that hats should stay in the dramatic-play area. Staff need to recognize that many learning centers are also take-out areas, whose materials are available to transport to other areas. In fact, without physical boundaries, many areas become take-out areas for infants and toddlers, because a favorite activity for this age group is transporting objects from one place to another, just for the sake of moving, carrying, pushing, or pulling them.

Infants and toddlers may not appreciate the logic behind adult definitions of areas. Especially when planning for younger, mobile babies, staff need to keep in mind that moving things around in space, fitting things inside other things, and generally altering the setup will be a priority, and these interests take precedence over whatever logical grouping of materials makes sense to adults. Staff need to be very flexible when children mix materials from different areas.

Characteristics of Learning Centers

Learning centers have size, shape, and height. The size of the area should be tailored to the desirable number and size of users and to the activities within. Learning centers can be as small as the size for one child, often called a *learning station*. If the area is too big, a larger group than is desirable may congregate in the area.

Areas may be as small as a tub or a rug or a window used to observe the outside or interior world, perhaps enhanced by a bird feeder or transformed by colored transparencies. When it comes to shape, adults typically square-off corners. However, round, triangular, and oddly angled areas are appealing to children. Areas of varying height created through the use of hanging fabric or umbrellas, canopies, platforms, and overhangs or by raising or lowering the floor add character, charm, and clear definition.

> **Learning centers have different surfaces.** Floor space, tops of tables or counters, and walls or dividers to mount materials on or to use as easels allow a variety of learning and play opportunities.

Learning centers can have personality and ambiance. Remember they are *sensory-scapes*. A mood can be produced by the combined effects of all the elements: businesslike, cozy, chaotic, cheery, noisy, bland, serene, perhaps even melancholy (a womblike place where children can go when they feel sad). The mood is created by the activities, lighting, sounds, smells, colors, textures, and feel of the place. Artwork, furnishings, ritual behaviors—all the things that create ambiance in personal spaces can be used in the room.

Learning centers can communicate and signal behavior. An easy message is OPEN or CLOSED, signaled by a gate, a sign, a sound, fabric over a storage unit, or a light. There are other signals that engage children, such as a new picture or object that catches their eye and gives the message CHECK ME OUT, or a smell or sound that sets off a stampede to the area!

Learning centers can have understood rules and behavior expectations. As children reach toddlerhood, one goal in a learning center is to help children develop expectations. How will tasks get done? How must the inhabitants interact? The more these expectations are built into the space through arrangements of furnishings, materials, and symbolic instructions and reminders, the less adults need to indoctrinate and supervise. Everyone, children especially, pays more attention to what actually happens than what is supposed to happen (witness how little highway speed limits are observed). If the rule is "No throwing things," but it is only enforced intermittently, children understand that it is not really a rule.

Keys to Effective Learning Centers

The right size and scale. Think baby-size. Learning centers can be as small as a bath rug. The size of the area should depend on what is to happen there. Work spaces should reflect the fact that many times toddlers do their work sitting or lying on the floor or standing up at tables rather than sitting down in chairs.

Open storage. Have sufficient open shelving accessible to children to display materials clearly and discretely; provide picture labels to encourage older children to return materials. With infants and toddlers, clear displays mean only a few items per shelf, and each item clearly separated from the others. Clear plastic containers or baskets that allow visibility reduce the amount of dumping or tipping out. Collections of objects in containers are just begging to be dumped out for inspection, so if that is not what staff want to encourage, then it is better to display items individually on shelves.

Adult storage. Props and other materials not in use should be located out of reach of the children in a place convenient for staff and close to where they will eventually be used.

Good boundaries. Boundaries define for children where actions will take place. A pit (depression), rug, low dividers, shelves, risers, or boxes can serve as defining boundaries. The more materials a learning center offers, the more useful physical boundaries are for containing them. Boundaries that require children to make a physical decision to enter or exit (for example, opening a gate or stepping up, over, or down) result in children spending longer times in that area. More symbolic boundaries (for example, taped lines and stop signs) can be useful for older toddlers and twos.

The right amount of seclusion. Creating some visual and auditory separation between children is important, because wandering and succumbing to distractions are primary problems for young children in group care. It helps to use furniture or low dividers to separate spaces.

Clear expectations for child and staff behavior. Clarify how materials can be used and how staff are expected to behave (for example, get down on the floor, supervise closely the use of particular materials, keep the material in the area). This assists in creating a relaxed atmosphere. A poster with pictures of what is expected is very effective.

Zoning. Planning the overall relationship of different areas and their impact on each other can minimize problems. For example, messy areas should be placed away from carpets and active areas away from quiet areas.

Sufficient number of areas and choices. Building in choices—some novel, some familiar—is important in engaging children's interest. There is no simple formula for deciding how many learning centers and what choices should be made; however, keep in mind that the aim is for children to be alone or in groups of two or three and to be actively engaged. Too many choices can be overwhelming; too few can be boring.

Rotation. Changes, even small ones, help keep children's interested. The rotation of play materials within learning centers, the alteration of arrangements in areas, even changes in their location within the space may be enough to stimulate renewed interest when children show signs of boredom.

Developing a Room Layout

In thinking about the best possible layout for a particular space, it helps to set aside preconceptions and knowledge of how the room has been used in the past, and to start with an empty room, either in fact or in mind.

Start by thinking about the fixed space: doorways, windows, bathrooms, sinks. Try to get a picture of the several kinds of primary flows: people traffic, food and supplies and ensuing equipment, noise, dirt, and cool and warm air. Think about how these affect the program and the children.

Think about what is going to take place in the room, what children and adults need to do: eating, motor activities, messy play, or quiet play. List absolutely everything, including events such as children undressing for water play, children and parents arriving and putting away their belongings, and parents and staff talking together.

Now ask what other possible spaces are available, such as the hallways or the outdoors, to supplement or replace the space in the room.

What are the essential activity settings, and what are the learning centers needed? Which areas need to be multipurpose? For example, table areas are typically used for eating, table toys, and messy play. Which areas are generally permanent (for example, dramatic play—which may be transformed—and the book corner)?

Given all of the above:

- What flow of communication and materials is necessary?
- What transformations are needed during the day to create spaces (for example, an eating space or a nap space)?
- What features exist in the setting that lend themselves to locating one area in a particular part of the space? Features may include the placement of windows, sinks, electrical outlets, doorways that lead to other parts of the center or to the outdoors, floor coverings, storage, and heaters.

Anita Olds suggested thinking of a *neighborhood*, a warmer concept than that of zones,

defined both by the fixtures they require and by their personalities. All the areas which need water should be grouped near the sink. But it is probably better to put painting, rather than water play, close to the reading corner. The movement and talk that occurs around a water table are distracting. In creating areas, think about separating messy and neat, quiet and noisy, expansive and contained activities (1984, 14).

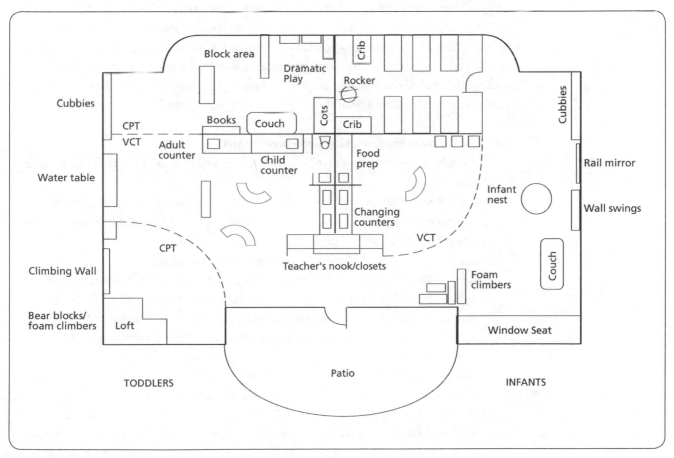

Room Layout Example

The next step is to consider what minor physical alterations would greatly enhance the space, for example, more wall storage, display space, or bench tops (see room layout example on previous page).

Keep in mind that all children (and most adults) give credence to the maxim, "Materials placed close together will be used together." Thus, for example, unless Squeaky the guinea pig can swim, keep him away from the water-play area.

Remember also that young children, use their whole bodies to perform a task. They need room; they are continually getting used to rapidly changing bodies that don't seem to respond quite as competently as they imagined they would. Children need the freedom not only to move about the space but also to use their whole bodies when engaged in activities, whether stacking blocks or grasping toys. When allocating space to a learning center, it helps to visualize children lying down spread out as they explore materials. Conflict, accidents, and messes follow within cramped spaces.

Furnishing the Environment

This handbook looks at appropriate furniture and equipment and considers equipment issues of environmental health and safety in chapter 14. In the present chapter, some important concerns in selecting furnishings and equipment are noted and some observations are provided on common equipment.

There is no one list of best furnishings for infant or toddler programs. Many decisions are a matter of taste and opinion because there are few developmental implications for selection of some items, and, in any case, professionals simply do not agree on the issues. With many issues, such as when to switch from cribs to cots, cots versus mats, at what age to introduce computers to children, the need for lofts or particular equipment, and so on, knowing prevailing practices in the community *and* parent and staff perceptions will result in the most effective purchases.

General Criteria for Selections of Furnishings
- *Durability*. How long will it hold up? Center use is at least ten times as hard as home use.
- *Safety*. Sharp edges or corners? Small parts to swallow? Toxic finishes? Straps to entangle? Will the item be pulled or tipped over? Will it wear or break in such a way that it becomes dangerous?
- *Health*. Does it allow for easy cleaning and disinfecting?
- *Size and scale*. Is it the right size and scale for projected and unanticipated use by every child and adult, including those with special needs?
- Is it consistent with the program goals (for example, autonomy, authenticity, lending itself to diverse uses, offering a balance of challenges and likely successes)?
- Does it facilitate the staff's competence?
- Does it add to the children's and parents' sense of security?
- *Aesthetics*. Is the design attractive? Do the color, size, and shape add to or detract from the room's overall aesthetic? For example, will its inclusion mean that there is too much primary-colored, plastic equipment in the room?

Some Thoughts on Common Furnishings

Equipment for food preparation and feeding:

- *Refrigerator.* This is essential in the infant room (even in programs with kitchens) for food preparation and medications; it is highly desirable in toddler rooms. Four cubic feet or more is desirable.
- *Bottle warmers or electric pots (with temperature controls).* These are essential in the room. *Note:* Microwaves are not recommended because uneven heating creates a serious danger of internal burns to the throat and esophagus.
- *Infant feeding.* The choice of high chairs, low-chair trays, "sassy seats" that attach under a table, or very small "me do it" chairs and tables should be guided by the program space available for equipment when not in use and for staff preference for sitting on the floor or on low chairs. High chairs typically take up valuable activity space.
- *Older infant and toddler feeding.* Developmentally, once the child can sit up independently, tables and chairs are preferable to high and low chairs with trays (which restrain the child) unless having tables and chairs inadvertently results in individualized mealtimes being replaced by group meals. Group tables with built-in seats are *not* recommended because they confine children and place them very close together.

Equipment for sleeping:

- *Cribs.* The important specific criteria for selecting a crib include small size, safety (including less than 2⅝ inches between slats), and adjustable mattress height or a drop side.
- *Cots.* Ease of storage is a key criterion in choosing between folding mats and cots, as well as easy cleaning and durability of stitches and fabrics.

Equipment for comfort and general functions:

- *Loveseats, easy chairs, and futons.* These are great for sitting on as well as for climbing up and on. Flexibility of futons and "flip" chairs and couches is a huge plus, but futons in frames are less ergonomically appealing to staff and so often result in fewer laps for snuggling. Specific criteria to pay attention to include size and stain resistance. (*Note:* using throws extends fabric life.)
- *Beanbag chairs.* These are useful for children age fifteen months and over, but not safe for infants under a year because of the threat of Sudden Infant Death Syndrome. Specific criteria to look for include durability of seams and washable covers.
- *Rocking chairs and glider chairs.* These are nearly essential. Well-designed gliders reduce the potential for pinched fingers and don't require the supervision of nearby children, as rockers do. Specific features to check include the spacing of slats and the safety of the rocker mechanism when subjected to inquiring fingers.
- *Infant bounce seats (air chairs).* These are somewhat useful but always subject to overuse. Particularly for younger infants, more holding and use of infant carriers (such as Snuglis) and less use of these chairs are desirable.

- *Chairs.* Criteria for choosing chairs include their fit within space requirements, whether or not they will stack, aesthetics, size, weight, and ease of cleaning. Child-sized armchairs light enough for toddlers to move and educubes that have multiple play uses are desirable.
- *Tables.* Tables have limited use for play, so it is not desirable to add tables beyond those used for meals, except for small tables with rims for loose-part play, tub or water tables, and nesting tables.
- *Play lofts.* These can be useful programmable play space (sites for planned experiences) for protecting nonmobile babies. Specific criteria for using them include portability and size relative to the rest of the space. Lofts that dominate the space or are permanently fixed in a location often drive staff crazy.
- *Nests or plastic wading pools.* These can be very useful additions to programmable learning areas.
- *Risers, carpeted cubes, planks.* These are very versatile and encourage children to climb in, on, out, and over.

Equipment for toileting, washing, and drinking:

- *Changing counters.* Changing counters should have at least 36–40 inches of length for an infant, 48 inches for toddlers, and a 3-inch lip or sunken surface to help prevent children from rolling off. Straps are not desirable because they are unpleasant for the child and give staff a false sense of security. Counters ideally should be in the room or in an alcove that provides visibility and easy access to the room. Steps up to a changing counter are preferred by some, but many (including the authors) are concerned about the risk of allowing children to climb up 36 inches over a hard, nonresilient surface, even under adult supervision. It is highly desirable to have the sink included in the counter (add another 18–24 inches to the length) or within arm's length.
- *Toilets.* Toilets appropriate to toddlers' height or potty chairs should be available to children aged eighteen months and older.
- *Sinks.* Sinks that children have access to should be 14–16 inches off the floor with handles that are easy to grip and use (preferably levers) and should be aerated, with low water flow and a basin at least 8 inches deep to reduce splashing. Hot water should be kept under 110 degrees Fahrenheit.
- *Drinking fountains.* It is desirable for toddlers to have access to a lever-operated fountain with mouth-guard protection, or to individual cups for independent use.

- *Equipment for transporting children.* Four- and six-passenger carts, single to triple strollers, and approved car seats for field trips in cars or vans are all very desirable to get children out and about (but not to replace "toddling walks").

Equipment to avoid:
- *Wind-up swings.* These swings are justified only when programs offer such poor conditions that they are in survival mode and have few means to cope with children's distress. They are nearly always overused to pacify infants. They are also not very durable.
- *Walkers, exersaucers, and jump-ups.* Walkers and jump-ups are not recommended because they have no positive developmental effects (and may slightly delay in the short-term) and can be dangerous (particularly walkers). Exersaucers are not dangerous but have no developmental advantages. They can offer protected space but at the same time tend to be overused and therefore limit active learning.

Evaluating the Space

As children get older, the composition of the group changes. Just as the daily timetable needs to be looked at critically every now and then, so does the arrangement of space. There may be bottlenecks, spaces that are underused or not used at all, places that are constantly messy and disorganized, and places where the play is not as constructive as it could be.

Watch how the children and adults use the space. Wandering, illegal climbing, using each other as playthings, or seeking tiny spaces all indicate what is missing in the space for children. Staff leave similar clues. Items left on changing tables indicate a need for storage surfaces. Fumbling around for tissues points to a need for greater accessibility. Constantly walking through play areas and interrupting activities there or stepping over babies says something about pathways.

Take a child's eye view of the space. What does a child see, hear, smell, and feel?

Use an outside observer. Periodically, not just in times of crisis, it can be very helpful to have someone outside the room observe it. They may notice concerns, as well as the effects of good arrangements.

A Quick and Simple Evaluation

Look at your space when all the adults and children have gone. Ask yourself the following three questions:

- Does this seem like a great place to be an infant or toddler—safe, secure, and full of learning opportunities?
- Does this seem like a great place to be with an infant or toddler—for the whole day?
- Does this seem like a good place to work—to be a good teacher and colleague?

If the answer to any of those questions is no, then the adults have to provide more daily magic to make things work. The more functionality and learning are built into the setting, the better the space will work.

Changing the Space

Because a familiar place is an important source of security, change should be made thoughtfully and major familiar landmarks should remain constant. Involving the older children and having all the children witness change make alterations to the space less stressful.

It takes time to tell whether a change in environment will have the desired results. Staff need to give most changes a few weeks for children, staff, and parents to adjust before deciding whether changes are helpful or unhelpful.

See Supplement: *How to Improve Your Indoor Space for Infants and Toddlers*

A Final Word: Preventing Over- and Understimulation

So much energy goes into making programs rich and inviting that it is easy to forget that human and physical environments and daily schedules can result in children (and adults) feeling bombarded by stimulation. The result is sensory overload. How much is too much? Too much causes distress or prevents children from getting involved.

It is fairly easy to judge when a child does not have enough to do. It is considerably more difficult to judge at what point a baby or toddler has too much to react to or interact with. The best guides are the child's involvement and mood. A child who is unhappy or distracted, who only interacts very briefly and superficially with toys and people, may have too many things to react to.

While younger children sometimes have the capacity to turn off or ignore things around them, overstimulation is nonetheless an ever-present concern. A child who frequently has to turn off excess noise, confusion, and activity in the room uses up energy and is also very likely to turn off meaningful experiences. This is particularly true of children with special needs.

Overstimulation is different for each child. Young babies, for example, may be startled and upset by loud or unexpected noises that a toddler would find entertaining. Some children are adept at filtering out irrelevant stimuli and pursuing their own activities, while others are more apt to notice and to respond to everything. Such children need more protection, more quiet time. Knowing each baby's characteristics will affect the way a sensitive teacher interacts with each of them.

Also keep in mind that mobile babies have more control over the kind and amount of input they are exposed to than do younger babies. Nonmobile babies often have too much or too little to react to.

Of course, understimulation is also common. Opportunities for exploration and learning may be lacking because of lack of resources, staff concerns about the mess or possible accidents, or resistance to adapting to the needs of children at the edges of an age span—those who are considered too young or too old for the room. Rooms need to fit the children, and not the reverse.

Exercises

1. Chart the paths of major traffic flow in an infant room. Do the paths cut across learning centers? What can you do about it?

2. What are the pressure points during the day—the times that are difficult for staff and children? Why is this so? What can be done to improve them?

3. Look at the arrangement of time and space In a center you are familiar with. What messages do the arrangements give about the qualities that staff value in children?

References

Ceppi, G., and M. Zini. 1998. *Children, Spaces, Relations: Metaproject for an Environment for Young Children*. Reggio Emilia, Italy: Reggio Children.

Olds, A. 1984. Quoted in "Fine Details: Organizing and Displaying Materials," *Beginnings,* Summer.

Prescott, E. 1979. "The Physical Environment—A Powerful Regulator of Experience." *Child Care Information Exchange* 7:1–5.

Resource for an extended discussion and visuals of infant and toddler environments:

Greenman, J. 2005. *Caring Spaces, Learning Places: Children's Environments That Work*. Redmond, WA: Exchange Press.

Chapter 8

Sharing Care with Families

εxcellence *The program values a partnership with every family and makes every effort to create and sustain the partnership. Every family is confident that their child is receiving excellent care that takes into account the family's needs, beliefs, priorities, and values.*

Do these comments sound familiar?

Why do we do all this for parents? Where will it stop?

They leave their kids here all the time. They object if we close for training. Why did these people have kids?

They always want us to be more "academic."

They "borrow" crackers for their commute home. They tie up the phone and get coffee from the staff room.

You know, my life would be much easier if children didn't come with parents.

Such laments are heard in centers across the country. In the real world of child care, parents are frequently considered a burden or even a necessary evil, a holdover from traditional school attitudes favoring sharp home–school boundaries and from all-too-common early education assumptions that children are sent to us for education on our terms. Fortunately, there is now more discussion of the need for child care to be family-friendly, a welcome recognition that children come with families, that what we do has implications for others in the child's life, and that we can have a positive impact on the family's appreciation and understanding of their child.

But family-friendly child care may not be enough. In the twenty-first century, child care centers need to go a step further and become real family centers, recognizing that the family is the unit of service and that child care for young children is the core service. What changes are necessary when a center defines itself as a family center? The family becomes the starting point for developing services and program content. Staff always consider the child in the context of the family surrounding the child. For example, the experience of six-month-old Denise reflects the understanding that her world includes her parents, Alex and Christina, her older brother, Steven, and her grandparents, Ben and Evelyn. Eighteen-month-old Sisi lives in two households with her parents and stepparents, siblings and stepsiblings. Two-year-old David lives with his mother, Emma.

See Supplement: *Parent Partnership: A Continuum of Quality*

The Program Serves Families

Child care is a family affair. Rather than taking over or substituting for families, child care supplements and extends what the family offers. Families have the most influence on a child—they are there for life—and parents are usually their children's primary caregivers. The job of child care is to work with families to meet the needs of children in the context of their family life. Good-quality child care is individualized for the child and the family and empowers both. The best programs work hard to share with families decision making and control of the child's care. The best experience happens when there is a true collaboration that recognizes the prerogatives and constraints of parents and staff alike.

Staff strive to nurture in children a sense of belonging to their family and to reinforce primary attachments to parents and other family members. How does this happen? It happens by welcoming families, involving them in decision making about their child's experience, and nurturing each parent's pleasure in and understanding of their child.

Good relationships, however, don't happen automatically—they aren't merely by-products of caring well for children or of just being nice people. They stem from trust built on a foundation of hard work, attention to detail, and good systems for promoting communication and real partnership. And nobody says it's easy!

But What about the Child?

When the focus shifts from the child to the family, do we lose the child? Aren't *child* development and learning professionals also *child* advocates? The assumption that the child gets lost and will suffer comes from our somewhat mistaken sense that we speak for the child. Don't we? Yes, we can speak about the experience of children in our care and probably know a great deal about them—their personalities, likes and dislikes, and

> ### Child Care in the Real World
>
> A parent introduced to another parent by a teacher as "Marika's mom" responded somewhat tersely, "I'm Jane—I have a name too." It is easy to fall into the habit of labeling and thinking of parents of the children in your care as parents only, even referring to them that way: "Marika's mom said that Marika was very tired this morning." Granting parents a separate identity is important in creating a culture of respect.

preferences. But do we really know more about them than their parents? How could we? So who *does* speak for the children? In a sense, both we and families do, not as opposing teams but rather as allies, in order to provide the best experience for the children.

Both parents and teachers need to be heard because each of them sees different "pieces" of the children and their lives. Teachers have special expertise, but their vision can be clouded by their narrow professional perspectives. Yes, parents can put on the rose-colored glasses and at times may make decisions that are not in their children's best interests as they try to balance family life—for example, too many eleven-hour days of care, overly protective concern about the normal bumps and bruises of childhood, or seeing their sick child as well enough to be in child care. But teachers wear rose-colored glasses too, especially while they work to balance their own resources, needs, and schedules. Like parents, teachers scramble and necessarily sometimes put children's needs second in order to cope with budgets, turnover, scheduling staff vacations, less than ideal staff-child ratios, and other trade-offs that are necessary in the real world of child care.

Teachers do typically know more than parents about children—children in general, that is. They may even know a lot about a specific child, and it may feel as if that knowledge is superior to a parent's knowledge. But this is a false superiority, because the focus is tightly on the child in front of them. They may edit out the home and family context and the child's past and future. Parents have broader and deeper knowledge, although they often are not aware of how much they know or how to help their child with the knowledge they do have. It is the teacher's job to bring out the knowledge that parents possess and figure out how to best use it to help the child. It is not the professional's job to judge the family.

Child Care Is Not School

There is as much learning going on in childcare centers as in schools, and in some ways, probably more, but child care is not school—that is, an institution organized to instruct children. Just as it is important not to think of child care as school, it is also important to stress that relationships between child care and parents are not the same as those between parents and most schools, even preschool programs. Schools generally assume responsibility for educating children in the manner they see as appropriate, and share information about the child's progress with parents on the same basis. The parents' job is mostly to keep informed about the child, support the professionals, and discuss any issues that the professionals wish to consult with them about. Parents' presence is usually on the perimeter of the classroom.

Child care is different. If parents' overall responsibility is to raise the child, be the expert on the child, and make sure the child is cared for in accordance with the values and standards of the family, culture, and community, then it follows that in child care it is the parents' job to pay attention to and influence the child's day-to-day experience.

This is an important point, and one that makes some professionals uneasy. Sharing information is one thing—sharing power is quite another.

To help make the conceptual shift, suppose that you are a parent with lots of money and you are looking for child care. You may hire a nanny or seek out the specific care you want from the best programs in the area. You would expect to have influence over your child's care, not simply receive information about it—in other words, you would expect to be able to buy exactly what you want. Your purchasing power backs up your parental prerogatives. If you want some advice and parenting education from the child care professional(s), you would certainly expect it to be given respectfully, in full awareness that what you do with your child is your choice. As the parent, you want control over the care, but as a typical sensible parent, you use your financial ability to find teachers you trust and respect and whom you rely on for their professional judgment on many decisions.

All parents, regardless of income or status, deserve the same choice and sense of control over their child's early care and education.

Going Beyond "Do No Harm"

The first imperative as a human service is of course the same lesson that health practitioners are taught: *Do no harm*. And just as is true in any other human service organization, it is easy for child care providers to *do* harm by

- contributing to the family's rat race
- undermining the family's values
- showing lack of respect for the family's culture and lifestyle
- being judgmental and causing parents to lose confidence in themselves or their children.

But the mission, of course, is to do much more than "do no harm." Our responsibility is to actively support children and families. The family center recognizes that all of what is done for the child is mediated by the family context. But note this: caring about the family, just like caring about the child, does not imply that early care and education programs should expect to perform social or therapeutic services or that we should allow parents to expect those from us. We can direct families to those services if need be, but trying to provide them ourselves without training and certification can cause harm.

There is support that we can provide families within our own realm of expertise. All it takes is flexibility, creativity, and the desire to help rather than watching parents struggle.

Extras Some centers provide extra services that may not even involve children. For example, they may provide parenting advice or assistance or help families balance work and life more effectively. With the latter aim, a program may adopt a "what else can we do for you" orientation, which can lead to convenience services that may not generate revenue but add value to the child care service: commute snacks, meals to go, dry cleaning pickup, copying services, and other conveniences. The critical concept is that services provided at a particular center are based on identifying or anticipating the needs of the families served, not starting from the fixed idea that we only do child care.

Is there a danger in expanding or enhancing services? Of course. If a program gets swept up in becoming something new and expanded, it can lose what is most important: the quality early care and education that parents expect—a great place for children to live and learn. But this can be prevented in the way that all mediocrity is prevented, by using active intelligence, which means always asking "Why not?" and "Why?" rather than operating on autopilot. A program can only do what it can do, restricted by budget, site, and family and client or board desires. Most family centers need not and will not extend services very far beyond what a child care center usually offers, but things such as having extra diapers on hand and snacks-to-go for the ride home (children can even help make these) are not unrealistic. A center that focuses on offering high-quality care and education to children in ways that support child rearing and that does not offer any additional services is still making a major contribution to family well-being, particularly its child-rearing responsibility.

"Them"

Parents easily become "them" or "the parents," not a collection of individuals. In every population, individuals range from near-saints to clear sinners. We often use the annoying and problematic behavior of the least agreeable to create our "them," against whom we rail. The parent who willingly places her child in care for forty hours a week but who only works part-time to pay for expensive clothing defines one "them" ("self-indulgent"), along with the chronically late parent ("rude and uncaring"), the one who forgets the diapers ("irresponsible"), the one who whines ("obnoxious"), and the one who wants her infant toilet-trained ("ignorant"). When some staff get together to talk about parents, you wonder if they are talking about a mutant species. Usually, however, the staff's bark is worse than its bite. Many staff who rail against parents actually behave in sensitive and accommodating ways while interacting with them.

This tendency to create "thems" is certainly not limited to child care professionals. It is a natural phenomenon that has to be fought—an occupational hazard of service-related professions. To resist the creation of "thems," all staff should help each other make it taboo to slide into generalizations and judgments. Do you suppose the parents ever talk about "us"?

Parents as Clients or Customers

Although negotiating children's experiences in child care—for many children, such care is a significant part of their childhood—is much more important than buying a product or purchasing many other kinds of services, it may help to understand what a good program tries to accomplish if we think of parents as clients or customers. As with any business or service, the program must meet the customers' needs and create satisfied customers. Children are consumers of the service, not its customer—except in the unlikely event that they pay the bills!

Does thinking about the parent as a customer seem to negate or diminish the importance and seriousness of the human service we provide? After all, we're caring for children, not selling clothes in a department store or meals in a restaurant. On the contrary, seeing parents as customers helps us focus on how we can improve their and their children's experience. It does not in any way undermine our credibility or expertise. If you were scheduled to have surgery, you would have lots of questions about the procedure, not because you're the medical expert who can perform the operation, but because it's your body. If we start from the premise that parents are responsible for their children, then they really are our customers, and we should treat them as such.

Does this mean the program can't apply standards and values to children that may differ from those of their families? Of course not. Just as conscientious electricians, plumbers, architects, and physicians won't go along with customers' or clients' wishes when those wishes conflict with their own professional judgments, neither should child care staff. Focusing on customer satisfaction does mean, however, that the foundation of the service is serving customers' needs. A focus on customers also implies that it is in our interest to define and promote our product—excellent child care—in ways that parents can understand. It also implies that we are accountable to parents and have an obligation to explain what we are doing in ways they can understand. It is also imperative to find out what parents want. Satisfied parents who feel good about their child's care are a fundamental ingredient in quality child care.

Even when parents do their job as customers, there are inherent tensions. What is our image of a good customer? Usually, someone who asks questions and makes demands. When parents behave like conscientious customers, they ought to be admired for doing what they should be doing, and their criticism should not be taken personally or responded to defensively.

Good Programs Support, not Supplant

Parents who use care do not want to be replaced in their children's lives. Teachers are not parent substitutes, except in the practical sense of providing substitute care during the hours that parents are unavailable. Having a baby in child care should not be seen by either parents or staff as "handing over" the child, but rather as engaging in provision of the best possible care for the baby.

Policies and Practice

As is true of all aspects of good-quality care for babies, it helps when program practices related to working with parents flow out of sound policies. Great policies don't make any difference if they are not reflected in daily practice. The importance of families and of shared care should feature prominently in the vision statement or statement of philosophy of the center. Many policies can relate to and strengthen partnerships with families, and a strong, clear statement should be made about collaboration, communication, and shared decision making.

In addition, there need to be clear procedures, expectations of mutual responsibilities, and a process for resolving conflicts between parents and staff.

Parent Involvement

Parent involvement is an all-purpose term that encompasses membership on parent boards and committees, volunteering in the program, participating in parent education activities, helping with fund-raising, coming to work days, and attending special events. Each center needs to find the right mix of opportunities to help families feel welcome and a part of the child care community. However, parents who use child care are almost

> **First Steps: Milestones for Whom?**
>
> Eric finally does it—he lurches across the room like a miniature sumo wrestler, and he does so at the center of the room. So what do you do? If you tell the parents, they may well feel left out and cheated of a major milestone, thinking, "I wish he had walked first for me." What if you don't tell them? Eric will eventually walk at home. In come Eric and his parents the next day, united in family pride. However, some parents, knowing that the center generally follows this practice, will want to be told; otherwise, they feel the center may always be holding back information. How do you know what each family prefers? Ask them.

always very busy and will have limited time to participate in the life of the child care center. The key to parent involvement is to make a variety of ways available to parents to become involved in the life of the center without making them feel that doing so is obligatory. Parents shouldn't feel guilty about not being able to participate.

While the partnerships and collaborations may involve parents in a variety of ways, parent partnerships are *not* the same thing as parent involvement. Parent involvement usually means parents doing things to support the service or becoming part of the experience, while partnership and collaboration are about relationships on behalf of the child's well-being. Parent involvement typically focuses on the program or the parents, while parent partnerships always focus on the well-being of the child. Most important, parent involvement typically allows teachers to be in the driver's seat, while partnerships involve sharing decision-making power and control.

The foundations of partnership are communication, decision-making systems, and daily interactions that promote sharing, negotiating, and mutual trust.

Parent Insecurity Is Normal

Parents of infants in child care are likely to be the most insecure of all parents. Many are new to parenting, some are new to marriage, and almost all experience some stress and fatigue from childbirth or the often lengthy process of adopting, returning to work, shouldering multiple responsibilities, and late-night caregiving. Every parent knows that simply leaving the house with an infant or toddler and all the necessary paraphernalia for the day can be a major effort. Parents, like their children, may respond in different ways:

- Some parents will be ambivalent or regretful about returning to work or school and leaving their child in care: *Am I really doing the right thing. Is it too soon? What if my _____ (parents, friends, in-laws, grandparents, or other critics) are right and I am being selfish?* Initially, they are likely to experience the real pain and insecurity of separation. After all, they are entrusting their most prized possessions—their tiny, vulnerable children who are unable to communicate what they are experiencing—to people whom they don't know well. Even if the center has a five-star reputation, parents are likely to initially feel insecure and to take time to learn to trust.
- The pain of separation felt by parents not only doesn't disappear quickly, it recurs throughout the child care experience (and beyond: when children go away to school, camp, college, and leave home). In the first two years of life, children change so fast, seemingly becoming new people every week. The loss of time with them continually pains many parents. Some parents have to leave their child in care but truly wish they could be home with them, while others are unsure about the decision to return to work or to use a child care program or family child care home rather than a relative. Other parents may be worried about being replaced in their children's affections. These feelings add to the complexity of parents' relationships with staff.
- First-time parents usually approach child care uncertain about what to expect, particularly about how much of a role their knowledge and wishes should play in the scheme of things.

- When a child has a disability, the parents are likely to be even more anxious, because they wonder about whether or not their child's cues will be responded to and her needs met and how other children and their families will react. They may still be coming to terms with the fact that their child is not developing typically, and their grief may affect their relationship with you. They are likely to be particularly sensitive to any implied or even unintended comparisons of their child to typically developing children.

- Parents of very young children, especially first-time parents, may be anxious about their child's development and behavior. They may wonder if their child is normal, and worry about unusual or undesirable behavior. "Why isn't my Tommy holding a spoon" (or walking, talking, playing chess)? Teachers' objectivity and experience with lots of babies can be very useful in these situations. We can reassure parents that little Angela's passion for sinking her teeth into the flesh of her playmates will not lead to her becoming a vampire, and that Sol's inability to share at age two doesn't mean he won't ever be able to. We know that the vast majority of things that children do lie within the wide and diverse range of typical behavior.

Staff can help families by talking about typical separation issues even during the initial tour of the center, and from the first conference on. By letting parents know that ambivalence about using care and having trouble separating while their child apparently isn't are perfectly typical.

Having a child in a group situation with other children approximately the same age is both an advantage and a disadvantage for parents. Parents can't help comparing, and they worry if their child doesn't seem to measure up. The staff's job is to help them appreciate their child's uniqueness and accomplishments, pointing out the child's expanding abilities—in short, helping them to appreciate their child and discouraging them from excessive comparisons with others. Of course, that means we have to refrain from making comparisons too.

Every Parent Is Different

All parents want the best for their child—and that is their job. This is important to remember, particularly when parents are demanding and seem to care too much, when they have a not-very-accurate picture of their child, or when they seem removed and care too

---

Common Insecurities

Both teachers and parents would be surprised to know that they may harbor similar insecurities.

Parent Insecurities

Many parents wonder

- What do I *really* know about raising a child? About the child care I chose?
- What do they think of me? Of my child?
- Do they understand my child care guilt?
- Do they know how complicated and hard my life is?
- Will they understand and like my child?
- Will they understand and respect me?
- Is my child attached to me? *Too* attached?

Teacher Insecurities

Teachers may wonder

- Do I *really* know enough about children?
- What do parents think of me?
- Do they know how complicated and hard my life is?
- Do they understand and respect me?
- Is the child attached to me? *Too* attached?

Parent and teacher insecurities have some of the same roots:

- There is no right way to raise children, so how do we know if we are doing the right thing?
- Children are complicated.
- Sharing love and responsibility for the same human being can be difficult.

An additional factor in teacher insecurity is the reality that some teachers are drawn to early childhood education because they prefer relating to children and feel less confident interacting with adults.

Not One, but Both

Often center staff see one parent much more often than the other. It is important not to fall into the habit of saving all important communication for one parent. When communication systems are carefully designed to ensure that communication reaches both parents, the program supports adult relationships.

The following example illustrates what can happen when communication is mainly with one parent:

Everyone in the room preferred to talk with Craig, Taylor's dad. The general consensus was that Taylor's mother, Susan, was, to put it delicately, *not right;* staff located her somewhere on the parent behaviorial continuum between peculiar and unbalanced. They thought she was extremely overprotective, critical, irrational, demanding, and unpredictable—sometimes sweet, but often stormy. After a while, it became clear that the staff went to great lengths to communicate with Craig alone. Survival-driven, they hoped to get Susan off their backs. But something else also became clear: tension between Craig and Susan was rising, and often Craig's child care decisions were a factor. He usually acquiesced to staff requests and took the teacher's side if there were any issues between center and family. The path of least resistance for staff was creating, or at least aggravating, a bumpy marital relationship, and it was not helping the relationship between Taylor and her mother. If staff had been trained to take a family focus, they would have made extra efforts to communicate with a parent like Susan.

little. Most parents want the same things for their child: success in school, work, and life; friends; a healthy lifestyle; self-esteem. But parents have different beliefs and values, and what they believe about how their children should attain these ends may differ from the teacher's or other parents' beliefs. Sometimes two parents of the same child have different views.

Staff must respect differences and try to accommodate them within the program. When parents' beliefs are incompatible with the program's philosophy and policies, our job is to seek common ground and try to work out solutions.

Cultural Differences

When there are cultural and language differences, the challenge to form a partnership can be even greater because of real or perceived differences in child-rearing practices. Expectations about children, nurturing routines, discipline, and giving praise and affection vary from culture to culture. The way members of a society care for children determines the characteristics of its adults, and the beliefs, values, and practices that hold communities together. For example, adults' responses to crying and other signs of distress differ from culture to culture. In some cultures, four-year-olds are expected to look after two-year-old siblings. The same children may be given freedom and responsibilities that many Americans would rarely give to a young child. In some cultures, it is very common for a parent to feed a child, even of preschool age, both to create an intimate bond and to demonstrate that food is a precious resource (food in such a culture would never be used for play). In many cultures, respect for elders is almost automatic. Children may be expected to automatically defer to older siblings and adults, to show respect by bowing the head when spoken to, or to smile when being disciplined. In many cultures, going outside in the rain is expected; in others, children may be expected to stay inside when temperatures drop. The importance of a neat and clean appearance, even in a play setting, also varies from culture to culture.

Every center should have a good understanding of the practices of the families who use it. Some of these practices will be based on cultural background. Although it is useful to have some information about cultural practices, too little information can be dangerous, in the sense that it is important not to overgeneralize and assume that the child-rearing practices of all parents will be based on cultural background, or, worse, to assume similarities among cultures when we do not understand the many differences between them (for example, among Vietnamese, Koreans, and Chinese, or between Iranians and Iraqis). While we are aware that practices within our own culture vary quite a bit, we tend to generalize about other cultures.

Parents are the best source of information about their cultural backgrounds and lifestyles. When information comes from them, you avoid the possibility of stereotyping or making assumptions based on general or outdated information. Openness and willingness to negotiate the child's experience will reassure families that their preferences will be respected. Learning key phrases in a family's language is a sign of respect and helps the child feel secure. "Welcome," "How can I help?" "Good-bye," "Thank you," and "I am happy that you are here" are useful and welcoming ways of communicating.

Every culture believes that what it does is right. Within each culture, there is usually a degree of consensus about what constitutes good care and normal child development. But cultures don't agree, which is understandable, because they are products of centuries of history, geography, language, and visions of the future. Child development experts who are raised and educated within a single culture can just about always agree on what is "right."

In working with parents, it is important to remember that there is often a cultural logic to their beliefs and practices. The logic may be based on cultural practices perceived as natural, and those are likely to feel just as right as our own closely held truths. Because this is so, we have a responsibility to listen and respect, to adapt practices when possible, and to clearly articulate the logic of these adapted program practices to both staff and parents. Most important, in our articulation of what we believe, we must be careful to distinguish between what we believe to be true (our cultural assumptions) and what is universally true.

Parents Take Different Roles

Parents' roles as protectors, educators, providers, and child care consumers influence their interactions with staff.

> **Child protector: What kind of a parent am I if I can't protect my baby from being chewed on by some ferocious toddler?** The most basic, primal role of parents is to protect their child. Parents who don't perform this function adequately are not well thought of. What kind of parents let their child run out in the street, fall down a well, or get injured by other kids? So what reaction should we expect from a parent whose child is bitten, injured, or seems to be in the throes of despair when left at the center? Would we really want a parent to say, "Hey, it's okay, just a bite—biting is natural"?

> **Primary educator: If my child grows up ignorant, no one will look to her child care teachers as the culprits.** Most parents are very concerned about what their children are learning in their early years. They hear that educational needs begin at birth, that the brain is busy wiring itself, and that the first three years are critical. There is contradictory information raining down on them from all sides. They hear both that children need more instruction and that they need more play and hands-on

experiences and less instruction; that intellectual development is key and emotional intelligence is most important. They want to make sure their child is well equipped for the future, especially for the not-too-distant time when their formal schooling begins. The result may be that the child care center feels friction because its curriculum doesn't seem to recognize parents' goals for their child.

Provider for the family: I want the best for my son Kevin, and sometimes that means working long hours and two jobs. I know that may mean some longer child care days than are ideal, but what can you do? Parents are told they have to begin saving immediately for college and retirement, as well as for braces, school activities, and all the other expenses that arise. Single parents may be feeling very real pressure to "do it all" with even fewer resources and time than other parents.

Child care consumer: When I buy a car, I'm supposed to look under the hood, slam the doors, kick the tires, take a test drive, and hit the brakes. As a child care consumer checking out a center where I may spend more than $40,000 for two kids over five years, shouldn't I be as demanding? Well, yes—but remember that we are under the hood, we are the tires, and we are the doors. Sometimes the conscientious, savvy, assertive child care consumer is an admirable parent who may also place great demands on the center.

These are tensions between parents' and staff's roles that are bound to create some friction in any center, no matter how wonderful individual parents, directors, and teachers are. Our job is to create a safe place that educates and challenges a group of children and that satisfies parents who may not fully agree on what is safe, what is appropriate education, and what are the right challenges. The parents' role is to choose a program that works for their child, not the group, and that seems in line with their beliefs and values. Given these aims, it is surprising that there is not more tension.

Parents Are Human (Like Us)

Parents are people like us: struggling to do the right thing in a busy, sometimes confusing world. Many are thoughtful and sensitive, whereas a few are not; some are open and easy to talk to, whereas some are more reserved; some are confident and others are not; some are experienced and others are novices; some have many stresses in their lives, whereas others seem to have everything under control.

No one is or will be a perfect parent. We face different challenges and make different compromises in balancing the real world of children, work, and family life. Parents have many roles (for example, employee, student, spouse, partner, son, or daughter) and many conflicting demands, some of which keep them from putting their children's needs first all the time. It is easy for teachers, whose task is always to put children first, to overlook this and to become intolerant or overly critical of parents.

It is not always possible (or desirable) for parents to make all the decisions about allocating precious resources (time, energy, and money) on the basis of what is good for their children right now. Over the course of our parenting lives, all of us will sacrifice and indulge, behave sensibly and not so sensibly, rise to the occasion and fail miserably, and be sensitive and thoughtless. This is called being human.

The daily choices parents make are often difficult. In interactions with parents and in conversations with other staff members, it is essential that you reflect an empathetic and supportive attitude toward parents. It is not our job to evaluate them and the choices they make. We may be completely unaware of some of the roles they play and the responsibilities they have shouldered. Our support should reflect our respect for the difficult choices they may need to make.

Although the partnership between staff and parents focuses on the well-being of their children, showing interest in other aspects of the parents' lives and sharing information about yourself builds the relationship. Always, of course, respect the parents' boundaries, do not be too nosy, and keep in mind that the core focus should be their child's experience.

"They Don't Care"

In child care, we often take our own institutional limitations as givens—certainly not as signs that we care less about the children. Ratios, center size, foods served, limits of services, staff turnover—"Sorry, welcome to the real world of today's child care." We usually can honestly say that we are doing our best, but we are not always so willing to accept parents' givens. Yet parents' real lives—long work days, finding time for themselves, money problems, difficulties sorting out what is the right thing to do in a diverse, guilt-inducing, materialistic culture—easily bring out the judgmental tendencies in us (particularly if we haven't had to face the world as parents ourselves).

"They don't care" or "They don't care enough" is perhaps the most common hidden thought lurking in the back of the minds of many child care teachers every time we look for extra clothes, cope with a sick child, or regret the poor turnout at an open house. This is often followed by "I wish they would get some parent education," while we piece together an image of the child's family life based on the child's behavior, on our disapproving glimpses of parent-child interactions, and on reports from the home front. As a director, one of the authors made sure the parent handbook at his center had a section asking that parents label their children's clothing because "Don't they realize how many clothes we have to go through and how alike all the clothing is?" But as parents, we inconsistently label our children's clothing because "Don't they realize how many clothes kids go through and what it takes to label each pair of socks?" As parents, we regretfully missed open houses and committed all the parent sins, but still cared deeply about our children.

Parents' Boundaries Differ

Different parents may want very different relationships with the center and the staff. Some want a lot of contact, a great deal of information about the details of child care, and opportunities to share much of what is going on in their own lives with staff. Others maintain a distance, seek and share far less information, and have much less contact. This may be because they want to know only enough to believe that they have made a reasonable arrangement for care. Parents have a right to set their own boundaries, as long as all needed information for the good care of the child flows back and forth.

However, remember that some parents may simply be shy or uncertain about their role or may have had experiences in which professionals showed no interest in their ideas and concerns. Staff should always look for ways to put these parents at ease so that they really feel welcome and comfortable in the relationship and believe that teachers really do want to hear what they have to say.

Some Parents Will Alienate Staff

Take any ten or fifteen people. A few will be difficult some of the time, and one will be impossible, while all will be difficult occasionally. This is true of staff and true of parents. The most difficult parents to form partnerships with are those who are critical of the center and staff, self-centered, always demanding or uncooperative, or neglectful of their children. Often, in spite of the fact that they are behaving in ways that are least likely to elicit help and support, these are the parents who most need those services. It is the essence of professionalism to serve these parents well.

Some Parents Harm Their Children

Family stress and dysfunction can have serious implications for a child's future, more serious than any of the direct effects of mediocre child care. A family center recognizes that reality and understands that families may be under a considerable amount of stress: divorce rates are high, there is increasing competition for family members' time and energy, and there are conflicting and mixed messages about appropriate family values.

Sooner or later, most centers will struggle with the issues of child abuse, neglect, and family dysfunction. Parenting is never stress-free, and each of us has the capacity to harm a child, either by acting out in frustration or anger, by becoming overwhelmed by circumstances, or by neglecting care. But most parents don't abuse or neglect children; instead, somehow most parents manage to control themselves and care for their children adequately.

Dealing with families under stress is undoubtedly the most difficult aspect of a teacher's job. Child care providers are required by law to report any instances of suspected abuse or neglect. Reporting abuse or neglect—in fact, even deciding whether there is enough to report—is a traumatic experience with potentially huge consequences for the family and the teacher-parent relationship. Sadness, confusion, anger, fear, and every other difficult emotion may cloud the decision, including doubt about whether reporting is best for the child. The center and individual staff must follow the state guidelines. Centers require training and thoughtful procedures to ensure that children are protected and that families are treated respectfully.

"You Can't Imagine How It Feels."

"You don't really know what it's like to suspect or discover that your new child is not like all the other kids until it happens to you," Marco explains. He is the parent of a child with a severe hearing disability. "You are in denial, in shock, and then angry and frightened. It's hard on the marriage, it's hard on her ten-year-old brother, who doesn't understand what's wrong and why. It throws off your social relationships with friends and family—some avoid us, we get sick of sympathy and pity, and some don't understand what it all involves. We have had wonderful child care, but it is always tricky; sometimes they think I'm too pushy, sometimes they feel we don't tell them enough, and sometimes they seem to expect too much. Well-meaning teachers have said things that upset me because they underestimate Sarah, and I've said things that upset them because they think I expect too much from them. I wouldn't trade Sarah for any other kid on the planet, but I also feel for any family in our situation."

Marco is a difficult parent, at times abrupt and demanding, at other times aloof. Serving children with special needs means serving parents who also have special needs. Like their children, they require extra patience and sensitivity.

This difficult situation is the ultimate test of the bond between parent and program. If there is a strong partnership and mutual trust, there is at least hope of weathering the storm and continuing to support the child and family.

The Parent and Teacher Partnership

Building a partnership with parents is probably the most challenging aspect of a teacher's job. It takes sensitivity and skill to maneuver through relationships with parents that are free from competition over the child's affection and claims or beliefs that one party knows what is best for the child.

Many parents approach the parent-teacher relationship with some guilt about using child care and some confusion from the conflicting messages they've received about

---

Benefits of Partnership

For the child:
- The experience of the special people in his or her life working together cooperatively, getting along with each other
- A feeling of security
- Consistent, sensitive, individualized care based on shared information
- Greater continuity between life at home and at the program
- Parents who feel empowered in caring for their child, which enhances feelings of attachment to the child
- Parents who feel confident about their child rearing
- Passionate advocates in both the parent and the teacher.

For the parents:
- Greater confidence in their decision to use care and in their parenting skills
- Belonging to a community of people who care about their child
- The support of early childhood professionals who listen, respect, and trust them
- The opportunity to contribute significantly to their child's experience even when they are absent
- Increased feelings of attachment to the child (in contrast to decreased attachment, which may occur when there is no partnership)
- Additional information about and a different perspective on their child
- Continual reassurance that they are the most special person in their child's life.

For the staff:
- Information about the child from an expert on that child
- A variety of help and contributions
- Affirmation of their importance and support for their work
- The satisfaction of knowing that they may be making a lasting, positive difference in a child and family's life.

"They Won't Leave Us Alone"

The flip side to "They don't care" is "They care too much" about some things. Cody's mother, Gloria, only twenty-two, is a high-school drop-out on public assistance and the mother of three children. She keeps appointments erratically and rarely provides an extra set of clothes for her children. Moreover, she was reported to the state for suspected child abuse for what looked like a burn on Cody's bottom. It turned out to be impetigo. When she becomes upset with the center about Cody's care or has questions about his education, some staff respond with an underlying, unspoken attitude, "How dare *you* (*an unreliable, irresponsible parent*) challenge *us* (*professional child development experts*) on our care decisions!" The more questions, the more staff become outraged.

Some of Gloria's questions and concerns:

- When will Cody be taught to read?
- Why does he get so dirty?
- How did he get that bruise?
- How could he lose two shirts and a shoe?
- Why do you let Cody get away with so much?

Gloria is loud and seems ill at ease and pushy to the staff. Because of this, many staff do not recognize that her questions and concerns are nearly always appropriate and are never frivolous.

Lupe's mother, Marta—a forty-two-year-old, fashionably dressed psychologist—is nearly the opposite of Gloria. Lupe is her only child. Marta is usually late picking up Lupe and is often slow in responding to staff's requests. When she asks questions or has concerns, which is frequently, she asks many questions that are similar to Gloria's. Staff response is less one of "How dare she?" than of "What a typical, neurotic, older yuppie parent." Like Gloria, Marta has questions and concerns that, while numerous and often minor, are never off the wall.

continued on next page

what to look for in a program. Many teachers, some of whom work with children because they feel more confident with children than with adults, bring the insecurity that accompanies low pay and status along with the same uncertainty about "what is the right thing to do" in the parent-teacher relationship. Others translate their insecurity into inflexible certainty about what is best. Most staff and parents come from America's individualistic culture, which is not great about sharing love and intimacy. Staff often develop feelings and perceptions that work against a partnership with parents. Those feelings are a natural outgrowth of the complex relationship and are present in nearly all programs.

Parents Are Experts on Their Own Child

The parent-child relationship is much longer, more intimate, and more intense than the teacher-child relationship. Parents observe their children across a range of very different settings and over a long period of time. Even when parents lack confidence, they inevitably possess insights and information about the child that staff do not. Are they always right about their child? No, their perspective is often distorted by love, hope, fear, and incomplete understanding of development and learning. But the teacher's perspective, while often wise because of greater objectivity, knowledge of development, and experience with a number of children, is not infallible, and teachers are often wrong as well.

Someone once said that a parent's job is to be the president of their child's fan club. When parents are advocating for their child, they are simply doing their job, and although it may sometimes complicate our lives, we should celebrate whenever we can see that a child is surrounded by people—or at least one person—who thinks he or she is the most special human being alive. It's the child who doesn't have such a person that we need to be concerned about.

Parents Focus on How the Program Works for Their Child

It would be a much easier job for staff if parents had the same perspective that we do—that is, an equal concern for all children and families in the program and an understanding that compromises are inevitable in order to make things work for all children and families in the program. However, this is unreasonable to expect. We don't behave that way in our own expectations of services we purchase, and parents won't, either. For example, have you ever said, "No, don't worry, Mr. Auto Mechanic, I don't mind that my car is not fixed, because you did a swell job on all those others"? It is the parents' job to look out for and advocate for their child. It is our job to balance the needs of and parental preferences for each individual child with the needs of the group.

Competition for the Love of the Child and "Child Saving"

It is hard not to compete with parents for children's affections. Teachers become attached to children and take pleasure in their attachment. Most parents appreciate the importance of their child being attached to the teacher. But "child saving" is a huge occupational hazard for those who work with children: the feelings that we would be better parents and that we somehow have to make up for the parents' real or imagined failings. Parents need to know that the staff who care for their children understand that the parent-child attachment is crucial; that parents are the most important people in their child's life; that the relationship between the teacher and the child will not be at the expense of the bonds between parent and child. How will parents know this? In their writing and conversations, teachers should express respect for and appreciation of parents' efforts and the parent-child bond and not overemphasize the child's bond with the teacher. There is a fine line for staff in doing this, because parents also want to hear about how much their child is liked and thought of as special.

Staff Competence and Parent Self-Esteem

The more competent staff are, the more parents may feel insecure about their own parenting, unless priority is given to forming partnerships. Teachers have two somewhat conflicting agendas: first, they want parents to feel secure leaving their baby with them, and therefore they want to demonstrate competence and understanding of the child; second, they want parents to feel important and needed. It is easy for teachers with good intentions to undermine parents by offering unsolicited advice, describing better behavior by the child at the center than the parents experience at home, or appearing competent and confident when the parents do not feel that way.

Parents Belong in the Room

Parents should be encouraged to visit, linger, and take the time to nurse or eat with their children, not just when they are new to the center, but always. Feeling at home is assisted by knowing the rules and the ways things work in the room. Parents need to know where to hang their coats and purses and what to do and not to do—for example,

> ### "They Won't Leave Us Alone," *continued*
>
> A fundamental parental role is that of child protector. Parents look out for their children, monitor their care, and advocate for quality care and education. In addition, our model for a conscientious consumer of an expensive and important service is someone who looks very carefully and demands satisfaction. Both Gloria and Marta play these roles as well as or better than many nicer or more easygoing and relaxed parents. When a parent is persistent or assertive, she (or he) may well seem obnoxious (at least to us), and we first use stereotypes to discredit her, and then extend our feelings about her to all "parents," thus creating a "them." Staff need to understand that parents' concerns or questions are always valid, although some may be ill-founded. Making requests or complaints is a legitimate aspect of the parental role.

Favorites

Nothing gets in the way of parent-staff partnerships more than parents' perception, whether accurate or false, that teachers have favorite children or parents—and it's not them! Nothing is also more likely in a setting in which personal contact is so extensive. It is inevitable that staff will take to some children and parents more than to others, and vice versa. Staff and parents may have personal relationships outside the center, or staff may babysit for families. A treasured teacher may be invited to a child's birthday party.

Some centers discourage any fraternizing or babysitting, but that seems neither realistic nor particularly healthy. Are there clear guidelines to avoid problems? Not really. These situations require sensitivity and professionalism on the part of teachers to keep professional and personal relationships separate. All parents and children need to feel that they receive friendly, respectful treatment and the best from their teachers.

The best approach is to acknowledge potential problems, accept the difficulty that a child, parent, and staff person will have in completely disassociating the special relationships, and be aware of any problematic situations. Teachers should be open about personal relationships outside the center, and staff should work as a team to keep each other honest, ensuring that all families receive equal treatment and that no child or parent has cause for complaint.

the procedures for changing diapers and where not to sit. It will also help parents if they have clear information about their responsibilities for their child when they visit, and if they understand what their role is in relationship to the other children in the program.

Some staff worry that if parents feel truly at home in the center, the environment will become too crowded, adult-centered, and busy. This can indeed happen, but such problems can be corrected if staff are alert and change the environment when it is adult-heavy. Staff can take some babies outside or on a trip through the center. If there are traffic jams because of too many parents, the problem should be discussed with parents as a group. They should be asked for good alternatives. Staff should not discourage parents' feelings of belonging.

Staff Behavior Teaches Parents What Is Really Expected of Them

Sometimes center staff make the mistake of assuming that it is enough to inform parents that they are welcome and that staff want to talk to them, and then back up these claims with written information. Unless such initial information is reinforced on a daily basis by staff, partnerships will not happen. Staff have to take the lead in continuously demonstrating to parents that they desire partnerships.

Staff, especially new or inexperienced teachers, may feel intimidated by parents and may find relating to them the most daunting aspect of their work. However, they need to remember that parents also feel daunted by the prospect of using care and wonder how they and their child will measure up. If staff and parents do not understand how the other feels, they may misinterpret what is actually a lack of confidence, reading it instead as aloofness or unfriendliness, to the detriment of mutual relationships.

Parents Won't (and Shouldn't) Feel Secure and Comfortable until They Know the Center and Staff

Staff who work in a center will be proud of their reputation for good work on behalf of children and may feel affronted when parents do not appear to trust them immediately. But not only is this to be expected, it is also a clear sign of the parents' investment in their children and the seriousness with which they accept their parenting role. Just as is the case in relationships with children, teachers need to accept that trust and feelings of security on the part of parents will build over time and with accumulated experiences and interactions. Trust cannot be rushed.

Partnerships Take Time and Work

Partnerships are not created by decree or by statements in a policy handbook. Like all meaningful relationships, they happen over a period of time through the ordinary give-and-take of interactions and communication. One of the biggest obstacles to forming good relationships between parents and staff is the fact that both are busy. Parents are often rushing at both ends of the day, which are often the most hectic times for staff as well. Each may perceive the other's hurried and busy demeanor as an indication of lack of interest in communicating.

If partnerships are to happen, staff schedules and communication resources should support parent-staff communication. They need to be in synch with primary caregiving relationships, and there needs to be sufficient staffing to allow conversation. Further, communication may have to extend beyond frenetic greetings and departures to phone calls, e-mails, and notes.

Parental Responsibility

All parents have a right to be involved in decision making about their child. Some parents may be willing to leave decision making up to staff. This may be a sign of confidence in staff, but the wise teacher should resist allowing parents to hand over all responsibility. Of course, when parents or families are in crisis, staff may compassionately take on increased responsibility for the child's care and well-being in order to support the parents and to lighten their burden. It is important that the center's special efforts to support parents, such as serving breakfast to the children, bathing them, arranging for immunizations and medical or dental checkups, or speaking regularly directly to the child's physician, are accompanied by continual efforts to maintain the parents' view of themselves as the main decision makers and most important people in their child's life.

Parents' Requests: A "Why Not?" Approach

All parents' requests should be met with "Why not?" thinking and a nondefensive attitude, an approach that grants legitimacy both to the parent's request and the teachers' limitations. When a parent asks for a change in their child's routine, a special activity, or a different way of doing things, staff should genuinely ask "Why not?" instead of immediately thinking or saying "We don't do that," "That won't work," or

---

"They Don't Tell Us What Is Happening at Home"

As a consultant, one of the authors sat in on a teachers' meeting at a small center and listened to staff talk about the children and families.

"What about [two-year-old] Jacob? He seems to be having a hard time and acting out a lot," noted the director.

"I found out through a mutual friend that his parents are struggling and may split up," his teacher Jane responded. "That explains a lot. I wish his mom had told us. How can we help their kids if they don't tell us what's happening at home?"

I asked the staff what they would have done if they had known what was going on with Jacob's mom and dad. They replied that they would have tried to give Jacob "more" and that they would have understood more. I asked Jane, "Suppose you were going through a messy divorce and you were under a lot of stress. And suppose you weren't getting along with Katie [the associate teacher] because she was on edge because she's drinking too much. Should we put out a memo to the parent so they could give you more and understand more?"

TO ALL PARENTS: The children in Jane's class may behave differently at home because of problems at child care—Jane's divorce and Katie's drinking have resulted in some tension and breaks in the normal routines, but don't worry, because care is still good and Jane's and Katie's on-the-job performance is acceptable. Please try to give your child some special attention, because she or he may be feeling a little insecure. We thought this information might help explain your child's behavior.

continued on next page

"They Don't Tell Us . . . ," *continued*

Of course, the staff were horrified at the possibility. Why would this memo be unforgivable? Because staff deserve confidentiality. The details of their personal lives are not the parents' business unless staff choose to share. It is tempting to justify knowing the details of a family's private life because it may help us understand or teach a child. But we have no right to know the ins and outs of family life any more than parents have a right to know about our private lives in order to monitor program quality or to better understand the center.

For the most part, what we need to know is that a child like Jacob is under unusual stress and needs us at our supportive best. Even in the absence of any information, when a child needs more of our attention and patience, we simply give it. Much of the time, it makes little difference in our response if the stress is due to family problems, fitful sleep, mild illness, or any of the other possible sources of children's stress. What we try to do is offer flexibility, warmth, and nurturing. If a child is older, perhaps talking about the situation may be helpful. But in that case, let the child or parent decide.

Respect for parents demands that unless the situation is one of abuse or neglect, the parents control what information they wish to share. If we come to know something about the family, as professionals we should ask the parents if they mind our sharing the information with colleagues or supervisors. In the case of Jacob, discussing his family situation as a staff, based on gossip and without parental permission, is just as unprofessional as a group discussion about a teacher's private struggles. When we have a relationship based on mutual respect and confidence, many parents will trust us with information about their private struggles.

simply "No." Unless a practice is definitely harmful to a baby or absolutely cannot be accommodated in child care, parents' wishes should be honored, even in fairly unimportant matters—for example, when a parent asks that her infant's food always be warmed before feeding.

A mother may request that her baby not be picked up if he cries when he is put down for a nap, especially if the baby has shown many signs of being tired, because she allows the child to cry for up to ten or fifteen minutes at home. Teachers should agree to see how this works. Doing so empowers parents and establishes a relationship in which the mother and staff can talk openly and honestly about issues related to the care of the baby.

This is different from "the customer is always right" approach. "Why not?" does not always mean "Yes." There are many legitimate "Why nots?" that will lead to a "No." A practice may be harmful to the child (for example, naptime bottles of juice), the center's budget may not allow it, it may be prohibited by regulations, or the complexity of the group may make it impossible. Perhaps teachers don't know how to accommodate the request or staffing does not permit it, to name two other reasons. The program has no reason to be defensive about unalterable givens that lead to program limitations.

When you cannot say yes to a request, it is very important to explain the reasons in a respectful manner, without seeming condescending to the parent or implying that the request itself was improper. Make it clear that it is always acceptable for parents to ask.

Often, excessive demands by parents come from a feeling of having too little influence over their child's care and a need to exercise some control. In some cases, discussion leading to a compromise or a new workable solution will be necessary.

The outcome of a "Why not?" approach is not unmanageable complexity, but thoughtful care, a foundation of mutual respect, and, in most cases, increased trust that staff are professionals committed to good care. Equally important, a "Why not?" approach leads to innovation and better care. Parents share important questions and concerns that are on their minds, as well as their expertise. Parents acting as informed consumers fulfill their responsibility to ensure that their children receive the care they deserve.

Giving Advice to Parents

It is important to be cautious in giving advice to parents, clearly making certain that you are making the distinction between opinion and fact and avoiding the impression that you are evaluating their practices. It may be difficult to refrain from giving unsolicited advice on child rearing, but unless keeping silent harms the child, it is best to wait until parents open the way for a discussion.

Teachers also need to recognize the limits of their expertise. Absolute opinions on what is the right thing to do for a child's development are rarely called for. When parents raise issues that lie outside the expertise of the center and its teachers, parents should be referred to appropriate professional help. Teachers are not social workers, therapists, or counselors.

The Value of Consistency

How important are consistency and continuity in the child's experience in home and in care? After all, people are different, and the child care setting is different from the home setting. Consistency between care at home and at the care program helps a baby feel secure and assists in learning. Just as important, striving for consistency affirms parents and ensures that each child is treated as an individual; for example, finding out how Jenny's parents soothe Jenny, and then doing the same.

While achieving consistency is hard because children change so quickly, the drive for consistency fuels the continuous flow of information between home and child care. If Jacob is learning to drink from a cup either at home or in child care, sharing this information and coordinating practices will make his learning process easier and affirm the teachers' and parents' sense of joint enterprise. Whenever possible, let parents take the lead in initiating new practices, or start them through discussion. In other words, avoid discussions that leave parents feeling as if you are always telling them what to do.

When families come from cultural backgrounds different from that of the staff, there may be home customs that are unfamiliar to us. Understanding and respecting the variety of good practices is essential. We all have biases, some of which we are aware of, some of which are more hidden. Staff may need help to look at their own biases about people in order to relate effectively to all the center's families. This is the first step toward working against bias and prejudice, or at least toward ensuring that they do not influence interactions with families.

What Is My Job?

In an employer-sponsored center, the employer liaison called the director. "I'm really concerned. Jean [a parent] just told me that the center called and she's got to go wash her kid Gino's hair—he's got head lice. Last week it was her sick baby, and she missed two days. I need her on the job, and she's lost six days in three months. I'm really pulling for her—she's a great employee and a single mom and works real hard to make her life work, but she might not make it. Can you do anything?"

"What can we do? Keep germs out of the center? Ban head lice? Wash his hair? What if we did that for every kid? We don't wash hair, we are educators. Why is this our problem?"

Maybe that isn't how we should think about this. Why not wash Gino's hair? Licensing won't allow it? After a call, it turns out that they will. If we had to do it for every child, how many heads a year would we really have to wash if we did it when necessary? Maybe a dozen at the most. Not a job for teachers? Maybe not—unless we also define ourselves as family supporters.

At a family center, we might wash hair if necessary because we are advocates for Gino and understand that Jean's success on the job is important to the family's economic security. It's bad for Gino and bad for his sister if their mom loses her job. It's bad for the family if she lives in a constant state of fear of that phone call from the center. Policies that allow Gino's mom to keep her job are probably more important to Gino's future than almost everything else we can do for him.

In general, some diversity in care practices is not harmful to children, and in fact it is inevitable. However, naptime, eating routines, use of pacifiers, and discipline should be handled somewhat similarly at home and in care.

When is consistency critical? First, it is critical when what a child learns in one place makes her dysfunctional in another setting. For example, if Suki is spoon-fed by her parents at home but encouraged to feed herself at child care, she may begin to feel incompetent or disobedient for behavior she has been encouraged to develop. At the very least, she will feel confused. Second, consistency is important when parents feel that certain practices are crucially important to their child's well-being—for example, at mealtime or if the child shows disrespect toward adults.

A Final Word

There's no doubting the fact that working in partnership with families is complex and demanding, maybe even more so than working with young children. Just as with children, individual differences play a big role, and the relationships and interactions must be tailored to each individual parent and family. Nevertheless, it's worth the effort to the child when a center comes across to families as respectful and eager to work in collaboration with them in the best interest of their child.

See Supplement: *Aligning Program Practices with Parent Wishes*

Exercises

1. List the elements of an ideal child care situation from the staff's perspective. Then do a similar test from the parents' perspective. Compare the two lists.

2. Make a list of those decisions about a child's experience that are
   • made by teachers
   • made by parents
   • the results of discussion and negotiation between parents and teachers.

3. List the ways that your center involves parents. Then make a list of all the practices that encourage and support partnerships. Are the lists balanced? Traditionally, many centers have placed more emphasis on involvement than on partnership.

Chapter 9

Establishing and Maintaining Relationships with Parents

excellence *The program has established policies and practices in order for all families to feel welcome and valued as members of the child care center community. Teachers in practice recognize that prime times with families on behalf of their child are as important as prime times with children.*

Parents want to like and trust their child care providers. They also want to be conscientious consumers, but many have an incomplete sense of what they should want. The first six weeks are the time to grow the relationship, set expectations for quality, and make sure that any issues come to the surface.

From Prospective Parents to New Parents

All prospective parents should be encouraged to visit the center and observe its program before making a decision to enroll their child. This visit can be very informal, with questions answered and information given. As with any relationship, first impressions count. Parents' experiences during a visit before deciding to enroll will provide impressions that color their future experiences. The tour introduces the program, staff, and vision of quality to the prospective parent. Many parents tour during a pregnancy and get on a waiting list. A second tour after the baby arrives should always be recommended, and parents should be invited to bring anyone else who might be helping them make a decision, such as the baby's grandparents, a friend, or another relative.

See Supplement: *Successful Tours for Prospective Parents*

The Enrollment Conference or Intake

Once parents have decided to enroll a child, an intake that includes the supervisor or primary caregiver should occur before entry in the program. The interview, a scheduled conversation to share information, to get to know each other better, and to complete necessary paperwork, should be relaxed, and the parents should be helped to feel comfortable about bringing the child or children to the interview.

More than a time to complete a business transaction, the intake is a time to begin the parent-staff partnership: for parents to share information about the child and their desires and concerns, and for staff to discuss the details of the program. It is a time to find out what expectations parents have of the center and to make clear to them what responsibilities the center has to them.

See Supplement: *Individual Personal-Care Plan for Infants and Toddlers*

It is important for staff to go beyond simply responding to parents' questions, because parents who are new to child care may not know what questions to ask. Staff should be prepared to highlight important information in the parent handbook. Topics to be highlighted in the beginning may include

- daily routines
- discipline policies
- learning environment and curriculum
- expectations of parents
- policies related to illnesses
- staffing practices
- possible sensitive issues such as biting and diagnosis of special needs.

See Supplements: *Twenty Steps to Partnership with Parents: Child/Family Checklist in Child's File* and *Twenty Steps to a Full Partnership with Parents*

Misunderstandings in areas such as when to keep a sick child home and the need to adhere to agreed-upon pickup times can create tension and ill will that are hard to overcome.

Parents need to know the areas in which staff will be guided by parents' wishes, those in which staff and parents negotiate an outcome comfortable for both, and those in which there can be no compromise. In fact, it is a useful exercise for staff to look at their program and make lists under those three headings. If the longest list is the no-compromise list, then a look at the program's attitudes toward parents is warranted.

The Parent Handbook

The Parent Handbook is a bible—a reference book for parents to check when they have a question or concern. It outlines the center's philosophy, policies, and operations (for example, fees, hours, dates of closing, and staffing structure). The handbook is a comprehensive statement about what the center stands for. Reading it, a parent should gain a clear sense of what to expect, including limits to the program's flexibility. The handbook should be a living document, updated regularly and reflecting current practices. Parents should receive the handbook before or at the intake. It is also useful to give parents access to it online.

Remember that much of the information in the handbook will become meaningful to parents only as time passes and situations arise. They may initially be overwhelmed by the amount of information given to them, and they will need tolerance from staff while they learn the ropes. They will also need explanations and gentle reminders of policies and practices when situations arise. It's similar to beginning a new job. Even though you may have a comprehensive introduction to a new job, you can't possibly take everything in. Certain information becomes relevant only when it becomes applicable. Frequently pulling important sections out of the handbook and including them in your newsletter helps bring policies to life.

Sample Parent Handbook Statement on Parents' Roles, Rights, and Obligations

Essential Roles of Parents

- experts on and advocates for their child
- advisors about policies, procedures, staff, and curriculum
- evaluators through polls and surveys
- promoters of the center.

Parents' Rights and Responsibilities

Rights:

- assurance that your beliefs, concerns, and values will be sought out, respected, and reflected in your child's care
- information about all aspects of the program in general
- information about your child's total experience in the program
- freedom to visit or observe
- freedom to ask questions of staff (at times when staff are able to respond without interrupting the program)
- confidence in the complete confidentiality of all matters involving the welfare of your child and family.

Responsibilities:

- knowledge of the handbook and acceptance of its policies and procedures
- updates of current important information (for example, a change of address or the results of the child's medical exams) and response to staff's requests for information
- daily review of your child's experience sheet and notes
- exchange of essential information about the care of your child with staff
- respect for staff as professionals who work with you to provide quality child care.

See Supplement: *Parent's Handbook: Sample Table of Contents*

Welcoming New Families

See Supplements: *Twenty Steps to a Full Partnership with Parents* and *Twenty Steps to Partnership with Parents: Child/Family Checklist in Child's File*

Once enrolled, each new family needs a relaxed, reassuring, warm welcome. The first few weeks are critical in establishing a partnership between parents and staff, and staff must take the lead. While staff may sometimes feel intimidated by parents, and new staff may not feel totally confident about their own skills, it is important to remember that parents may be equally intimidated by staff and the newness of the situation.

The teacher or primary caregiver assumes responsibility for introducing the parents to all room staff, and all staff need to make an effort to put parents at ease. The primary caregiver should be assigned and all necessary preparations carried out before the child's arrival:

- Assign and label cubby, crib, or mat.
- Put a picture on the cubby.
- Make a welcome sign with child's and parents' first names.
- Post all information necessary to individualize the child's care.

Parents should be encouraged to spend time with their child at the center when they begin (see chapter 12 for more information). This can be reassuring for everyone concerned. Staff have a chance to see how the parents interact with and care for the child. Parents get a better picture of what child care is like. It is important, nonetheless, to use the time when the parent is present to form a relationship with the child. It may be tempting in a busy center to just leave the child and parent alone, but doing so misses a valuable opportunity. It is important to acknowledge that many parents will not be able to stay with the child. Also, parents who stay may need to be reassured that the child is still likely to show some distress when they leave.

See Supplement: *New Family Homebase Satisfaction Questionnaire*

Welcoming Parents into the Room through Photographs Another way of welcoming parents and making the child's room theirs is using photographs of parents, siblings, and grandparents in the room on a regular basis. Pictures of all the members of the child's family in the cubby area makes it a family space and also introduces parents to other parents.

The First Six Weeks

Following the first day, each parent should receive a congratulations note or e-mail from the primary caregiver. In the first few weeks, the primary caregiver should make an extra effort to ask parents how things are going for them and their child. During the third or fourth week, the director might write a personal note asking the parents how things are going and extending an invitation to talk. At the end of six weeks, the primary caregiver should give the parents the six-week questionnaire, read their response, and pass on the form to the director.

See Supplements: *Sample First-Day Congratulations Note or E-mail, Sample First-Day E-Mail and Photo, Sample Director's Third-Week Note to New Family,* and *New Family Homebase Satisfaction Questionnaire*

Note: For parents new to the room but not to the center, staff should follow the same procedure, omitting the congratulations note and the director's note.

Maintaining Parent-Teacher Partnerships through Good Communication

Partnerships are founded on communication. Effective communication is a result of using naturally occurring opportunities and understanding that everyone today is bombarded with information, much of which we ignore or quickly forget. Good centers communicate but don't overcommunicate; instead, they try to understand the best ways to reach overloaded parents.

Daily Room Communication

Regardless of the range of other strategies used, parent-teacher relationships will be made or broken during the daily moments of arrival and departure. The partnership hinges on the accumulation of those few moments of interaction. Some hints for successful daily contacts, in addition to those in the discussion of arrival and departure routines in chapter 12, include the following:

- Greet *both* the parent and the child as they arrive.
- If you are busy when a parent and child arrive, greet them and let them know that you will be with them as soon as you can.
- Be sensitive to cues from the parent that indicate they are in a hurry. If they look as if they are and there is nothing urgent to talk about, don't keep them.
- Try to have the room set up in an inviting way so that there is something attractive to engage the child upon arrival. This helps the child make the transition from home to child care. As you get to know the children in your care better, you will begin to know which ones may need extra support during separation. You can anticipate this and have activities ready that will appeal specifically to those children.
- If the parent has a concern and you are very busy, explain this and agree on a specific, mutually convenient time to talk about it. If the arrival time for a parent who typically wants to talk is always hectic, suggest how a slight change in arrival time may allow you more time to talk.
- Communicate a tone of openness. Display the menu and the daily program, letting parents know when students or other visitors will be present. Inform them of staff changes. All these messages communicate not only the information contained in the message, but also "What happens here is your business too, and we want to keep you informed."
- Invite parents into the room and be ready for them. Encourage them to nurse, play with their child, or simply observe. Help them feel comfortable.
- Occasionally, very talkative parents take the teacher away from the group for more time than is necessary. At other times, conversations can lead to the parents asking questions about other children, center politics, or other areas that violate center confidentiality. Teachers should politely assert the need to get back to the children. A teacher shouldn't feel compelled to interact with parents just because they are present.
- Some children have an easier separation when the parent establishes a routine for this time. It may be setting the child up with breakfast, a quick story, or even

just waving good-bye from a specific window overlooking the parking lot, perhaps while the child is being held by the teacher. The teacher may want to suggest a routine or help new parents establish one. Modeling understanding and sensitivity and offering practical suggestions build a partnership.

Daily Experience Sheets or Journals It is important that everyone caring for a child has a sense of the child's experience, both at home and in the center. Staggered scheduling of staff makes the daily experience sheet or journal, which provides written information on the child's experience at the center and at home, a critical communication link. But note that these are a supplement to informal, daily communication between teachers and parents and should never be thought of as a substitute for it.

Besides transmitting information, these communications assure parents that their child was well cared for and affirm the program's belief that parents should know about their child's day. A well-written note or journal entry demonstrates that their child was noticed, well cared for, and appreciated.

In writing daily sheets, try to give an accurate sense of the child's day without either sugar-coating it or making parents feel bad. Always look for some positives—information that will make parents feel happy about their child's experience. If the child had a bad day, phrase it in an understanding way that focuses on the child's struggle, not on the effect on staff or other children. For example, writing "Johnny had a hard time with limits today" is easier on the parent than "Johnny constantly annoyed other children and pushed the limits." The more parents are informed and helped to know about their child's experience, the more respect and support they will give to staff.

Writing daily notes is an art. If you need help on a sensitive issue, ask other staff to suggest wording. Teams can brainstorm and compile note starters to give your communications variety and interest. Having an assortment of opening sentences helps prevent "____ had a good day" from being at the top of each and every note. A catchy and personal introductory sentence will keep parents reading: "Tyler made me laugh," or "You should have seen Anita with the guinea pig!"

Ongoing Communication: Room Letters, Newsletters, E-mails, and Other Notes

Periodic letters and informal newsletters supplement daily information. Mixing information about activities, tales of development, and parent news with the inevitable reminders of policies and homebase needs makes for a more readable result. Room newsletters can be as brief as one page that recounts current events. Newsletters are an effective way to present more extensive information on the center's operation and to elaborate its philosophy and policies, specific aspects of the program, and the broader context of child care. A simple newsletter of a page or two can involve contributions from parents, or perhaps parents can even take responsibility for it. If you mention a child's name, make sure to include all of the children's names in the letter. Set each child's name in bold—no parent will ignore a newsletter in which they can expect to read about their child.

The key to effective partnership is good communication. The key to good communication is to use a range of methods for conveying information. At the same time, recognize that parents will choose different ways of communicating and that their interest will vary. Don't get discouraged if occasionally a newsletter does not seem to be read avidly or if only a few parents notice a new sign in the lobby.

Other communication tools include

Web pages. Center Web pages are useful vehicles for communicating with families. They can contain calendars, news, notices, community events, art shows, curriculum, center policies, the parent handbook, even interactive, online registration. Web pages are likely to become standard in the next few years.

Notice boards and signs. Notice boards in hallways, room entrances, and the foyer are useful and necessary for communicating news, daily events, staff changes, holiday closing dates, visitors, and other up-to-the-minute information.

Parent mailboxes. A number of devices are possible for use as parent mailboxes: clips or clipboards on a cubby, mail slots, or fabric pockets are all common. Whatever is used should be easily accessible to parents and staff. *Note:* Take a proactive approach and solicit parents' feelings about what communications should be private, such as notes about their child.

E-mail and voice mail. Both e-mail and voice mail are great vehicles for parent-teacher communication. Again, inquiring about what is comfortable and preferred by individual parents allows you to reach them most effectively and keep them informed.

Documentation panels. Documentation panels and displays are essential communication vehicles for chronicling experiences: what children are doing, learning, and thinking about, and the perspectives of staff and parents.

From the Panda Toddler Room: Sample Newsletter Copy

What a great month we had. We saw the weather change from windy and cool to pretty hot. We love being out on the grass picking dandelions. Toddling along barefoot, watching butterflies, and watering plants are three of our favorite activities. Swinging outside and putting our feet in the water puddles keep us giggling. We also like bringing out pillows, lawn blankets, sun umbrellas, books, and wagons.

As we move outside, we are entering the wet and messy season and appreciate the extra clothes you bring. Let us know if you have any concerns about sun and sunscreen.

We welcomed *Jonathan* and *Celina*, and said sad good-byes to *Alex, Tara,* and *Brittany.* Alex and Tara moved up to the Dandelions, and *Maria* moved to a new house with her mom and dad because *Amber* got a great new job. Congratulations, Amber!

Some of the amazing things we love to do these days:

- *Malik:* Collects everything he can and files it away in his cubby.
- *Jonathan:* Loves to be on Betsy's lap and read books.
- *Kim Li:* Is very serious about easel painting.
- *Celina:* Tries really hard to keep that food on her spoon as it heads for her mouth.
- *Emma:* Wants to climb, leap, and run at every opportunity.
- *Tyler:* Loves to cook and makes great peanut butter cookies.
- *Kemal:* Builds terrific block structures, including airports.

Many thanks to *Steven* (Celina's dad) for fixing the wagon and *Kate* (*Sara's* mom) for sewing the pillows. Thank you all for taking the time to chat in the morning and evenings.

The Kindness of Strangers?

Suppose you are talking with a friend who's a parent and ask her who is watching her child, and she replies, "Some nice blonde woman named Kim and a friend of hers who helps out." Would you feel secure? Parents need to know who cares for their children, no matter how much they trust the center. This includes new staff and substitutes. It should not be acceptable for a parent to arrive and be greeted by an unfamiliar adult.

Use name tags. This may not be necessary in small programs, but it is essential in large ones. The slight formality of name tags can be alleviated by their style.

A staff display, including pictures and short biographies, is important. This does not have to be fancy; in fact, if it is too fancy, it will be difficult to update. It is best to place the display where all parents can see it, not just in a single room.

Notify parents of staff changes: comings or goings, new substitutes and volunteers. Always do so in advance, even if it's only in the form of a note on the door where parents enter.

Nobody likes to communicate unpleasant information, and this fact often leads to avoidance or inappropriate notes. Teachers have to think through how best to communicate information that may be potentially distressing or complicated for parents. While a note has the advantage of giving the reader a chance to react in private (and the sender a chance to avoid delivering the news in person!), verbal communication is often gentler, because words on paper have a way of seeming harsher. What approach to use depends on the complexity of the message, the time available, the skill of the teacher, and her knowledge of the parent. Often, a discussion backed up by a simple written note avoids miscommunication.

It is important to anticipate those instances in which we would expect a parent to be upset. For instance, when a child has been bitten, had an accident, or been injured, call the parents if possible so they won't be surprised when they come to pick the child up. If they know that they will be notified when something difficult occurs, parents feel more secure. Be sure, however, to communicate in ways that are reassuring; do not alarm or worry parents unnecessarily.

When parents find out about changes after they've occurred (for example, in staffing or routines), particularly if they become aware of them just by observing them, they may understandably feel annoyed or anxious. Letting them know about changes as soon as possible acknowledges the partnership; in trying situations, it helps by not adding fuel to the fire.

Staff Expressing Sensitive Concerns to Parents When teachers have concerns about either child or parent behavior that they need to discuss with parents, supervisors, and in most cases the director, should be involved before the parent-teacher discussion takes place. It is important that staff's concerns and expectations are expressed clearly and are consistent with the center's philosophy and policies. Concerns about child abuse and neglect should be consistent with reporting policies established by the state. Some states forbid notifying parents of a report prior to its being investigated.

Random Kindness and Senseless Generosity: Delivering Good News Nothing is more endearing than unexpected acts of kindness and generosity, such as a card on a parent's birthday or an unexpected, appreciative e-mail or note. A phone call to a parent stuck at home with a sick child empathizing with their plight and voicing concern for the child is a powerful expression of caring. You might e-mail or send home a photograph of the child or a card marking the anniversary of the family's time at the center. You might simply make an offer of tea, coffee, or a bagel. If you seek out ways to make a family happy, the result will be stronger parent-staff relationships. This kind of connection will help you, the center, and the relationship weather nearly any storm that arises—and storms will arise, circling around biting or aggression, care and educational concerns, or other differences in beliefs.

Parents Expressing Sensitive Concerns Parents will not always feel comfortable expressing a concern to their primary caregiver or staff in the room. They may choose to use a supervisor or the center's director. Don't be discouraged! Channels of communication should be as flexible and open as possible, so long as staff share information with other staff who need it, while respecting parents' concern for confidentiality.

Cardinal Sins in Interactions with Parents

- Diminishing parents' sense of hope for their child or family
- Diminishing parents' sense of joy about their child and family
- Diminishing parents' sense of confidence and competence in their parenting.

Parent Conferences

The parent conference is an important part of the center's overall communication plan. It acknowledges that *we are all in this together*. It is a scheduled and formal effort to ensure that the child and family experience is satisfactory, to update the profile of the child collaboratively, and to develop goals for the upcoming months. While parents should be encouraged to request a meeting with the primary caregiver any time they want one, the primary caregiver should invite parents to a conference three to four times a year, especially during the period when the teacher is helping a child make the transition to a new group.

It is important that the conference be a real discussion about the child and family experience, not just a report by staff to parents. Conferences are a coming together to share observations and perspectives, to create an accurate picture of the child's development, and to explore the child's and family's experience at the center. The tone of the conference should be friendly, relaxed, and informal, with faculty communicating caring and compassion for the child and respect for the parent and family.

> See Supplements: *How to Conduct Parent-Teacher Conferences* and *Parent-Staff Conference: Report Form*

Engaging Parents

Ideally, a center offers a range of opportunities to allow parents to match their involvement with their time and interests.

Parent Polling You may find it useful to take quick polls on curriculum, field trips, enrichment activities, and more. Polling accomplishes three things:

- Provides useful input
- Facilitates parent buy-in with particular issues
- Educates parents about issues and policies.

One useful polling structure is a weekly mini-poll—a single question that takes less than a minute to answer. Some examples:

Are you satisfied with the new mailbox procedure?
What's the best thing you have observed this week at drop-off?

If you keep your questions direct, your format easy to answer, and don't overuse polling, parents will be glad you ask their opinions.

Polling can be done through e-mail, a quick questionnaire at the sign-in area, or on a portion of the center newsletter. As an incentive to have more parents complete the poll, offer a chance to win a prize in a raffle, such as a gift certificate for a local coffee shop.

Center Newsletters A newsletter or e-letter can be an effective medium for presenting more extensive information on the center's operations, specific aspects of the program, the broader context of child care, and center philosophy and policies. A simple newsletter can involve contributions from parents.

See Supplement: *A Note to Parents: Living with Diversity*

Parent Events—Large and Small When teachers plan parent events, consider the parents' perspective. Parents are busy, and there may be few good times for events. Evening programs are difficult for parents because they conflict with their desire to get their children into bed. For that reason, some centers schedule events at mealtimes so the parents and children can stay at the center rather than have to leave and come back. Some centers have been successful holding Saturday morning parent-child activities and social events. These can work well if your families live in the surrounding community. Another advantage of weekend mornings is that some of the workday pressures are eliminated.

Plan a mix of events, and don't expect all parents to attend. A room tea, a center-wide barbecue, a wine-and-cheese night, and a special program are all good things to do, as are parent work days, fund-raising events, and parent-child activities. Parents who choose not to attend should not be perceived as problematic or be less valued.

Parent Education Parents often are interested in a session that gives them a chance to learn more about child development and child rearing. Most effective are informal sessions that allow parents the chance to discuss concerns and share their experiences with the center's experts and other parents.

A resource library with books, magazines, pamphlets, and DVDs is a useful resource for parents and teachers as well.

Parent Donations and Contributions of Time or Skills Encouraging parent donations and involvement allows parents to feel a sense of belonging and connection to the center. It creates a community feeling and produces valuable resources. However, if the practice results in a forced sense of obligation among parents who contribute or in guilt in parents who don't, it may not be worthwhile.

Parent Partnership Group Committees

Parent partnership committees require a higher level of involvement than the ideas we've just covered. No matter what the formal governance structure—public or private owner, corporation, university, or social service—having some kind of parent group structure is important. Why? Because parents are the experts on their own children, and involving the consumers of child care will help ensure better care. It also brings parents into the center, and their ownership can lead to support on a number of levels. There is a third value: there will be many issues about which parents won't agree—for example, lunch menus or when to hold parent-teacher conferences. If the center leadership can set the acceptable parameters for decisions and involve parents to reach consensus, it prevents the leadership from having to be the bad guy on issues when it's hard to please everyone.

Participation in the management of the center may be one option for parents wanting to become involved. While this suits some center managers, boards of directors, and parents, it should not be viewed as the best or most effective vehicle for parent involvement. If parents are involved in managing the center, it is important that they see themselves as representing other parents as well. There should be mechanisms for canvassing other parents' views and for sharing information between parents and management. Keep in mind that parent participation in the management of a center, even management by parents alone, should not necessarily be equated with the idea of partnership discussed earlier.

The Structure of Parent Partnership Committees

There is no best way to structure parent advisory committees. Unless there is a formal function of governing, elections usually are not necessary and an open system of seeking volunteers and achieving balance by room or by age group of children is probably most desirable. Within reason, little is gained by limiting the number of parents on the committee. A very effective structure is a parent representative system in which parents represent rooms or age-group units. This is a system that assumes parent reps will contact their constituents—for example, parents in the same room—prior to the meeting and solicit concerns, ideas, and appreciations. All parents should be invited to participate in meetings and on committees and task forces. The minutes of parent representative meetings serve as vehicles for airing issues, explaining policies, and circulating parents' appreciation of center staff.

Soliciting Information

Parent reps might volunteer for about a year. They join with one or more other parents from their child's room to call other parents from the room to see how things are going and to respond to any specific topics that have been identified by the director or anyone else. The only topics excluded would be those that require confidentiality about a particular child, parent, or staff member.

Possible topics might include:

- Questions:

  "How do you determine when children move up?"

  "How are parents' fees established?"

  "Why do children have to go out in cold weather?"

  "Why does it take so long to fill a teaching vacancy?"

- Suggestions or ideas:

  "We'd like the twos to go on field trips"

  "What about extending the hours to 7:00 PM?"

  "Why don't we use the multipurpose space differently?"

  "What about more meals from a variety of cultures?"

  "Can't there be more food we know the kids all eat?"

- Concerns or complaints:

  "The bathrooms don't seem very clean."

  "I worry about the supervision when children are outdoors."

  "What are you doing to make sure my child will become a good reader?"

  "Why can't I get my new baby in?"

  "Is there enough training of teachers?"

  "My child has a disability. How do I know she will receive the experiences that she needs?"

  "Why is there so much biting among toddlers?"

- Compliments and appreciation:

  "The toddler staff are really doing a wonderful job."

  "The new substitutes seem much better trained."

  "There has been a lot of improvement in the variety of meals."

  "I think Carrie did a great job helping Addie get through her first few days in the infant room."

Parent Partnership Meetings

Six to ten times a year, parents representing each constituency get together with representatives of the administration and board of directors (or sponsor) and any interested parents to discuss how things are going, raise any issues or concerns, and plan any desired special events or activities. The topics discussed stem from the information collected by parent reps, the director, or others.

Ensuring Positive and Productive Meetings When there is a commitment to honest discussion and problem solving, parent meetings are positive. Participants need to accept the fact that there will always be real issues and concerns and honest questioning of policies and decisions. At the parent meeting, individual concerns usually become the starting point for discussions of policies and practices. There should be a commitment to work through "why we do things the way we do" and to meeting the needs and interests of parents—a "Why not?" attitude. There should be open recognition that the right thing to do is not always clear or immediately possible and that "we are all in this together," with each person representing a legitimate perspective.

It is also important to make sure that meetings don't focus on those issues much better handled by individual communications between parents and teachers and that they don't become discussions of a staff member's individual performance, a specific parent's participation, or a particular child's behavior.

Excerpts from the Minutes of a Parent Representative Meeting

Toddlers: Concerns, Ideas, Suggestions

A parent was concerned about how hectic it was at pickup time and felt she never had time to talk with her child's primary caregiver. A second parent always felt that the end-of-day experience was a hassle, and they never ended the day on a relaxed note.

Response: It has been hectic lately, and we are brainstorming alternatives. Sometimes by adjusting your arrival and departure times by a few minutes, you can avoid a traffic crunch. We are working on tinkering with the environment and late-afternoon activities to make the transition more relaxed and to free up staff. Remember, if you want more communication, feel free to call or ask for a phone call mini-conference (or a longer face-to-face conference).

Two parents felt that transitions from infant to toddler rooms were not as smooth as they could be.

Response: We agree. We had it all worked out and then had to shuffle because of staff illnesses and the change in plans of two families. We will try and learn from this and work out some contingency plans.

A parent didn't understand why we let sick children stay. Her child would then get sick.

Response: As we explain in the Parent Handbook, our exclusion policies are based on the American Academy of Pediatrics Model Health Policies. It is important to understand that the spread of infection from the illnesses that we are experiencing now (colds, mostly) occurs before a child shows any symptoms. Excluding any child with a cold who can participate in the program does nothing to reduce the spread of infection. There is a copy of the Model Health Policies in each room.

Appreciations

- Jenny does a terrific job helping me with Byron's clingy behavior.
- I was sorry to see Georgia move to the preschool but think Talia is a great addition.
- Thanks for the great daily experience sheets.

A Final Word: Common Sense, Respect, and Systems to Ensure Great Relationships

Good relationships with parents grow out of common sense and thinking through the realities of child care. They stem from staff with a genuine belief in partnerships, the skills and knowledge to make them happen, and sound policies and practices, which bring partnerships to daily life in care.

When we respect parents, focus on their perspectives, sensitively share our own, and think creatively about how to overcome the real challenge of busy people trying to work together, parents become allies and their children benefit.

See Supplement: *Family Room Departure Questionnaire*

Exercises

1. What are major obstacles to partnership in your center? How could they be removed?

2. List all the ways your program communicates with parents. Are there ways that could be added? Improved?

3. How does your center find out what parents like about their child's and their own experience and what they are concerned about? If the center relies exclusively on informal feedback, are there other communication vehicles that could be tried?

Chapter 10

Good Places for Staff

Excellence *Staff genuinely respect, enjoy, and appreciate the children they work with, and feel secure, valued, and respected as professionals and partners with parents. Roles and responsibilities are clear and understood. Teamwork and collegiality are valued and supported. Staff are supported through good supervision, a supportive work environment, and opportunities for professional development.*

Quality rarely happens unless the center is a good place to work. In the words of an experienced teacher,

> *I have worked in three programs in the last ten years. All had pretty good people, but only one was a great place to work. The center, not just the director, just seemed to care about staff—personnel policies, the way staff people treated each other, respect from parents, the staff room (even if it was almost a closet), all made a difference. They expected a lot from us, but they were always up-front and listened. I think the kids got better care because of it.*

She went on to say,

> *Of course, part of being a good place to work was the pay and benefits. It was the real world of child care, so none of the centers paid all that well. But the center I liked clearly was doing all it could to improve salaries and benefits: educating parents about the need for better salaries, looking for more funding, and involving us in some of the decisions that had a budget impact, like whether to switch toddler ratios from 1 to 4 to 1 to 5.*

Good People for Infants and Toddlers: Staffing the Program

Good programs know how to recruit, support, and keep good people and how to help them become an effective team. As discussed in chapter 3, the organization and culture of the center shape the quality of staff efforts.

Who Are "Good" People?

All sorts of people work effectively in child care, so there is always a risk in defining necessary qualities. However, as a guide to selecting staff, consider these characteristics:

- Good physical and mental health. Group child care is demanding, and children arrive with lots of needs and lots of germs.
- Sense of humor. Sometimes laughing is the only way to cope.
- Openness to new ideas and willingness to learn. There is never a settled right way to do things that applies to all times and all children, parents, and coworkers. Quality is a product of thinking and rethinking on a continuous basis.
- Enough self-confidence to be flexible and to accept and offer suggestions and criticism. Defensiveness blocks professional and program growth.
- Acceptance of the fact that many days are much the same, combined with the ability to get excited about little things and to appreciate small accomplishments. Daily life in child care can become mundane and routine without a mature perspective. Staff who find joy in all the small victories and wonders of ordinary life, just as children do, are the most satisfied and successful.
- The ability to function under pressure, to be calm amidst periodic tumult. Faced with crying children, upset parents, substitutes, dirty diapers, and "Taylor ate all the paste," a teacher has to be an island of calm.
- The ability and willingness to work with other staff and parents. Adult relations are as important as child relations, so empathy, respect for differences, tolerance, and tact are important.

Qualities Necessary for Working Effectively with Infants and Toddlers

Working with children under three years old is demanding on staff, physically and emotionally. In addition, staff may be faced with outdated attitudes that put them at the bottom of the educational ladder: "What does an infant or toddler teacher *teach*, really? Isn't it just caring for and playing with them?" In other words, the impression is 80 percent lap, 20 percent brain. In truth, finding good teachers for infants and toddlers is often more difficult than for older age groups. A good infant/toddler teacher

- likes and respects infants and toddlers, enjoys their company, and appreciates all that they can do at the moment, not just what they will be able to do in the future. Sensitive teachers appreciate the significance of a wobbly baby's reach for a toy, first sounds and first words, a fifteen-month-old patting a distressed child gently on the hand, a baby stacking two blocks together or drinking successfully from a cup
- knows about very young children and early development; understands where babies are and where they are heading

- adapts to infant/toddler time; accepts the fact that sometimes life with infants and toddlers is slow, and at other times there are brief moments that require a lot of effort
- is interested in getting to know each child (and family) and prizes all children (even at their most difficult times)
- has empathy and can see the world through the child's eyes; has compassion for separation, teething times, dubious assertions of "No" and "I can do it myself," and all the other times young children struggle with life
- is warm and affectionate; expresses affection in a manner appropriate for each child
- is creative in play with infants and toddlers; helps children explore what the world has to offer and understands the power of small changes to keep children interested.

Roles and Responsibilities

The highest-quality care is the result of teamwork in which the strengths and talents of all staff are developed and used fully. Tasks are assigned based on interest and talent rather than people being locked into roles. For example, keeping track of and ordering supplies may be assigned to Ben, who is highly organized. Selina, a new teacher, may take responsibility for redoing the housekeeping corner, while Kelli volunteers to look after children's files. Nevertheless, it is critically important that roles and responsibilities are clear.

Confusion over roles and responsibilities is often a source of tension. As one teacher said, "I'm an assistant teacher, Nikki is a teacher, and Alika is a lead teacher. We really work like a team here. We share all the work; I help with planning. I have nearly the same qualifications. It bothers me that we have different titles and salaries."

Differences in Roles and Responsibilities

An early care and education homebase is a complex work and social setting. For it to operate smoothly, all staff must have a deep appreciation of the need for teamwork and be willing to help each other. There are overlapping responsibilities, even between an experienced, highly qualified staff person and an inexperienced worker with no formal qualifications. Everyone usually changes diapers, interacts with the children, helps set up and clean up, and talks with parents. Each staff person may serve as a primary caregiver. Complicating the situation, in practice in many programs there are only slight differences in staff qualifications that separate head teachers and assistant teachers. But in well-organized programs, in at least two important ways staff are usually not equal:

Authority and supervision. The responsibility for the room and the performance of the staff team is usually invested in the lead- or head-teacher role and entrusted to the individual with the experience and expertise in leadership and supervision.

Curriculum planning. Although everyone contributes, the person who is ultimately responsible for planning the environment and curriculum and who determines the child's educational experience should be both the most expert and the most responsible—the lead teacher.

Titles and salaries reflect levels of responsibility. A leadership role carries with it responsibility for the work of others and for the experience of children and parents, even when the leader is not present. The director is held accountable for the center at all times. If everything collapses when she is off-site or on vacation, the director is usually accountable and has to answer questions about poor planning or delegation. This should also apply to the lead teacher and to the room or rooms she supervises, or to the teacher in charge in the absence of the lead teacher.

The Lead Teacher (or Program Coordinator) The lead teacher or program coordinator has the following responsibilities:

- Provision of a warm, nurturing, and educational environment that meets the needs of each child
- Supervision of room staff and assignment of primary staff
- All necessary administrative tasks as delegated
- Oversight of the development and implementation of daily curriculum
- Development of program goals (working with the director and with input from others)
- Close collaboration with parents to ensure that each child's needs are met and parents are satisfied with the program.

The lead teacher may be in charge of one or more rooms (a useful distinction may be to use the term *head teacher* if there is only one room to supervise). Much like the center director's role in relation to the center as a whole, the lead teacher is a team leader and is responsible for making sure all the necessary work gets done through her own efforts and through motivating, supervising, and delegating to staff.

The lead teacher does not necessarily have to be the most accomplished teacher in the unit, but she does have to be an effective leader and curriculum planner. The prior experience, training, and credentials that can be expected vary, depending on the available talent pool. But regardless of experience and training, lead teachers need the following qualifications:

Commitment to the program vision: understanding the program's philosophy, culture, and practices ("what we believe and do here") and the ability to articulate them.

Professionalism: ability to accept responsibility and to commit to a standard of performance that sets an example and earns the respect of others.

Leadership: ability to inspire others through knowledge, expertise, enthusiasm, and efforts in order to maximize the talents, skills, and efforts of the staff.

Supervision: willingness and ability to supervise staff. Good supervision involves communicating clear expectations, providing encouragement and support, delegating responsibilities appropriately, and addressing issues of unsatisfactory performance. Good supervisors are able to deal directly and fairly with sensitive issues.
See Supplement: *Tips for Supervisors: Questions for Poorly Performing Employees*

Capacity to work well with adults: ability to create quality experiences for children and parents through working with the teachers they supervise, not just through what they do directly with children.

Initiative: ability and desire to make things happen, solve problems, uncover and raise problematic issues, and come up with new ideas.

Planning skills for the homebase: knowledge and expertise in planing a high-quality learning/caring environment that offers individualized, personalized learning and caring.

Respect for children, parents, and other staff: ability to put oneself in the place of others, understand their values, ideas, and perspectives, and behave respectfully at all times.

Teachers and Associate Teachers Teachers and associate (or assistant) teachers have the following responsibilities:

- Team with the lead teacher to provide a warm, nurturing, and educational environment that meets the needs of each child
- Assist in planning and implementing the daily curriculum
- Assume responsibility for the group in the lead teacher's absence
- Work closely with parents to ensure that each child's needs are met and parents are satisfied with the program.

Good teachers' qualifications are similar to those of lead teachers—they too should share the program vision, perform professionally, enjoy working with adults, show initiative, plan caring and learning environments, and respect and understand the perspective of others.

Participatory Decision Making

Collaborative decision making generally produces better decisions and empowers staff. With delegated power comes ownership and responsibility. The key to participatory decision making is that it takes place in a context in which underlying program philosophy, principles, and objectives are clear and shared. Adequate time is made available for discussion.

A system for staff representation similar to the parent rep system may be a useful structure for involving all staff in decisions, keeping them aware of policies and issues, and promoting positive center morale. It offers chances to ask "Why?" and "Why not?" and to promote morale-building initiatives, voice concerns, make suggestions and observations, and express appreciations. With the ability to influence decisions come responsibility and the need to take into account the wider perspective of parents, the center as a whole, and budget realities that otherwise only directors would have to worry about.

Recruiting and Selecting Good Staff

Finding and keeping good staff is not easy in an industry that is relatively low paying and has a limited career ladder. Well-trained and experienced infant and toddler staff, particularly those in leadership roles, are perhaps the rarest commodity. Because young women have increasing choices in the workplace and there are still relatively few men entering the field, competition for good people will probably increase. To compete, centers will have to become good places to work as well as make good hiring decisions.

See Supplement: *Recruiting and Hiring Tips*

Who Are "Good People"?

Ida was eighty-six years old and still working at the center. To everyone, she was Grandma Ida. She worked her fifteen hours a week for $5 an hour and was, by and large, loved. The average age of the rest of the staff was twenty-four. Ida was very sweet and a good worker, but not surprisingly, she was occasionally old-fashioned, not always politically correct ("You sure are all boy, and ornery today, too"), and occasionally a little bit crotchety with other staff. But she never was offensive, harmful, or more than an occasional pain in the neck (not unlike the other staff!). When a coworker (age twenty-two) complained to the director (age twenty-five) that Grandma Ida was more trouble than she was worth, the director asked the teacher to think about the worth of a grandmother figure to children largely cared for by young women.

Understanding Your Talent Pool

A talent pool is the population that staff is drawn from—all the people who might want to work for the program. It is defined by a number of factors:

- salary and benefits
- location
- the official requirements for qualifications for employees—for example, experience and credentials
- unofficial (sometimes unconscious, often unfortunate) criteria—for example, age, gender, race, and personality factors
- the definition of the job

Some centers consciously limit the talent pool to the college-educated, but in the selection process they actually become more selective; for example, they always end up with white women between the ages of twenty and fifty. This usually is not deliberate so much as it is a limited vision of who is likely to be best at the job. Such decisions may mirror the current staff's own characteristics—their language, style, values, and general way of being. Candidates may self-select themselves out because the center doesn't feel like a compatible place to work. Out of a concern for diversity and the need to increase the number of potential applicants, those in a position to influence decisions should ask themselves:

- What training or credentials are actually required by licensing or to gain accreditation?
- What training is necessary for the performance of the job?
- Is this a place that welcomes diversity—for instance, a good place to work if you're an elderly person, a man, or someone from a minority culture or another ethnic group? Is this a place that is accepting of differences in interests, physical abilities, and personal style?
- Is our definition of good caregiving too narrow (too young or old, too white, too female, too based on matters of style, preference, and familiarity)?

Staff Recruitment

Recruiting staff is essentially marketing: becoming known, seeking out potential employees, and selling the idea that your program is a good place to work. Do all prospective employees know about your center? In most cases, the answer is no. How do those who are familiar with your center learn about openings? Why would they want to work for you? Usually the answer to both questions is word of mouth, advertising, and working with local training institutions and colleges. Word of mouth is often neglected when a center is having problems finding staff. Actively soliciting current and past staff and parents to spread the word often brings good results. Broadening your talent pool often means rethinking how you recruit staff. To attract people from different cultural or socioeconomic backgrounds than you currently employ, you may have to advertise in different locations; seek out employment counselors, training programs, and job fairs; and find community networking agencies that can advise you on recruiting.

Wages and Benefits

Compensation for child care staff is typically very low, because almost all centers are supported primarily by fees paid by parents or by parent-subsidy dollars. Unfortunately, caring for children has never been valued economically, and historically child care providers have been at the bottom of the ladder, competing with the voluntary care provided within families. The educating function of the child care teacher has been perceived as only slightly more valuable than other aspects of the job. While early care and education teachers deserve the respect and compensation that school teachers have won, even with the minimal compensation for staff, child care is a major expense for most families, typically $5,000–$15,000 a year per child. Changing the status quo will require political support and much more financial support from society, either in public dollars or in support from employers.

What a center can do on its own is to develop its budget carefully to maximize revenue and to provide the best and fairest compensation plan possible. All centers have a business function. Good business practice to maximize enrollment and develop stable and growing revenue from parent tuitions and subsidies is important. Providing benefits and annual salary increases to all full-time staff should be a basic fact of life. Centers have to acquire the business skills necessary to plan for possible eventualities rather than to merely react to events.

Selecting Staff

There is no one right way to hire, but there are lots of wrong ways. A good process for staff usually includes

- an initial assessment of the person on paper, in the form of a résumé, application, and references
- interviews with the director and others, including parents
- some observation of the applicant with children and parents.

Involving a few people in addition to the director is good not only in order to obtain a number of viewpoints, but also as a way to invest those participants in the success of the new employee.

How much influence should parents and staff in the room with the staff vacancy have on the selection? This is a complicated question and depends on the circumstances and the center's culture. Two factors lead to limiting staff and parent input and to not investing the people in a particular room with too much power. Generally, it is important to assume that you are hiring an employee for the center, not for a particular room, because the new person may eventually end up elsewhere . Second, the room may need someone who complements existing staff and brings in new ideas, skills, or a different perspective or background—someone the team wouldn't necessarily choose.

Selecting the best person available requires a clear sense of what the best might look like at that time and involves understanding the what and why of what you are looking for. Educational planning ability, knowledge of a particular culture (for example, Indian, Vietnamese, or Latino), maturity, energy, parent relationship skills, or other specific skills and knowledge may be particular needs. Efforts to diversify the staff often fail because of a limited vision of who can do the job. Visions are usually filtered through our personal biases and our often-limited experience with other cultures, disabilities, or other individual differences. Visualizing who good people might be in the broadest sense helps encourage inclusiveness.

Interviewing

Interviews are the time to discover what a person thinks and if her or his values and philosophy are compatible with those of the program. It is also important to find out about the kind of person the applicant is—does he have a sense of humor, does she listen, is he thoughtful? The more relaxed the interview, the more likely you will find out about the real person in front of you. Generally, interviews with more than one interviewer and fewer than five are best, with questions scripted in advance. Often, the best questions are those that ask how applicants have behaved or handled situations in the past, rather than what they would do in a hypothetical situation. Some useful questions are:

- Why do you want to work with babies? What do you find exciting about an eight-month-old (eighteen-month-old, etc.)?
- What is your vision of quality care? Have you achieved it in your work experience? How? Why not? Apply that vision to feeding, toilet training, and coping with biting.
- If you were a parent thinking about child care, what would you worry about?
- Describe what you see as your relationship to parents in the program.
- Describe a difficult situation you have had with parents, and how you handled it.
- Respect for diversity is a talked-about issue. What does that mean to you as a teacher, a collaborator with families, and a coworker? Describe situations in which you learned from the experiences of people with different backgrounds. What were the challenges?
- Tell us about a time when you had to change your thinking or behavior based on new learning.
- What are you excited about learning in the next few years?
- Describe yourself as a coworker, and what is important to you as a team member.
- What kind of commitment can you make to the job?

The last question is important. It is important for everyone to find people who will stay. A great person with great credentials who is looking ahead to her next job is no bargain.

Choosing the Right Person

When filling a specific position, it is important to recognize that you are hiring for the program, not the room, and that you are looking to the future. Will this person be able to work with other teams, other age groups, and possibly grow into a leadership role? A new staff member should complement the qualities and strengths of others.

Sometimes an applicant really stands out, and there is no doubt what an asset to the program she (or he—even though we have been using the feminine pronoun throughout for convenience, male applicats should, of course, be welcomed) will be. The only concern in this situation is whether she will take the job, and if she does, will she stay or will she be looking for another job soon. Typically, though, candidates raise a few questions, and the center has to look closely at the shortcomings she presents. When this happens, keep in mind:

- Some professional skills and understandings are subject to change, such as knowledge of child development and appropriate activities, caregiving practices, or language skills. If the center has the time and access to resources and the individual is willing and able to learn, taking a chance in these areas offers pretty good odds.
- Some important character traits or strongly ingrained beliefs or values are unlikely to change. Flexibility in thinking and behavior, ability as a team member, and strong beliefs about or attitudes toward parents or children may be difficult or impossible to alter.
- The capacity for leadership and supervision is essential in a lead teacher or director. It can be grown, and often must be; many applicants will have never had the opportunity to test that side of themselves. But the seed has to be there: the confidence to lead others, the strength to make unpopular decisions, and the ability to adopt a broader perspective.

In general: *hire for attitude, train for skill*. You can't train enthusiasm, loyalty, integrity, willingness to learn, and drive.

Supporting Quality Staff

The adult work environment plays a major role in influencing the quality of care for children. It affects the morale, motivation, and growth of staff, as well as staff's level of professionalism. Staff cannot focus on meeting the needs of children when their own needs are not being met. Paula Jorde Bloom (1997, 4) lists and defines the principal dimensions that contribute to a positive, organized work environment:

Collegiality: extent to which staff are friendly, supportive, and trusting of one another. This measures the peer cohesion of employees and the esprit de corps of the group as a whole.

Professional growth: degree of emphasis placed on personal and professional growth

Supervisor support: strength of facilitative leadership that provides encouragement, support, and clear expectations

Clarity: extent to which policies, procedures, and responsibilities are clearly defined and communicated

Reward system: degree of fairness and equity in the distribution of pay, fringe benefits, and opportunities for advancement

Decision making: amount of autonomy given to staff and the extent to which they are involved in center-wide decisions

Goal consensus: degree to which staff agree on the goals and objectives of the center

Task orientation: emphasis placed on good planning, efficiency, and getting the job done

Physical setting: extent to which the spatial arrangement of the center helps or hinders staff in carrying out their responsibilities

Innovativeness: extent to which the organization adapts to change and encourages staff to find creative ways to solve problems.

Supportive Work Space

Staff are more productive in work settings that support all aspects of their performance, including their thinking roles: team member, creator, planner, evaluator, and communicator. A staff room with teacher workspace and computer access, a room with space for meetings and conferences, a teacher's nook or desk in the room with a telephone, and ample storage are important. How is confidentiality possible without a private space for conferences? How can creativity flourish without adequate storage? How can teachers get along if there is no in-room storage? Who really likes to share everything, especially when members of the team often have very different abilities to stay organized?

Supervision

Good supervision is a fundamental element in quality. The fundamentals of good supervision are clear expectations of the employee, maximizing the employee's talent, ongoing evaluation, and follow-through with support.

See Supplement: *Rate Yourself as a Supervisor*

Orientation and Training of New Staff

Orientation is the first step in establishing clear expectations. It is both a short- and a long-term process. There is a temptation to pack everything the new staff person needs to know into the first few days of work, but this creates overload that may prevent absorbing much information at all. A better strategy is to have a list of everything a new employee needs to know, and then prioritize the items on the list, identifying those things that need to be learned at the beginning and those that can wait.

The more information available in writing the better—for example, job description, program handbooks, and policies and procedures. Written material still must be supplemented by discussions with supervisors.

Can you afford to take time off the floor to offer an orientation? Do you need to include the new person instantly to meet the ratio requirements? It may feel as if taking time to orient a new employee and allowing her time out of ratio to learn the job are luxuries. But many programs have found that if they don't orient employees well, turnover increases and employees are less likely to perform up to their best abilities.

See Supplement: *Staff Handbook: Sample Table of Contents*

Follow-up with New Staff

Much of what has to be learned will be learned on the job. A program culture that encourages new staff to feel free to ask questions, even seemingly simple or obvious ones, is important. The director and homebase staff should continually communicate that they know there is a lot to absorb and that questions are expected and welcomed. Having information to read or DVDs to watch, followed by discussion, is an effective way to present information to new staff.

Teamwork and Communication

A typical homebase has a team of three to five staff over the course of the day. No matter how sensitive or talented the individuals, several people just doing their own thing will not result in good care. It is how they work together that counts for children and for parents. Effective teamwork does not just happen but is the result of effort, experience, lots of communication, and time. Good teamwork is like a dance in which partners seem to understand what is happening, what will happen next, and how they fit together. After people have worked together for a long time, little may have to be said— they just know. If one is sitting with a child helping her eat, the other knows she should get up and help the other children start clearing the table. If one is caught up with a child in distress, the other knows she should keep a particularly watchful eye out for everyone else in the group.

This unspoken, intuitive support in good teams is not to be confused with the silence that comes from mindlessly doing things the way they have always been done, from doing them "by the book," or from staff working as individuals with little regard for others. Staff often have strong views about doing parts of their job in particular ways, based on their own past work experience, their experience as parents, or their own childhoods. "Mindless doing," "by the book," and "doing your own thing" are often coping responses to help people avoid discussion or controversy and to mask differences in beliefs and values. It is more constructive to bring differences out in the open in order to reach consensus or compromise. It is important to recognize that every program needs a unified philosophy and approach that result in shared caring practices—a center's way of doing things. At the same time, recognition that of course there are other ways to do things is also healthy: "Our way is not the only way, it is just what we believe should be done here." While there is certainly room for some diversity in teachers' behavior, it is important that staff agree on and follow basic principles and practices and give consistent information to parents.

Good caregiving teams

- understand that there is not usually one right way to do things
- think, reflect, and discuss
- pat each other on the back and share successes and accomplishments
- share concerns and issues
- share less desirable tasks
- help all members improve
- give and receive help during difficult times
- expect that there will be periodic tension and conflict to work through
- communicate openly and directly
- trust and respect each other and the work they are doing.

Teams come together over time as trust and understanding develop. Teamwork requires frequent communication, much of it on the run while staff are working with children, but there also has to be time to sit down together to talk, evaluate, and plan. Group meetings can be supplemented by mini-meetings of fifteen minutes or fewer, exchange of written information in notebooks and on whiteboards, and, perhaps increasingly, use of audio messages and voice mail.

See Supplement: *Steps to a Winning Team: Working Successfully Together*

Empowerment

Much of what has been discussed is intended to empower staff and acknowledge their capacity to be thoughtful, make decisions, take responsibility, and think as well as do. Empowerment takes a number of forms:

Opportunities to be heard: Structuring mechanisms for staff to be heard allows them to influence decisions and helps the center leadership assess staff morale. In larger centers, a staff rep system or staff morale group allows staff a structured opportunity to raise center-wide issues, suggest ideas, and express appreciation. It gives the director, board, or owner an opportunity to hear from staff at all levels. Polling staff about particular issues or polling them about more general "What's on your mind?" questions offers them a way to present their views anonymously. Rules that outline appropriate boundaries to protect confidentiality and prevent personal issues being addressed are important.

Opportunities for recognition: Compared to working with preschoolers, caregiving for babies may seem fairly repetitive and routine after a time. Staff may lose sight of the importance and meaningfulness of what they are doing. The rewards of working with babies, and some would add toddlers, are more subtle than those of working with older children. And working with parents of babies is often more extensive and intense than with parents of older children. Staff need to be reminded regularly that theirs in a very important and highly skilled job. This recognition can take many forms, from director's notes to a mention in the center newsletter to simple, positive introductions to visitors by the director when parents are being given a tour around the center. Awards of excellence and awards ceremonies recognizing great practice can also be effective.

Opportunities for more responsibility: A good organization provides opportunities for employees, when they become interested and ready, to be involved in areas that extend beyond the group they work with. These may include assisting in developing or reviewing center policies, presenting workshops or leading discussions with other staff, or representing the center on a committee outside the center.

Learning to advocate: One of the skills that early childhood professionals need is the ability to articulate their practice: that is, to be able to speak clearly, strongly, passionately, and dispassionately about children and their work—the why, what, and how of doing their job well. Infant and toddler care has traditionally been devalued even within the early childhood profession. It is important to assist staff to understand what they are doing and why and to be able to talk about it with each other and, even more important, with parents.

Professional Development

No teacher is a finished product. Regardless of the qualifications and experience brought to the job, ongoing professional development through workshops, conferences, coursework, and professional literature are important. Good programs have budgets that support staff libraries and assist staff in obtaining further education and training.

However, just as important as access to training is a culture that establishes the center as a place for professional growth: consolidating previous learning, gaining new skills, facing challenges, reflecting critically on practice, and engaging in debate. Disagreements must be accepted as inevitable and as potentially positive when it is constructively dealt with. If a center's culture has fixed ideas about "the way we do things here" or invests the director or other powers-that-be with unchallenged wisdom, mindlessness and apathy eventually set in. If the atmosphere is one of constant learning and becoming in order to do a better job, if staff can be open about problems or questions they have, and if there are channels for constructive criticism as well as praise, not only will people be more excited about their work, they will also be less defensive.

Professional development does not simply happen by inexperienced staff observing and absorbing the expertise of highly skilled staff: modeling must be coupled with opportunities for discussion that result in directed attention and reflective analysis. The difference between good and not-so-good practice with children is subtle, and inexperienced staff may not know what to learn from watching someone else. Very often the demonstration will be lost in the busy atmosphere. Suggestions and ideas for improvement must be made explicit.

Effective modeling requires that lead teachers and more experienced staff be perceived as credible mentors but not be set up as models of perfection. Part of their credibility stems from their leadership, and part from a culture that values constructive criticism about everything. Successes as well as failures are used as a basis for discussion in order to improve practice.

Identifying the professional development needs of staff individually and collectively should be built into the ongoing evaluation of the program and of the teachers. Staff and program development plans should include provisions for in-center mentoring as well as outside workshops and courses. Helping train others is a very effective way of making staff aware of their own expertise and competence, as well as providing them with an incentive to grow in knowledge.

See Supplements: *Employee Counseling Procedure* and *Tips for Supervisors: Constructive Critcism*

Staff Evaluation

Evaluation is an essential component of professional development and contributes to high-quality individual performance. It is an ongoing element of good supervision. Other elements include clear expectations, recognition and praise, critical analysis, suggestions for improvement and performance, and goal setting. Evaluation also offers an opportunity for meaningful two-way communication about the job, the employee's performance, and supervision.

A good evaluation process has five elements:

1. Establishing the criteria for employee performance from the start: job description, program handbooks, supervisor memos, employee goals
2. Collecting data from multiple sources: employee self-evaluation and portfolio, parents, coworkers
3. Analyzing, reviewing, and discussing the evaluation between employee and supervisor
4. Identifying goals for job performance and professional development
5. Offering an opportunity for the employee to evaluate the supervision

Performance evaluations are serious business. They not only affect the nature and quality of the employee's work, but also often affect salary and promotion. If clear expectations for performance and support have been established, the supervisor and the employee can maintain a good relationship and still have honest, if sometimes painful, discussions. The following categories for levels of performance are useful for supervisor and employee alike because they allow for more objective analysis:

Inadequate performance: Does not perform according to the requirements of the position. Requires close supervision and a performance-improvement plan in addition to the usual annual goals to improve in order to continue in the position.

Adequate performance: Frequently requires close supervision and extra support to meet job requirements; little evidence of growth, extra effort, or more than adequate achievement of responsibilities.

Good performance: Understands and consistently implements the program's objectives during daily interactions with children, parents, and coworkers; some initiative shown for professional growth.

Exceptional performance: Either extraordinary effort or extraordinary achievement and otherwise consistent professional performance; evidence of commitment to the center as a whole and to professional growth; understanding and commitment to the program's philosophy and goals; above-average attendance at nonrequired center meetings and events.

Outstanding performance: Extraordinary effort and extraordinary achievement—for example, "the employee throws herself into the job with exceptional performance results"; provides leadership through role-modeling, enthusiasm, professionalism, commitment, and performance with children, parents, and coworkers; clear integration of the goals of the center into employee's own needs and values.

See Supplements: *Teacher Evaluation* and *Staff Resignation/Termination of Employment*

A Final Word: Change Takes Time

Improving as a workplace takes a center as much time as improving as a place for children and parents. But accomplishing the second requires the first. It is important to keep pushing along, writing and improving job descriptions and handbooks, and making time for meetings and training.

When it all comes together, children and families will benefit and staff will inevitably demonstrate the following:

- Belief in the work they are doing. It is not "just child care" but rather a positive influence on children and families.
- A sense of themselves as growing, learning, and becoming professional, no matter what their training and how long their experience.
- Confidence and trust in themselves and the children they care for—the attitude "We know each other, we like each other, we can live well together, we can handle any situation."
- The work is fun (much of the time) and always worth it.

"Why Did You Stay?" Creating Stayers Who Perform

I have now been at the center for nine years through two directors, at least eight coteachers, a facility renovation, biannual budget crisis, a divorce, and finally finishing my BA. There were times I wanted to quit, and times I can't imagine why I wasn't fired (I was so angry throughout my divorce that I was no fun to be with). But I'm glad I'm here—although I'd like to make a lot more money!

Sherry, the teacher quoted above, is a stayer. Fortunately for the center, she now stays not out of lethargy or minimal job prospects but because she wants to. She stayed with the center, and the center stuck with her through thick and thin—sometimes more thin than thick.

I stayed and I think I grew because it was a place where I was respected and cared about and quality did count—which was sometimes painful, if the push for quality meant that I had to shape up. We went through a lot and accomplished a lot, and it felt like "we" did it—particularly accreditation. Over the years, I learned a lot about working with adults (parents and staff)— that was always the hardest part—and how to take things in stride.

Staff stay when the center feels like a good place to work and makes a long-term commitment to them.

exercises

1. Assess the talent pool available for a particular center. How would you recruit staff?

2. List what you think is important in your work environment.

3. Evaluate for clarity and comprehensiveness the expectations of performance found in your job description and in staff handbooks.

4. Develop a new staff orientation list and reorganize its contents into the following categories: first day, first week, first month, first three months.

Reference

Bloom, P. J. 1997. *A Great Place to Work: Improving Conditions for Staff in Young Children's Programs*. Washington, DC: NAEYC.

Part 3

Quality Care and Learning

Chapter 11

Good Care for Infants and Toddlers

ɛxcellence *All children are cared for in a warm and affectionate manner and are provided with the learning experiences that best suit their own natures and needs. All children learn that no matter how young, old, messy, fussy, angry, active, or challenging—no matter what—they will be loved and well cared for. All children have a primary caregiver who develops a special relationship of mutual trust and respect with them and their families and who works with all the program staff to ensure positive child care experiences for the children and their families.*

Human interactions are the heart and soul of a good program for infants and toddlers. Nothing is more important than creating a place that is fueled by adults' simple enjoyment and satisfaction in actively caring for each child in an engaging and respectful manner.

Essential Qualities of the Child's Experience

Good care and education happen when teachers stay focused on the important elements of each child's experience. Teachers are always jugglers, with many priorities to balance as they plan curriculum, routines, and parent connections. Which of those glass balls can they not afford to drop?

Time Alone with the Primary Caregiver
Each child should have the opportunity for some time each day alone and truly engaged with the primary caregiver (see discussion of a primary caregiver system

that follows). What the two do together is not nearly as important as how they do it. The child should be treated as an important person who can bring pleasure to others. This helps develop the child's positive sense of self.

Beng waddles over with a forbidden paper clip. His teacher smiles and accepts the paper clip, and together she and Beng put the paper clip out of reach on the counter, all the while talking together.

Alexander is desperately sad and afraid after a bout of being wholeheartedly angry. Bobbie, his teacher, accepts his outreached hands and holds him; their physical contact and her soft words help him understand that the storm inside him is gone.

Eight-week-old Talia spends a good deal of the morning nestled in a carrier against the chest of Maiya, her primary caregiver. Maiya goes about various tasks, continually responding to Talia's sounds and movements with rubbing, cooing, and smiling.

Warmth and Affection

Infants and toddlers need to be cared for in a way that lets them know they are special individuals with their own needs, preferences, and moods. Pleasurable experiences shared with caregivers over time will foster the development of positive relationships.

Vijay likes to have his head rubbed as he falls asleep. Hannah prefers the warmth of a teacher's lap, without being touched or stroked. Nolan enjoys a quick hug for assurance, and then toddles off to play.

Individual Care

All infants and toddlers deserve caregiving and teaching practices specially tailored to them rather than ones that come with the expectation that children must fit into the program. Yes, the developmental goals for each infant or toddler in a group will be similar, but the ways of achieving them will vary, depending on each child's needs and characteristics. Children will have a range of temperaments (for example, easygoing, slow to warm up, quick to startle, and hard to settle), energy levels, and parent preferences for caregiving practices.

Jacob hates to be hurried, whereas Anna is always in a hurry and gets fussy when diapering goes on too long. Ramón is always wary and weary late in the day, whereas Keisha is still raring to go.

Continuity and Consistency of People and Practices

Only a small number of people should be regularly involved in the care of each child. Why? Warm, responsive, individualized, *consistent* care teaches the child that the caregiver can be trusted and that the world is a somewhat predictable place. Being able to anticipate experience gives the child feelings of power and control.

> ### It Isn't What You Give, It's What They Get
>
> Have you ever had someone who loved you try to show you love and care, but you didn't feel loved or well cared for? It is the love and care the child *feels* that counts, not what is given. This is a much harder standard of quality to achieve; it means that when we're evaluating our interactions with children, we not only should be aware of our own words and actions, but we also have to be in tune with the child's reactions.

Elena knows exactly where Lee likes to be tickled, when Tommy is likely to get cranky, and that Chai is ready to retreat when the room gets too active.

Responsive Care

Responsiveness applies to every aspect of care and education, from providing toys geared to children's developmental capabilities, to providing food when children signal they are hungry, to responding with a smile and words to children's smiles and sounds. Infants and toddlers need to make things happen, to learn that they can exercise some control over the social and physical world. A teacher's job is to understand children's capabilities and to provide them with opportunities to do something interesting to the world instead of always being done to and for. It is most important to care for children in a way that helps them learn they can affect other people and that certain words and behaviors usually lead to predictable responses.

Responsive care does not mean that adults do not initiate, try something new, or introduce something that is beyond the child's experience. As mentioned in the discussion of Vygotsky's ideas in chapter 4, teachers need to be on the lookout for receptive moments to enhance or extend the child's experience.

When Mei Mei is fixated on the sound of the wind chimes, Rafel, her primary caregiver, adds ribbons to the chimes to bring Mei Mei within reach of them.

Learning from Everything

Every experience is a learning experience, and young children should be cared for in ways that optimize their opportunities for learning (including social interaction) during routine daily activities. Babies learn attitudes and feelings about people as well as information about the world and ways of solving problems from the way they are cared for. Since routine activities occupy a large part of the child's day, teachers should view these not as chores to be done as quickly as possible but as learning times, as prime times.

For each child, Yuenan has a special diaper song, a wake-up-from-nap song, and even a you're-not-feeling-well song.

Respect for Each Child's Disposition to Learn

Babies are born with a disposition toward viewing learning as a pleasurable activity. How can you maintain and enhance this disposition? Probably most powerful is a teacher's own enjoyment of teaching and her own capacity for pleasure in learning. Teachers should be aware of what is pleasurable to children and encourage their reactions. If learning is a pleasurable experience, more learning and exploration will take place. Discovering how to learn with pleasure involves a special kind of social interaction with the teacher.

I always loved to be with babies—they were funny and loved you right back! But since taking courses and getting my CDA, I began to find them interesting. Why did Davi spend so much time with the brushes (or put the cookie in his diaper)?

—Suhara, an infant teacher

Protection from Overstimulation

How much stimulation is too much? It varies from child to child. If infants or toddlers have too many things around them to play with, touch, listen to, and look at, they may become overwhelmed. They need a balance of sameness and variability in order to engaged and learn effectively. Infants and toddlers need time to absorb new information and consolidate new skills, and this cannot be done under the constant bombardment of new experiences. By being aware of the atmosphere and staying calm, quiet, and gentle during even the busiest times, a teacher can to a large extent influence the atmosphere of the room. A toddler teacher said,

> *I think of part of my job as provisioning: adding things for learning and taking things out; not unlike when I was a waitress and paying attention to my customers' needs for food and drink.*

Protection from Prolonged or Excessive Distress

Distress indicates need. Very young babies may need help quieting themselves, and all babies need help and warm support to learn to manage their distress. When adults respond to distress promptly and appropriately, babies learn to manage their own distress instead of crying excessively to get what they want. Does this mean that distress should always lead to babies' getting what they want? No. It means that crying is a legitimate way to communicate and that babies should never be allowed to cry for a long time or to become hysterical. A director said:

> *I noticed in my infant rooms that sometimes infants had to work themselves up in a tizzy to get noticed. We developed a goal that every baby showing any sign of real distress was responded to verbally within 15 or 20 seconds, and physically within a minute—unless it made sense to not respond and let the baby work it through. The key thing is we became much better at being alert and noticing and being intentional in our responses.*

Pleasure in Other Children

Infants and toddlers often enjoy and learn from interacting with other children. For very young babies—noncrawlers—this means frequently placing them near each another. At the same time, older infants and toddlers will need help and support from adults as they begin the difficult task of learning how to interact. Teachers must help older babies, who have little self-control and no understanding of or ability to share. It is also important to give babies lots of opportunities to do their own thing, and to avoid putting pressure on them to get along with others. Children need some protection from each other and some places where they cannot be intruded upon by other children. While surprisingly cooperative and caring interactions will happen between children and should be acknowledged and encouraged, they should not be expected. *Note:* While children enjoy time together, this shouldn't be taken as an endorsement of valuing group mealtimes or activities over individualized schedules.

Learning to Live with Others

Children need our help learning to get along with others, and there is a lot to learn. What is appropriate behavior varies by the context—the place, the time, and who is around—and inappropriate behavior can be almost indistinguishable to very young children, who have no sense of private, gentle, personal boundaries, or, for that matter, good hygiene. They don't have words to make the world work for them, yet they must learn to control their emotions, bodies, and bodily functions. The difference between a pat and a slap, what it is polite to point at, what exactly is an "inside voice" or "running feet," and when "behind the bush" serves appropriately as a potty are sophisticated learned behaviors that require our patient guidance.

A Connection between Home and Child Care

Good child care programs ensure some consistency between the ways the child is cared for at home and in care. Teachers must respect the parents' right to make decisions about the care of their child, and try to follow the parents' practices. Arrangements should be set up to ensure that parents and teachers can talk with each other daily about the child.

> *Six-month-old Josh likes to hold a baby spoon in his hand while he is being fed. Lisa, twenty months old, totes around a well-worn laminated photograph of her family. Twelve-month-old Katherine holds her mother's scarf whenever she is upset or tired, because it carries a faint scent of her mother's perfume.*

Primary Caregiving

A primary caregiver system ensures that every child has a special person and that each parent has a primary contact. How is a teacher who is the primary caregiver "special"? She becomes an expert on the child, an advocate, and a coordinator of the child-and-parent experience. Remember, the primary caregiver–parent relationship is as important as the primary caregiver–child relationship.

A primary caregiver's relationship with the child and parent should begin on the child's first day, or even earlier at the intake or first meeting. While a child is adjusting to being in care, it is easier to initially get to know one new person well rather than several.

The teacher's caregiving is primary in two senses. First, much but not all of the caring and nurturing and communicating with parents is provided by the primary caregiver. Second, the care is primary in the sense that prime times, those most intimate and personal of times, are the major responsibility of the primary caregiver, although not to the exclusion of others.

Primary does not mean exclusive. The child should not become dependent on the presence of one person in order to have a good day. *Primary care is not the same as a small-group structure,* and children do not spend the day at their teacher's side, like chicks with a mother hen. Other staff develop a warm relationship with the child and have caring and learning interactions with the child while the child explores the learning environment.

Key Roles of the Teacher as Primary Caregiver

Primary caregivers take on key roles that require them to:

Communicate. Share information about children with families and appropriate staff. Primary caregivers are the essential link in the communication chain between family and program, and children and program. They ensure that each day children's experiences are communicated to parents—not just what they witnessed, but what others observed or enacted as well. They relay parents' concerns and suggestions to other staff.

Advocate. Speak for children and families within the program. They empower parents and children by translating individual concerns and needs into action through the efforts of all program staff. They are the vehicle that ensures that the program wraps around children and families, rather than requiring a child and family to fit the program.

Nurture. Care affectionately for children. They tune in to children and develop a special bond that ensures that all needs are met. They ensure that prime times empower children, and they establish a sense of security and basic trust.

Teach. Help children learn. They care for each child in a manner that maximizes language experiences and learning potential. They ensure that the learning environment and routines work for each child, providing a balance of developmentally appropriate experiences and neither too much nor too little stimulation.

Observe, monitor, and evaluate. Ensure that children and parents have a positive experience. By continually assessing the child-and-family experience, they make certain that children's experience in the program is positive and that parents' concerns are addressed. Methods include observation, discussions with other staff, talks with parents, and assessments of actual experiences of children and families—that is, that the care was received, rather than presumed experience or intended care.

Assigning Teachers as Primary Caregivers

Children can be assigned to a primary caregiver by the director or lead teacher based first on compatibility with parents' schedules, plus a combination of the following factors, listed in order of importance:

1. Roughly balanced number of children for each teacher. With infants, this probably works best with a mixture of younger and older babies so that one-to-one time can be individually scheduled.
2. Likely demands on the teacher. For example, when some children or families have special needs, these children and families should be distributed among the teachers.

3. Compatibility of parent, staff, and child—"a good match."

Once assigned, children should not be reassigned while they remain in the group unless staff changes or other pressing reasons make it absolutely necessary. The goal of the system is to promote security through continuity. Reassignment results in the opposite.

Concerns about Assigning Teachers as Primary Caregivers

The match. How important is "the match" between teacher and child, between teacher and parents? Clearly, the eventual relationships are critical, but matchmaking is logistically difficult and doesn't guarantee results. It might be useful to think of the arrangement as similar to an arranged marriage or an adoption, rather than a love match. Teachers and parents have a huge interest in trying to make the relationship work, as do children (although they don't know this!), and most often it is successful. If there are characteristics that suggest a particular match, such as a common cultural background or other commonalities, and if schedules and the number of children per teacher work out, matchmaking is probably a good thing. Compatibility of culture and values is a particularly relevant characteristic.

Competition for "the best" primary caregiver. Will all parents want the most highly qualified primary caregiver—the one with the most training or the highest position? Will parents feel that the best primary caregivers are teachers or lead teachers with the most formal education? Maybe, but not if they understand that the primary care system is just one system that promotes quality care and education. The primary caregiver is not supposed to determine the child's learning experience. The educational experience of all the children is the major responsibility of the person most qualified by training and experience to provide it—presumably the lead teacher. That is, planning the learning environment, activities, and guidelines for adult-child interactions is her job. The qualifications for a good primary caregiver are those we would expect from any caring teacher: sensitivity, skill, and understanding of the program's philosophy and practices.

> *I was disappointed that Miss Carlotta was assigned to be Aiden's primary caregiver. She had no degree. I wanted Miss Tameka, who had a BA and was the head teacher. But Carlotta turned out to be a joy, and now, four years later, I am insisting she be assigned to Alice, even though she still doesn't have even an AA or a CDA.*
>
> —Aiden's and Alice's Mom

Primary caregivers aren't perfect. Many of us have an image in our head of the ideal teacher. She may look like a grandmother, a sister, or some other idealized image. That image may not be a man, someone who speaks with an accent, a person with few literacy skills, or someone who is nineteen or sixty-two years old. But if we look beyond our image to reality, high-quality teachers come in all shapes and sizes, speak different languages, and possess the usual assortment of human imperfections. Programs need to help parents recognize the qualities that justify each teacher's place in the program.

> *She could barely write. Her daily experience sheets were pretty atrocious—sparse, poor grammar, and worse spelling. When she spoke, her syntax was scrambled, and sometimes I had trouble understanding her. But I was so glad that she was Mikey's primary caregiver. I knew that Shirley would love him to death and watch out for Mikey as if he was her own. I cried when Mikey moved up.*
>
> —Mikey's mom

> *Lawrence, my husband, was opposed to having Ben (or any man) care for Tamara, and I wasn't sure myself. But we reluctantly decided to try it out. Ben was wonderful—very gentle and thoughtful—and I actually came to really appreciate that Tamara had a male teacher. He was different: more exuberant, more physical, and he encouraged Tamara to be adventurous when she became a toddler. He even won Lawrence over.*
>
> —Tamara's mom

Avoiding ownership. "Would you change Marcel's diaper? He's your primary." Primary caregivers do not own the children they care for. All staff have some responsibility for all children as well as collective responsibility for maintaining the learning and caring environment. An overzealous or rigid system of primary caregiving can work against children's best interests by creating excessive delays in attention and encouraging children to become so dependent on one teacher that they find it difficult to function without her. Staff may become so attached to particular children that they resist caring for other children or allowing their primaries to move to another group. The best way to avoid exclusive ownership is to openly acknowledge the issue as a natural tendency and to discuss it frequently when the problem arises.

Primary Caregivers' Blunders

The primary caregiver system is designed to ensure that every parent and every child feels secure. Used mindlessly, it can make everything worse.

> *My baby was assigned to Min, and we really liked her. But she went on maternity leave six weeks later, and we got Amber, who went on vacation for two weeks within a few weeks of her assignment. This is continuity?*
>
> —Rasheed's mom

Assigning a child to a teacher who is about to go on vacation—or worse, on maternity leave—is clearly not in the best interest of the child or the parent. A few weeks may not feel like a long time to the staff, but to a baby or a new parent, it's a huge chunk of their child care experience.

Here are some other blunders to avoid:

- Assigning a child to a teacher whose schedule is such that parents never come in contact with her—for example, the teacher works 8:00 to 4:30, and the child is in care from 7:30 to 5:00.

- Creating relationships that are so close or exclusive that the child has a horrible day when the primary caregiver is not present.
- Having all communication break down with parents when the primary caregiver is absent—no daily experience sheets, no casual conversation.

See Supplement: *A Note to Parents: Primary Caregiving*

Alternatives to the Primary System?

There are times when primary caregiving systems may not be good alternatives, chiefly when there is high staff turnover or uneven staffing. The best alternative is to consider how to enhance the sense of a community of caring in which each child is known well and knows others. This may involve pairing rooms or changing the role of a program coordinator or assistant director. It may involve discussing children more frequently among staff, posting more information about children, communicating more with families, monitoring and evaluating more often, or creating more opportunities for staff to have one-to-one times with the children in their care. It is important to identify what is missing when staff do not have a knowledgeable, anchoring relationship to each child and family.

Guidelines for Quality Interactions

In their wonderful book *Infants, Toddlers, and Caregivers* (1992, 9–24), Janet Gonzalez-Mena and Diane Widmeyer Eyer developed guidelines for caring for children that emphasizes respect for children and the primacy of caregiving moments as the bases for developing trust. The following is an adaptation of their principles:

Involve babies in things that concern them; respond to their interests. Involve children in feeding, diapering, dressing, searching for toys; use language and respond to their efforts to communicate: "Here's your spoon," "Let's reach for the cup," "Hold your boot," "*Ooops*—you dropped your boot!" Encourage children's fascination with zippers, buttons, and shoelaces. Don't work around them or distract them to get the job done faster.

Invest in quality time; give them your full human presence. Don't settle for being with them but only half there. Be on the floor, the grass, the furniture with them. Good teaching is not about overseeing children but about being with them.

Acknowledge in practice that the most powerful moments are true give-and-takes. These are reciprocal actions, communications through which we connect: singing a child to sleep, playing hide-and-find, setting up lunch together.

Learn children's unique way of communicating (cries, words, gestures, movements, facial expressions, body positions), and teach them yours. A cry with a particular sound may mean "I'm hungry"; a sudden burst of activity may signal tiredness that is being resisted. A gentle touch from you or a look and a smile across the room can come to mean to the child "I see you need me—I'll be there as soon as I can."

Don't underestimate or ignore their ability to communicate. Examples: Maria's enthusiasm is clear when she arches her body and waves her chubby fist, whereas

Arthur demonstrates his by puffing out his cheeks and grunting. When Matilda is tired, her sunny disposition sours and she clings and whines.

Invest time and energy to build a total person; don't strive just to make the child smart or nice. Better babies are not babies who walk or talk first, who do tricks or are quick to respond to activities. Better babies are babies allowed a range of active experiences with people, things, and their own bodies that will motivate them to keep exploring and experimenting.

Respect children as individuals; don't treat them like cute dolls or objects to be manipulated. Tell children what is happening or what will happen: "I'm going to check your pants now," "Let's look for some dry clothes," "We have to wait for a cracker now; I know you're hungry."

Be honest about your feelings and authentic in your interactions; don't pretend to feel or not to feel something. It is okay to tell children that their actions are annoying you or making you angry. Your body language clearly lets them know it, anyway, and trying to hide it in your voice is only confusing. "I know you are only experimenting with gravity by dropping your spoon, but it's annoying me. Stop, please, or we are finished!" Obviously, teachers need to control their anger while interacting with children. But it is appropriate to use words to tell them how we feel. It is not appropriate to act out strong negative feelings of anger, frustration, or impatience.

Model the behavior you want to teach, and use words to describe what is happening. "Molly, Marie is sad because her mom just left, so let's get her favorite book and read it together. That will make her feel better."

Don't preach or scold. Fourteen-month-old Jason is exploring ten-month-old Emily fairly roughly. "Gently, Jason, like this," says the teacher, as she gently strokes both Jason and Emily.

Let children learn to solve their own problems when appropriate; don't take away valuable learning opportunities. Don't step in right away when Elena meets George on a narrow ramp, or Stevie tries to pull the toy out from under the couch and cries out in frustration. When you decide that you need to step in, look for a way to provide the least amount of support that may help resolve the situation.

Build security by teaching trust; don't teach distrust by being undependable or incomprehensible. Keep promises. "I can't pick you up right now, but I'll do it as soon as I finish changing Marina's diaper." "I'm leaving now, but I'll be back." "We are going to go inside in a minute." "I'm making your bottle right now." Predictability and communication teach trust.

Be concerned about the quality of development at each stage; don't rush babies toward developmental milestones. Who was the first to walk, talk, or learn to use the toilet in your social circle? Does it matter to you now? Better isn't faster; better is fuller and richer experiences and appreciation for all the milestones, whenever they occur.

See Supplement: *Ensuring a Child's Positive Experience*

Infants and Toddlers in Distress

The sensitivity of your caregiving practices may be instrumental in influencing the skills a child develops for expressing needs, getting attention from adults, and coping with frustration. In life in general and in group settings in particular, periods of distress are givens. Nevertheless, good planning and sensitive caregiving will greatly reduce the stress that infants and toddlers experience.

What Causes Distress in the First Few Months?
Infants and toddlers cry for many reasons, and the reasons change as they grow older. There is typically more crying from younger babies. As they get older, instances of crying may become fewer but more sustained and intense, and the reasons for crying become more obvious. Sometimes an infant's reason for crying is not obvious, and teachers will have to respond in a trial-and-error manner, even with a child they know well. The teacher's manner should be gentle and soothing, for both she and the child are likely to be feeling impatient with each other and themselves at the time. Very young babies often cry because of

- hunger
- tiredness
- wet or soiled diapers
- pain (for example, gas, teething, colic)
- other discomforts (for example, clothing that is too tight, too warm, too cold; an uncomfortable position; removal of clothing)
- boredom
- overstimulation
- sudden change (for example, a loud noise, sudden loss of physical support, bright lights, being placed in water, being picked up abruptly).

As Infants Grow: Causes of Distress and How to Handle Them

Early frustration. As babies become increasingly aware of the world around them, they seem to develop some awareness of their limited repertoire of skills. A good example of this occurs in the early stages of reaching, when a baby's aim is not accurate and any efforts are fumbling. After several unsuccessful attempts to obtain an object, some infants and toddlers seem to become very annoyed with their own ineptness and may cry vigorously. Some become markedly less irritable as their competencies increase. Nevertheless, as infants become more mobile and take more active, assertive, adventuresome approaches to the world, they are certain to attempt many things they cannot do safely, and get themselves into difficult situations. New frustration and some bumps and bruises are inevitable.

Often infants become more impatient and easily upset during a period when they are attaining a new skill, such as walking. Their tolerance for frustration in most areas seems to drop while they direct their efforts toward developing new competencies. Infants also become distressed when something pleasurable is terminated, such as an adult's attention or the disappearance of an interesting toy. Crying sometimes indicates impatience because needs are not being met fast enough.

There needs to be a balance between helping children by making the situation easier to cope with, rescuing them, and letting them work things out themselves. For example, when nonmobile babies are upset because toys are out of reach and they cannot move to retrieve them, you should move the item closer to them. On the other hand, always accommodating children who do not like being put down after being held or who loudly protest the end of the applesauce at lunch may encourage them to use excessive crying to get their own way. A better response to this kind of crying is to engage children with something else.

Distress at naptime. Crying or less intense fussiness and whimpering may be the major cues babies use to indicate readiness for a nap. If children are not asleep when put down in the cot, they may cry. They may be irritated at having been taken away from the action. When babies reach nine to twelve months, they become used to the routine and seem to accept napping or resting when tired, so the job of getting them to sleep may become easier. Because of their new motor skills, they may also become physically tired more readily.

If teachers are fairly certain that children are sleepy, they should leave them for a while. What is a while? That depends on each child, the level of distress, and what has been discussed with the family. Teachers who know children well can tell when they have reached the point at which they are unlikely to quiet themselves and therefore need help.

Firm, affectionate, consistent handling is especially necessary with infants and toddlers who resist naptime.

Unpleasant encounters with other children. As babies begin to move around, opportunities to interact with other babies increase. Many pleasurable play situations occur when babies discover each other. However, occasions inevitably arise when infants and toddlers upset other babies by exploring them too roughly or by taking away another's toys.

Teachers should view these situations as times to help babies begin to learn how to interact, rather than as occasions for moral judgment and discipline. Both children in such a situation need support and help. Sometimes separating them is best. A duplicate toy may be introduced.

Fearful response to strangers. Sometime during the last half of their first year, many babies go through a period of reacting negatively to strangers. This period should be respected and the baby's feelings considered.

When a stranger is present, stay close to a baby who is reacting to the stranger with concern, or hold the baby and let the stranger know about the child's concern. Unfamiliar people viewed from a teacher's lap are less threatening than those seen from the floor. Of course, teachers have to be careful not to be overly protective of babies who are distressed by strangers. If a teacher runs to hold a baby protectively whenever a stranger approaches, and encourages the stranger to stay at a distance or to leave the room, the baby may learn that new people are to be feared. Instead, using her relationship of trust, the teacher is in an excellent position to help the child begin to react positively to new people. Teachers can also help adult visitors adjust their behavior so that they do not create a roomful of anxious children.

Excessive confusion and change. Crying contributes to and reflects the atmosphere of the room; for example, its noise level, its activity level, how crowded it is, and its calmness or confusion. Some babies are much more adept than others at filtering out stimulation. Obviously, staffing changes and new children may cause distress.

Helping a Child in Distress: The Teacher's Role

Crying always has meaning for the child—infants and toddlers don't cry for no reason. Sensitive teachers always react to crying by noticing it, considering its meaning and the implications for how to react to it, and then responding appropriately. This does not mean that a good teacher always intervenes immediately when an infant or toddler cries. On the contrary, she may decide to wait for a time to give the child an opportunity to self-quiet. A child may be crying not because anything is wrong physically, but out of desire to be held close or played with. Respect these needs and attend to them as you do children's needs for food, rest, and dry diapers. When infants and toddlers feel hungry, tired, confused, frightened, or insecure, they need to be nurtured. They need reassurance, holding, laps, hugs, smiles, and touches. Children in distress don't benefit from indifference or slow responses. If they're crying and you can pick them up, do it!

Are there exceptions to this? Yes, some babies seem to need to wind down by crying themselves to sleep. In this case, crying isn't vigorous and does not go on for a long time.

You may not always be able to solve the child's concern, but at least you can acknowledge the feelings and respond sympathetically. For example, you can say something such as "I know that you are having trouble waiting for your bottle" while rubbing the child's stomach. Making eye contact and physical contact reassures the child that at least the world cares.

How you respond to distress is critically important. Your sensitive response helps children learn to trust other people, to trust that needs will be met and help given when requested. At the same time, you are helping them develop resources for coping with some unpleasant situations by relieving their own distress.

> See Supplements: *A Note to Staff: Helping Infants and Toddlers in Distress* and *Teacher Reactions to Children's Distress: Performance Guidelines*

Responding to Distress: Considering Children's Individual Differences

There are many individual differences among babies in the frequency, intensity, and cause of distress episodes. While all typical babies cry sometimes and under some circumstances, there are not specific cries for particular situations that are typical of all babies. But you can become sensitized to the meaning of particular kinds and intensities of cries in individual babies—that is, whether they indicate hunger, pain, tiredness, or a rather halfhearted attempt to protest.

Kids Move in Mysterious Ways

"Why is Joey crying now?" We don't always know the source of distress, but we usually come up with a reason that satisfies our need for explanation: change of routine, something at home, the weather, a cold. Sometimes the cause becomes apparent a few days later, when the child develops a cold, ear infection, or some other illness; often it does not. Parents and teachers can be helpful to each other in looking for explanations, and, more important, in trying to alleviate the child's distress.

There are vast differences in the ways babies show distress, just as there is great variability in the way they show pleasure. Of course, this is true for adults as well. For example, a fairly mild cry by Thea, who seldom gets upset, would be more cause for concern than that same cry by Damien, who is often irritable.

Babies also differ widely in their ability to quiet themselves when upset, and therefore differ in the kind of consolation they require from caregivers when they are upset. Some young infants (less than three to four months old) become excited easily and are generally very "fussy." They may need much direct help in quieting themselves, including being picked up, carried, rocked, or, more indirectly, by being cared for in a serene, consistent, predictable setting. Some infants, even if they become very distressed, seem to be able to calm themselves relatively easily, whereas others seem to have to "cry themselves out" or require adult intervention in order to stop. For some infants, this intervention may mean a few comforting words at a distance, whereas for another child in the same situation, the caregiver will know that she has to pick up the child.

Do not worry about spoiling a young infant by responding quickly to crying, for this responsiveness and help will aid in the development of later skills for self-quieting. Some infants can quiet themselves and should be given the opportunity to do so; some cannot. Your response depends on your understanding the individual baby and the cause of his distress. From the beginning, the way you react to the baby's crying builds a relationship.

Responding to Distress: Considering Cultural Differences

As in almost everything, cultural practices differ regarding adult response to crying and other signs of distress. Some cultures typically attend to distress quickly and consistently, whereas others respond only to some crying. Some cultures believe that some crying is a sign of good health and exercises the lungs, whereas for others it is a sign of parental inattention. Every center should have a good understanding of the practices of each baby's family; some practices will be based on cultural background. While it is useful to have some information about cultural practices, a little information can be dangerous. It is important not to overgeneralize and assume that child-rearing practices of all parents will be based on cultural background—or worse, to generalize among ostensibly similar cultures (for example, Vietnamese and Chinese) when you do not understand the many differences. We know that practices within our own culture vary quite a bit, but we often tend to generalize about other cultures.

There are some common issues that arise in relation to crying and distress. Some cultures keep babies close: the baby is held or strapped to the mother's back or front (usually the mother, but sometimes a grandmother, sister, or aunt), fed on demand, and toileted by anticipating their need to urinate or have a bowel movement. Mothers in such cultures become particularly tuned in to their babies' needs and anticipate them before children become distressed. These babies seldom cry at home. When they experience the very different reality of group care, they may have trouble adjusting unless the program accommodates their expectations by holding and using infant carriers.

When and where babies cry may be significant in some cultures, and elicits different responses. For some Chinese, it is especially bad luck if a baby cries on New Year's Day, as it is thought to bring bad luck to the family for the entire year, so a lot of care is taken on that day to prevent distress. In some cultures, crying in public is considered inappropriate. Also, crying in the crowded family living conditions experienced by many new immigrants results in adults taking great care to prevent distress.

While centers cannot always accommodate what babies are familiar with, it is important that staff are sensitive and understand that it will be hard for some infants and toddlers to adjust to being on their own, to experience new levels of distress, and to calm themselves.

See Supplement: *A Note to Staff: Acknowledging and Responding to Cultural Differences Regarding Child Distress*

Discouraging the Crying of Toddlers

There are times when it is appropriate to briefly withhold attention from toddlers in order to avoid reinforcing negative behavior or to give them a chance to solve their concerns by themselves; for example, when they are experiencing frustration with a toy or a peer. But it is important that this controlled noninterference doesn't turn into less responsive nurturing.

Caregivers have a lot of demands on their time and energy, and it is not unusual to see programs in which infants get attention only when they cry, act out, or their teacher finds it convenient. Guard against this! As babies become toddlers and develop other ways to communicate, you don't want them to learn that the most effective way of getting attention is to cry. If children do not receive consistently positive responses to such communications (for example, being picked up when holding out arms, being smiled at when smiling), then they may learn to rely primarily on crying as a means of getting attention.

There are times when children want more attention than teachers can possibly give. If you feel the needs of a child have been met and the child is receiving a lot of quality individual time, you may decide to ignore distress and see if its frequency decreases over time. But cooperation between parents and child care staff is essential in order to expect real changes in the child's behavior.

Keep in mind that there is a whole continuum of responses to distress—it isn't simply all or nothing. When you know a child, you can choose your response, from an empathetic or reassuring look, to a vocal response, to picking up the child.

Young children need to learn to work out minor irritations on their own, but they need our support to do so. It is difficult but wise for teachers to respond by saying something encouraging and doing nothing when children complain about small problems that teachers believe they can work out on their own. Allowing children to do so is one way that teachers can provide appropriate challenges that help young children develop new competencies and skills.

Prevention of Distress

Obviously, the prevention of distress is important, in part because distress is contagious. The best strategy for preventing or keeping distress at a minimum is to anticipate needs before they occur. Some methods of doing this include:

- knowing a child's schedule and being alert to early signs of hunger, sleepiness, or irritability

- providing a safe, interesting environment that is neither overly stimulating nor overly restricting
- helping children learn to have pleasurable interactions with others and protecting them from hurting each other
- providing many opportunities for success
- giving children encouragement and help.

Many potentially distressing situations can also be avoided by knowing and respecting children's limitations. What gets in the way is seeing children's distress as a deliberate test or as making an unreasonable demand. For instance, children whom a teacher believes should not be hungry may become upset if they have to stand by while other children get fed. Rather than ignoring the problem or punishing children for being unreasonable, you can make the situation easier for distressed children to tolerate by encouraging them to become interested in other activities or by giving them a cracker while the other children are being fed.

Coping with a toddler's distress is a major source of teachers' distress. A child's crying tends to have a negative effect on everyone who can hear it, and brings out a gamut of adult feelings—sympathy, anger, frustration, even embarrassment. "How come my babies are always crying?" lamented one new teacher. A period of prolonged fussiness and crying will wear down even the most patient and understanding staff. Punishing (and this includes ignoring) a child for crying is not acceptable. A teacher working with an irritable or distressed child who will not be quieted needs other teachers to provide support and relief, because these are perhaps the most difficult periods of the day.

Caring Well for Children with Special Needs

Inclusion of children with special needs means much more than simply accepting their presence. It means recognizing, welcoming, identifying needs and strengths, and accepting them for who they are. It means working hard to make every child and family feel like a full member of the community and a full participant in what the program has to offer.

Identifying Children with Special Needs

Many special needs are not evident when infants or toddlers first enter the program. Because the typical range of development is quite wide, it is not easy to know when to become concerned about a child. If you have a concern that someone in your program may have a condition beyond what is typical and may benefit from early recognition and intervention, try the following:

- Observe the child closely and identify the behavior or absence of behavior and when it occurs.
- Compare the child's behavior to developmental norms.
- Consult with the lead teacher or director, while respecting the child and family by limiting discussion of your concern with other staff.

The Importance of Beauty and the Child *with* Special Needs

It took a long time for me to admit that I used to look at my daughter Sophia and feel disgust sometimes. I saw her as ugly and clumsy and embarrassing. She wasn't like the other twos—she couldn't walk, she slobbered, she couldn't do much, and she cried easily. And she was mine. Where was the beautiful baby I was sure that I would have? I felt sorry for myself.

It's funny. When she moved out of the church basement center and got to go to the new center, and I saw her everyday in a beautiful place with big windows, trees and flowers, pretty pictures, and people who told me what a doll she was and what she could do, I had those feelings less and less. She was beautiful, and, yeah, she was mine.

Children with disabilities and children from at-risk homes need and deserve to be in physically attractive settings among people who think they are wonderful. It helps everyone to see them in a different light.

- Carefully discuss the concern with parents, recognizing the potential for their emotional reactions. If necessary, rehearse the conversation with the lead teacher or director.
- Develop a plan with the parents for more observation, consultation with an outside resource, or screening. Always consult with the parent before bringing in resources external to the program.

See Supplement: *Caring for Children with Special Needs*

Caring for and Teaching Children with Special Needs

It is important to remember that your responsibility is to provide quality child care, not therapeutic services, to children who have special needs. In other words, it is the caring that allows children to succeed in your center, not the professional services that their condition may require. When caring for children with special needs, keep in mind:

Recognize and understand your own feelings. Teachers' thoughts and feelings about children with special needs are usually complicated, often a mixture of positives and negatives. Teachers at a workshop generated the following list of the emotions they felt when they began working with children with special needs:

- *Sadness.* "I almost cry when I think of the life she will lead with cerebral palsy."
- *Pity.* "I felt so sorry for Billy and his parents that it got in the way of seeing him as a complete child instead of just the blind kid."
- *Anger.* "Sometimes I find myself tired and mad. Why is this kid here if he can't control biting other children? And I get really mad at his mother—it was her drinking when she was pregnant that caused the problem."
- *Disgust.* "I hate myself, but sometimes I am revolted by the drooling and crying."
- *Denial.* "She's really okay. I just want to fix her, work really hard, and give her everything she needs, and then she will be better. She will be normal."
- *Ignorance.* "I really had a lot of misconceptions about babies with heart monitors, and I was scared to death all the time."
- *Vulnerability, incompetence, and fear.* "Why me? I can't manage this child and my other babies. The parents are going to blame me if something goes wrong."

It is natural for teachers to struggle with a variety of feelings as they move toward acceptance and appreciation of a child with special needs, particularly before they interact with the child. Being able to acknowledge and share feelings with other staff is usually helpful, as is knowing that acceptance and ease may take time.

Learn about special needs and use the parents as a primary resource. There is a lot of information about children with special needs available from local and national resource centers, schools, and advocacy organizations (see Resources at the back of the book). For physical disabilities and health conditions, often the best places to start are with information obtained from other professionals, from children's parents, and from parents' firsthand experiences.

Adapt the program to fit the child. Serving children with special needs demands the same adaptability that's needed for other children: the program must adapt to them—the environment, the routines, and the caregiving and teaching practices. Adapting the program does not mean overprotecting or segregating children. Children with disabilities need opportunities to be challenged and they need to undertake manageable risks, to learn to get along with other children, to manage limits, and to experience success and failure. Realistic expectations are important. If goals are set too high, they invite failure; if too low, they diminish children's potential.

Develop an individual care plan for the child. As for other children, infants and toddlers with special needs should have individual plans developed for them in partnership with their parents in order to ensure their success at the center. The special care plan should include any special medical, diet, or other care requirements.

Work with other professionals involved with the child. Families of children with special needs frequently use professional resources beyond child care and must juggle a challenging number of relationships in a variety of settings. Child care professionals need to communicate clearly with these other service providers to maximize the effectiveness of the resources offered to families and their children with special needs.

Work as a team. Teamwork with parents, other staff, and other professionals is essential, but may be challenging. There is more to communicate, more emotions, more of a tendency for primary caregivers to become possessive about children with special needs, and more of a tendency for other staff to cede care to the primary caregiver. Complications may occur when working with other health and human service professionals. Child care staff often feel that their knowledge of children with special needs is not accorded enough respect. Unfortunately, they are usually correct. It is important to understand the value of all those persons who support and care for the child, and to recognize that the coordination of these many parties' efforts is logistically difficult.

A Final Word: The Challenge of Good Care and Education for Every Child, Every Day

Providing every child with consistently good care and education and every parent with feelings of satisfaction every day is a challenge. Success depends on staying focused with sensitivity and patience on the characteristics and experiences of individual children and their families. Life demands that we cope with a wide range of circumstances and no small amount of stress. Helping infants and toddlers develop the self-esteem and skills that fit their unique personalities and that enable them to manage daily life provides them with the foundation for social competence and well-being.

Exercises

1. How would you explain the role of a primary caregiver to a parent?

2. List examples of how primary caregivers can make a child feel special.

3. List examples of how primary caregivers can make parents feel special.

4. When do you feel poorly cared for or unloved? What is missing in the care you receive at those times? Can you find parallels between your care experiences and the care experiences sometimes received by babies in group care?

5. When are children most likely to be in distress in your program? What changes might alleviate their distress?

Reference

Gonzalez-Mena, J., and D. Widmeyer Eyer. 1992. *Infants, Toddlers, and Caregivers.* New York: McGraw-Hill.

Chapter 12

Prime Times: Caring Routines

εxcellence *Caring times are recognized as prime times for children to develop a sense of well-being and personal worth and to learn. These times are individualized, relaxed, and gentle, full of conversation and self-help opportunities, never assembly-line-like, impersonal, or institutional.*

The term *prime times* indicates the critical importance of good care in a child's life in a program. The idea of good care carries with it not just being taken care of in a physical sense, but having warm interactions with an adult. Caring times include the interactions between teacher and child during feeding, diapering, toileting, dressing, washing, nurturing, arrival, and departure, as well as during other care activities. These are prime times for care and learning. During these times, adults address infants' and toddlers' primary human needs for food, sleep, disposal of bodily waste, bathing, clothing, nurturing, and learning. Since these times occupy a large portion of a child and teacher's day, caring times should be conducted at a relaxed pace, with one-to-one contact between teacher and child. The caring times should be full of language, physical touch, and give-and-take. These are prime times for developing a strong sense of personal worth and power, language, and a basic trust that the world is a good place. When children are actively involved in their own care, respected as people, and get their personal needs met, they develop a sense of autonomy.

Prime Times and Teachers

Teachers *are* caregivers (and caregivers are teachers), whether you use one term or the other. Education, or teaching, is only one aspect of a teacher's role; that very important role is as intrinsic to caring routines as it is to planned learning experiences. As we've said many times in this book, infants and toddlers are learning all the time.

Designing and planning caring routines that empower children and enhance their development are huge challenges in group care. Some staff lament, "We spend almost all our time caring for the kids and never get to teach them." For infants and toddlers, caring times are an essential part of curriculum. Don't rush through them to get to "the curriculum"; instead, see them as components of curriculum. Because of the influence of schools on our thinking, we find it hard to recognize that caring times are also prime learning and teaching times. They are. Consider these examples:

Let's change your diaper so you'll feel more comfortable. First we'll take off the soiled diaper, then we'll wash you up, and last we'll put on a clean diaper. The soiled diaper is wet, and the new one is dry. Doesn't that feel better?

In this scenario, the child learns:

- *Trust:* The teacher is responding to the child's needs.
- *Respect:* The teacher is speaking to the child, not ignoring him, not speaking to other adults, and not just mechanically changing the diaper.
- *Affection:* The teacher is helping the child in a gentle and loving way.
- *Sequence (Math):* First, we take off the dirty diaper; second, we wash; and last, we put on a new diaper.
- *Opposites (Science):* A dirty diaper feels wet. A clean diaper feels dry.

I'm so sorry that you got hurt when your friend pushed you. Here's a big hug to make you feel better. She wanted your ball. Next time, use your words and tell her "No" if she tries to take the ball.

In this scenario, the child learns:

- *Compassion:* The teacher is expressing concern for the child.
- *Nurturing:* The teacher is comforting the child.
- *Problem-solving skills:* The child can say "No" if someone is trying to take her toy.

In both scenarios, children learn that they are important people.

The major goal of a rich, built-in learning environment (this will be explained in chapter 16) is to engage children in play independently of adults. When children can do so, staff have relaxed time in which to diaper or nurture them: we can touch, talk, listen, and play all the call-response games that children set in motion. Imagine if every child experienced daily the intimacy that Nikki Giovanni describes in her poem "let's take a nap," which appears on the facing page!

Making Caring Routines Prime Times

What makes caring routines prime times? These occur when you:

Take your time while working one-to-one with a child. Don't feel as if you have to rush through tasks just so they can be completed. We all like to get things done—to have all the diapers changed, for example. But the diapers will get wet again. Go as slowly as circumstances permit. These are the one-to-one times that count the most.

Tell the child what you are going to do. Talk to and physically handle the child with respect. Approach even the youngest baby as a person; tell the child what you are doing and why: "Alfonso, I'm going to change your diaper, okay? You'll feel much drier when we're finished."

Offer the child the opportunity to help. Help children develop positive self-concepts and autonomy during care activities by offering them choices to do some things by themselves. "Would you like to dry your hands with the towel, or do you want me to help you?" "You can eat the banana pieces all by yourself. Good job. I'll help you with the squash."

Talk directly to the child, not to other staff. Avoid talking about children across the room to other staff, as if the children were dolls or were not there. For example, saying, "You change those two and I'll change those," or "Carter's wet. Would you change him while I check Alicia?" treats children as if they are invisible or incapable of hearing. Even babies can sense when we are talking over or about them.

Speak positively to children about unpleasant care routines. Don't let your attitudes toward food, bodily wastes, or dirt and grime turn prime times into negative experiences. "Why don't we clean you up?" is much better than "You're a mess." Avoid using words like *dirty* and *smelly* when talking to children, especially about elimination.

Acknowledge your personal feelings. Know yourself. Staff have different tolerance levels for noise, crying, smells, and physical appearances. Be aware of your personal feelings about prime times and how they may have been shaped by your own past experiences.

Be willing to compromise your own personal feelings for safer and more consistent care. Adults bring strong feelings, opinions, and attitudes to prime times from their own family experiences. Group care often means submerging some personal

---

let's take a nap

by Nikki Giovanni

almost every day
after my lunch
after my milk
after i go to the potty
and teddy and piggy, my green turtles,
have been fed
and i can't think of anything to do quick enough
mommy says "come on chocolate drop"
'cause she thinks i don't remember what she wants
"let's take a nap"
just cause i'm a little feller don't mean i'm dumb!
then she takes off my shoes and pants and hops me
into her big bed
and i have to:
    climb on her chest
    be tossed in the air
    get tickled under my chin
    hear this little piggy three times
    and get the bottom of my feet kissed
    at least twice
before i put her
to sleep

feelings and preferences in order to care for children consistently. For example, parents vary widely on how they react to minor bumps and scratches, from ignoring them entirely to showing great concern. Consistent staff reactions based on knowledge of children and their families is desirable.

Pay attention to your body language. Negative body language, such as rolling your eyes or throwing your hand on your hip, can be more powerful than words, especially for children. Do you wrinkle your nose, grimace, or handle children roughly during some routines? You may not even be aware of it. Ask another teacher to let you know if your body language is inappropriate.

Focus on the needs of the child rather than on your own feelings. Concentrate on the child's experience of discomfort or fear instead of your own feelings of sympathy, disgust, fear, or overwork. Think about how you would want to be treated if you were in a similar situation.

Remain aware of the needs of other children while you are working one-to-one. As you are interacting with one child, keep your eyes and ears on the rest of the group and try to spot opportunities for giving other children moments of your entire attention. If another child approaches you, for example, you should acknowledge his presence: "I see you have a book. I'm helping Sienna wash her hands right now. We can read the book when I finish."

Respect parents' views about caring routines. Routine activities related to eating, sleeping, using the toilet, washing, and dressing are all areas in which parents, because of cultural, religious, or personal preference, are likely to have strong views. Because of this, they are likely to want to participate in decision making. While this makes caregiving more challenging, it is critically important for a variety of reasons that parents play a major role in making decisions about their child's routine care (see the detailed discussion in chapter 8).

The goal of the daily schedule is to allow individualized care and learning to go smoothly and predictably. It may appear to be easier for staff when all children eat and sleep at the same time, but it is better for children when feeding, diapering, and sleeping follow individualized schedules. Not all toddlers can go all morning without a nap. Post each child's typical daily schedule for eating and sleeping as a guide, but don't let this get in the way of reading cues from children about their needs. Young children's schedules are constantly changing as they grow.

Nineteen-month-old Simon rarely takes a morning nap, but today he is lying on the pillows in the book area and is not interested in climbing on the slide, as he usually does. His primary caregiver puts out his mat away from the area where the other children are playing. Simon lies down and takes a twenty-minute nap.

Flexibility demands organization, communication with other staff, and teamwork. Individualizing is not as simple as just sitting back and being responsive: it requires allocating staff's tasks. A checklist of jobs for staff to do on a daily, weekly, and as-needed basis will help. Equipment and supplies must be accessible and plentiful.

An obsession with order and neatness will interfere with providing high-quality care; at the same time, continually tidying and restoring order are important to make the environment attractive and functional for children and staff alike. The quality of interactions and play deteriorates in a disorganized environment.

See Supplements: *Ten Essentials to Turning Caring Routines into Prime Times* and *A Note to Staff: Connecting with Infants and Toddlers: Prime Time Opportunities*

Separation and Reunion: Arrivals and Departures

Children's arrivals and departures are not always included in lists of daily routines, but they are important aspects of every child's experience. Actually, the ways children start the day in the program and reunite with their parents later may determine the quality of their day in the program and their time at home afterward.

Arrivals and departures, particularly the difficulty or ease of separation, may also determine the quality of the parents' day. Because arrivals and departures provide parents with the majority of their contact with staff and the program, these occasions play major roles in parents' feelings about the program, staff, and the value of the center's services.

Separation Times Are Prime Times

Helping children and parents arrive and separate should be prime times. Instead, these are often hectic times for a program, when full staffing may not be present and those staff who are present are very busy. Consequently, parents may be overlooked during staff planning. Children's arrival and departure times are likely to be fueled by workday rush hours, so they are controlled more by parents than by staff. Programs should consider providing more staff during these times. If parents have more flexibility, you can encourage them to arrive during off-hours or at other less busy times, when they are likely to receive more focused attention from staff.

Separation and reunion need to be thought of as family affairs—that is, as times that are important to the feelings and well-being of children *and* parents. There is great value in talking with parents when they drop their children off, even when the conversation is very brief. A system of exchanging written information between staff and parents on a daily basis is valuable too, as long as it supplements but does not substitute for face-to-face communication.

Sometimes separating at the beginning of the day can be more painful and difficult for parents than for their children. Parents' feelings are as legitimate as their children's, and need to be acknowledged with respect and empathy. This may be challenging for teachers, who sometimes feel that the parents' behavior and feelings are making separation more difficult for their children and life more difficult for the staff. When such feelings occur, remember that child care serves families.

Separation on a Daily Basis Separation distress recurs throughout children's and parents' experiences, sometimes unexpectedly and for no apparent reason. Often nothing can be identified in the home or at the center that is likely to cause distress on a particular day. The likely explanation is that the children's cognitive powers are developing so quickly that even familiar situations seem to change overnight. Separation takes on new meanings, or children develop new understandings of it, and these can cause distress. This is true for adults as well: for example, in new love relationships, people begin to develop new perceptions, understandings, and hopes. When these occur, even a brief separation can become very painful.

Good-byes Are Often Painful Staff need to acknowledge that the pain of separating is real for parents and children. This is so even for a child who has been coming to child care for some time and is apparently settled in. Even when a child knows the teacher and the program, enjoys his time at the program, and at some level knows that his parent will return at the end of the day, the act of parting can still be painful. It may be tempting for staff and parents to deny the reality of such distress.

It is the teacher's job to help parent and child separate. Greeting and welcoming parents and children makes it easier for children to make the transition from home to child care and reassures parents. For children, saying good-bye to loved ones is much easier within the arms of another special person.

Help Parents Separate and Get Off to Work

Encourage parents to plan a leisurely drop-off when possible. Saying good-bye is easier for a child if the parent does not race in and race out and the staff aren't rushing on to other responsibilities. It works best when parents and staff can be flexible and can have relaxed conversations.

Help parents overcome their ambivalence and assist them in saying good-bye. When a child is distressed, parents may feel as if they should not leave until the child has become happy. Sometimes parents are reluctant to leave because they are uncertain about leaving their child in your care—or in any care, for that matter. They may say several times that they are going to leave but then don't; they may actually leave and then reappear. Parents who have difficulty separating require sympathetic assistance from staff, not criticism. Some parents will need gentle but direct advice about leaving if they are clearly floundering and don't seem to know when and how to depart. This does not mean that staff should make the decision for them. Instead, staff should offer to help parents leave at the point when they decide to leave. They may need reassurance that being consistent helps a child adjust. Parents will be reassured when staff call or send them e-mails at work that report how the child is doing. Photos of a happy child are the best reassurance.

See Supplements: *A Note to Parents: How Our Feelings about Transition Can Affect Our Children; A Note to Staff: Helping Parents with Separation;* and *A Note to Parents: Daily Separation*

Try to prevent parents from sneaking out. Parents may be tempted to sneak away without saying good-bye, thinking either that this will be best for their child or that by doing so they will avoid the pain they feel when leaving their distressed child. While showing sympathy for parents' pain, staff should help them understand that it is never best to leave without saying good-bye, because doing so diminishes a child's feelings of trust and security and may in fact cause the child to become even more clingy.

Encourage parents to communicate with you during the day. Parents should be encouraged to phone or e-mail during the day to find out how their child is doing. Staff should see this as an important aspect of building trusting relationships. Reports to parents at these times should be positive and optimistic but honest. If the child is still upset, say so. Reassure the parent that this type of behavior is typical and that things will get better.

Support Children by Acknowledging Their Feelings Staff should help children through hard times by acknowledging their feelings, comforting them, and framing their feelings in words. One of the many things children learn from adults in the early years is what feelings are appropriate in different situations and how to recognize and acknowledge their feelings. Children need to have their feelings validated, not ignored or denied. Simply distracting them to stop the distress is inappropriate unless it is preceded by communicated acceptance of their feelings. Acknowledge their feelings by saying something such as "I know you miss Mama. Are you very sad? Mama's working, and you'll see her after snack. Should we go look for a truck to play with?" instead of "You're okay—let's go play with the truck," which ignores their unhappiness.

Use Rituals and Special Objects to Help Children Cope with Separation A special ritual or routine for the child who is settling in can be comforting, such as helping the child engage in play, waving to the parent from the window, providing a kiss and a hug, or making a comment. "I love you, Sweet Pea, and I'll be back" works for twenty-month-old Elena. Such a routine gives the child a feeling of control, a feeling of "I know what is going to happen now—when Dad leaves, my teacher Mary and I always go over and feed the fish, and then we find a good toy to play with." Encourage the child to play an active rather than a passive role in the separation; this often helps. A structured departure ritual helps many parents and children.

> *Sixteen-month-old Samantha sits in her teacher's arms, and together they open the door for Sam's mom to leave, then wave good-bye and look out the window as she leaves.*

> *In the morning, when the father of two-year-old Ryan is about to leave for work, the two exchange photographs. Ryan gives his dad a picture of him at the center, and his father gives Ryan a picture of him at his desk. In the afternoon, they swap photos again, and leave them at the center until the next day.*

It is natural for children to miss their parents during the day. Children new to the program may be comforted by having an object that belongs to the parent—for example, a scarf or handbag, accessible to them during the day. For some children, this seems to serve as an indication that Mom or Dad will definitely come back. This is a good example of how the minds of young children often work differently from those of adults. We adults know that the parent will definitely come back to get the child, whereas for the child it makes sense that Mom will return to get her handbag! Having a photo of the family in a place accessible to the child can also be reassuring. Staff should talk about the parents with the child during the day in a natural way. Because it is such a positive way to build parent-child relationships, parents should be encouraged to visit during the day if circumstances permit, even if the child is sometimes distressed by a second separation. Parents who make time for their children should not be discouraged from doing so. If separation distress is prolonged, parents and staff should work together to resolve any concerns.

"Soon" to Whom? It is tempting to comfort children by saying that Mom or Dad will be back soon. *Soon* is a word that has many interpretations, depending on the context in which it is used. Children have a good sense of sequence (what comes after what) but not of time. "Your birthday will come soon" may mean in two weeks; "Lunch will be here soon" may mean within thirty minutes; and when the teacher says, "We'll have to go inside soon," she may mean within five minutes. Consequently, saying to a child whose parent is due an hour from now that "Daddy will be here soon" can easily be misinterpreted and result in frustration and disappointment. For an older toddler, it may help to list all the events that will take place before the parent arrives. Saying, for example, "We will have a nap, then some afternoon tea, go outside, and when you have had a little play outside, your daddy will come" gives a more accurate sense of time to that child than *soon*. The safest thing is to avoid using the term.

Reunions: They Do Love Parents Best!

While it is more likely that attention will be given to separations at the beginning of the day, reunions at the end of the day can be equally challenging. By the end of the day, staff, parents, and children are all likely to be tired. Children have usually had enough of being in a group, and as other children start going home, they begin to anticipate the arrival of their own parent. It may be difficult to be one of the last to leave. It is important to provide interesting things to do, as well as extra cuddles and attention, for those children who are not among the first to leave. Saving some special books or play materials for the end of the day can make the time special. In fact, the end of the day, if staffing is adequate and tasks are organized, can be a pleasant time, with fewer children and therefore more opportunity for prime times.

At the end of the day, parents no doubt want an enthusiastic welcome from their child and a smooth and pleasant exit from the center. Unfortunately, for a variety of reasons, it doesn't always turn out this way. Instead, on some days several other possibilities await parents:

- A child may look up briefly from what she is doing when her parent greets her and then return to her activity.
- A child may see his parent and become distressed.
- A child may act up and engage in behavior that isn't allowed.
- A child, even one who did not want to stay in the morning, may actively resist going home.

None of these situations is what parents have in mind! They may think, "Well, it's happened—she likes these people better than she likes me; she'd rather be here than at home." The teacher may be thinking the same thing. The parents may be embarrassed, sad, or annoyed. Of course, it is not always possible to say what a child's behavior means, but the least likely interpretation is that a child actually would prefer staying with the staff. Children do love parents best. Parents need to know that.

From an adult point of view, here are some possible reasons that children may act peculiarly when parents arrive to pick them up:

Ignoring the parent. Ignoring a parent or giving only a cursory greeting may actually be a sign that a child has adjusted well, feels secure at the center, and knew all along that her parents would return. In other words, this behavior could simply mean "I'm glad to see you, but it's no big deal. I knew you'd come back, and so I'll just continue with what I was doing." This is not unlike the way older children respond to being reunited with their parents, or the way adults respond to short-term separations from people they are close to.

Falling to pieces. Falling to pieces may be a natural reaction to the sight of the person a child is closest to. It takes a lot of internal strength and stamina for young children to cope in a group all day, and by the end of the day, most of them are tired and their resistance is low. Seeing that most special person, the one they know will love them no matter how awful they act, may serve as a cue to act the way they feel—and the way they feel is *miserable*. Again, this is not unlike the way we adults cope with difficult days: we maintain a professional demeanor with colleagues and exhibit our best behavior, but when we get home with the people we are closest to and feel the most comfortable with, we let it all hang out and act the way we feel. Parents need to be reminded that children consistently behave better with staff than with them; they save their worst behavior for their parents. It's like that old song: "You always hurt the ones you love, the ones you shouldn't hurt at all."

Acting out. Acting out (behaving in unacceptable ways, breaking rules, and defying limits) may be the young child's way of testing an interesting situation. Two people, the caregiver and the parent, are now setting limits and enforcing the rules. "So who's in charge?" Unable to articulate the question with words, the toddler asks the question through behavior. In fact, unless it is talked through with parents and expectations are made clear, parents will be uncertain and may think that while the child is at the center, the staff are in charge. The staff, thinking parents are responsible when they are present, may be looking critically at parents and wondering why they don't give the child some much-needed discipline.

Resisting going home. Resisting going home may mean one of several things: The child may be expressing a wish for the parent to stay awhile in this place that is special, to just be here. The child may be resisting the sudden end to an engrossing activity. The child may be saying something such as "I didn't like it when you dropped me off here rather abruptly this morning, so I'm not going to go easily tonight." The toddler, anticipating the hustle and bustle that may characterize his world from this point until bedtime, may even be voting with his feet to stay in this child-centered place!

It is important that staff share these possible explanations with parents so that parents understand that their children are complex little social scientists who use their behavior to experiment with how the world of other people works and what their place in it is.

See Supplement: *A Note to Parents: End-of-the-Day Reunions: They Do Love You Best!*

Clear and Honest Communication with Parents Letting parents know clearly through daily communication that you enjoy caring for their children and that you know about the positive aspects of their children's day makes separation and reunion easier. Communication should

- *be honest, but sensitive.* For example, "Lisa cried this morning when you left, but she quickly started playing with the blocks. She loves building things these days; she mentioned you again at naptime when she said, "Mommy at work."
- *convey that the staff like the child.* For example, "We love seeing Daniel smile; he gets such pleasure out of everything."
- *share the child's struggles in a tactful way.* For example, "Ralston was hesitant about playing with the paint today, but once he started rolling the toy car wheels through the paint, we couldn't get him to stop."
- *avoid staff problems and struggles.* For example, don't say "If we had more staff, it wouldn't be so hard to deal with Sanji's constant crying."

Bottles, Meals, and Snacks

For children and most adults, what is more primal and important than eating? Mealtime and snacktime demonstrate for babies the level of quality in a program. The pace, atmosphere, and extent to which such times are used as prime times are a good indicator of the overall quality of the program.

For young babies, in addition to satisfying nutritional needs, these times offer opportunities to have the teacher all to themselves, to be talked to, to be close. The nature of the feeding experience changes greatly during the first year of life. The close, peaceful time when a primary caregiver holds a drowsy infant and gives a bottle soon changes to a much less serene, more exciting scene after the infant begins eating solids. Eventually, the child takes over much of the responsibility for self-feeding, sometimes with more enthusiasm than skill.

For older infants, feeding also becomes a time to find out about new tastes, textures, and colors; to begin learning the names of common objects; to begin mastering the difficult job of holding a spoon, maneuvering it into the dish, balancing it all the way from the dish to that elusive target, the mouth, and then savoring the wonderful feeling of having mastered a new skill. Learning to hold their own bottles and eventually to manage spoons and cups represent early and important achievements in babies' increasing efforts to master their worlds.

For older infants and toddlers, eating becomes a much more social situation involving peers. Mealtime and snacktime for older babies and toddlers are moments for eating, learning, and practicing small-motor skills; developing a sense of independence and autonomy; and having conversations. Staff need to be relaxed and flexible if eating times are to be pleasant.

Involving Parents in Making Decisions about Feeding Their Children

Parents are likely to have definite views about feeding their children, and should be involved in almost all decisions about feeding infants, including timing, breast milk or type of formula, and all aspects involving the introduction of new foods. The supplement *Individual Peronal-Care Plan for Infants and Toddlers* will help you elicit important information from a child's parents.

It is important to know what the food practices and patterns are at home. Knowing when and how much an infant ate before coming to child care each day allows the primary caregiver to anticipate cues of hunger. It is essential with young babies to keep an up-to-date record of foods introduced along with any special information, such as food allergies. Written records of daily food intake should be provided for parents. The introduction of new foods should occur at home, or, if at the center, following a discussion with and after receiving permission from the parents. Parents need to let staff know when a new food has been introduced at home. Foods should be introduced one at a time, in case there is an allergic reaction.

Parents may have special food requests because of cultural or religious background, a child's medical condition, or personal preference; these should be respected. Parents may be asked to provide requested special foods for their infant when these cannot be provided by the center.

Breast-feeding should always be encouraged, and the parent should be made to feel welcome and provided with the degree of privacy requested.

See Supplements: *Making Prime Times of Toddlers and Twos Mealtimes: A Quick Assessment* and *Ten Mealtime Tips for Toddlers*

Mealtimes are some of the most complex times of the day. In many groups, depending on the age range, there may be young infants who are being bottle-fed or who must be fed solids, infants beginning on finger foods in high or low chairs, and some older infants or toddlers at tables. Without planning and preparation, mealtimes can be chaotic, disordered, and no fun for anyone. If possible, feeding should always occur individually or in small groups and in a relatively quiet place, especially for those children who are easily distracted by what is going on in the room. Whenever possible, meals should be attended to by the child's primary caregiver.

Individualized Schedules What determines when an infant gets fed?

- Information from the child's parents.
- The primary caregiver's knowledge of the child's typical schedule.
- Cues from the child.

Cues may include crying or fussiness, finger sucking, or sucking movements. It is likely that young babies' schedules will be different enough that all babies will not be hungry at the same time. This should be encouraged rather than discouraged.

Individualizing schedules may extend mealtimes, which are prime times for caring and learning, by reducing the number of babies eating at one time, thus allowing for more personal attention. Meal routines depend on careful planning, and all staff members should know their roles. Post all information on routines, including individual children's eating habits, so that nothing essential is locked away in an absent staff member's head. Specific information about each child's eating habits helps to make mealtimes personalized and comfortable for infants. For example,

- at mealtime, six-month-old Tara prefers to eat all of one food before eating another. She likes to eat all her squash before her teacher feeds her green beans.

- nine-month-old Jonah doesn't like the feeling of a plastic bib tied around his neck, so staff always use a cloth one.
- at nine months, Yasmina is determined to feed herself, and does a good job, but she makes a real mess. Yasmina's mother gets upset when she becomes too messy. Her teacher puts an extra shirt over Yasmina's clothes so she can eat with joy and her clothes stay clean.

Many programs believe in individualized schedules in theory, but do not individualize them in practice. (Most often this is due to the need to maintain staff-child ratios, accomplish staff chores, or enable children to go on walks or participate in other activities instead of sleeping through them.)

But occasionally, individualizing is put aside to promote positive group experiences at mealtimes. In most instances, except with older twos, this makes little sense. There is more value in the individual pacing of sleeping and eating schedules than in group engagement. Yes, older infants and toddlers often enjoy the sociability of mealtimes, but they have similar experiences throughout the day.

Holding Bottle-fed Infants Bottle-fed babies should be held while they are drinking, because this is an important time to be close. A child being given a bottle deserves the same one-to-one attention and physical closeness that a breast-fed child receives. It is a time when babies and primary caregivers bond.

Staff usually have a preferred arm for holding infants and feeding them their bottles. However, if a baby is drinking breast milk, try switching the child from the cradle of your right arm to the cradle of your left arm, and vice versa, to better emulate true breast-feeding. This movement from side to side is what a child experiences when drinking directly from her mother's breasts, and such shifting allows an infant to receive cuddling and warmth on both sides of her body.

When children choose to hold their own bottles or more than one child is being fed at a time, some physical and eye contact are particularly important. For example, place an infant who is holding her own bottle next to you on the floor while you feed another child. Propping up bottles is not acceptable. Help children holding their own bottles into a more upright position because drinking in a reclining position is bad for the health. *Note:* The difficulty of feeding more than one infant at a time is one reason to value individualized schedules.

Assisting Infants with Self-Help If a child rejects a food one day, make a mental note of it and perhaps reintroduce the food in a week or two, at a time when the child is hungry. To the extent possible, let the infant determine the pace of feeding. Some babies eat and drink very quickly and efficiently, whereas others are slower and may lose interest or become tired before they have had enough to drink. Babies should not be rushed, and staff should respect their differences.

Some young babies like to assist the teacher with feeding by putting their hands into their mouths, which may already be full of solids, or by grabbing or batting at the spoon. Feeding solids is no job for the fastidious, especially when babies are learning to feed themselves. By the end of the meal the child, the chair, and the teacher will often need to be wiped clean. Feedings must be free from unreasonable demands on the child for neatness, attention to the job, and persistence. As in other areas, staff should take their cues from the child's interest in grabbing the spoon or from signs that the child is ready to learn to self-feed. Obviously, finger foods are easier to manage than spoons.

Of course, some ability to self-feed or interest in trying does not mean that the baby is ready to manage the entire job, and these behaviors should not be viewed as signals for adults to withdraw their attention. Some children will need help with feeding because they may tire of the challenging task before they are full.

As with all aspects of infant feeding, parents are partners in determining what the best practice is for their baby. Family and cultural practices differ with regard to the value of encouraging infant self-help.

Toddler Mealtimes

Toddlers may find it difficult to move from active play to sitting down and eating. It will help if the transition from playing to eating is peaceful and proceeds at a gentle pace, so children can relax. Calming music, minimal wait times, and calm adults will help the children relax.

Mealtimes are one of the few necessary group times for toddlers. Ideally, waiting at the table is kept to a minimum, and children can sit down when the food is ready to be served. When waiting becomes necessary, fingerplays, singing, or storytelling can occur instead of waiting for group times to offer these experiences.

Children should be allowed to leave the table when they have finished. To require them to wait until everyone has finished only creates frustration for those who have finished, and often puts pressure on those children who need more time.

The Physical Setup at Mealtimes Children (and adults) respond better to pleasant and comfortable atmospheres for eating than to bleak ones. The goal for mealtimes is to encourage competent, developmentally appropriate self-help and a bit of conversation. How do you support children's competence?

Appropriate child-sized furniture. Table heights should be slightly above waist height, and chairs should allow feet to touch the floor—having your feet dangling in midair is very uncomfortable. If you need convincing, try sitting on a bar stool with no rungs, let your legs dangle, and you will find that very soon you start to squirm, wrap your legs around the legs of the stool, and generally feel uncomfortable. Toddlers are not very good at sitting still during the best of times, and uncomfortable furniture only makes doing so harder.

Chairs with solid sides give young toddlers support and help them remain seated. Individual feeding tables that surround the child with a rimmed tray work well for older infants and young toddlers. Putting older infants or younger toddlers at tables with other children too soon may require more mastery from them than they possess. Managing eating, staying balanced in a chair, and relating to others close by may be too much to ask of a one-year-old! If toddlers must eat on carpet, a sheet of plastic or linoleum under the eating area makes cleaning up easier.

Small groups of children. Putting toddlers in small groups with plenty of space between helps them avoid interfering with each other and helps mealtime go smoothly. Although what is on someone else's plate may be identical to what is on theirs, toddlers may not be able to resist another person's food if it is within arm's reach.

Appropriate child-sized plates and utensils. Toddlers can learn to hold cups and spoons and to serve themselves. Spoons should have short handles and rounded bowls. Cups should be sturdy, wide-bottomed, and wide enough in circumference to require two hands to hold. Dishes with sloping sides rather than flat plates make self-feeding easier because food is confined. When toddlers decide they want to use cutlery, it helps to be able to push the food against the side to get it onto the spoon. Very small pitchers give toddlers the chance to practice pouring. At the end of the meal, they can take their dishes to a cart.

Providing spoons is a good idea, but staff should be relaxed about whether fingers or spoons are used. Eventually all toddlers become interested in the fine-motor activity of getting food on a spoon and maneuvering it into their mouths, so they don't need any pressure to eat properly; they will take control of this important activity when they are ready to feed themselves. (See discussion about self-help below.)

Food. Food should be simple but attractive, nutritious, familiar, varied, and tasty. Foods should reflect the cultural backgrounds of the families in the center and those in the local community. Familiar foods can be comforting to a child who is coping with a very different environment.

The amount children eat will of course vary, but a general rule of thumb is one serving spoonful for each year of age. Initially, small servings, with the possibility of seconds if they are wanted, work best.

Offering some finger foods on a plate—for example, pieces of fruit or biscuit—gives older toddlers the chance to make their own choices rather than having the food placed in their dish. Desserts should be treated as normal parts of meals and should be nutritious. This does not necessarily mean that they have to be offered along with the main course, but staff should avoid giving the message that the last course is the most special.

Assisting Toddlers with Self-Help Toddlers require the patience, good humor, and appreciation of the staff when their emerging skills and drive to experiment come alive at mealtime. The behavior that may drive us crazy—dropping, flinging, smearing, and imitating each other, for example—is a result of their drive to learn. Allow for some messiness, which, after all, is really experimentation, exploration, and sensory play and is essential if they are to move beyond this stage of eating to a more socially acceptable phase.

The importance of toddler self-feeding and the use of utensils (as opposed to wasting food and cleanliness) is again an area in which family and cultural practices vary. It is important to ask families for their views and to come to an understanding about the program's approach.

Encouraging an "I Can Do It!" Attitude in Toddlers

Focus on modeling good manners rather than teaching them. While toddlers begin to learn some conventions about eating, a focus on learning table manners is inappropriate. Table manners and eating conventions, which vary tremendously among cultures, are eventually learned through modeling. Trying to teach them too rigidly and too early will only result in frustration for the adult and the child.

Gently discourage excessive messiness, but allow for exploration. Staff can gently discourage excessive messiness and outright playing with food during mealtime, but children need to explore textures, and the mess that inevitably results from efforts at self-feeding should be accepted.

Remind children to eat. Staff may need to remind children who are distracted by what is going on around them that they need to eat, lest they forget that they are hungry and that the business at hand is eating. Excessive playing with food is usually a sign that children are not hungry or have had enough to eat.

Expect and prepare for spills. Spills and inadvertent messes should be responded to very matter-of-factly. A wet cloth and sponge should be kept nearby.

Encourage but never force children to try new foods. Children should be encouraged to try new foods but should never be forced to eat or to try foods that they vigorously resist. Ultimately, the right of refusal must be honored. Giving children choices builds autonomy and reduces power struggles.

Do not use food as a reward or a way to quiet children. Care should be taken not to use food to appease, occupy time, or reward children for behaving well (for example, "Eat your squash or no dessert").

Remind toddlers to sit down. Out of consideration for hygiene and safety, toddlers should be required to sit down to eat. They will need regular reminders, because they get irresistible urges to wander while they are eating, but most of them will eventually get the idea if reminded.

Sit down and enjoy eating with the children. A well-planned routine and reliable timing should allow staff to sit and eat with the children. Adults should avoid hovering over children while they eat and assisting from above or behind their heads. As toddlers finish, individuals or small groups can be cleaned up rather than making everyone wait at the table. Once again, individualization is the key.

See Supplement: *Making Prime Times of Toddlers and Twos Mealtimes: A Quick Assessment*

Snacktimes All of the suggestions about mealtimes apply to snacktimes as well, except when teachers choose to serve snacks informally to older infants and toddlers. Instead of having a particular time of day when all activity stops and all children sit down together, you can bring out snacks and invite children one by one or in small groups to come over and have some.

Diapering, Toileting, and Washing Up

Children learn good health habits in the same ways that they learn most things: through modeling, demonstration, patient coaching, and consistent expectations. Children are children, with runny noses and hands in mouths (and other places), and we don't expect them to become models of good sanitation. Nevertheless, parents and teachers can patiently instill healthy habits in them that will last a lifetime.

Assembly-line diapering and toileting are never good practices. Would you want to be treated that way? Check regularly to see if diaper changes are needed, because some babies seem not to be bothered by wet or soiled diapers and will not indicate that they need changing. As a reminder for staff, it may make sense to specify on the daily timetable several times when staff will ensure that each child has been checked. These should only be reminders, not diapering schedules.

Waiting is not something toddlers do well. In addition to planning routines to allow for individualization, use the environment to engage children who have to wait for the toilet or for a diaper change. Create a space near the bathroom or changing counter for a small interest area—perhaps a water table, paper attached to the wall for coloring with markers, or a music center with songs on CD.

Diapering

It takes organization to make diapering proceed smoothly for child and adult and become a successful, one-to-one prime time.

Typical diapering of a responsive baby may involve the following learning experiences:

- *Motor activity:* kicking vigorously while the teacher removes confining clothes.
- *Cognitive activity:* the teacher's face disappears behind the diaper and then reappears.
- *Language activity:* the teacher and the baby talk, coo, and laugh together.
- *Social activity:* the teacher talks to, laughs with, and gently touches the baby, responding to smiles and babbles.
- *Sensory experience:* the feel of being free of clothes; the soft, fresh, dry feeling of a new diaper replacing a cold, wet one.

Most important, the gentle manner of the adult and a need met without delay increase a baby's trust in people.

As described in chapter 6, an ideal changing area supports relaxed, focused, and sanitary diapering. There should be ample counter space with a 3-inch lip; a sink with a spray large enough to bathe a child; and ample, compartmentalized storage an arm's length away. The changing routine should be posted at the changing area. Proper sanitation is critical, including following universal precautions for bloodborne pathogens. Chapter 13 on health and safety details the changing routine.

Toilet Learning

Staff have to work together to avoid putting too much emphasis on toilet learning. There may be pressure to get toddlers to reach this developmental milestone as early as possible. (Admittedly, changing the diapers of toddlers who enjoy a wide range of foods is not exactly the highlight of anyone's day!) However, the process should be undertaken with a minimum of fuss, and treated as just one aspect of a varied program.

When to begin helping a child learn to use the toilet should be a decision made largely by parents, based on signs of readiness from the child and with the teacher's advice, if requested. Cultural expectations vary, and it is important for staff to know about these. Beginning too early often leads to frustration and power struggles between children and adults.

The importance of individualizing the age at which children learn to use the toilet cannot be overstressed. Typically, sometime between sixteen and thirty months, children can be prepared for learning to use the toilet by being taught about elimination and given words for urination and defecation. Parents and staff should respond to individual children's cues and signs of readiness. What are the signs of readiness?

- learning to pull their own pants down
- learning to sit on a toilet or potty chair
- showing readiness by staying dry longer
- showing an interest in the process of using a toilet
- telling you they are urinating or defecating while they are doing it

Somewhere between two and a half and three years old, most children learn to stay dry most of the day. Before this age, there is wide variation in their interests and abilities in toileting, and these should be respected.

A relaxed pace and nonjudgmental approach are essential. Because children are struggling for self-control at this stage, possibilities exist for all the complicated emotions of power, shame, failure, and accomplishment. The teacher's job is to be calm and supportive and to reduce the pressure that children feel. As they show readiness, adults can respond with help and encouragement.

If children are truly ready and adults are relaxed about toileting, then training is not really necessary. Adults need only provide assistance and support over a period of time, and learning will happen. This process is enhanced when toddlers are in a group, where they learn much from each other. They may develop an interest in sitting on the toilet when they see others doing this.

Toilet Training Infants?

Is early toilet training possible? Is it desirable? There are groups promoting the "elimination communication" method. Parents learn the signs that the baby is about to go, and respond to these cues by taking their baby to the toilet instead of the changing table. "Elimination communication" relies on parents' ability to read and recognize the signs that their infant needs to eliminate, much as they learn to recognize that their child is tired or hungry. This method is used in a number of cultures in which there is a great deal of intimacy between parents and infants.

Does it work? It may work if a parent or teacher has the time and focus to intently observe the baby and is able to respond instantly to cues. But the child's muscles and nerves are not mature enough to be able to hold in urine and stool consistently and to relax for spontaneous voiding and stooling. Developmentally, this doesn't usually occur until after they reach two years; earlier than that, children are unlikely to recognize the need to go. The adult is the person who is actually becoming trained.

So is it a good thing? In some families, it may result in a close parent-child bond and a diaper-free child at 18–24 months, much earlier than the average of around 30–32 months. But there is a danger that adults' unrealistic expectations may create an unfortunate power struggle. One positive advantage of waiting is that when toilet learning occurs later on and children have control over their bodies, they can own the activity and the success.

Children can learn on potty chairs, on child-sized toilets, or (less preferably because of their size in relation to the child's size) on standard toilets with potty inserts. What is important about the equipment is that it is accessible, comfortable, and easy to sanitize. Clothing that is easy to pull up and down provides greater autonomy for children.

See Supplements: *A Note to Parents: Good-bye Diapers, Hello Underwear—Ideas for Successful Toilet Training* and *A Note to Parents: Toilet-Training Accidents: Successful Ways to Cope*

Hygiene

Hygiene is critical to good health, and good hygiene habits should begin when children are very young.

Washing Up Washing up is another prime time that is sometimes forgotten. When they need washing, children are too often treated as things rather than as people. Washing infants' hands or helping toddlers and twos wash should occur throughout the day: when they enter the room, before and after meals, after diapering, after handling pets, or when their hands are soiled or come into contact with bodily fluids (their own or those of other children).

Helping children clean up is a time for talking about body parts. It is also a time when toddlers learn important self-help skills if they are allowed to use soap, paper towels, and washcloths independently. Be sure to use a clean washcloth or paper towel for each child. Child-height sinks with soap dispensers and faucets easily manipulated by small hands and mounted 16 to 18 inches off the floor, make both the teacher's and the child's job easier. If a stool or platform is necessary, make sure it will not slip and that it can be easily cleaned underneath.

Sponge bathing can be a wonderful time for many infants, although some seem to find it uncomfortable. A slow, gentle sponge bath, during which the child is told what is going to happen next and is allowed to anticipate and help, is as educational and positive an experience as a child can have in group care. "Doesn't the water feel nice and warm? Would you like to hold the sponge?"

Covering Coughs and Sneezes Older toddlers and twos can begin to understand and practice the basics of good hygiene by starting with coughs and sneezes. Covering their coughs, sneezing into tissues, or coughing or sneezing into the inside of their elbow can become habits as children grow in self-control.

Toothbrushing Children aged two and older can begin to learn toothbrushing. While toothbrushing at the center is not something of critical importance for toddlers, programs that can incorporate it into mealtime routines in a relaxed and sanitary way should do so. Not only does the ritual of toothbrushing build up the habit of good dental hygiene, it also gives children a sense of accomplishment.

Sleeping and Resting

Moving into and out of sleep are times when children are often vulnerable. If there is ever a time to be relaxed and gentle with children and to treat them as individuals, it is while helping them move into and out of sleep. It is a time for individualized schedules and patience, which give toddlers some leeway in settling down and waking up while they make the transition to a group nap schedule.

If sleep times are based on the needs and styles of each child and variations are expected from day to day, napping becomes a natural, even pleasant activity, rather than an arena for confrontation. Some babies go to sleep easily and predictably, whereas others resist sleep from a very early age and have difficulty making the transition from one state to the other. Even with babies of the same age, there is great variation in the amount of sleep they require and when they require it. Sometimes knowing that a child needs a nap determines what the teacher does more than how the child acts. Some babies need a wind-down period of quiet play before they can relax and go to sleep. Cues that children are sleepy include rubbing eyes, showing disinterest in play, clinging to adults, sucking thumbs, putting their heads down, becoming clumsy, slowing the pace of activity, becoming easily frustrated, and becoming fussy for no apparent reason. Tension, excitement, or change may affect children's ability to sleep.

Like adults, toddlers vary in energy level and pace. Some children need to crash in late morning, whereas others will not sleep for more than an hour midafternoon. The program's space and schedule need to take into account children who don't fit the 1:00–3:00 naptime.

Parents may have concerns about their child's sleep pattern, both its timing and amount. Some may want their child to sleep more, others may want them to sleep less, and still others may want their child placed on a regular schedule. This is another matter about which communication is critical. Parents and staff must work together to make children's entire day go well.

Gently into Sleep

When possible, put infants down to sleep the same way their parents do at home—rocking or patting, for example (see "Back to Sleep" in chapter 13). Such gestures not only reassure children, they help parents retain a sense of control and continuity. Even as adults, we have our own individual going-to-sleep rituals. Of course, it is not usually possible for staff to engage in a one-to-one extended ritual with each child, so they should avoid locking themselves into them, lest other children become restless and impatient while awaiting their turn. For toddlers on cots, naptime may include back and temple rubbing and, after naptime, helping children slowly rejoin the world.

It is common for some babies to react to being put down for a nap by crying vigorously. Babies differ a great deal in their ability to quiet themselves after becoming upset. Consistent, predictable handling and allowing babies to work things out with appropriate support will help them develop the ability to put themselves to sleep. There is no rule for how long babies should be allowed to cry before being picked up again; staff have to know the individual.

Sometimes children who cannot sleep will rest quietly on their cots for a while with a few toys or a book as quiet entertainment. Some babies want a special comforting object—for example, a blanket—when they are going to sleep. Others find music calming. Darkening the room may also help.

Some babies wake up slowly and need a gradual reintroduction to the brightness and activity of the playroom.

Cribs and Cots

While it would be nice to plan the crib-to-cot move based on parents' preferences, the timing is often based on when children are scheduled to transition to a toddler room. But they must show signs of being able to stay on their cots and not fall off or get up to roam around. This decision should be made in consultation with parents.

Young children should view sleep and rest times as relaxed and comforting times. Cribs or cots should never be used as places where children are put for misbehavior. The use of sleep or rest as a kind of punishment teaches children that it is something unpleasant and should therefore be avoided or resisted.

Transition Times during the Day

Good infant and toddler programs minimize or eliminate the need for extended group transition times when activity ceases and the group moves from one segment of the day to another. Individualization of the program means that there will be few if any times when everyone is doing the same thing, when children are waiting or roaming around aimlessly, or when play abruptly stops to prepare for some other activity. *There is no place in a good program for infants and toddlers to be lining up.*

When materials or equipment have to be put away, children should be warned ahead of time that they will soon need to finish what they are doing. Enlisting the help of toddlers should be done in a gentle and inviting way, with sensitivity to the limits of their interest in tasks and without expectation that they will have the same interest in restoring order that adults do! Toddlers can be encouraged to help put things away, but there is no point in forcing it. With an individualized program, there should be few times when everyone has to stop their play and either help or sit idly by while a major cleanup takes place.

Ongoing tidying up by staff minimizes the need for massive cleanup.

Beginning Care: The First Few Weeks

The first few days and weeks in child care set the tone for the total child care experience. Beginning group care for the first time or even coming to a new place after experiencing another program is unsettling, at the least, and can be very frightening for children and parents. The routines for children described in this chapter and the approaches suggested for working with parents in chapters 4, 7, and 8 are designed to build relationships that help children, parents, and staff withstand the wear and tear of group living. From the beginning, parents need to feel that the staff want to form partnerships with them on behalf of their children. Parents will not know what is expected of them in such areas as providing information, asking questions, being present in the center, helping out, and making requests. They will be guided by what they are first told and, more important, by what messages they receive from their daily experiences. Let parents know what to expect of their children while they settle in, and let them know the value of a smooth transition from home to child care each day, even after their children have been enrolled for some time.

Children Adapt to Change Differently

Some children show obvious discomfort when new to the group. Others show very little. These reactions also vary by age. An eight-week-old baby is very different from an eight-month-old or eighteen-month-old child. Staff and parents need to remind themselves that it is perfectly normal and expected that babies who are over about six or seven months of age may react negatively to new people. There are great individual differences among babies, just as there are among adults, and some adapt more easily and quickly than others to change, new people, and new places. Some just need time to adjust, whereas others actively resist and protest any significant change. Even when they show no obvious signs of discomfort or fear, young infants notice everything that is different—sights, sounds, and handling. These changes can be stressful.

Some children seem at home right away and become involved in activities, whereas others want to observe from the sidelines for a time until the place becomes familiar. Staff should not necessarily interpret lack of involvement as a sign that children are unhappy and therefore need to be pushed to participate. Staff should continue to interact with them and to invite participation without pressuring, allowing individual children to adjust at their own pace.

Encourage Parent Time in the Room

Parents should always be strongly encouraged to spend some time in the room with their child during the first few days, gradually tapering off as the child's stay is extended. Ideally, when parents first leave their infant or toddler, they will leave for a short time, several hours perhaps, rather than for a whole day. The interval that parents are away should be long enough that the child has a chance to get over being distressed and to become settled. While this is not always possible because of work commitments, parents who have a choice should understand that it is beneficial both for them and for their child. When parents stay around for a few moments in the morning, it helps their child settle in, increases their own sense of

---

Inserimento

In Reggio Emilia, *inserimento* is the term used for the welcoming and settling-in period of transition and adjustment for the child and family. In contrast to typical American concerns about parents spending time to ease child separation, *inserimento* conceives of the period as one of forming new relationships between baby, parents, and staff:

"During the families' very first days at the infant-toddler center, during the period of transition or *inserimento*, we, as teachers, want to create a truly welcoming environment within each classroom and throughout the infant-toddler center. We want to communicate a sense that children and parents are welcome, expected, and considered important. We ask the parents to be present with the children at the beginning because this very first transition needs to be supported by them. We want this first beginning to be shared by parents, children, and teachers together so that we can better support the children in this very important moment when new relationships are formed at the infant-toddler center. The transition in small groups of children and families has to be a strategy that creates a sense of communication and reciprocal knowing between children and adults and among adults; teachers and parents together construct this sense of belonging and trust. . . .

"I think it is very important for teachers to listen to children from the beginning. . . . It is important to listen carefully and observe what the children are communicating to us through many languages such as gestures, facial expressions, or other signals that may show curiosity, interest, or well-being. Together we also have to share and understand signals like crying and other moments of difficulty." (Gandini 2001, 57)

belonging to the center, and builds a closer partnership with staff. When parents spend time in the room, they:

Become familiar with the staff. Parents get to know the staff, become familiar with how they work and care for children, and learn how the day goes in the room. The result is that when they are not present, they have more of an idea about what is happening than the tiny slice of life at arrival and departure.

Chat with the staff about their child. Staff have the chance to chat with parents and extend the discussion begun at intake about their children's likes and dislikes and to observe how the parents actually care for their children while feeding them, helping them go to sleep, comforting them when distressed, and disciplining them. In short, it helps staff become knowledgeable about children much sooner than they would without parental contact and they become more aware of the care that children are familiar with.

Reassure their children. Having someone familiar and loved around makes it much easier for children to adjust to new people and a new place. Children will be less fearful of a strange person if that person is observed relating in a friendly way to their parent(s).

There is no best plan for settling in all children. The important thing is to have a plan developed by the parents and staff that takes into account the needs of parents and children. Everyone should understand that despite a plan, there may be ups and downs and it may be a matter of days for some babies and weeks for others before it all goes smoothly.

Occasionally parents and some staff may support the notion that the best way to orient children is to throw them into the deep end and let them sink or swim, a harsh metaphor that allows for no gradual introduction: just bring them to child care, leave them there, and get it over with. While it is true that it is possible to drag the process out so long that it becomes counterproductive, taking into account the perspective of children and the need to help them feel comfortable and secure benefits everyone—children, parents, and staff—in the long run.

Understanding the Parents' Perspective Putting a child in child care, especially a baby, and especially on a full-time basis, is a big decision for parents. For many parents, the decision is made reluctantly. Even when they are sure that it's for the best, they usually have some doubts and uncertainties. Staff need to remember that while they may know they are competent and worthy of parents' trust, parents have no reason to believe that until their first child has been in the program for a time and until they have experienced for themselves how good the staff are. This may take a long time.

Loving Good-byes

"I can't believe it. Allison's mom saw I had my hands full, but she wouldn't just put Allison on the couch or the rug—she had to hand her to me. Parents are so irrational!"

This teacher is right—they sure are. But so are we all. Love is not rational. How do you feel about parting and separating from loved ones? When you travel by airplane, even for just a few days or weeks, do you let your spouse/lover/parent just drop you off and pick you up at the curb, which is eminently practical? Or do you want them there for that final good-bye as you go through security? A physical exchange of the baby is important to many parents; their level of concern is a wonderful thing. Programs need the staffing and resources to accommodate such exchanges.

Because infants and young toddlers cannot report on their day or on how they are feeling about child care, parents may be anxious.

Some parents will come to the program certain that they are doing the right thing, whereas others will be ambivalent. It is important to remember that some who use child care would much rather stay home with their children, but they do not have that option. Some parents are subjected to criticism about their use of child care and may feel that using child care means they are not good parents. To make things more complex, whereas some parents are aware of their feelings and may communicate them to staff, others are not comfortable doing so or may not even be aware of their feelings.

Parents may feel ambivalent about the fact that their child apparently separates easily. While professionals may see a smooth separation as a good thing and be critical of parents who, as staff often see it, "seem to want to make their child cry when they leave," parents may instead believe that a no-tears, happy separation means that their child has become more attached to the primary caregiver than to the parent. Staff need to help these parents see that this is not the case, and reinforce the program's position: the staff will not and do not want to replace parents in their children's affections.

Some centers find it helpful to have new parents talk not only to the director and to staff but also to parents who have used the center for a time and are familiar with it. Other parents may give a different perspective on the center from that given by staff. New parents may feel more comfortable asking other parents some of their questions.

Settling in and separating is a big deal for parents and children and should be treated as such by staff. Written policies as well as initial and ongoing communications with parents should make clear that, although staff will try to form special relationships with the child, they do not see themselves as taking the parents' place. Discussed in much greater detail in chapters 8 and 9, the partnership with parents is critical and depends on parents knowing that staff believe parents are the most special people to their children and that child care outside the home does not change this.

Welcoming New Families

Once enrolled, each new family needs a relaxed and warm, reassuring welcome (see chapter 9 and the Supplement *Twenty Steps to a Full Partnership with Parents*). The first few weeks are critical in establishing a partnership between parents and staff, but staff must take the lead. While staff may sometimes feel intimidated by parents, and new staff may not feel totally confident about their own skills, they need to remember that parents may be equally intimidated by staff and by the newness of the situation.

The lead teacher or primary caregiver assumes responsibility for introducing parents to all homebase staff; homebase staff need to make an effort to put parents at ease. The primary caregiver should be assigned and all necessary preparations carried out before the child's arrival:

- Send a "what to expect on the first day" note.
- Assign and label the cubby and the crib or mat.
- Put a picture of the child and parents on the cubby and elsewhere in the room.
- Make a welcome sign with the child's and parents' first names, and post it prominently.

- Post all information necessary to individualize the child's care.
- Begin a portfolio to collect observations and artifacts.
- Prepare a note for parents.

See Supplement: *Twenty Steps to a Full Partnership with Parents*

No Surprises As with other potential sources of parent stress or unhappiness, the best time to begin helping parents work through an issue is before they are in the middle of it. Talk about separation and other painful issues during the parent intake conference, and prepare parents for what might happen. Have a handout available on the subject, even if the same material can be found in the parent handbook.

The First Six Weeks In the first few weeks, the primary caregiver should make an extra effort to ask parents how things are going for them and their child. At the third or fourth week, the director should write a note asking the parents how things are going and extending an invitation to talk. At the end of six weeks, the primary caregiver should give the parents a six-week questionnaire, read the response, and pass the form on to the director.

See Supplement: *New Family Homebase Satisfaction Questionnaire*

Transitioning Children and Parents to the Next Age Group

Sooner or later, children move to the next age group. For some children, parents, and primary caregivers, this is a time of anxiety. For others, it is a time eagerly anticipated and there are few tearful looks back.

As discussed in chapter 6, successful transitions depend on good planning and recognizing and understanding the perspective of children and parents. Some principles to implement and make sure families know about include:

Make the experiences fit the child regardless of the child's age. Sometimes children cannot move up until there is a space in the next group. These children get stuck in a group waiting for an opening. Sometimes children get moved up a little earlier than expected to take advantage of an opening. Because of this, it is important to make sure the group works for children at both ends of the age spectrum.

Keep in mind that moving up does not indicate advanced development or intelligence. Care must be taken to avoid giving the impression that there is something competitive about moving up, that it is like graduation or some indication that the child has superior skills and abilities.

Facilitate ample child and parent visitation in the new room. Most children need more than a few days of visiting a new group to feel comfortable. Preparing for transitions is an ongoing process that begins a long time before the actual move.

Be flexible when considering transitions. Parents should get the message that while the child is ready to move, if the child doesn't have to move or cannot move because of age or development, or if family situations dictate the timing of the transition, staff will adapt the situation to fit the child.

Ensure that there are ongoing relationships between rooms—a community of caring. Ideally, even in large centers there is a sense of community and relationship between different age groups and different rooms. A child in an infant room comes to know the toddler staff and the toddler rooms through visiting, shared activities, and shared common space. The same is true of toddlers and twos or preschool groups. Through the newsletter and other communications, parents come to know the people and the aspects of life that their children will soon become a part of.

Keep a "children ready for transition" list. Once a child is actually ready to move, regardless of whether space is clearly available, or a few months before a move is anticipated, staff in the two rooms or modules should make a concerted effort to begin the transition. This involves the child visiting (accompanied by the primary caregiver) sharing activities, and making other efforts to gradually become familiar with the new room. At the same time, parents should be made aware of the approaching transition and be given information on the child's soon-to-be new homebase.

Implement a plan for the last few weeks. When the move date is known, the current primary caregiver and the newly assigned primary caregiver should get together and map out a plan for daily visiting in the new group, and ensure that parents have all the information necessary to feel secure about the move. Each child's and parent's needs are different.

Make the child and the family feel welcome in the new group. The first week in the new room should follow the lines of the first week for any new child and family: picture on the cubby, welcome sign, first-day note to parents, and a reassuring phone call if necessary. It is also important for many children to keep in contact with the old room. Cold-turkey transitions are not a good idea.

See Supplements: *A Note to Parents: How Our Feelings about Transition Can Affect Our Children* and *A Note to Staff: Transitioning Children and Parents to the Next Age Group*

Leaving the Program

Just as it is important to be sensitive while helping children and parents settle into the center, staff should work with parents when a child is going to leave the program to ensure a smooth transition. For some infants and toddlers, gradually decreasing the amount of time spent in the program may be helpful, if parents' schedules allow it. It is important to acknowledge the feelings of the teacher and parents as well as the child; these often include a sense of loss and, in the case of parents, anxiety about the future. Good programs keep in touch, at least for a while, after a child leaves a program.

A Final Word: Thoughtful Routines—Every Child, Every Day

Planned, well-prepared routines are essential if all the tasks associated with good child care are to be accomplished. Good routines can integrate noninstitutional, personalized care if staff focus on the goal of the routines: consistent, high-quality, personalized care. Routines need to be continually monitored and evaluated, and consistency should be balanced with flexibility. When routines become mechanical and mindless, tasks may get done, but essential quality gets lost.

Exercises

1. List what a child learns while being: (a) bottle-fed and (b) diapered by a primary caregiver.

2. Observe naptime routines at a center. How are individual differences acknowledged and accommodated?

3. Describe a transition you have made in your life (for example, to middle school or high school, camp, or college) and consider its parallels to child care transitions. Discuss this with one or two other adults who went through the same transition to discover individual differences between your reactions.

References

Gandini, L., and C. P. Edwards, eds. 2001. *Bambini: The Italian Approach to Infant/Toddler Care*. New York: Teachers College Press.

Giovanni, N. 1985. "let's take a nap," In *Spin a Soft Black Song*. New York: Hill and Wang / Farrar, Straus & Giroux.

Chapter 13

Safe and Healthy Environments for Infants and Toddlers

εxcellence *A safe and healthy environment designed for infants and toddlers allows exploration and challenge without threat of serious injury or illness. Parents and staff have confidence in the equipment, materials, and continuous monitoring of the physical environment, and in the careful caregiving practices and appropriate supervision of children.*

Certainly infants and toddlers are the most vulnerable children in group care. They are new to the world, and their bodies and minds haven't accumulated the experience yet that will eventually allow them to live safely among unseen germs and accidents waiting to happen.

Daily living in a group setting presents continuous opportunities to exchange germs and incur injuries. The more personal, warm, and relaxed the setting, the more possibilities for transmission of disease. The more encouragement of active sensory and motor learning, the more apparent risk of injury.

Can child care centers be safe and healthy for their youngest inhabitants? Yes—with an understanding that *safe and healthy* does not mean a sterile world free of germs, bumps, and bruises. A safe and healthy center is one that minimizes children's exposure to illness and the threat of injury as it provides for developmental needs.

Health and safety issues often test the strength of the parent-staff partnership because there are many issues for which there is no easy answer and no clear compromise but plenty of strong feelings. The mutual respect, trust, and empathy that parents and staff build up are often required when issues of illness, exclusion, and accidents arise.

Health and safety practices are highly regulated in most states and Canadian provinces. There are differences of opinions and emerging research that make definitive recommendations seem increasingly unlikely. Licensing and health guidelines should be the first place to look when evaluating policies and practices.

Health Policies and Practices

Babies are highly susceptible to respiratory and gastrointestinal illnesses. Their immune systems are undeveloped, and their drive to mouth and touch everything leads to frequent transmission of potentially infectious matter. It is common for many babies in group care settings to have eight or more illnesses during the first year of life: five or six respiratory (ear, nose, and throat) and two or three gastrointestinal (stomach and gut) infections. In a program with poor health and sanitation practices, children may experience even more illnesses. Children in group settings with good health practices probably experience about the same number of illnesses in their childhood as children cared for primarily at home. More of those illnesses occur in the first two years if children are in group care because they receive earlier exposure to more children.

Healthy settings depend on a number of factors:

- Thoughtful, strictly followed sanitary routines that are regularly monitored and evaluated. Careful diapering and toileting procedures, regular hand washing, and proper food handling are key.
- Careful attention to the stress placed on each child and to adaptations and routines that can reduce the stress.
- Policies on staff and child illness and contagious conditions that minimize the likelihood of infection.

Essential Resources

The following resources are comprehensive references on health and safety in infant and toddler programs:

- *Caring for Our Children: National Health and Safety Performance Standards: Guidelines for Out-of-Home Child Care, 2nd Edition* (2002) is the most thorough guide to good health and safety practices. It is available online and is updated regularly. See http://nrc.uchsc.edu.
- *Model Child Care Health Policies* (2002) is a support tool for site-specific policy development in out-of-home child care facilities. Created for easy adaptation to various child care settings, this guide includes essential information on health and policy topics such as sanitation, emergency plans, discipline, field trips, authorized teachers, and much more. It also includes appendices containing hundreds of forms, charts, and checklists. It is available in book form or on disk from the National Association for the Education of Young Children (NAEYC).
- *Healthy Young Children: A Manual for Programs* (2002) is another terrific resource on creating a safe and healthy environment.

Child Care Licensing, Public Health and Public Safety Departments, and NAEYC Accreditation Most health and safety policies and practices are regulated by state child care licensing, local public health and fire regulations, and building codes. NAEYC accreditation has criteria on health and safety as well. Regulations vary; what is considered a best or acceptable practice is usually a subject of some debate and changes over time. It is always important to uncover the regulations or suggested practices that apply to a particular program. *Note:* The content of this chapter may reflect standards either higher or lower than those in a particular jurisdiction, or may not reflect information or research published after 2007.

Partnering with a Health Consultant When at all possible, infant and toddler programs should have a relationship with a health professional familiar with early care and early childhood education. The consultant can advise the center on health, sanitation, and safety issues and visit the program regularly to support the staff and make any recommendations for improved health and safety practices.

CPR and First Aid Training At least one staff member who is trained in cardiopulmonary resuscitation (CPR) and first aid should be present on-site at all times. Although the cost of training may make it prohibitive, training all staff in CPR and first aid is highly recommended. Even better is to offer training to parents as well.

Daily Admission and Exclusion

When is an infant or toddler too ill to be in child care? This is probably the most difficult and sensitive health issue, and it often becomes a source of tension between parents and staff. It is a concern to everyone: the parent, who may not be able to go to work; the staff, who must care for the sick child; the child, of course; and the other parents, who look at each sick child as a potential threat to their own child's health. Parents and teachers, even different teachers in the same program, may look at the same child and reach different conclusions about his health. The parent who can't afford to miss another day of work sees a recovering child who will do fine. The teacher who has to care for an unhappy child or one who has diarrhea sees an obviously ill child who should be at home.

There are always issues over how strict or flexible exclusion policies should be. *Model Child Care Health Policies* and *Caring for Our Children,* a set of guidelines developed by the American Academy of Pediatrics, are designed to ensure the health of the individual child and all children in the group. These guidelines point to a critical fact: *Exclusion often has little effect on the spread of many respiratory and gastrointestinal diseases because children are infectious before they exhibit the symptoms of the disease.* This is a point that cannot be emphasized enough. By the time the ill infant or toddler is actually showing signs of illness, the germs are in general circulation. Excellent sanitation will reduce the spread, but given how infants and toddlers explore the world, some germs will spread no matter what we do.

> *Exclusion of children with many mild infectious diseases is likely to have only a minor impact on the incidence of infection on other children in the group. Thus when formulating exclusion policies, it is reasonable to focus on the needs and behavior of the ill child and the ability of the staff in the out-of-home child care*

setting to meet those needs without compromising the care of other children in the group.

—*Caring for Our Children* (2002, Standard 3.065 Inclusion/Exclusion/Dismissal of Children)

Exclusion is necessary at times for certain conditions: chicken pox, measles, rubella, mumps, and pertussis are highly communicable diseases for which routine exclusion is warranted. It is also appropriate to exclude children with treatable illnesses such as conjunctivitus or pinkeye until treatment is received and until treatment has reduced the risk of transmission. The presence of diarrhea, particularly in diapered children, and the presence of vomiting increase the likelihood of exposure of other children to the infectious agents that cause these illnesses.

Undiagnosed rashes and infestations such as head lice usually warrant exclusion until treatment is under way, but check for current research available from the American Academy of Pediatrics (www.aap.org).

Daily Admission Procedures An important part of the greeting process is assessing the suitability of the child for group care that day and communicating with parents about any current medications the child may be taking. Children arriving with symptoms that suggest possible illness should be referred to the supervisor for possible exclusion. If children who may be mildly ill are admitted, it is advisable to request that their parents leave phone numbers where they can be reached (if they lack cell phones) and that they call or e-mail during the day to ask about their children. Each day, ask parents to indicate on the daily experience sheet (see Supplements: *Infant Daily Experience Sheet* and *Toddler Daily Experience Sheet*) any special health considerations and to fill out request forms if any medications need to be administered. Staff can use the daily experience sheet to inform the parents about their child's disposition and behavior throughout the day and about any medicine that was administered.

When a Child Becomes Ill at the Center It is always important to contact parents as soon as possible when a child shows signs of illness, even if these are minor and the child does not have to be sent home. Let parents know the child's condition. Understand that parents are not always able to drop everything and leave work. It is wise to save your requests

"That Child Does Not Belong Here!"

Teachers usually prefer strict, black-and-white policies that exclude children, particularly infants, with most signs of illness. Many centers have policies with no flexibility. One instance of diarrhea, one temperature reading over 100 degrees, and it's "Please come pick up your baby immediately," even if it's 2:00 PM and the child is due to be picked up in a couple of hours, or if the child is resting comfortably. A program that looks at the child in the context of his or her family and recognizes the realities of parents' lives will understand the guidelines cited above, and behave differently. "Able to participate in the program" is a key factor that calls for judgment. In a program that accommodates differences in pace and schedule and has cozy places to pause, a mildly ill child may not require exclusion.

When parents relay the advice of their pediatrician, different standards may come into play: parents may be advised by one pediatrician to keep their child out for five days because of a particular illness, whereas a different pediatrician may counsel that it is acceptable to send the child to child care once the fever breaks or once the child is on medication and can participate in the program. Because pediatricians have a range of views and expertise on out-of-home child care, it is valuable to make it known to parents and staff that the books *Model Child Care Health Policies* and *Caring for Our Children* are the program's definitive resources.

for immediate pickup for conditions that warrant it. Some mildly ill infants and toddlers simply need to rest, snuggle, and be kept comfortable until parents arrive; others are unable to be comforted even with one-to-one care. Ask a parent to come immediately if teachers are unable to keep the child comfortable or if the child's condition requires exclusion.

Common Health Conditions of Infants and Toddlers

High fevers: Infants and toddlers run high fevers more easily than adults. Fevers over 102 degrees are common in response to viral infections of the throat and ears. It is important to pay attention to temperature and behavior in determining the seriousness of the situation. A child with a high fever who is acting sleepy and apathetic is much more of a cause for serious concern than an irritable child who is fairly active and eating well. In very young infants (children under four months), fever alone may pose a serious medical condition, and these children should be referred to a medical professional immediately.

Vomiting, diarrhea, and dehydration: Dehydration is a life-threatening condition, particularly in infants. The body needs fluids, and vomiting and diarrhea can quickly cause dehydration. Outward signs of dehydration are dry mouth, dry and papery skin, crying without tears, and sunken eyes. Teachers and parents should always take diarrhea and vomiting seriously.

Middle-ear infections: Anyone who works with babies soon becomes aware that ear (and to a lesser extent, throat) infections are common in infants and toddlers, both as by-products of colds and on their own. The telltale signs of pulling on ears and running a fever should lead to a doctor's visit, because ear infections can lead to permanent hearing loss. Some toddlers who have many infections eventually have tubes put in their ears to drain fluid and pus.

Avoid feeding children prone to ear infections while they are lying on their back. Be alert to any sign of hearing loss or problems with speech. After children have had tubes inserted in their ears, keep water out of their ears to avoid introducing new infections.

Common colds: Colds are infectious diseases caused by hundreds of different viruses. Germs are everywhere, spread by people before any symptoms become evident. Colds are not caused by cold weather, rain, drafts, or insufficient clothing. It is possible to get one cold after another from different viruses, and they can last for up to two weeks. Runny noses, stuffy noses, coughs, and low fevers are symptoms. Rigorous sanitation and limiting contact with large populations may reduce the number of colds a child is exposed to, but unfortunately no matter how much care is taken, colds tend to run through group living environments.

continued on next page

Common Health Conditions of Infants and Toddlers, *continued*

Diaper rash: Prolonged wetness, rubbing from wet diapers, and urine and feces combine to create diaper rash. The best treatment for diaper rash is to let the child sleep without a diaper and give sitz baths containing a small amount of vinegar. Change diapers often and increase the child's intake of liquids, particularly acidic fruit juices such as cranberry.

Thrush: A severe form of diaper rash that can also occur in the mouth, thrush is caused by a fungus and appears as milky patches on the skin. It requires antifungal medication.

Teething: Teething occurs around six months and may cause irritability, biting, and drooling. Drooling often leads to diarrhea, since the extra saliva causes babies to overdigest their food. Chilled rubber teething rings or teething biscuits are good chewing alternatives. Massaging the baby's gums will soothe the child (wash your hands before and after).

Other Health Issues of Concern

HIV/AIDS, Hepatitis B, and bloodborne pathogens: Bloodborne pathogens are bacteria, viruses, and other disease-causing organisms carried in the blood and sometimes in other bodily fluids. The best known are human immuno-deficiency virus (HIV) and hepatitis B virus (HBV). Every center should have written policies on the admission, exclusion, and care of children with HIV, HBV, and other viruses transmitted by blood. The likelihood of transmission of HIV between children in child care does *not* warrant exclusion from child care or disclosure of the condition. The latter violates the child's and family's privacy. Because of the seriousness of illnesses like HIV and HBV and the fear they generate, up-to-date knowledge about transmission and universal precautions is critical. The center should take care that all staff and parents understand the issues.

The most important response to the threat of bloodborne pathogens is to adopt the universal precautions recommended by health authorities for handling exposure to blood and blood-containing body fluids. *Caring for Our Children,* available online and in book form, details the proper use of nonporous gloves, hand washing, and disinfecting blood-contaminated areas.

Sudden Infant Death Syndrome (SIDS): Infants are susceptible to Sudden Infant Death Syndrome, also called *crib death.* It is an invisible killer and the leading cause of death between infants aged one month to one year. SIDS is most common in children two to four months of age and in male infants. It is more common during the winter months. Research has shown that putting infants to sleep on their back reduces the incidence of SIDS, and all infants

continued on next page

Common Health Conditions of Infants and Toddlers, *continued*

should be placed to sleep on their back, unless the family signs a liability release also signed by a physician. (Even with such a release, the procedure may not be allowable by licensing.) If children are physically able to turn over, they should be allowed to continue to sleep in the position they find comfortable. Eliminating pillows, heavy blankets, and large stuffed animals from cribs and barring the use of beanbag chairs for infants is also important. If an infant sleeps with a light blanket, the teacher should place the infant at the foot of the crib with the thin blanket tucked around the crib mattress and reaching only as far as the infant's chest.

The "back to sleep" campaign has been very successful in reducing the incidence of SIDS. Sharing information about sleeping positions with parents is important. There is ample information available for families on the National Institute of Child Health and Human Development Web site at www.nichd .nih.gov/sids/sids.cfm/.

Because today infants are spending more time sleeping on their backs and upright in seats and car seats, it is important for them to have supervised tummy time two or three times a day, when they can be placed on the floor on their stomachs to strengthen their arm, shoulder, and neck muscles.

Child Abuse and Neglect: Teachers in all infant and toddler programs need training to identify possible cases of child abuse or neglect and to learn how to address such issues sensitively with families. Teachers are mandated reporters, legally required to notify child protection authorities of instances of suspected abuse or neglect. The potential ramifications of reporting on the parent partnership and staff relationships are so serious that knowing what behaviors or patterns of behavior, injuries, and conditions suggest abuse or neglect is critical. Training is often available from public health departments.

Children's Health Records

Every child in group care should have a health appraisal form completed by a pediatrician. Most states require this form to be placed in a child's file before or shortly after enrollment. NAEYC accreditation standards require a completed physical within six weeks of a child's enrollment in a program. This form must confirm the child's good health and suitability for group care and verify that required immunizations have been completed. With the exception of religious exemption, all immunizations must be kept up-to-date. It is a good idea to require annual health appraisals for each child.

The health appraisal form should also provide complete information on any special health needs. If special care is required, a detailed special care plan should be developed by the parent, pediatrician, and center.

Medications

The administration of medication is an important aspect of child care health practices and requires careful attention to detail. Infants and toddlers can easily be harmed by the failure to develop and follow proper procedures. While some centers refuse to give medications and require parents to come to the center to do so, that practice seems unfriendly to children and working parents. Rules outlined by the state licensing authority must be followed. Important aspects of a medication policy include:

- Medications for children must be accompanied by a medicine authorization form signed by the parent that includes the child's name, doctor's name, dates for administering the medicine, dose, name of medicine, reason for medicine, and name of pharmacy. Some states may require a doctor's signature as well.
- Medicine must be in the original pharmacy container. Parents should request a second container that is also appropriately labeled from the pharmacy so the original can remain at the center.
- Nonprescription medicines should be administered following the same procedure. Because many over-the-counter medications do not have standard doses for children under age two or three and instead recommend consulting a pediatrician, a note from a child's pediatrician for that medication or preparation should accompany the parent's permission. *Note:* It is important to use sunscreens to prevent sunburn. Parents' permission and instructions for use are required for sunscreen just as for any other over-the-counter medications.

Each center should work out a medicine administration routine and training that ensure:

- Appropriate locked storage of medicine, easily accessible to the teacher but not to children, and refrigeration of many medications. *Note:* Even medications in the refrigerator must be stored in a locked container.
- Teachers carefully trained in administering medication, with a written performance evaluation of the five right practices for administration of medication updated annually by a health professional. This training also includes awareness of center policies and immediate recording of administered doses in a log and on parents' daily experience sheets.
- Schedules structured whenever possible so that medicine can be given around lunchtime and in late afternoon (that is, three times a day, with parents administering the first dose).
- An individual authorization form for each medicine. No medicine should be given without an accompanying authorization form.

It is critically important to ensure that the center's policies conform to the health and licensing rules governing the center.

Staff Health Issues

In order to ensure that staff are both physically fit for their jobs and free from contagious illness, employees should successfully complete a pre-employment physical, including a Mantoux or chest x-ray testifying to the applicant's good health and a satisfactory immunization record.

Staff health records should include results of the pre-employment physical, physical updates at regular intervals, records of work injuries, instructions for special needs, and emergency instructions that include information on the staff member's special health needs (for example, allergies), physician, and contact instructions. Again, licensing rules may contain additional requirements.

Staff Illness Staff illness is often nearly as sensitive an issue as child illness, given the frequency of exposure to illness and the difficulty of finding substitutes. Staff should not attend the center if they are known to be in the contagious stage of an illness, if they are physically unable to perform their job because of illness or injury, or if their job is likely to exacerbate an illness or injury.

Management of Infectious Disease

The critical factors in infection control are rigorous hand and mouth hygiene, sanitation routines, and appropriate response when an infectious condition is discovered.

Every center should have a trained staff member capable of reviewing symptoms for infectious illness to supplement the basic training of all staff. When a contagious condition is suspected, the parent must be contacted and the requirements for the child outlined (including when exclusion is necessary and when return to the center is possible). Center policies should detail the steps needed to prevent the spread of the illness (for example, identifying ill children, disinfecting the environment, and changing sanitation practices or routines). When appropriate, a sign notifying all parents of exposure, symptoms, and precautions for this illness should be posted, or a letter should be sent to parents.

Sanitation Policies and Practices
Young children need to learn about health and safety as a natural consequence of daily care. Infants and toddlers will begin to learn about proper hand washing and sanitary practices in food handling, meal preparation, and toileting procedures from well-planned routines. The curriculum for older toddlers can include developmentally appropriate information about germs and other important health topics. Workshops and written communications for staff and parents are excellent vehicles for health and safety education.

Hand Washing Hand washing is the single most critical aspect of good sanitation in an infant/toddler program. In a good program, staff feel as if they are washing their hands all the time. To protect against the spread of illness, all participants at the center should wash their hands with soap and running water on arrival, every time they enter another room or reenter their own room, before eating and after toileting, after diapering or assisting children with toileting, when cleaning or administering medication, after nose blowing, following contact with any body fluids or contaminated material, after handling animals, and after engaging in water play with the children. It is also highly recommended that all adults, including parents, visitors, and other center staff, wash their hands upon entering the center and before entering an infant or toddler room. A poster on proper hand-washing techniques at each hand-washing sink can serve as a helpful reminder.

Children should wash hands upon entry, before and after meals, after being diapered or using the toilet, after coughing or sneezing, after visiting other rooms, after handling animals, and before and after contact with body fluids. Teachers should wash the hands of babies and help older children, teaching them proper techniques. Toddlers who can stand at a sink should follow the same hand-washing procedure as adults, with the teacher assisting them and ensuring that they complete all the steps. For infants who cannot stand or be held at the sink, teachers should wipe their hands with a wet paper towel with a drop of liquid soap, then wipe their hands with a clean, wet towel until all the soap is gone, and finish by drying the children's hands with a fresh towel. Wipes and hand sanitizers are not advisable when running water is available but may be the best alternatives for room-entry sanitizing for adults and for outdoor use.

Using Latex Gloves Latex gloves are necessary under certain conditions:

- while changing the diaper of a child who has diarrhea or a very messy diaper
- while changing the diaper of a child with gastrointestinal illness
- when contact with blood-containing fluids is likely (especially if a teacher's hands have open cuts or sores)
- while cleaning materials or surfaces contaminated with body fluids such as blood, vomit, or feces.

Gloves should be removed by pulling them off from the wrist and turning them inside out to prevent further contamination. Gloves should be disposed of in a hands-free, step-on container, or in a plastic bag when teachers are on the playground or off-site. After the removal of gloves, teachers must wash their hands vigorously, using the hand-washing procedures outlined above.

Wearing gloves is *not* a substitute for hand washing. It is not necessary to use gloves for every diaper change. In fact, it may even be harmful to sanitation, because staff may forget that gloves only protect hands. If staff touch other surfaces while wearing gloves, they may contaminate those surfaces.

Staff should always bring latex gloves on trips and to playgrounds to be used in case of injury.

Diaper Changing Even in the best-designed facilities, it is a challenge to diaper children without contaminating the surroundings. In developing the routine, consider the following:

- Disposable diapers should be used unless a child has a medical condition that requires the use of cloth diapers.
- Diapering should take place only in designated areas.
- A poster outlining the correct diapering procedures should be displayed at the diaper-changing table.
- Diaper-changing areas should be sanitized (sprayed with bleach solution or other disinfectant) after each use and allowed to air dry. Soiled areas must be cleaned with hot, soapy water, wiped dry, and then sanitized.

Diapering Routine

All diaper routines should be adjusted to the particular setting, but the essential steps are similar:

1. Wash hands and gather supplies needed for changing, including a change of clothes if necessary.

2. Put a clean sheet of diapering paper (for example, nonporous examination or computer paper) on the table.

3. Place the child on the changing table. Always keep a hand on the child.

4. If gloves are needed, put them on before continuing. *Note:* Gloves should be required in instances when contact with blood or gross contamination is likely.

5. Remove and double-bag soiled clothes and put them out of reach of the child. Remove the diaper. If using a disposable diaper, fold it inward and place it in a covered, lined, foot-operated can. If it's cloth, double-bag it and place it in the container, out of reach of the child and away from clean clothes.

6. Cleanse the diapered area of the child with wipes or a wet paper towel and dispose of the wipes in the can. Clean away urine and stool, wiping backward from front to back and using a new wipe each time.

7. Powder or cream the diapered area only if requested by a parent.

8. Wipe your hands using a disposable wipe or paper towel, and use another wipe to clean the child's hands.

9. Re-diaper and clothe the child.

10. Wash the child's hands at the sink. If the child is too young for this, use an additional wipe and follow the handwashing procedures for infants.

11. Remove and dispose of the diapering paper.

12. Wash the changing table and pad with soapy solution, then sanitize and air dry them.

13. Wash your own hands again, using the paper towel to turn the faucet off.

14. Record diaper changes on daily experience sheets or in the journal. Note diaper rashes or uncommon contents.

- All diapering supplies should be kept near the changing table and out of children's reach.
- Nothing—not toys, clothes, or supplies—should be placed on diaper-changing surfaces, even briefly.
- Used diapers and diapering materials should be placed in a container with a tight-fitting, hands-free lid that is kept closed and inaccessible to children.
- Straps and restraints should not be used while diapering, and a hand should always be kept on the child.

Diaper creams and powders are not necessary for most children and are actually discouraged by many health professionals, although parents may wish to use them. If used, they should not be shared among children. It is important to prevent inhaling powders and cornstarch.

If an emergency arises when a teacher is changing a child, the teacher should place the child in a safe place, on the floor, or take the child with her.

It is important to keep in mind that diapering is a prime time during which eye contact, play, conversation, and contact are important.

Toileting Toilets should always be kept visibly clean and be disinfected daily. Health authorities strongly recommend *against* the use of potty chairs because of the risk of spreading infectious disease. They are banned in some states. Unfortunately, some centers find it necessary to use them. Wooden potty chairs should be avoided because their porous surfaces make them difficult to clean. After each use, potties should be emptied, cleaned, and disinfected by staff wearing latex gloves. Great care should be taken to avoid contamination in the process of cleaning them. Potties need to be cleaned in a utility sink not used for other purposes.

After accidents in which clothing becomes contaminated, double-bag the clothing and send it home with the child.

Naptime Hygiene Infants should have their own cribs and toddlers their own cots or cribs, plus blankets that are labeled with their names. Crib sheets will need to be changed frequently, and mats and cots should be sanitized weekly. Bumper pads (if used) should be laundered every two weeks. Blankets should be washed weekly or when soiled.

As we've already noted, cribs or cots should be separated by at least 24 inches or by a barrier that prevents transmission of infectious material. (*Note:* The authors believe that a recommendation of 36 inches between cribs or cots is both unwarranted and unrealistic—the play space of children simply becomes more compressed.)

Save Money: Use Bleach

There are a number of commercial disinfectants available, but chlorine bleach and water is as effective as any of these and often more effective than sanitizers claiming to kill germs. Before using any other product for cleaning, the state licensing agency should be consulted.

Use ¼ cup of bleach per gallon of cool water. Mix daily, and throw out any unused solution. *Note:* Disinfectant kills germs by oxidation, so it is effective only when the surface is allowed to air dry. Wiping dry after use negates the disinfectant's effects. The solution is not harmful to skin.

Washing Clothes and Toys Children's soiled clothing should be bagged in plastic bags until it can be washed at home or at the center.

Once a toy or cloth item has been mouthed by a child, it should be removed from circulation until it has been sanitized or laundered. Toys may be sanitized in a dishwasher or washed in warm soapy water, dried, then sprayed with a disinfectant and air dried. Each room should have a system of separating contaminated toys from clean toys. A dishwasher for toy washing near infant and toddler rooms (which are often located near the washer and dryer) is a great help.

Cover Your Coughs and Sneezes As noted in the previous chapter, coughs and sneezes are a major route for transmitting infectious materials. Teachers should always cough or sneeze into a tissue, or into the inside of their elbow when no tissue is available. Toddlers can begin to learn these habits if adults model and gently coach good hand and mouth hygiene.

Nutrition and Health

Ensuring adequate nutrition and sensible food policies and practices is important for healthy development. Guidelines for healthy nutrition are widely available. *Healthy Young Children* (2002) is a good resource. Here are a few guidelines to consider:

- Programs that prepare and serve foods should post menus for families and also make copies available. Menus should also be kept on file.
- Teachers should feed infants whenever they are hungry, but avoid feeding them as a form of comfort.
- Infants should not drink cow's milk until twelve months of age.
- Toddlers should drink whole milk between the ages of one and two years.
- Only 100 percent juice, not exceeding four ounces per day, should be served to infants and toddlers. The excessive intake of juice and fruit-flavored juice drinks is a factor in childhood obesity, and children need to learn that water is the best beverage to drink when thirsty.
- Juice should not be placed in bottles.

Food Allergies

Food allergies occur in 2 to 8 percent of children and are often first discovered during their time in infant and toddler care. Allergic reactions can range from mild skin or gastrointestinal symptoms to severe, life-threatening respiratory and/or cardiovascular reactions. Detailed care plans and ability to implement such plans to treat reactions are essential for all food-allergic children.

> *Successful food avoidance requires a cooperative effort that must include the parents, the child, the child's health care provider, and the child care staff. The parents, with the help of the child's health care provider, must provide detailed information on the specific foods to be avoided. In some cases, especially for children with multiple food allergies, the parents may need to take responsibility for providing all the child's food. In other cases, the child care staff may be able to provide safe foods as long as they have been fully educated about effective food avoidance.*
>
> (*Caring for our Children* 2002, Standard 4.010 Care for Children with Food Allergies, 154)

All adults who may care for a child need to be constantly aware of the child's food sensitivities and allergies. Information from parents about each child's food sensitivities should be posted and clearly visible to new staff and substitutes. Staff need to be trained in recognizing and responding to allergic reactions.

Food Handling and Mealtimes

Disease is easily transmitted during food preparation and meals unless strict sanitary procedures and continual monitoring are observed. Most important:

- Procedures for bottle and food preparation, feeding, storage of food, and cleanup should be detailed in writing, then posted and monitored by a health and sanitation professional.

- From a health standpoint, food handling and diapering should be carried out by different teachers. Because this is often not possible, it is critical to keep the two functions distinct and separate by distancing changing areas and food areas and by rigorous hand washing. For a healthy center, teachers must learn to think of any casual transition between the two as taboo.
- Food, juice, and milk should be stored appropriately. All partially used food and drink should be discarded. Any spills should be cleaned up with hot, soapy water and the area disinfected.
- Food spills during mealtime should be wiped or vacuumed up immediately.

Feeding: Breast, Bottle, and Baby Foods

Infant feeding should be based on parents' instructions. The best food for infants is breast milk, and teachers need to be supportive of mothers who wish to nurse their children. There should be a comfortable place that meets each mother's requirements for privacy to nurse and to pump breast milk. Careful procedures for the handling and storing of breast milk and other bottles is very important. Because of the possibility of transmitting HIV and other viruses, it is critically important to have procedures such as color-coding bottles and careful monitoring to prevent children from sharing bottles. These systems will make it much less likely that a bottle of breast milk will end up being drunk by the wrong child.

Because of the range of parental preferences and individual differences, even centers with food programs usually ask parents to send food from home. Unfortunately, there is no consensus on the best way to handle formula brought by parents—should the parents or the center prepare the bottles? To ensure each child's health and safety, licensing regulations should be adhered to, along with the following guidelines:

- Accept only formula in original containers, and reconstitute it according to package directions or use bottles prepared by the child's parent.
- Prepare formula in bottle warmers or Crock-Pots, using water heated in bottles to the child's preference. *Never* heat bottles in a microwave oven. Microwave heating is uneven, and a bottle warm to the touch may contain scalding milk that permanently damages the child's esophagus (which is about the width of a straw in a young baby).
- Label bottles and caps with each child's name.
- Do not place solid foods in bottles.
- Color-code bottles of breast milk.
- To preserve nutritional components, gently mix but do not shake breast milk.
- Do not store defrosted breast milk for longer than twenty-four hours.
- Discard unused prepared formula at the end of each day.
- Refrigerate all prepared bottles.
- Keep partially used bottles at room temperature for no longer than one hour and do not put them back in the refrigerator for later use. Keep bottles out of the reach of other children.
- Place used bottles in a basket clearly labeled USED BOTTLES.
- Never serve commercial baby food out of the jar. Use a serving dish and a cover. Date and refrigerate open jars of baby food and use the contents within forty-eight hours of opening.

- Record the type and amount of food each infant consumes and give that information to parents each day.

Foods to Avoid

Teachers should not serve infants solid food or fruit juice unless the child's health professional recommends an alternative feeding practice and the parents agree. Infants and toddlers should not have hot dogs unless they are sliced in half the long way and then sliced again in very small pieces. Teachers should avoid giving children whole grapes, nuts, popcorn, raw peas, hard pretzels, raw carrots, and any food cut larger than ¼-inch squares for infants or ½-inch squares for toddlers.

Dental Health

Good oral care starts at birth. Even before children have teeth, infants' gums can be cleaned with a soft infant toothbrush and water. With parents' permission, teachers should wipe an infant's teeth and gums with a disposable tissue after the child eats or drinks anything except water. For children older than one year, teachers should provide an opportunity for brushing teeth. Fluoride toothpaste should not be used until two to three years of age. At about two years, children can be taught to brush their teeth on their own, but they will still need an adult to assist and to ensure that all their teeth have been cleaned. When toothbrushing is not possible, drinking water after meals helps to remove food particles from teeth.

Baby-bottle tooth decay is caused by giving an infant or toddler a bottle of milk, juice, or other liquid (besides plain water) as a pacifier during naptime or at bedtime. Pediatric dentists suggest that children be offered juice only in cups.

Thumb sucking or pacifier use generally presents no dental health or developmental issue unless a child continues beyond five years of age and into the onset of permanent teeth.

A Healthy Environment

Some of the important environmental properties that help improve the health of young children include:

- good ventilation and lots of fresh air
- draft-free temperatures of 65–75 degrees
- adequate humidity (30–70 percent relative humidity)

No Sweets at Birthday Parties?

Baby birthdays are universally prized events. Food policies can often turn into a battleground when adults differ on what standard of nutritional purity applies, what foods should be presented, how much children should have to eat, and what foods are appropriate at celebrations. Expert advice may divide staff and strain the parent-teacher partnership. Centers with food programs may have to balance their concern for good nutrition (low fat, high fiber, few sweets, lots of fruits and vegetables) with ethnic variety, parents' concern about children not getting enough to eat if the food is different from what they eat at home, and, of course, cost. What do you do?

A good program will accept the challenge and strive for balance and moderation. All the occasionally conflicting concerns mentioned above are legitimate. What is important is defusing the righteousness that seeps into attitudes, and recognizing that group life involves compromise.

Birthdays and holidays are times that typically are celebrated with treats. Centers might encourage parents to minimize the use of sweets and empty-calorie foods and to celebrate in other ways, using special decorations and activities. But here, too, a pure policy is at odds with mainstream culture and may lead to more conflict than warranted by the positive effects of the policy.

- a smoke-free environment
- clean air and water, free from toxins and allergens
- a setting free from infestations of vermin
- pets (hamsters, gerbils, guinea pigs, and birds that are not from the parrot family) free from disease and vermin and kept in clean cages.

Get Out, but Take Care

Infants and toddlers should get outside every day for fresh air and physical activity (not just stroller and cart rides), except in bad weather. As is true for adults, layered clothing makes sense; young children typically require only one more layer of clothing than adults.

When taken outside, babies under six months of age should be kept out of direct sunlight and dressed in lightweight clothes that cover their arms and legs because they should not wear sunscreen. They should also wear a brimmed hat. Current advice is that for children over six months, sunscreen with an SPF of at least 15 should be applied to children thirty minutes prior to going outside, even on cloudy days. All children must have a written consent form on file that gives their teacher permission to apply sunscreen.

Shoeless Environments While a matter of dispute (including among the authors of this book) and uncommon outside the United States, shoeless environments are now recommended by *Caring for Our Children* and NAEYC. NAEYC accreditation criteria (Standard 5.c.06) state:

> *Before walking on surfaces that infants use specifically for play, adults and children remove, replace, or cover with clean foot coverings any shoes they have worn outside that play area. If children or staff are barefoot in such areas, their feet are visibly clean.*

Emergency Preparedness

Emergencies do happen, and infants and toddlers are the most vulnerable populations at every center. Each program should have a plan for emergencies that is posted in each room in a central location. Emergencies typically call for evacuation (for example, in cases of flooding, fire, or toxic air) or staying inside in a safe place (for example, during an earthquake or tornado, or in other dangerous external conditions). Common emergency procedures include preparing for fire, severe weather, internal or external environmental emergencies, power outages, potential violence, and medical emergencies. An entirely different sort of emergency is preparing for a health crisis like a flu pandemic. Plans should include at least:

- two diagrammed evacuation routes
- instructions for each adult in the room
- evacuation cribs for children under fifteen months
- a gathering place and temporary site following evacuation
- information on how to call emergency medical help
- first aid instructions, including infant CPR
- a complete communications process for exchanging information with families during an emergency.

Both the office and the room should have up-to-date files with staff's and children's emergency information. Each room should have a well-stocked first aid kit that is clearly marked with a red cross to identify its contents. The program should have necessary communications equipment such as cellular phones, personal digital assistants (PDAs), battery-powered radios, and emergency supplies.

Evacuation and Interior Emergency Shelter Drills

Evacuation and interior emergency shelter drills should occur once a month and should be scheduled to occur at times that might present problems, such as toddler naptimes. For safe evacuations and shelter:

- All adults should have assigned roles, with support staff commonly helping in infant and toddler rooms.
- Infants and other nonambulatory children should be transported in cribs designated as evacuation cribs with reinforced legs and wheels (or in a crib substitute, such as a mail cart).
- Blankets, jackets, shoes, and emergency information should be stored in a manner that permits quick removal during a fire drill.
- Designated staff should check each room prior to leaving the building or moving to the safe interior site.
- A designated person should account for each child and adult listed in attendance that day.

Medical Emergencies

Medical emergencies are not uncommon in child care. Emergency procedures should be posted in every room and by every phone. Sufficient staff should have up-to-date training in first aid and infant CPR to ensure that a trained staff person is available at all times. First aid training should include management of dental emergencies. Frequent refresher training is required to sustain a state of preparedness.

A designated staff member should assess all injuries and identify who should administer first aid, carefully following specified procedures. As an example, see the "Guidelines for Handling Medical Emergencies" in the supplement.

A first aid kit should be available in a convenient but secure place and should be well marked with a red cross in each homebase, in the kitchen, at playground doors, in any vehicles, and in the office.

First aid kits and children's emergency information cards should accompany all outings, both to the playground and off center property. A designated staff person should ensure that first aid kits are well stocked.

Procedure for Life-Threatening Emergencies

- Remain calm, render first aid, and call for help.
- Do not move injured or sick persons unless their safety and health are at risk.
- Call 911 for emergency medical services and report the incident, or request that someone else call.
- Stay on line with the dispatcher and provide information as requested.
- Assign an individual to meet the emergency medical personnel to guide them to the location.
- Have someone retrieve from center files the medical release form of injured persons and provide them to the emergency medical personnel upon arrival.
- Assign a teacher to accompany anyone needing hospitalization.
- Notify the designated emergency contact of the ill or injured person(s).
- Insure that the appropriate paperwork is completed.
- Contact the parents or the designated licensing representative to report the incident.
- For progress reports, maintain communication with the teacher assigned to stay with the ill or injured parties.

Reporting Injuries All significant injuries should be described by an observer on an incident or accident form, with a copy sent to the parents or the injured child. Parents should be called and informed of all injuries. When the injury is more serious than day-to-day scrapes and bruises, call parents prior to pickup and tell them about the injury and the care the child has received. Minor bumps and bruises may be reported in an "Ouch" or "Bump" report (see Supplement: *Ouch Report*), and a copy given to the parents and put in the child's file.

Biting should be treated like any other injury. If it is minor, complete an Ouch Report. If it is more serious, call the child's parents and complete an incident report.

In the event of a very serious injury or emergency, the parents should be notified either at the same time as the emergency medical service (EMS) or 911, or after the EMS has been called.

Tracking Injuries Preventing injuries depends on having an accurate picture of what is actually happening—where, when, why, and to whom. It is important to maintain a central file of incident reports and not just disperse them in children's files. They should be reviewed regularly and analyzed to identify hazards, problem times or locations, and children who seem prone to problems. Reviewing these can help you take steps to prevent future injuries.

Providing a Safe Experience Safety is, of course, a top priority for every program. Infants and toddlers don't recognize most of the dangers that accompany daily living. Yet if young children are to actively explore, investigate, and use the skills they are so rapidly developing, they will inevitably experience the normal bumps and bruises of childhood that come with exploration and physical learning. The challenge for staff is to strike a good balance between safety concerns and a rich learning environment. Your job is to minimize the chance of accidents, however small, and to make sure that virtually no threat of serious injury or harm can occur in the form of cuts, concussions, and broken bones.

Remember, anything that can happen probably will happen over the span of the hours, days, and years that a program operates. A center with twenty-five infants and toddlers will have more than twenty thousand diaperings in a year. In five years, what are the odds of a child falling off a changing counter if there is no focus on safety? Eliminating accidents depends on several factors, including:

- Staff that are trained to continually think safety and to keep informed about possible hazards.
- An environment continually monitored and evaluated for safety concerns.

Major Safety Hazards

Not surprisingly, infants and toddlers are susceptible to a host of dangers because of their drive to explore the world with their mouths and bodies:

Ingestion (choking, poisoning, internal burns)
- small objects, coins, safety pins, buttons
- small wads of paper
- pushpins (particularly colored ones)
- pills and medications
- toxic plants
- toxic liquids
- plastic bags and balloons
- large food pieces (for example, raw carrots), nuts, popcorn
- foods causing allergic reactions
- too-hot foods and liquids

Strangulation
- necklaces or hooded sweatshirts with strings
- loose bedding and crib furnishings
- entrapment openings from 3 to 8 inches wide
- hanging cords, ropes, straps, loose netting

Falls
- changing tables
- stairs
- stacked storage units, chairs, tables
- platforms, lofts, climbers, couches
- child walkers and stairs

Falling objects
- unsteady storage units
- poorly attached cabinets
- equipment with hanging cords
- heavy equipment or toys stored on upper shelves
- desk- and tabletop items

Cuts, eye injuries

- sharp corners and edges on doors, cabinets, furniture
- sharp objects
- protrusions (handles on windows, knobs, etc.)

Pinches

- doors, cabinet doors, car doors, and windows
- rocking chairs and glider chairs

Burns and electrocution

- electrical outlets, exposed wires
- hot liquids (tap water, coffee and tea, soup, grease)
- hot foods (especially those heated in microwaves)

The Politics of Risk

Infants and toddlers will get bumps and bruises. The world has risks, and fortunately their bodies are designed to withstand the normal insults they receive as they learn to become mobile, active participants in human society. Each program has to draw its own lines on what level of risk is appropriate. For instance, infants and toddlers need to crawl in, on, and over. Carpeted risers and cubes and rocking boats are great for that. Can a child get a bump or a carpet burn from a 12-inch fall? Possibly, but they are built to withstand the common tumbles that result from the exploring they need to do.

It is one thing for us to write that children need to be allowed to explore the world and risk the normal bumps and bruises of childhood. It is quite another to be a teacher talking to the upset parent of a bruised child. Teachers cannot be left to struggle with the issue alone. The program as a whole has the responsibility to help parents buy into a vision of active learning and to trust the program's ability to protect their child from unreasonable risk. Every program needs to decide where it stands on the continuum described here, and conduct open discussions on what is acceptable.

See Supplement: *Ouch Report*

Safety Depends on Staff Awareness It is easy to become desensitized to unsafe conditions. Safe settings depend on staff remaining vigilant about safety concerns and periodically asking others to watch for safety concerns by:

- Checking equipment for rough, broken, or unsafe parts.
- Keeping in mind that babies will use anything available to pull themselves up to stand, to hold on to while walking, and to climb on, so equipment needs to be secure and heavy enough that babies cannot cause it to fall.
- Ensuring that there are proper surfaces under climbing equipment to cushion falls.
- Covering electrical outlets.
- Making heaters and fans inaccessible.
- Installing childproof railings and banisters on stairs and other raised areas.
- Moving medications, purses, and other potentially unsafe materials out of the reach of children.
- Ensuring that floor surfaces, both indoors and out, are nonskid, especially in areas that get wet or covered with sand.
- Having places where young infants can watch or play safely.
- Observing the environment throughout the day for hazards (for example, toys on the floor).
- Observing children's behavior and adjusting the setting to make play safe (for example, eliminating items from the reach of a child).

This vigilance extends to vehicles used to transport children. Transportation safety requirements tend to be regulated by state law. Infants and toddlers should ride in approved safety restraints rated for their weight. Vehicles used for group transportation should be equipped with a first aid kit, a telephone, and preferably be accompanied by a backup vehicle.

Every program should develop a site safety checklist and check it monthly for safety purposes.

Learning from Experience Often a safety concern comes to light because of an accident or a close call. The reaction is often to make a snap judgment about cause and effect to try to solve the problem. This may result in unnecessarily limiting equipment or coming up with a solution that has more negatives than the original conditions. Instead of jumping to a quick solution, ask:

- What happened? What was going on around the incident? Look at the child's behavior and the behavior of other children. Look for crowding, equipment concerns, transition confusion or stress, fatigue, and supervision concerns.
- Was it avoidable? Can the chance of it happening again be reduced?
- Was there a chance of serious injury? If there was, how can the situation be modified to eliminate the risk?

Faulty Logic: You Can Be Too Safe!

It is not unusual for the tunnel vision-logic that seems sensible when applied to child care health and safety issues to break down in the real world. Take the issue of supervising infant crib areas: there are legitimate concerns about SIDS and about leaving children for long periods of time in their cribs. This has led to some states insisting that there be no separate crib areas, to others insisting on separations no higher than a half wall (the height from the floor to the bottom of a crib, or 24 inches), and to yet others stipulating that babies be checked every five minutes. Are such guidelines necessary? Even if these rules are extra cautious, can any harm come from requiring these levels of vigilance?

Yes. Policies often have unforeseen consequences.

How do babies sleep at home? How much surveillance do they receive there? Has anyone ever recommended that parents maintain 24-hour vigilance on babies sleeping in cribs? Is it irresponsible or neglectful for parents to sleep while their baby is asleep in the crib, even in another room or on another floor? While there is a distinction between taking care of one's own children and the children of others, current regulations reveal a dramatic difference in assumptions. If a surveillance logic were applied to them, all parents might appear neglectful.

Where's the harm in regulating health and safety? The harm lies in this: encouraging very little separation between crib areas and activity areas has a large and negative impact on the quality of infant care and learning. A close examination of most infant rooms would find that many, if not most, programs are better at nurturing—soothing, calming, and quieting—than at encouraging active, exuberant infant exploration. In good programs, moderating exploration means the ample laps and open arms of teachers; in not so good programs it means overuse of restraints: high/low chairs, bounce/air chairs, exersaucers, cribs, playpens, and so on. In rooms that have little or no separation between activity areas and crib areas, three very negative phenomena are widespread whenever teachers must act to keep the area—now the whole room—quiet:

1. Teachers moderate the active behavior of babies, often leading to restraints or an increase of staff "No"s, because a 24-inch barrier or crib bottom makes a great pull-up bar, and cribs are fun to shake.
2. Teachers often move toward less individualized sleep schedules.
3. Teachers increasingly believe that older, mobile infants need to be separated and are "too old for the room." The consequence is more age segregation (young baby/old baby), which usually leads to less continuity of teachers.

But what is the harm in an every-five-minute checking policy? If the aim is for teachers to be nurturing, to go slowly in caring, and to focus on individuals, a rigid checking and charting system changes the dynamics of interaction to an artificial schedule imposed on a sleeping baby.

Instead, let's look at health and safety issues in the context of the real world of child care, compare them with the assumptions made in the other settings where children spend time, and then consider the trade-offs.

Many safety problems are less the result of poor equipment choices than of poor planning, crowding, inappropriate use or location of equipment, and children not having enough to do.

A Final Word: Health and Safety—Always a Work in Progress

A coherent approach to health and safety in group care for infants and toddlers is always a work in progress. Health professionals provide new information and advice, and changes in public perceptions and events at the center change the views of parents and staff. The balance of challenge, safety, strict health policies, and accommodations to the real world will continually change. The key to creating a safe and healthy center that is a great place to be a child and where parents can feel secure when leaving their child is to never stop thinking about it. Always ask how sanitation can be improved, spread of disease reduced, accidents eliminated, and preparation for emergencies made more effective.

Exercises

1. Observe a number of diaper changes and toilet learning incidents, watching carefully for possible contamination and lapses in safety. List occasions when contaminated fingers or clothing are likely to have spread germs.

2. View an infant and toddler room with the eyes of a new staff member or substitute. How easily would you learn about the individual health and nutrition needs and concerns of each child in that room?

3. Discuss what constitutes acceptable risk with three or four teachers in relation to motor activities that may lead to bumps and bruises, indoors and out.

4. List those areas of the site where accidents are most likely to occur. What times of day are most likely to produce accidents?

References

American Academy of Pediatrics, American Public Health Association, and National Resource Center for Health and Safety in Child Care and Early Education. 2002. *Caring for Our Children: National Health and Safety Performance Standards: Guidelines for Out-of-Home Child Care Programs.* 2nd ed. Elk Grove Village, IL: American Academy of Pediatrics and Washington, DC: American Public Health Association. Also available at http://nrc.uchsc.edu.

Kendrick, A., R. Kaufmann, and K. Messenger. 2002. *Healthy Young Children: A Manual for Programs.* Washington, DC: NAEYC.

Pennsylvania Chapter of the American Academy of Pediatrics. 2002. *Model Child Care Health Policies.* Washington, DC: NAEYC.

Chapter 14

Guiding the Behavior of Infants and Toddlers

εxcellence *Children are helped to learn self-control and how the world works in a relaxed, positive atmosphere of support and understanding that recognizes the child's struggle. Discipline is viewed by adults as an important aspect of teaching and learning. Children are accepted as they are, not as immature creatures whose deficits and weaknesses need to be fixed right now. Development is viewed as a process of growing, in which each age and stage has its own characteristics, its own challenges and needs.*

The thought of disciplining an infant may seem ridiculous. Yet every time a baby reaches up to tug a teacher's hair and she gently removes his grasp, or he pulls an unsafe object to his mouth and she intervenes, she is setting limits, she is redirecting, and she is disciplining. Discipline is about teaching infants and toddlers how to act in a socially acceptable way and how to acknowledge their emotions. Discipline helps children learn how to control their reactions, how to understand the way the world works and their place in it, and it helps them learn to take care of themselves and others. By guiding children's behavior in positive ways and thinking about discipline as a series of teachable moments, not punishable ones, teachers are more likely to help children learn and succeed.

One teacher who had just started working with infants and toddlers said, "I used to think that the children were always misbehaving. Then I realized that they're just learning to do what is right. They don't know. I have to show them. They really are just acting their age."

See Supplement: *A Note to Parents: Disciplining an Infant—Are You Kidding?*

Learning to Live in the World

Learning to behave in a mysterious world is a tremendous challenge, full of complexities and confusing messages. Young children strive for understanding, independence, connection, belonging, acknowledgment, and self-control. They learn by exploring, experimenting, testing the limits of their environment, and experiencing the consequences of their behavior. Through these they begin to understand how the world works, what their limits are, and appropriate assertiveness. This learning is a pretty tall order, unmastered even by some adults, and so by age three, children will have only just begun the journey. In this drive to understand, they need adults who can set limits for them. Teachers should

Keep children safe. Teachers keep children from harming themselves, other people, and the physical environment.

Nine-month-old Dana is fascinated by the way the cabinet doors open and close. She swings the door back and forth, delighting in the banging sound each time she slams it closed. She doesn't know that she can hurt herself. The teacher moves her away, saying, "You really like the loud noise you made, but I don't want you to hurt yourself. Let's find something else you can bang."

Twenty-month-old Jalen sees a group of other toddlers playing. He excitedly runs over to the children, pushing two, as if to say, "Hi! I'm here. I want to play." Jalen doesn't intend to hurt the others; he just wants to play too. The teacher helps keep the other children safe by intervening to stop Jalen's pushing and to help him deal with the social situation. She says, "You're really excited to see your friends. Use your words to say hello next time instead of pushing." She then helps him find a toy so he can play along with the others.

Help them feel safe and secure. Teachers help infants and toddlers feel safe and secure. They can find their own lack of control frightening, and they need to know that an adult will stop them if they can't stop themselves.

Kia at thirty-two months has temper tantrums a few times each week. She often lies on the floor and kicks and screams. The teacher slowly approaches her, saying, "You're really upset. Let me help you calm down." She gently touches the girl's back and the child starts to breathe more slowly. The teacher pulls her on her lap saying, "Sit with me, and let's figure out what you want."

Michael, twenty-four months old, also has tantrums, but the teacher knows from experience that if she touches him he will become more upset. The teacher simply goes over to Michael and sits down near him, saying, "I'm right here, Michael. I'll stay until you calm down and feel better." Michael starts to settle down. He feels comforted by her presence.

Help them begin to understand behavioral expectations. Teachers help children begin to get an idea of what behavior is expected from them; that is, to begin to read the expectations of other people.

Eighteen-month-old Alex hits another child when the child tries to take his toy. The teacher makes sure the child who was hit is all right, and then turns to Alex. "You get angry when he tries to take your toy. Use your words and say 'No.' Hitting hurts."

While sitting at the lunch table, twelve-month-old Simi grabs the food of the child next to her. The teacher says, "You must be hungry." To get her attention, she points to Simi's plate of food and says, "This is Simi's food."

Teachers Are Children's Allies

Imagine driving in a world without traffic lights and signs, one in which parking lots lack lanes and marked parking stalls. The police expect you to comply with complicated rules, and they often issue directives you don't fully understand. When you foul up, you are punished and issued new directives.

Children must feel like this as they navigate the complex world of child care. When they misbehave, our first inclination is often to see the children as problems and to try to change them through guidance or punishment. But it usually makes more sense to change the environment (for example, provide duplicate toys) or the situation (for example, spread the children out to reduce the incidence of the behavior or to regulate the behavior). Yes, the situation is still imperfect. But environmental planning can certainly cut down the chaos, even though some motorists still run stop signs and park illegally.

The long-term goal of this disciplinary approach is for each child to become capable of self-discipline and to be motivated by understanding, concern for others, and a desire to do the right thing rather than by a desire to escape the painful consequences of doing only what she wants.

Discipline involves a mix of gentleness, understanding, and firmness. Relationships with young children include unpleasant moments, times of tension and disagreement, and times when the children may drive you crazy. Those are the times that you, as a teacher, have to keep in mind that you are on their side—you are an ally, not an adversary. Toddlers in particular have a way of engaging adults in struggles and confrontations, and teachers can easily become invested in winning or in teaching them a lesson.

Yes, discipline involves firmness, but it also involves empathy, negotiation, and sometimes compromise. When there is a struggle, look for a solution in which neither the adult nor the child loses face, but from which the child learns something that makes it less likely that the behavior will occur again.

Two-year-old Amy had worked for thirty minutes making a large, gooey mud cake decorated with leaves, sticks, and stones. She insisted on bringing it inside and playing with it on the table where the toddlers were having lunch. She became upset when her teacher, Ming, told her she could not. Resisting the urge just to take the precariously perched cake away from Amy and leave it outside, Ming explained that it wouldn't fit on the table with the food. She quickly took a cardboard box and created a lunch table for dolls so they could share the picnic cake together outside.

Guidance and Discipline Are Teaching and Learning

Discipline is simply one of the many kinds of teaching that adults do with young children, so we can apply what we know about teaching in other areas. Discipline is not punishment. Punishment is an unpleasant reaction by adults after children do something that is not acceptable. While discipline helps children identify unacceptable behavior and reduces the chance of it occurring again, it is much more than that. Discipline teaches children what to do by letting them know when they do something teachers approve of, such as showing care for others, controlling themselves, or cooperating.

The Goals of Guidance and Discipline: Self-Control and a Positive Group Environment

The program's goals are to promote children's independence, autonomy, self-esteem, and caring for themselves, others, and the physical environment. The basis for these is a secure, orderly, developmentally appropriate caregiving environment—a positive, "yes" environment that allows children to experiment and test their behavior within clearly defined limits. The program's environment is geared to children's competencies and interests. This approach is based on respect for very young children and an appreciation of how hard it is for them to learn to guide their own behavior. Teachers often have to provide the self-control that infants and toddlers lack.

It's important that in creating environments teachers don't do things that can create disciplinary problems and set up children to fail.

Settings with the following characteristics are guaranteed to produce discipline problems, regardless of who the children or adults in the program are:

- too high expectations for self-control
- too little space or too much open space
- too few materials or too little equipment
- materials or equipment that are too challenging or too simple
- too much waiting time
- inflexible routines, spaces, schedules, and people
- too little order or predictability
- too much change
- too many temptations—that is, objects and places that are forbidden
- too much noise
- excessive requirements for sharing
- long or frequent periods of sitting still
- lots of times when children are expected to just look or listen instead of becoming directly involved
- inconsistent responses from adults.

Not only will children have trouble coping, but their constant inability to meet expectations may also lead to defiant, difficult behavior.

Discipline Begins at Birth

Is it surprising that discipline is an appropriate topic to consider in relation to infants? (No one is surprised that it is a major topic of interest in relation to toddlers!) If we accept that early interactions with people and inanimate objects help children learn about themselves and the world, and that the basis of learning to control one's own behavior is feeling confident that one's own needs will be met, then discipline begins at birth. It begins when adults interact with babies in ways that help them feel safe, secure, and cared for. These actions lay the basis for learning how to wait, give, trust, love, and care for others.

Concerns about disciplining infants and toddlers are likely to arise over three issues:

1. **Encounters with others.** Group care offers children very early opportunities to begin learning the give-and-take nature of relationships with other children and adults.
2. **Learning to wait and to control impulses.** A challenge for young children is learning to stop doing something that is both interesting and unacceptable.
3. **Protection.** Young children need adults who intervene to keep them safe and to protect others and the physical environment around them.

Positive learning can come from these experiences if teachers understand the limitations on infants' and toddlers' abilities to guide their own behavior. Teachers can encourage children to be active, curious explorers rather than "well-behaved children."

See Supplements: *First Steps in Infant Discipline: How Do I Rate?; Creating a Positive Discipline Environment for Infants and Toddlers; Steps to Successfully Guide Inappropriate Behavior; The Cardinal Sins of Guidance and Discipline;* and *Principles of Effective Guidance and Discipline*

The Importance of Consistency

Discipline is an aspect of care about which adults often have strong views borne from their own experiences as children, teachers, and sometimes as parents. At almost every center, there will be differing views about appropriate behavior and effective methods of discipline. These views may vary greatly, depending on cultural preferences, socio-economic background, and individual beliefs. Some teachers and parents value assertiveness and an active approach to the world, while others value acceptance and cooperation. Some adults have different standards for boys and girls. How we behave, even more than what we profess to believe, is often based on how we were raised.

How important is consistency in guidance? Among adults at the center, consistency is critical; the program needs a consistent philosophy and approach. It is destructive not only to children but to the whole idea of a program culture to allow a variety of approaches to child guidance. It is important for staff who work together to discuss discipline and air their differences away from the ears of children and parents and to reach agreement about ways to respond to the children in their care. Consistency is easier to achieve when adults understand that the program's philosophy and practices are not "the truth" or "the right way"—only an agreed-upon way that best fits the program.

Consistency of responses to important behaviors requires teachers to recognize that children are different and that different expectations apply to different developmental stages. For example, responses to a child who is smearing pumpkin on the table at lunch should differ depending on whether the smearing is being done by one-year-old Jimmy or by two-and-a-half-year-old Gloria. Exploring and touching a gooey food is an appropriate behavior for a one-year-old. Although a two-and-a-half-year-old will also find the smearing actions tempting and enjoyable, Gloria should be redirected by her teacher and given opportunities to explore smearing at other times. Look at the differences that drive this distinction:

> At lunchtime, twelve-month-old Alexandra takes the just-served pumpkin from her plate and begins smearing it on the table. The teacher responds, "Does that feel squishy? The pumpkin is for eating." She proceeds to feed Alexandra a bite to taste.

> When two-and-a-half-year-old Ryan begins smearing the just-served pumpkin, the teacher responds differently because of her expectations of a toddler at mealtime. "The pumpkin is for eating, Ryan. Let's not play with it. Here's a towel. Can you help me clean that up?"

Another dimension of consistency is follow-through. When teachers tell children there will be a particular consequence for an inappropriate action, they must follow through. It is not helpful to say to a baby who is tipping her juice on the table, "If you keep doing that, I will take the cup away," and then to ignore her while she continues to do it.

Consistency between home and child care is desirable because it simplifies a child's task of learning appropriate behavior. But the more diverse the families attending the program, the harder it is to achieve consistency between home and the program. Children can and do learn that different settings have different expectations. However, teachers and parents need to understand and tolerate children's confusion while they are learning that there are different rules in different places. When there are differences, mutual respect is essential to avoid parent-staff conflict because damage to a parent-staff relationship is even more harmful to a child than inconsistency is.

Discipline and Culture

It is clear that the ideas presented here in *Prime Times* reflect a predominantly western European/English/American/Australian point of view.

In her invaluable book, *Multicultural Issues in Child Care* (1993, 71), Janet Gonzalez-Mena discusses the fact that "good discipline" is an inherently culture-bound idea. She writes:

> *Good early childhood practice, much of which is influenced by the value systems of white Americans with northern European background, dictates that any discipline measure has behind it the goal of self-discipline. . . . Though the adult starts with externalized controls, the idea is that they will lead to "inner controls," a term often used by early childhood practitioners.*
>
> *In some cultures, however, externalized controls are not expected to lead to inner controls. Children are always watched—not just by parents, but by the whole community. A misbehaving child away from home will be guided and directed by whoever is around.*

What does this mean for your program? Do you have to discipline each child and help each with social skills based on the child's home culture? Not really—in fact that would be impossible. It does mean, however, that above all else, good teachers must recognize that cultures vary and are equally worthy of respect, but that differences may result in difficulties for some children and parents while they struggle to make sense of program practices. The practices outlined in this book are not the right way ordained by God or experts. This book (and NAEYC accreditation) is culture-bound. When children and parents behave in ways consistent with their culture, they may present for us. That does not make them (or us) wrong. It means that we must strive to work through problems without judgment or condescension, because we respect the child and her parents. In a culturally diverse program, we may have to modify our practices considerably. In a program that serves predominantly one culture, the least we can do is respect and understand the legitimacy of any minority cultures.

Hurting a Child Is Never Okay

Although adults' personal childhood experiences may have included being slapped on the hand for grabbing, or being bitten back by an adult for biting, or even being spanked for inappropriate behavior, these actions of physically hurting a child are never acceptable in a child care program. Neither are verbal assaults or shaming. These behaviors may be thought suitable by members of some cultural groups or families in the program. Parents may suggest them to staff when their child misbehaves in the program. When these differences arise, staff must respectfully but firmly inform the parents that those practices are not allowed at the center in order to ensure the physical and emotional safety and trust of each child.

Since some parents' disciplining techniques are limited to their own experiences, this may be a good opportunity to expose those parents to alternative ways of redirecting and guiding children's behavior that do not include physical punishment.

It is also the responsibility of the teacher to observe, document, and report any suspicions that children are being abused by their parents or other teachers. Whenever a teacher has the slightest suspicion about a child's safety, she should approach the program director immediately (see chapter 13 for more information).

A Question of Balance

Imposing restrictions, setting limits, and helping infants and toddlers learn controls must be balanced with encouraging active, curious, exploratory attitudes toward the world. Too much emphasis on control and too many restrictions tend to discourage children from exploring. An adult working with young children should not be overly concerned about teaching them to behave properly, although older toddlers are certainly ready to learn some controls.

Teachers need to be sure they are not encouraging or rewarding undesirable behavior. Young children need attention, and they may learn in group care that the best way—perhaps the only way—to get attention is to do something that will be disapproved of. It is often not possible to ignore undesirable behavior, but teachers need to be astute enough to see when behavior is being used to obtain attention, and to then ensure that sufficient attention is given at other times to reinforce appropriate behavior.

Appropriate Expectations

Behaviors considered inappropriate in older children may be natural in infants and toddlers, who are still exploring and expressing curiosity, doing their job of coming to know and understand the world.

Infants When infants first begin to move around, they seem to relate to each other not as people but as interesting objects to explore. Don't assume that they intentionally try to hurt other children. Gentle redirection is called for. Similarly, infants have no sense of property rights and are not born with the notion of sharing; therefore, they are likely to take toys from others. "This toy belongs to all of us" is meaningless to them. When infants younger than approximately ten to twelve months take something from another child and their victim does not mind, it is probably best for the teacher not to intervene. As infants age and become more aware of others, or as their victims learn to protest, the teacher should intervene and direct their energy and attention in ways that teach these young children that interacting can be pleasant for everyone. Remember that mouthing is the major way infants explore the world around them, and when they chew crayons, eat more dough than they manipulate, or suck paintbrushes, it indicates that they are not yet developmentally ready for such materials.

Older infants can begin to learn some controls. The teacher may, for example, show an eleven-month-old some ways of interacting with another infant that are likely to be received more positively than pulling hair is. Around the age of ten to twelve months, infants become more sensitive to reactions of approval and disapproval from adults.

Toddlers Are Not Preschoolers Some of the characteristics of toddlers—for example, their need to assert their autonomy—contribute to the difficult situations they find themselves in. When toddlers and twos are uncooperative, even defiant, they need adults who are gentle and firm, who enforce reasonable limits, and who understand the difficulty they are having.

Active, curious toddlers are often labeled as aggressive because they frequently interact with other children in ways that other children may find unpleasant or hurtful. Much as infants explore people as objects, toddlers explore others as social scientists: "If I do this, what will he do?" The casual push, smack, and poke may be motivated by a simple desire to see what will happen. Labeling such behavior as aggressive is inappropriate, because toddlers have little understanding of the impact of their behavior on others. And while they may set out to achieve a certain aim—for example, to get the toy back—they do not willfully aim to hurt another person. Most of the hurtful things toddlers do to others are the result of characteristics of their developmental stage:

Toddlers and twos can be egocentric. Toddlers mostly believe they are the center of the world. They learn gradually as they get older that this is not quite true, albeit this is a lesson many individuals and humanity in general never quite seem to grasp. This egocentrism makes life in groups hard. It is often like the frontier, ruled by the idea that if you want something, you take it; if someone is in your way, you move them; if you find the reaction you get interesting when you push or hit someone, then you do it again. Toddlers have a very hard time putting themselves in someone else's place. They are beginning to develop empathy and apparent understanding of others' feelings; nevertheless, their empathy is unpredictable and should not be expected on a regular basis.

Toddlers can lack understanding. In the process of exploring other people, infants and toddlers may hurt them. In some cases, they do not understand that it hurts because they are unable to see another point of view. At other times, it's because they do not notice cause and effect: they are unaware that their actions cause another child's distress.

Toddlers may have good intentions but bad implementation. Toddlers often do annoying or unhelpful things with good intentions. That is, they may mean to help, to show affection, to investigate or find out, but their lack of understanding or clumsiness means that their execution of their good intentions is not so good! A poke in the eye may be a clumsy greeting; a spilled cup may be inept self-help. In these situations, show encouragement and appreciation of the good intention while trying to teach a better way to accomplish the task at hand.

Toddlers often lack self-control. Sometimes, even when toddlers sense that what they are doing will not be approved of, they simply cannot stop themselves. There is a difference between knowing what you should do and having the willpower or self-control to do it. Young children are like hungry dieters confronted with heaps of their favorite food. This is why they often require adults to supply the willpower they lack.

See Supplement: *Do I Respond Appropriately to Toddlers' Unacceptable Behavior?*

Good Teachers Pick Their Battles

Toddlers' teachers should decide which issues matter and which ones can wait. Similarly, your reactions should tell the child something about the seriousness of the offense. For example, hurting another person is much more serious than knocking toys off a shelf, and your reaction should be much sterner and more consistent for the former offense. Minor infractions and acts deliberately designed to test limits usually require a bit of humor and lightness on the part of the teacher. Working with toddlers will be very heavy going if every misdeed is treated as an occasion when the child must be taught a lesson.

Minimizing Conflict If the facility and routines have been designed with very young children in mind, most limits and prohibitions will have to do with interactions with other people, not with harm to materials and furnishings. Teachers can minimize the number of occasions that call for repeated "No"s and restrictions. In all these situations, teachers sensitive to children's limitations will alter conditions to make them more tolerable, rather than expecting children's behavior to change. Some examples of ways to do this are:

A ten-month-old is obsessed with trying to climb onto the rocking chair. His desire to do this far exceeds his ability to do it safely. The teacher, who is busy feeding another baby, cannot be with him to assist his efforts. She moves him to another part of the room while telling him that he cannot climb on the chair. She places him near some safe, low, climbing equipment, and removes the rocking chair temporarily from the room. She also makes a note of his particular interest in climbing.

An eight-month-old notices that another baby is playing very busily with a toy that happens to be her favorite. She cannot sit by and idly watch this, so she crawls over to take it away. The teacher, understanding that the situation is very frustrating for the infant, sees this as a good time to involve her in a game.

Two babies are together on the floor. One is very irritable and reaches out to pull the other's hair over and over at the slightest frustration. The teacher understands that the child needs some time alone and so she puts her in a semisecluded quiet corner nest with some toys.

Two toddlers are losing interest waiting for their turn to stir the gelatin. The teacher gives each of them a small bowl for stirring, noting that in the future she should restructure the activity so that children can stir simultaneously.

Two-year-olds Cate and Roberto are always dumping everything. Teachers create a dumping pit with lots of containers and loose materials like blocks. They also note that many of the items Cate and Roberto have dumped are not readily recognizable in their containers on the shelf. They buy some clear plastic containers that reduce the dumping, but toddlers still love to dump.

Children with Special Needs

Some children may be more of a challenge in a child care setting because they have a special need that results in challenging behavior—for example, an inability to calm themselves, distractibility, aggressive behavior, or hyperactivity. The principles for helping them succeed in the setting are the same as those for other children: understand the child, partner with the parents to determine what works best, adapt the setting, and keep the special need in perspective—it is, after all, only one aspect of the child.

It is easy to lose perspective. The special need may be based on a physical condition caused by prenatal exposure to alcohol or drugs, the result of abuse and neglect, or other atypical conditions. In any case, the child is more than the special need, and teachers have to avoid the inappropriate but understandable they-don't-belong-in-my-group attitude. Most infants and toddlers with special needs can be successfully mainstreamed in good centers because their challenging behavior is similar to that of most children, just more frequent or more intense.

Principles for Effective Guidance and Discipline

Effective guidance is based on principles that guide every interaction:

Discipline is not punishment. Discipline is a matter of planning, setting clear limits and expectations, redirecting, and pointing out logical consequences—not punishing.

Discipline includes prevention. Good discipline is also a matter of prevention—anticipating situations and heading them off at the pass.

Discipline helps children learn self-control. The teacher's job is to gently encourage and support self-control, to protect children, and to help children learn how to behave reasonably.

It is appropriate for children to be curious, to experiment, and to test the limits. It is natural, not naughty, for babies to poke, push, hit, and even bite each other, especially if there is nothing more interesting to do. It is natural for babies to experiment with food and materials—to drop, tear apart, smash. It is natural for toddlers to test limits and assert themselves in order to discover their own powers.

The environment and routines should prevent crowding of children. The teacher's job is to keep the children interested and the room arranged in such a way to prevent children from bunching up, since the more bunching there is, the more unpleasant incidents there will be. When unpleasant incidents do occur, it's best to resolve them calmly and patiently.

All children, including challenging ones, deserve respect. All children should be respected as special individuals who even at their worst are not little criminals but are very young persons struggling to achieve self-control. It is not appropriate, accurate, or fair to characterize children as *bad, mean,* or *nasty,* or to use other terms we sometimes apply to adults.

Do not label children. Labels stick. Avoid labeling children, because children believe what we tell them about themselves, and we end up believing what we tell ourselves and others.

Praise good behavior. Catch children when they are behaving well. Let them know with your attention and approval when they are behaving in acceptable ways such as showing caring, self-control, or another characteristic you would like to see more of.

Model appropriate behavior. Children learn by identifying with and imitating our behaviors. Shouting at children to keep the noise down does not make sense, nor does handling them roughly while trying to teach them to be gentle with others. When very young children are treated fairly, shared with, comforted, reasoned with, and otherwise cared for sensitively, they learn important and lasting lessons about how to treat other people.

When possible, let children try to work out their struggles themselves. When there is little risk of harm, let children try to resolve for themselves.

Limit the use of the word *no*. Overuse of the word *no* renders it ineffective. Instead of telling children only what not to do, tell and show them what is acceptable.

Have a consistent adult response for redirecting behavior. Children learn what is acceptable more quickly if all adults react the same way to the same behavior.

When young children are acting out—that is, are hurting another child, damaging the physical environment, or about to hurt themselves:

Tell children in a firm but friendly voice to stop. Whenever possible, speak at close range to such children, not from across the room, making eye contact at their level. An adult's tone of voice can effectively communicate approval or disapproval even before infants understand the words.

Give a brief explanation of why the behavior is unacceptable. Give brief reasons why the behavior is unacceptable, keeping in mind the limits of young children's understanding of their own behavior. Explaining helps us stay calm and builds children's understanding so that they can gradually make judgments themselves and guide their behavior. Reasons may be obvious to us but not to children. Why can the ball be thrown but not the wooden block? What is the difference between dropping and throwing? Why can we run outside but not inside, and what is running anyway, as opposed to fast lurching? Why can we pour water at the water table but not pour juice on the table at lunch? What is wrong with trying to pick up the baby? Answers to these questions may be obvious to adults, but not to toddlers.

State the appropriate behavior, and then model it. State and model the acceptable behavior: say, for example, "Be gentle with Taj," as you stroke Taj's arm. Find an acceptable alternative when appropriate. If you are stopping children from doing something, don't just tell them what they cannot do—tell them what they can do as well.

Validate emotions. Always recognize and acknowledge as legitimate children's feelings of anger, confusion, or hurt. "I know that makes you angry when Tommy takes your toy, but you can't hit him. Tell him 'No.'" "It's frustrating when you can't get the toy to work the way you want it to. May I help you?"

Help children stop unacceptable behavior. Redirect them to a new activity, or physically remove them, the object, or the victim, if necessary. Often your words are not enough. Even when children understand the directive to stop, they may not have the willpower to do so. Giving a number of verbal warnings is not helpful, and in fact can provide some children with an incentive to continue doing what they are doing.

Offer choices. Offer children reasonable choices whenever you can. For example: "Do you want to finish your drink or get down and play?" "Would you like to go outside and throw the ball or play with the blocks?" Avoid implying a choice when there is none. "Would you like to give Brad a turn on the swing now?" is not appropriate unless either a resounding "No" or a happily swinging toddler is acceptable. When there is no choice, be prepared to help the child go along with the decision you have made.

Recognize your own inability to deal with a particular situation. Take a deep breath or seek help if you are about to lose control or are too angry to handle the situation.

The Dos and Don'ts of Discipline

The Dos

When a young child hurts another child, damages the physical environment, or is about to hurt himself, we always

- make clear that it is the child's behavior and not the child that is unacceptable.
- help the child with appropriate language to understand the problems with his behavior.
- use redirection, logical consequences, or cool-down time, depending on the age of the child, the misbehavior, and the child's observed state.
- assist and encourage children to use language to express their strong feelings.
- try our best to appear confident, even when we are not, knowing that our manner will affect the child's decision to cooperate.

The Don'ts

When a young child is hurting another child, damaging the physical environment, or about to hurt himself, we do not

- shame or humiliate the child. Even saying "You wet your pants again" can be a form of humiliation and shame. Instead, try "Let's get you into some clean clothes."
- shake, jerk, squeeze, or physically indicate our disapproval. Working with infants and toddlers is a challenging job, physically and mentally, but it is never okay to indicate your disapproval physically.
- use "bad girl" or "bad boy" or otherwise imply that the child instead of the behavior is unacceptable. Also avoid the use of *good boy* or *good girl* for acceptable behavior.
- moralize or let too much anger come through. Teachers may tell a child they are angry, but they should never react in anger, because this will make the child fearful and anxious. "It makes me angry when you hit me. Please touch me gently, like this."
- use "No" too often. Use the positive ("Hold on to the cup") and words such as "Stop" or "Please don't" instead of "No."
- use bribes, false threats, or false choices. Avoid using food or scheduled activities like going outside or on field trips to reinforce or punish.
- make children say they are sorry. Uttering the words is an empty and meaningless gesture unless the words reflect true sentiment. Until toddlers fully understand what they have done, they are not likely to actually feel sorry. Requiring "Sorry" as a standard response to unacceptable behavior can be interpreted by the child as a way of magically undoing the thing he or she has done. Thus some two-year-olds utter "Sorry" just before the wrongdoing.
- retaliate. Never retaliate—that is, do to children what they have just done to someone else. Remember, children learn the most from us through watching what we do.

Logical Consequences

When children behave in an inappropriate manner, the most effective discipline is for them to experience the specific logical consequences of their behavior.

> Two-year-old Ahmad can't play at the water table without splashing other children. The teacher warns him several times: "Please keep the water in the table, Ahmad. Your friends don't like it when you splash them." When he continues to splash, the teacher directs him to other play until he can play with water without creating a mess.

> When twenty-two-month-old Qian continues to draw on the wall with markers, the teacher redirects her to paper. When she attempts to draw on the walls again, the teacher tells Qian, "You can't use the markers if you are going to draw on the wall. You may draw on paper or play elsewhere."

Young toddlers may not have the ability to always make the link between their behavior and the consequences. It is important that the consequences be enforced in a matter-of-fact way that helps the child learn rather than in a punitive, I-told-you-so way, which serves mainly to fuel the adult's feelings of power and control over the child.

A logical consequence helps teach children what is acceptable behavior and what is not by preventing them from continuing to participate in the activity if they cannot proceed appropriately. Generalized punishment—for example, sitting in a chair for a period of time—teaches children little or nothing. If older toddlers refuse to accept the consequences, they may need some quiet, relaxing time to pull themselves together.

Cool-down Time for Older Toddlers

Both the term and the concept of *time-out* are somewhat out of fashion. Unfortunately, time-out has become associated with fixed-time punishment or the time-out chair, rather than with a neutral, voluntary withdrawal from an activity to cool down and get oneself together. There will always be times when children are not capable of self-control and need a teacher to redirect them or to suggest some time to settle down. Cool-down time is not punishment. It is not the same as sitting children down or isolating them for violation of a rule.

Instead, cool-down time is just what it sounds like: a quiet, relaxed, neutral break; a cooling-off period during which children can regain self-control. Cool-down time is used when a child loses control and refuses redirection—for example, when acting aggressively, having a tantrum, or being totally defiant. If children have violated a rule without losing control or have regained control, they should experience the consequence of that behavior, not be forced into cool-down time.

Cool-down time should occur in soft, cozy, peaceful places—perhaps an easy chair or an area with pillows. One center calls this spot the "peace place." While children have to be compelled to take cool-down time, the ultimate goal is for them to achieve the control to take the time on their own whenever it is needed. Often an adult will need to help children regain control. If the adult approaches cool-down time with an adversarial stance, children will see it as something negative and unpleasant, and the cool-down time simply becomes ineffective punishment. If the adult maintains an attitude of alliance and understanding, then even though children may initially resist, they will eventually get the correct message: "This is something I need right now, and since I don't have the self-control to do it myself, my teacher is helping me."

Note: Cool-down time is not appropriate for infants and young toddlers. It is appropriate only after children begin to have some sense of how they can help themselves, usually around age two. If children are unable to relax and calm themselves down, cool-down time should always occur in the presence of a nurturing adult.

Positive Steps to Cool-down Time

1. After children repeatedly refuse to cooperate or to stop inappropriate behavior, the adult says gently but firmly, "You need some cool-down time."
2. Without there being any moral overtones, place them in a comfortable cool-down time area at the edge of the room, with some materials or books to occupy them. "I know you are really angry, but you need to cool down on the couch here before we can play some more. Tell me when you are ready to talk." Pay the minimum attention necessary so that they remain in the cool-down time area while regaining control. If you need to hold a child, try to do so in a neutral manner, neither warmly nor angrily.
3. When the child regains control, say something such as "Are you feeling okay? Are you ready to come and be with us?" If you leave the cool-down time area, children should be told to come to you when they feel okay.
4. Help children express the feelings leading to the cool-down time by putting words to emotions and behavior: "You got very angry when you couldn't get a wagon, didn't you? You really wanted that wagon." Give them the physical nurturing they need.
5. Explain your position: "I know how upset you are, but I won't let you hurt people and I won't let people hurt you. Next time, if you get really angry, you can take some cool-down time and I'll spend some time with you."
6. If children regain control quickly, acknowledge it.

After Cool-down Time

- Adjust the environment to avoid the situation the child had trouble with.
- Praise the child for every instance of self-control.
- Be prepared to catch situations before the child loses all control, and encourage the child to take self-initiated, quiet, relaxing time.

Remember: *Cool-down time is not punishment.* This is so important that it bears repeating. *Cool-down time is not punishment.* We had to throw out a perfectly good term, *time-out,* because it became synonymous with a punishment chair. Cool-down time is simply time during which the child, and sometimes the teacher, can settle down.

When a Child Is Struggling

What do we do when children are really struggling and their actions are causing harm to other children or to themselves? Parents of other children may become upset and question whether or not such a child should be allowed to stay in the program. The parents of a struggling child are often as upset or more upset than the other parents in the program. It is necessary for the teachers to help a struggling child while keeping other children safe and while balancing the emotions of all the people involved: the struggling one, other children, all the parents, and the teachers.

See Supplement: *Steps to Help the Struggling Child*

Supporting a Struggling Child

A systematic approach to dealing with a struggling child is essential, involving parents and program leadership from the beginning.

Step One: Observe

A. Observe the child in the environment, including:
1. the child's approach to activities
2. the child's attention span and interest in activities
3. the amount of energy the child uses
4. the child's mood and general demeanor
5. how well the child gets along with others
6. how the child begins and ends an activity
7. what the child's relationship is with you and other teachers.

B. Observe how the environment affects the child. Note and chart everything about the specific room situation that the child experiences, including:
1. activities that are occurring
2. other children's activities or interactions
3. the general atmosphere of the room
4. how often activities change
5. how the child functions during transitions in daily routine
6. the time of day
7. signs that group or individual activities are creating a problem.

Step Two: Synthesize observations

A. Identify patterns in observations.
B. State concerns clearly.
C. Bring concerns to the director's attention.
D. Ask for help if necessary.

Step Three: Modify the room

A. Make program modifications based on informal observations.
B. Evaluate your concerns after attempting program modifications; keep the director well informed.

Step Four: If the problem persists, ask the director to observe the struggling child.

See Supplements: *Observation Slip (long form)* and *Observation Slip (short form)*

continued on next page

Supporting a Struggling Child, *continued*

Step Five: With referral from the director and written parental consent, consider finding outside help—for example, ask the local child care resource and referral agency or the United Way.

A. Create a program plan involving the parent, director, teachers, and outside resource people.

B. Maintain ongoing communication with all parties.

C. Schedule frequent meetings to evaluate progress, or lack of it, with a timetable for improvement.

D. If the plan is unsuccessful, encourage and assist the parents in finding alternate child care arrangements.

Step Six: Make a plan and provide support to parents if there is a decision that the center cannot meet the child's needs and/or if the child is unable to function successfully in a group setting.

A. Determine the period of time before termination of child care.

B. Try to give parents at least two weeks' notice that child care will no longer be available.

C. Help parents understand that the termination resulted from the program's inability to adapt to the child's needs and that it is not the child's failure.

There will always be toddlers who struggle with the dynamics of a same-age, toddler group setting; after all, it is hardly an ideal situation. After all, there are good reasons why group settings of toddlers aren't commonplace in human history. A systematic approach incorporating careful observation and a strategy for changing the environment, the teacher's responses, and the child's behavior is the best method for helping the child and for making life manageable for staff and other children.

Asking Families to Leave the Program

When do you decide that you can no longer serve a child? If the child is continuing to exhibit aggressive, hurtful behavior to himself, other children, or adults on a regular basis then he may need to be placed in a different setting or may need the help of specially trained professionals in an environment more appropriate than the one the center offers. Document the child's behavior, using the steps outlined above. With the assistance of the director, share the information with the parents, and seek outside help to develop a strategy for helping the child succeed. If the program lacks the resources to help the child while maintaining the safety of other people, the director may conclude that the child will not benefit from the program. Asking a family to leave is a difficult decision, but if your program is confident that you have made every effort to help a child, then that child may be better served somewhere else. Think of your decision not as casting a child out or as the child's failure but rather as redirecting a family to find a program in which their child can function successfully while receiving the help he needs.

Terminations should occur only when the program has done what it can to adapt the program to fit the child. The stronger your partnership with parents and the more effort you have made to adapt the program, the more likely it is that all children will fit in. Strong relationships also mean that if the program cannot serve a child, the decision to withdraw that child will likely be made mutually or with little acrimony.

Biting

It is evident in the eyes of staff and parents when an epidemic of biting breaks out. Tension hangs over the room like smog, a demoralizing haze of fear, anger, and anticipation: *When will it strike again?*

Children biting other children is an unavoidable consequence of group child care, especially among toddlers. It happens in the best of programs, but it happens much more frequently in mediocre programs. When biting occurs and continues, it's pretty scary, very frustrating, and very stressful for children, parents, and staff.

Group living is hard—people rub up against each other, literally and emotionally, and children in child care need and want attention from adults. Sadly, for some children, negative attention is more desirable than being ignored. A bite is powerful and primal, quick and effective, and usually inspires immediate and dramatic reactions. Size and strength are not required; even an infant can inflict a very painful bite. Once begun, biting is hard to get rid of quickly. One child bites, another child imitates, and soon it's an epidemic. Parents become very upset about biting, and the problem escalates.

Why Do They Bite? Biting is a horrifying stage some children go through and it can be a major problem or crisis for a group. For the biting child, it's a natural phenomenon that has virtually no lasting developmental significance—unless adults end up defining the child on the basis of the biting. Biting derives its significance from the group care setting. It sounds obvious, but children who are not around other children are unlikely to bite—both the causes and the opportunities are absent. *Biting is not something to blame on children, parents, or teachers.* A child who bites is not on a direct path toward becoming a discipline problem, a bad person, or a cannibal. Yes, biting is an antisocial act, but it is an act of an individual just beginning life as a citizen and not yet equipped to be fully social.

So why does one child bite and another child does not? Were you a biter? There are a number of possible reasons that children under age three bite, and those reasons do *not* include a bad home, bad parents, or bad teachers. Sometimes we think we have a good idea of what is causing the biting, but most of the time it is hard to assess what is going on in the child's head. Some of the likely reasons children bite:

> **Children may bite while they are teething.** When teeth are coming through, applying pressure to the gums is comforting, and babies will use anything available to apply that pressure. If this is a likely cause, then a teething ring or an object to bite on will lessen an infant's need to bite others.
>
> Roxana has molars coming in and wants to bite. Carrying a washcloth around gives her something to bite on.

Children may bite because of impulsiveness. Babies sometimes bite just because there is something there to bite. This biting is not intentional in any way, but rather a way of exploring the world. Children may bite each other's chubby arms as readily as they will bite into a plastic squeeze toy in their path.

Children may bite to make an impact. Young children like to make things happen, and reactions when they bite someone are usually pretty dramatic. It's easy to get everyone's attention by biting another child.

Children may bite when they are excited or overstimulated. When very young children become very excited, even happily so, they may behave in out-of-control ways.

Carlos loves moving to music, and after a session with music and scarves and everyone twirling and enjoying themselves, it is very predictable that he will bite someone if an adult does not help him calm down.

Children may bite when they are frustrated. Too many challenges, too many demands, too many wants, too little space, or too many obstacles may stimulate children to bite, especially before they possess the capability to express frustration through language.

On the playground, Samantha likes to go in the fort under the slide, but when too many children crowd in and she is unable to get out quickly, she is likely to bite if the teacher doesn't assist her in moving.

See Supplement: *A Note to Parents: Children Who Bite*

The Politics of Biting—Who Is to Blame? Although there should be no blame, the program must accept responsibility for children's acts of biting and other hurtful acts such as hitting or scratching and not place responsibility on the child or family. Good programs recognize biting as a natural developmental and situational phenomenon in the same way that toileting accidents or tantrums are.

What does accepting responsibility mean? It means that the program has chosen to provide a group setting for children who are at an age when biting is a common response to life in a group. Knowing that biting is likely in group care, the job of the program is to create a positive experience for all children, removing the stresses that often lead to biting. Some children become stuck for a while in the biting syndrome, and it is frustrating for the parents of victims when teachers are unable to quickly change the child's behavior or are unwilling to terminate the biter's child care. Empathizing with parents' feelings of helplessness and their concern for their children is essential as teachers educate and reassure parents about their efforts to extinguish the behavior quickly. *Note:* No parent looking at a blazing bite mark on their baby's cheek wants to hear that it is normal or natural. Balance your commitment to the family of the biting child with that to the center's other families.

Parents are not responsible for children who bite, nor are they significant factors in the "cure." Parents are encouraged to work with staff on a strategy for change at the center and to reduce, when possible, any stresses their child may be feeling. It's important to remind parents that any such stresses may have little or nothing to do with why their child is biting.

It is the center's job to provide a safe setting in which no child needs to hurt another to achieve goals within the normal range of behavior—and biting is within typical range in group care. The names of children who bite should not be released, because doing so serves no useful purpose and can make a difficult situation even more difficult. Punishment doesn't work to change children who bite: neither delayed punishment at home, which children will not understand, nor punishment at the center, which may make the situation worse.

Sometimes nothing works and a child becomes so stuck in biting behavior that she has to leave the program. In that case, there's no reason to place responsibility for the inability to find a solution on the child, her family, or the program—the situation is unfortunate for all.

Before the Biting To reduce the emotional fallout that biting can produce, it is best to educate parents about biting before it occurs. When families enroll in the program, as early as the enrollment conference, prepare parents for the possibility that any child, including theirs, can either be a biter or be bitten. Make sure parents are aware of all the steps you take to minimize biting and to end a biting crisis. Parents need to know that your understanding of biting as a natural and common phenomenon does not mean that you throw up your hands in resignation—instead, you take every bite or other hurtful act seriously. Finally, determine how long you will continue to work with a child who is biting, and communicate that to the child's parents right away. Fear of a sudden loss of child care adds to the tension. Again, it is better if parents know about this before a crisis occurs.

When Biting Happens In all biting situations, regardless of the likely cause, it is important that adults show strong disapproval through words and manner. Teachers can try to minimize the behavior through a number of approaches:

- Let the child know in words and manner that biting is unacceptable. Reserve your sternest manner and words for acts such as biting. "No biting. Biting hurts."

Biting: A Crisis for Parents

When a room is under a siege of biting, everyone suffers. It is important to keep in mind the perspective of parents.

Memoirs of a Parent of "That Child"

I still have vivid memories of that horrible period that began when she was nineteen months old. It was awful every day, walking into her room and waiting to find out who Jenny had bitten. Four bites in one day, twenty-five in June alone. Life was hell. We slunk in and out like the parents of a criminal. Was it us—some flaw in our home or some mutant gene?

Jenny was such fun as a toddler, this tiny red-haired mop top with great bouncy enthusiasm. Even at her biting worst, she was happy. We never saw her bite at home— there weren't very young kids around.

We would have these meetings with her teachers and the director. We were all desperate. Even though we were doing everything we could, we all became defensive, sometimes disbelieving each other. Maybe she was bored (their fault), troubled (our fault), immature (her fault).

I knew that other parents were upset. After all, their children were coming home with Jenny's imprint (thankfully, this was before the time of AIDS). I saw them look at Jenny, and at us. Finally one mother began yelling at me, shoving her son's arm in my face with the incriminating two red half-circles.

And then at about twenty-two months, Jenny stopped biting. Part of it was all the stuff that the staff were doing and that we were doing at home. But probably she just grew out of it. Now I look at Jenny and see

continued on next page

Biting: A Crisis for Parents, *continued*

this good high-school student with lots of friends, and I can laugh about what we went through. But I remember wondering then how she could ever have a normal life.

The Other Side of the Mirror: "My Child, the Victim"

If I can't keep my baby safe, keep him from being some other kid's snack substitute, what kind of mother am I? One day there is a bite on the cheek, the next day on his arm, and then even a bite on his bottom. The teachers would sympathize with me and then say, "Biting is normal at this age." Yeah, I know that toddlers bite, but mothers protect, and I couldn't protect my kid. It may be normal to bite, but it is not normal to be gnawed on every day.

"We're doing all we can," they said. So? Was I supposed to live with that? I wanted those biters out. How long was I supposed to let my child suffer at fourteen months old? I was told, "Stevie is so curious and friendly that he is the most common victim." I blew up. So it's his fault?

I left the center with hard feelings. Not because it was the center's fault or even because they wouldn't throw out the biters. They were trying so hard to solve the problem, but they didn't seem to understand what it was like to be in my shoes. We had to leave.

- Avoid any immediate response that reinforces the biting, including dramatic negative attention. Remove children who bite from the vicinity with no emotion. Focus the caring attention on the child who was bitten. The child who bit is not allowed to return to play until after being talked to at a level he can understand. Communicate that you understand the child's frustration or needs for exploration or teething relief, and are willing to help him achieve self-control. "I know you're frustrated when you can't go first, but you can't bite. I'll play with you until it's your turn."

- Work with the child who bites on resolving conflict or frustration in a more appropriate manner, including using language, if the child is able to understand: "When you feel like biting, use words," "I'll help you to not bite." Don't assert "I won't let you bite" unless you can deliver on that promise.

- Examine the context in which the biting occurred and look for patterns. Was it crowded? Too few toys? Too little to do? Too much waiting? Is the child who is biting getting the attention and care she deserves at all times, or only when she acts out?

- Change the environment, routines, or activities if necessary.

- Try to observe the child who is a short-term chronic biter to get an idea about when the urge to bite occurs. Some children, for example, may bite not when they are angry or frustrated, but only when they are very excited.

- Do not casually attribute willfulness or maliciousness to the child. Infants explore anything that interests them, and that includes other bodies and limbs!

- Observe the group closely until a pattern of biting emerges; this may help you find a solution if biting continues.

- Empathize with all of the parents and staff involved. It's a difficult situation for everyone.

Responding to an Epidemic of Biting When biting changes from a relatively rare occurrence, perhaps a couple times a week, to a frequent and expected one, it should be considered an epidemic or a health emergency—a serious threat to the well-being of the children in the room, including those who bite. In health and safety emergencies, teachers should apply extraordinary resources to the crisis. Do the following:

Meet on a daily basis. The staff in the room should meet with the director or other supervisory or support staff on a daily basis throughout the crisis for advice and support, and should maintain a perspective devoid of blame directed at children, parents, or staff.

Document every bite and every attempted bite. Chart every occurrence, including attempted bites, and indicate location, time, participants, staff present, and circumstances.

Evaluate staff response. Immediately evaluate staff responses to each biting situation in order to forge appropriate intervention. Provide comfort to injured children and treat their injuries. Use a cool, firm, disapproving response to the child who has bitten, and avoid inadvertently providing reinforcement to further biting.

Look for biting patterns. Analyze your biting chart and profile the behavior patterns and the environmental context of children who frequently bite and children who are frequently victims.

Have one teacher stay with the child who bites at all times. Shadow or stay with children who indicate a tendency to bite.

In addition:

Anticipate biting situations.

Teach nonbiting responses to triggering situations, and reinforce appropriate behavior in potential biting situations.

Adapt the program to better fit the needs of children who bite.

If appropriate, transition the child who bites to another room. Consider early transition of children stuck in a biting behavior pattern to a changed environment, if it is developmentally appropriate and allowed by licensing statutes.

Change the room environment. Consider changes to the room: its environment, schedule, routines, and/or the expectations of children and staff. Minimize
- congestion
- commotion
- confusion and disorder

> ### "I Dreaded Going to Work"
>
> The lead teacher in a room undergoing a rash of biting described what it was like:
>
> *You don't know how lousy it feels when biting gets out of control. Four bites today, three bites yesterday, two bites last Friday. I went through periods of feeling like a terrible teacher. I didn't want to face the parents of the children who weren't biting. I'd get angry at the biting kids and see Ben and Becca as if they were these little monsters. I wanted to kick them out. And I was even more angry with their parents! They had to do more, take more responsibility, be more structured, more loving, more something. All these feelings swirled around, although only my husband had to hear the wails and moans. I knew the feelings weren't fair, and it took all my professionalism to stuff them down.*

- competition for toys and materials
- wait times
- frustration levels
- competition for adult attention
- boredom.

Work with children in small groups. Avoid large-group activities and routines and break into smaller groups.

- Use the playground, walks, and other spaces in the center.
- Within the room, spread out activities and staff to avoid bunching up. Also use the nap area.

Make children feel secure. Look for ways to promote their sense of security and stability.

- "No surprises": maintain a predictable schedule and ensure that children understand and anticipate the progression of the day.
- Ensure that each child has some prime times with their primary caregiver.
- Ensure there are warm, cozy, semisecluded places to be.
- Avoid staffing changes.
- Develop and maintain individual and group rituals.

Help children become involved in the program. Look for ways to engage children more effectively in the environment.

- Analyze choices as children might see them.
- Analyze the developmental appropriateness of choices.
- Provide duplicates of toys and materials, and multiple options for activities.
- Consider increasing the motor and sensory choices available.

Balance active times with quiet times. Look for ways to calm children after periods of excitement, including

- relaxed transitions
- calming music
- calming physical contact with teachers.

Group children to avoid biting. Group children to avoid combinations that may lead to conflict or biting.

- Avoid grouping children who bite with likely victims of biting.
- Avoid grouping children who will compete for toys.

Have other adults observe the biting epidemic. If necessary, bring in outside observers to help you analyze the entire situation, not just the children who are biting.

Maintain a positive relationship with parents during biting epidemics.

- Let all the parents know that there is a biting problem and what you are doing to resolve it.
- Remind parents of your philosophy of working with children in crisis.

- Work together as partners with the parents both of children who bite and their frequent victims to keep them informed and to develop joint strategies for change.
- Prepare the parents of the child who bites for the worst if suspension or termination from the program may be necessary, and suggest they make contingency plans. Having to leave the program is a terrible consequence; having to leave with little warning is even worse.

See Supplement: *A Note to Parents: Children Who Bite*

Hanging on during an Epidemic Magic feathers helped Dumbo fly, but there are no magic feathers to solve a biting crisis. Sometimes nothing works, and children grow out of it or leave the program. Doing all we've suggested above should help alleviate or shorten the crisis. Maintaining good relationships with parents during a biting epidemic requires all the trust and goodwill built up by good program practice before biting ever occurs.

Because biting is a natural and inevitable occurrence, like illness, earthquakes, and floods, teachers can prepare for biting and maintain perspective while it is occuring. This is the time when the expertise, professionalism, and character of teachers is put to the test.

Temper Tantrums

Going to pieces, becoming out of control, or having a momentary breakdown are all ways of describing temper tantrums. Unfortunately, these are common experiences for toddlers (and older children—and some adults!). Ever try to work some new sort of electronic gadget, only to find yourself tossing the manual, stomping your feet, and contemplating hurling the gismo out the window? That's the adult version of a tantrum.

A temper tantrum is an irrational, immature way of expressing anger or frustration. Having a tantrum often involves exactly what the expression *throwing* a tantrum implies: children hurl themselves on the floor, complete with kicking, screaming, and crying. While tantrums are inappropriate, they are perfectly typical for children aged one to three years. (By three years, tantrums become less frequent because children are learning other coping skills for dealing with anger and frustration.) Tantrums can be quite powerful and therefore frightening, not only to other children and adults but also to the child who is having one. They typically come as the culmination of fatigue, frustration, too much excitement, or the confrontation of a number of obstacles or barriers. Frustration is a normal developmental part of children's lives while they are learning how the world works. Tantrums are fueled in toddlers by their inability to use words to express their strong feelings. Imagine a bottle of champagne that has been jostled and shaken to the point that it finally blows its top with a powerful explosion. When that is finished, it becomes still and flat. With a temper tantrum, a seemingly insignificant event can become the straw that breaks the camel's back.

Temper tantrums, like crying, are real expressions of distress, not something most children do deliberately. Most toddlers in the throes of a temper tantrum need help to get out of it. The sort of help that will be effective varies with the child. Some children need to be held to get back in control. But for others, being held will feel like restraint and will only fuel the tantrum. These children may respond positively to an adult staying close by and talking calmly. Adult anger is not an appropriate response to a tantrum, which calls for calm firmness that shows children that the adult will help them regain control. A tantrum can be physically and emotionally exhausting, and afterward children may want to engage in quiet soothing activities, such as looking at books, playing with sand or water, or even resting or sleeping. Teachers may want a nap too!

Unfortunately, there are always a few toddlers who have learned that temper tantrums are effective ways of securing something they want. Usually these tantrums are more controlled than the ones previously described. As long as children who are having tantrums do not hurt anything or anyone, the teacher may decide to ignore the behavior. As is true with biting, temper tantrums should never be a successful way for children to get something they want. They may nevertheless be signals to teachers that certain children need attention and a reminder to give attention to those children when they are behaving appropriately.

See Supplement: *A Note to Parents: Temper Tantrums*

Responding to Temper Tantrums When teachers are in the throes of a child's tantrum, it's hard to remember that such outbursts generally diminish as children get older and develop better coping skills. When tantrums erupt, try talking to the child if her tantrum is just beginning or is not too violent.

Validate the child's feelings.
"It's hard to wait for food when you are hungry."
"I know you wanted to be the first one to paint."
"It's frustrating when you don't want to come inside."

Help the child express herself by offering assistance.
"I understand you want to tell me something. Show me what you need."
"I know it's hard to work this toy, but you'll get better at it. May I help you?"

Tantrums can be scary to children: during a prolonged tantrum, verbally encourage and reassure the child.
"I can see you are very angry. I'll leave you alone until you cool off."
"I know you are very upset. I am here if you need me."

In some cases, help the child regain self-control through physical contact.
Children who are having tantrums may not be able to regain control by themselves, except through extreme exhaustion. These children will do better if we help by holding them. If they are not too large or violent, try approaching them from behind and gently place your hands on their shoulders. Move your hands down their arms to steady them. If children have thrown themselves on the floor, try sitting near their head to avoid being kicked, and gently place your hand on their back.

When the tantrum stops, comfort the child and offer alternatives to tantrum behavior.

Teachers' care and respect for children should be unconditional. After a temper tantrum, hold, hug, or verbally let the child know that you want to reassure and comfort him: "You were really angry. Next time, use your words and tell me what you want." "I want to help you, but I can't do it when you kick and scream. Next time, point to what you need."

Do not give children what they want as a result of a tantrum.

Giving in to children's temper tantrums may momentarily cause them to stop their behavior, but it greatly reinforces acting in an inappropriate, angry way and it demonstrates that tantrums get them what they want.

Document the occasions when children have tantrums.

Record the time and circumstances of each tantrum. Study the information to determine if there are times or situations in which a child is more likely to have an outburst. Use this information to anticipate and help each child avoid a tantrum. If the child is more likely to have tantrums before a nap, schedule an earlier naptime.

A Final Word: Life in Group Care Is No Picnic

Is this approach to discipline too soft for toddlers, delaying their learning the hard facts of life about waiting, sharing, taking turns, and controlling themselves? Absolutely not. Even in the most accepting, gentle, individualized program, group care creates numerous occasions that require extraordinary self-control, delay of gratification, and other behaviors that we want to cultivate in children. It is not necessary to build in extra opportunities for children to test their self-control.

It's easy to get into power struggles or battles of will with children, even the youngest infants. Group living is tough, especially with a collection of little egos struggling for self-control and intent on exploring how the world works. The key is for staff to help each other maintain a perspective that accepts much of the troublesome behavior as natural, while trying to smooth the waters and come up with strategies to build more peaceful tomorrows.

Exercises

1. Observe an infant room and a toddler room. In each room, what undesirable behaviors did you see? Note the following for each incident:
   - Was the behavior observed by staff?
   - Why do you think the behavior occurred? Consider the situation, the child's exploration, and the child's mood.
   - Was there a consequence for the unacceptable behavior?

2. In those same rooms, look for and note any unnecessary "No" conditions that work against the creation of a "Yes" environment.

3. Make a list of the limits or rules that operate in an infant or toddler room. What is the rationale for each? Do they have to do with adult convenience or the well-being of children? Are they justifiable?

Reference

Gonzalez-Mena, J. 1993. *Multicultural Issues in Child Care.* Mountain View, CA: Mayfield.

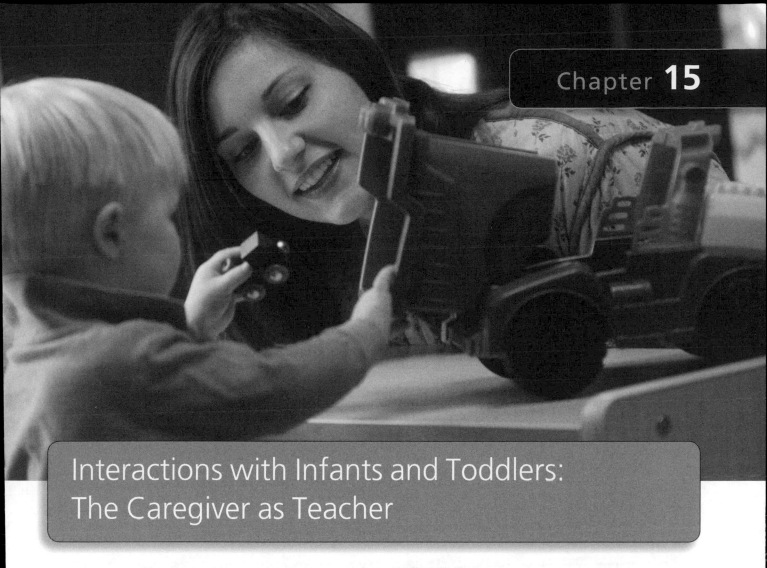

Chapter 15

Interactions with Infants and Toddlers: The Caregiver as Teacher

εxcellence *Teachers recognize and value all prime times for learning interactions that maximize one-to-one moments with individual children, and they aim to create many of these throughout the day. Teachers understand and appreciate that children are constantly learning and doing their job exploring and playing, even when teachers are not intentionally teaching. Interactions are authentic and personal, responsive to the children's invitations, rich with language, and follow children's interests and developmental capabilities. Group activities are scaled to the children's development in frequency, size, and duration. Large-group experiences are avoided with infants, and are rare with toddlers.*

What does it mean to teach infants and toddlers—to be an infant or toddler teacher? The fact that the word *teacher* conjures up all sorts of images that don't really seem to fit has led some to abandon the title and instead to use *caregiver, educarer, child care provider,* or *infant/toddler specialist.* As we discussed in the introduction, while *caregiver* is certainly an appropriate term, in the real world of parents and schools, it reduces the status of those who work with infants and toddlers. Like it or not, the term *teacher* confers educational legitimacy. *Educator, educarer,* and *specialist* are used too infrequently to imply the same status as *teacher.*

Are caregivers of infants and toddlers really teachers? Although the real world may view the interactions of caregiver and child as less educational than those of school-teacher and child or even teacher and preschooler, a true educator is a facilitator of learning regardless of the age of the student. Good infant and toddler caregivers who create an appropriate learning environment for children, supply materials for exploration, develop a relationship with each child, ask questions, and provide children with developmentally appropriate challenges are educators and deserve the title of *teacher*.

Why might there be some discomfort about the term *teaching*? Because many people associate teaching with lessons, structure, and sitting children down to learn something an adult thinks they need to learn. In other words, in some people's minds teaching is something that is adult-initiated and -directed, imposed on children, and has little relation to what children indicate they are interested in.

See Supplement: *A Note to Staff: Are Caregivers of Infants and Toddlers Really Teachers?*

Teaching and Learning through Play and Exploration

The notion of teaching embraced in this book is based on the belief that infants and toddlers are learning all the time, including during routines and transitions. Only rarely and briefly does teaching in the sense of instruction have any part in the child's experience in the program. Infants and toddlers acquire new skills and understandings about the world and themselves through play and exploration and living each new day. Good teaching often happens spontaneously, but flows out of planning and preparation (discussed more fully in chapter 16). Structured, adult-imposed lessons, activities, and special exercises to teach specific skills are not needed.

For example, children will learn the names of colors in natural conversation as the teacher talks about the colors of food, children's clothing, or pictures in books. Children learn shapes by talking about the shapes of their toys and what they see and touch, indoors and out. Skilled teachers weave in learning experiences throughout the day, mindful of Vgotsky's zone of proximal development (discussed in chapter 4). This refers to the distance between what children can accomplish during independent problem solving and what they can accomplish with the help of a teacher. Using their awareness of children's emerging skills and interests and probable next developmental steps, good teachers provide an environment filled with opportunities, encouragement, and conversations. They make careful decisions about whether to intervene to alter or enhance an experience, creating a *scaffold* that helps children move forward and build new competencies.

In preceding chapters, the emphasis has been on the teacher's role as the adult who provides the security and stability that frees young children to explore, be curious, and get involved in play. Children who are not sure their needs will be met, or who have to adjust continually to new teachers, new places, and new routines, will not become involved in active play and exploration. The subject of this chapter is the critical role of the teacher in supporting children's learning through interactions, interventions, and language. The chapters that follow will focus on the third critical role of the teacher, as an architect and engineer preparing a *world-at-their-fingertips* environment for learning, so that children can do their job of developing fully (see chapter 4). Teachers need to maintain an environment for free and structured play that provides developmentally appropriate challenges.

Follow the Child

Play should be driven by each child's interests and timetable, even if the child spends a lot of time engaging in only one kind of play. Children's major interests often reflect their emerging motor skills. For example, a baby who is learning to crawl may for a few days be interested almost exclusively in crawling, and only rarely will anything else hold his attention. Getting into everything is driven by the child's new mobility and dexterity and by the important realization that the world is rich with objects to explore.

Curriculum—the formal organization of what is provided for infants and toddlers and the opportunities given to them—should be based on deep understanding of the principles of good early childhood practice, information about development in the first three years of life, and sensitive awareness of the styles, interests, and competencies of individual children. Curriculum (discussed more thoroughly in chapter 16) is the framework and rationale for doing what you do, not a list of activities.

Supporting the Play of Children

The most important teaching happens when adults interact, talk, play, and work alongside children. These create prime times. Good teachers stay with children: on the couch, on the floor, on the grass, sitting, lying, sprawling at their level, listening, conversing, touching, observing, and figuring out good moments to engage children and moments when it is simply better to watch them. At the same time, teachers are looking after the physical and emotional safety of each child, observing development, identifying strengths and interests, and of course, helping children manage their behavior. Clearly, the idea that *being with* children is easier than *instructing* them is way off base.

Times when a teacher and a child play together are prime times offering many benefits. The child learns a number of things:

- I am special.
- I can trust people.
- We are in this together.
- It feels good to spend time with people.
- I have lots of ways to get attention (a smile gets a smile in return).
- I can do things new ways, understand more, and get new ideas.

Respect

Samantha had worked diligently to attain a degree in early childhood education, and had the student loans to prove it. But now that she was out of school and working as a teacher in a child care center, the world didn't seem too impressed with her job compared with those of her friends who were working in banking or retail. At social gatherings when people asked Sam, "So, what do you do?" she received varying responses to her answer, "I am an infant teacher." The most common response was, "So you're kind of like a babysitter?" It irritated Sam that people didn't understand or appreciate the importance of her role.

Sam decided she should change her title to *NDS* to gain respect. What's an NDS? A neurodevelopmental specialist. Because that's exactly what Sam is, as is every other teacher—a person who nurtures the development of young brains. Although at times the world may not appreciate the tremendous contributions of infant and toddler teachers, the children do, and, for the most part, so do their families. Accolades for a good teacher may not appear in the forms of prestige, financial gain, or even credibility, but they present themselves in the forms of an infant's thankful smile, a toddler's hand reaching out, and the satisfaction of a job well done.

Daily Life Is Filled with Education

Because group care can be physically and emotionally demanding for teachers, they often forget that daily life at the center is filled with language, math, science, and other educational content. The steady beat of rain on the window and the rhythmic whirring of the washing machine are musical experiences. Putting two sheets in the dryer is math: "The sheets are wet when they go in and come out dry." The evaporation of

water and the change in the feel of sheets from wet to dry is science. "Put them in the dryer and take them out." The prepositions *in* and *out* show direction and location. "Smell the warm sheets, help sort and fold the laundry, and push the laundry cart into the room."

It is important for teachers to hear the music and take advantage of the language, number, and classification opportunities around them during routines and play. However, teachers should not be so concerned with educational concepts such as numbers, letters, and colors that they miss the pure enjoyment and texture of everyday life. If teachers are constantly articulating, enhancing, elaborating, reflecting, classifying, and counting, genuine pleasure and authenticity will fade, and children (and teachers) will overdose on teachable moments!

Guidelines for Quality Interactions

Playing with children as an adult differs from playing with children as another child does. While teachers participate in the caring or play activity, they are also responsible for keeping up the flow of interest, recognizing efforts, finding the novel experience, asking questions, and thinking ahead to the next transition. Good planning makes all these possible.

The teacher's role changes with the age of the child. In general, the older the child, the easier it is to know how to play with her. As a child gains more skills, she becomes more of a participant in play and less of an observer. As a result, most teachers feel more comfortable. At the same time, as infants and toddlers become older, they become more capable of entertaining themselves and should have sufficient time alone and with other children. The natural tendency of adults is to spend more time than is appropriate with older children because they respond in ways adults can better understand, such as pointing or speaking, and less time with the younger ones, particularly if there is any external pressure to teach.

Be Responsive and Reciprocal

Adults and children initiate social interactions and respond to and influence each other. Even very young infants initiate social interactions through crying, looking, tracking with their eyes, and, later, through vocalizing and gesturing. Also, from birth, infants respond to social approaches from adults. Distressed infants will often quiet when they are picked up. They become still while they listen to a teacher talk or sing, and they smile and coo contentedly when touched and talked to.

Responsiveness to a child's social initiations is critical during caring routines and play. All social overtures by a child should at least be acknowledged with a look or gesture and responded to as soon as possible. It is never appropriate to ignore an overture from an infant or toddler—for example, by refusing a block being offered, ignoring a smile or a wave, or not answering a babble or some other verbal communication.

Teachers have to be careful not to overwhelm very young children with their own activity. Instead, opportunities should be created by adults for infants and toddlers to respond to. Responses should be encouraged by showing pleasure or by responding in turn.

> Sienna, helping an infant stand up from a sitting position, does not repeatedly pull him up to standing by the arms and then sit him down again. Sienna might do this once or twice, but then she waits to feel the baby pushing up or trying to pull himself up by holding on to her.

Playing is not something done *to* babies: it is done *with* them.

Adapt Interactions and Play to Children's Cues Signs of interest become more obvious as infants get older. Their moods and behavior suggest the most appropriate kind of play. For example, when they are becoming tired or are at loose ends near departure time, they might enjoy close, quiet times with their teacher and a favorite book.

Infants and toddlers also give clues about their interests. For example, infants who are mouthing everything should not be given materials that are unsuited for chewing on. Toddlers who have discovered the thrill of hurling objects through space need lots of materials that are suitable and safe for throwing. Stackers need objects to stack, climbers need things to climb, and toddlers driven to fill and dump or transport objects need appropriate materials for those activities.

Good teachers are flexible enough to drop their preconceived plans and follow children's leads.

> Than has nine-month-old Ned in her lap and is helping him learn to play pat-a-cake. Ned claps his hands together for the first two lines of the verse, but instead of "rolling it and patting it," he begins to pat his cheeks, then his knees. Than understands this as an initiation, a creative variation by the baby, and she drops pat-a-cake at least temporarily to imitate Ned, expanding on his variation by naming cheeks and head and hands as he touches them.

> Ben has set up a painting activity for his two-year-old group. Large-appliance cartons have been placed outside, and thick, bright paints and large chunky brushes are nearby. A basin of soapy water, some sponges, and cloths for cleaning up are also available. The toddlers are mildly interested in painting the cartons but very interested in the soapy water and sponges. With great enthusiasm, they begin cleaning some nearby large play equipment. Ben, though disappointed, is flexible enough to allow this to become the activity and to provide some additional cleaning supplies.

Teachers must guard against becoming so invested in the experience they have planned that they forget the children.

Communicate in Many Different Ways Communication with infants and toddlers includes looking, moving, holding, rocking, touching, singing, smiling, laughing, listening, and talking, talking, talking! One of the marvelous virtues of body carriers like Snuglis or slings is the responsive communication that occurs when teachers move about and work with young infants secure on their chests.

> Monique has six-month-old Itai strapped securely in a sling that positions the baby on her hip. As Itai moves or gurgles, Monique responds with a reassuring sound, touch, and adjustment of her body to the baby's movement.

Overuse of body carriers is a concern only when children go from carriers to cribs, high chairs, or other restraining equipment and have little unrestrained time.

Recognize the Individual Style of the Child at Play, and Adapt Your Style to It

Some children need more help than others to get involved. Children who tend to stand or sit back may need the support, encouragement, and possibly the help of an adult to become involved. They do not need pressure, however, and individual differences must be accepted.

> Eighteen-month-old Emma typically watches from afar before trying something new, and often dabbles a bit before becoming fully engaged. In contrast, Mumtaz throws herself into whatever is available and needs help to stop flitting from one novel experience to another.

Be Authentic: Differing Personal Styles Have a Place Infants and toddlers become quite adept at recognizing artificial enthusiasm and interest. A discrepancy between your words and body language may confuse, cause anxiety, or ultimately lead toddlers to discount what you say. Some teachers are naturally bubbly and speak in a somewhat high-pitched voice when interacting with babies. Others are more matter-of-fact and less animated. Both styles are fine. The world is full of all types of people, and children benefit from the opportunity to interact with teachers with differing personalities and dispositions.

Help Infants and Toddlers Learn New Ways to Master and Meet New Challenges

With careful observation, teachers can give infants and toddlers just the amount of help they need to meet challenges, whether those consist of crawling out from under a table or zipping up a coat. They can also demonstrate new or better ways of doing things—for example, testing puzzle pieces or removing a cap from a jar. Demonstrations are a last resort and should be used only when children are about to give up on solving a problem. The aim is to encourage young children to be curious and to explore and discover the world on their own.

Twenty-four-month-old James is visibly frustrated that he cannot zip up his coat. Janelle, his teacher, observes his frustration and approaches him, saying, "May I help you with the zipper? I'll get it started and you can do the zipping."

Show Pleasure in Children's Play, but Use Praise Discerningly Showing pleasure and enjoyment in infants' and toddlers' play encourages them to persist. However, indiscriminate praise for everything they do has much less impact and begins to sound empty after a while. Sometimes simple acknowledgment or a comment about their work is all they need:

- "You put all the puzzle pieces in the container. That was a lot of work. Good job."
- "Look what you discovered! The ball goes through the tube and comes out on the other side. You're a smart thinker."
- "You've dropped one, two, three, four corks into the water!"
- "You must like that book—you've been looking at it a long time."

Let Children Explore the Uses of Materials In presenting a new play material or arrangement of equipment and materials, teachers should let children figure out what to do with it rather than direct their activities. Teachers should join in or suggest new possibilities only after children have had a chance to try it out. Children should not be deprived of the fun of discovering what can happen when they act on their world— that a mobile dances to its own music when it's touched, that pulling a string attached to a toy car will bring it closer, that water will not stack higher than the sides of a container, that balls bounce but a round piece of playdough does not.

Sensitive teachers rarely say "No" in play with infants and toddlers, reserving it for occasions when they might harm themselves, someone else, or something in the environment. One of the major goals of play in the child's first three years is to nurture curious assertive approaches to the world. To accomplish this, teachers must allow children freedom to explore within a secure setting.

Encourage Infants and Toddlers to Persist, Work Hard, and Achieve Reasonable Goals Good teachers provide challenges that are difficult but achievable for children and encourage each child to work at them. They intervene with help before babies become upset and quit when it seems appropriate, but not before children have wrestled with the problem.

Sooner or later, children with interesting, challenging environments are bound to find problems they want to solve but cannot. They frequently get stuck when they can't figure out their next move. Adults can then step in and provide the smallest possible bit of encouragement, the tiny link or boost that allows children to move forward again.

One-year-old Sarah is struggling to climb out of the wagon and is rescued just as she is about to dump herself out headfirst. David gives up the same task without as much effort as Sarah, and Fareen will never stop until she is successful.

Giving the right kind of help in the right amount at the right time is a characteristic of an excellent teacher.

Sometimes a teacher can encourage other children to help, or motivate a child who is flagging—for example, by saying, "Tyler and Gina, let's help Byron find that car." Infants and toddlers have valid reasons for stopping an activity: they may be tired of it, or the activity may be too difficult for them. There is no reason to persist in trying to maintain children's interest if there are signs that they are no longer interested, but sometimes encouragement revives their interest.

Help Infants and Toddlers Enjoy Other Children Infants' and toddlers' interest in relating to each other often exceeds their ability to do so. Teachers need to remain physically close to ensure that most interactions are pleasant ones. At the same time, teachers are modeling and talking about appropriate ways of interacting. The environment can assist them in helping children get along. Infants and toddlers often play better near, not with, each other, sharing experiences but not materials. Teachers facilitate learning when they provide duplicates of toys, tubs with sensory materials for each child, back-to-back toddlers' easels instead of side-by-side ones, and tables for one to three children instead of group tables.

Keep Children Safe and at the Same Time Allow Them to Take Risks Children exploring their emerging physical powers need to be able to stumble and take tumbles. Occasional minor bumps and bruises are inevitable, but more serious injuries are not acceptable. As discussed in chapter 13, finding a good balance between keeping children safe and allowing them to explore and use all their skills is a challenge for teachers.

See Supplement: *Playing and Exploring with Infants and Toddlers*

The Importance of Language

Language does more than simply represent our thoughts and feelings; it shapes and directs our thinking and feeling. A language-rich environment is important in encouraging cognitive and emotional development during the early years.

Children are tuned in to language from birth. The first feeding begins the lifelong give-and-take of communication that ends in dinner parties years later. The infant gurgles; the adult smiles or murmurs in response. The adult soothes; the infant sighs in response. From sighing, cooing, and babbling to first words, an infant learns that language is a powerful tool in human society. Children learn language by being with people who encourage their efforts to communicate and who look for opportunities to communicate with them.

Talking with Infants and Toddlers

Children learn language not only by living in a language-filled environment but by direct personal communication and eavesdropping—by listening carefully to the dialogues of others. Teachers should seize opportunities to talk one-to-one with children and to eliminate unnecessary noise. As reported in chapter 5, the frequency of communication in the first two or three years of life matters forever! Permanent cognitive capacity is increased through language interactions, and limited language interactions may permanently limit a child's language cognitive development (Hart and Risley 1995).

There is little value to baby talk. From birth, infants should be talked to in a natural manner. Adults sometimes oversimplify the ways they say things to babies ("See, big dog"), almost as if they have toned down their speech to speak as toddlers do. Of course, avoiding baby talk does not mean ignoring the cooing and babbling of young babies or the silly nonsense words of toddlers. This is valuable conversation for the youngest speakers. Young children like to hear their own emerging voices and words. They can be quite flattered when teachers join in on the repetitive game of imitating sounds and words.

> Six-month-old Andrea lies on her back, saying, "ma, ma, ma, ma." Her teacher, Shaun leans over and imitates Andrea's sounds, repeating, "ma, ma, ma, ma." Andrea smiles and repeats the sounds again. Shaun then changes the sound to "Ba, ba, ba, ba." Andrea eagerly imitates the new and similar sound.

In helping young children learn to use language, it is easy to lapse into teacher talk or artificial uses of language. Sometimes adults ask too many simplistic, closed questions—for example, "What color is that?" or "Where's the ball?" Or in their enthusiasm, they may talk too much, bombarding children with chatter so that there is no space for them to respond. Children may just turn off and tune out.

It may not feel natural at first to converse with infants who do not understand words or who cannot respond with words. However, this feeling is soon replaced by pleasure at their positive responses. With practice, natural, authentic conversation with infants becomes second nature.

Language Development in Young Children

As children try to learn to communicate fully, their language development moves from the perceptual to the conceptual, from sensation to thought. Children's thoughtfulness and curiosity arise from conversation or dialogue, from talking with adults and being listened to. They need much more than being asked concrete questions with singular answers: "What's that?" "How many?" and "What color?" They need questions that encourage divergent thinking ("Why?" "What if . . . ," "How?") and a willing listener as they search for answers to problems they are interested in. Genuine questions, prompted by children's interests, and conversations about a world with a past and a future, not just the here and now, characterize a good program. Conversations help endow events with meaning:

> "Kira's crying," said twenty-two-month-old Joey. "Why is she crying?" asked their teacher, Ellen, rather than explaining Kira's distress. "Sad!" said Joey. "She's sad that her daddy left, I think," Ellen explained. "What do you think, Joey?"

Guidelines for Good Language Interactions

"It is hard for teachers of older children to understand how much I talk during the day," says Linda, who staffs an infant-toddler class. "With young babies especially, I'm always putting words to their actions and sounds, so I am talking for two. I say things like 'José, you really like that milk,' or 'Look at you reach for that ball, Benji!' I'm always singing, chanting, telling them what I am doing, and reflecting their feelings—of course, I listen a lot too."

Children learn language in environments where it is valued as an integral tool for expression and for organizing the world. Good teachers:

Listen and respond. Take conversational turns that encourage give-and-take. Talk *with* the child, not *at* the child; watch for times that the child initiates conversation, and then respond. Let the child control the interaction sometimes.

Model language. Infants and toddlers need modeling, not correcting. Use words along with or instead of gestures, and use names: "Maya, please come sit in the chair," instead of "Sit here." Use nouns instead of shortcut pronouns: "Katie, take the ball" instead of "Take this." Adjectives enrich conversations and directions. Say "Justin, find the red duck," instead of "Go get it."

Share books with children. Looking at or reading books with infants and toddlers connects sounds and words with pictures. Share books regularly, even with young infants, who will enjoy the interaction with the teacher, the sounds, and the pictures, as well as the story line. It is never too early to start using books with infants.

Label and enhance the child's language. Give names to things and experiences. When an infant makes sounds or points, connect the experience to words. When an infant laughs at the sight of a biscuit, say, "You like the biscuit, don't you, Hakim?" When an older infant points and says, "Ba," say something like, "Oh, yes, look at the ball, Michael." When an infant is hungry, upset, or delighted, use language to label the emotion: "Oh, Lin, that makes you so happy when you find the ball." This is using language in a natural way to teach.

Extend the child's language. As infants combine sounds, teachers can extend their sounds into words without correcting them. When the child says, "Kitty there," respond, "Yes, Rohan, the kitty is right over there by the apple tree."

Play with sounds and words. Language is a marvelously expressive tool. Whispers, squeaks, chants, rhymes, songs, and other sound play encourage children to explore the range and the pure fun of language.

Comfort with language. Use words to help children identify their strong feelings and to help them feel better: "It makes you angry, Ella, when Gao knocks over your tower." Language is a powerful tool that can affect feelings dramatically.

Create experiences for using language. Provide objects and experiences that give children opportunities to talk about animals, people, familiar objects, and make-believe.

Use directives carefully. "Please come here," "Let's go out," "Time to eat," "Please clean up," "Cate, would you like to help me?" and other phrases that direct children's activities fill the environment with language. A high proportion of responsive comments and questions are characteristic of good caregiving and teaching.

Encourage questions. Ask toddlers questions to clarify and seek more information. Even before children have large vocabularies, it's important to encourage their questions by responding to quizzical expressions, gestures, and simple words.

Help children learn the give-and-take of conversation. Help children listen to each other and ask each other questions. Help them attend to other children who are attempting to communicate with them.

Know when to be silent. Give children some silent space in which to experiment with language. "The more teachers talk, the better" is true only up to a point.

A Final Word: Give Each Child Your Full Human Presence

Infant and toddler caregivers deserve the title of *teacher* and much more when they are present for children and use their full knowledge of each child. When they give children their full human presence—their language, which creates conversations; their nurturing physical contact, which supports a sense of personal worth and emotional and physical security; their ability to think on their feet, which creates and takes advantage of teachable moments—then they are educators in the best sense of the word.

See Supplement: *Do I Maximize Learning Experiences for Infants and Toddlers?*

Exercises

1. After working with children for thirty minutes, jot down all the teachable moments you noticed and can extend to scaffold the children's learning.

2. Make a list of the opportunities for learning about the world of numbers in the daily life of a group of toddlers on a typical morning.

3. Choose three children and compare and contrast their styles of playing.

4. Record your conversations with children for fifteen to thirty minutes. Listen to the recording and analyze how much of your language was directive, responsive, or conversational. Did you use open-ended questions? Did you use more nouns *(the ball, Maya)* than pronouns *(it, her)*?

Reference

Hart, B., and T. Risley. 1995. *Meaningful Differences in the Everyday Experience of Young American Children.* Baltimore: Paul H. Brooke.

Chapter 16

Curriculum and Learning

Excellence *The child's entire experience in the program is considered important; there is no clear separation between learning and being cared for, between play and work. There is an awareness that children are learning all the time as they go about their job of developing: education does not fit into a tidy time or space. The curriculum incorporates all parts of the day and the child's experience. Group activities are scaled in frequency, size, nature, and duration to the children's interests and abilities; large-group experiences are rare.*

Curriculum is the term used for the provisions made for children's learning experience—the way a learning environment, both its physical and human dimensions, is planned and organized, the caring and learning experiences and routines, and the interactions and relationships that occur. The fundamental premise of a curriculum is that children are active learners who learn best from activities they plan and carry out themselves. Children are recognized as explorers, scientists, and builders, as acrobats and artisans who need active experience with the world of people and things, and opportunities to plan, set goals, and take responsibility. It is understood that the spirit of learning, not the informational content, is the prime concern.

The curriculum is designed to

- empower each child to become a confident, lifelong learner and a secure, caring person who approaches the world as if it is an invitation to learn
- promote all aspects of development: large and small motor, cognitive, perceptual, social, emotional, language, creative, and expressive

- nurture a positive self-concept, which includes acceptance of cultural and family background
- be free of racial or gender bias and stereotypes, and to encourage children to accept and enjoy diversity
- provide a wonderful place for a childhood
- promote parent partnership and awareness of the child's learning and development.

Staff are expected to provide the routines, environment, and materials that children learn from, and to stimulate their questions and curiosity. Staff support and encourage children, provoke their questions, have interesting conversations with them, and help them find answers and new challenges. Teachers also help children achieve the confidence and self-discipline to develop increasingly more sophisticated skills and knowledge.

In order to teach children what the world is like, how it works, their own important place in it, and what they are capable of, an environmental approach to early education addresses furnishings, equipment, materials, the ways time and space are structured, and all the ways adults and children behave. Schedules, routines, learning centers, and learning are built into classroom furnishings (for example, different patterns, textures, and furniture to interact with—not the artificial learning of garish ABC rugs), and outdoor play areas are planned to encourage children to explore, discover, and learn independently through developmentally appropriate play.

> **The Child's Job**
>
> - **Make sense of the world**
> - **Learn to communicate fully**
> - **Discover and develop all bodily powers**
> - **Understand how everything works**
> - **Deeply connect with people**

The Infant and Toddler Curriculum

The first two years of life are when children need to acquire what psychologist Erik Erikson called *basic trust*—a pervasive sense of the essential trustworthiness of oneself and others. This is the sense of safety and security that comes from responsive, predictable care from familiar others to whom one is attached. Without this sense, the world is far too scary a place to cope with and learn about.

Each child also needs to develop a sense of autonomy, a sense of being a separate, independent self. This comes from being treated as an individual and being allowed increasing opportunities for independence. The toddler's "No" is an assertion of autonomy that leads to freely saying "Yes" and to developing the power to begin controlling body and feelings.

Only when children feel a sense of personal power ("I can affect (influence) things") and competence ("I can achieve things") can they step out into the world as active learners and problem solvers prepared to cope with whatever will come.

To ensure that each child develops a strong sense of basic trust, autonomy, power, and competence, the curriculum needs to be based on two concepts: prime times and a world at their fingertips. Together, these two elements ensure individualized care and active, developmentally appropriate experience.

In addition, children need to develop a sense of connection and belonging—to family and to the group. Along with independence, children learn interdependence and begin the challenging lifelong task of negotiating their own needs and rights alongside those of others.

Encouraging Prime Times through a Well-Designed Environment

A well-designed learning environment that supports child choice allows staff to focus on prime times, those moments of one-to-one care and learning that lie at the heart of healthy development: caring, nurturing, learning moments or conversations during which there is total engagement with people and things. A rich, built-in learning environment allows teachers relaxed time to feed, diaper, dress, ease into or out of sleep, and otherwise nurture a child: to touch, to talk, to listen, to play all the call-response games the child sets in motion. These moments are the most important prime times for learning.

A World at Their Fingertips Young children need a safe world, rich with opportunities they can actively explore and enjoy. They need to see, hear, feel, touch, and move in a world in which, according to psychologist Jerome Bruner, a child "is encouraged to venture, rewarded for venturing his own acts, and sustained against distraction or premature interferences in carrying them out" (1973, 8).

Infants and toddlers are sensorimotor beings who make sense of their experiences by exploring with their rapidly emerging bodily powers. Long before they understand concepts like *under* or *far* with their minds, their bodies are learning to navigate the up and down, over and under of the physical world.

Infant and toddler environments are planned and organized to maximize

- *large- and small-motor experiences.* For younger babies, these include looking, reaching, grasping, holding, crawling in, out, over, under; for toddlers, these include gripping, throwing, manipulating, walking, climbing, pushing, pulling.
- *sensory experiences,* which includes explorations of texture, color, sound, size, shape, smell, taste, weight.
- *cognitive experiences,* which includes object permanence, spatial relationships, classification, collection and dumping, cause-and-effect experiences, problem solving.
- *language,* which includes adult-child conversations, labeling, books, music, rhyming, and sound explorations.
- *social experiences,* which include one-to-ones with teachers, child-initiated interactions, guiding and modeling positive peer interactions.
- *expression,* which includes art, movement, doll and soft-toy play, imitation, and beginning dramatic play.

With all these, the emphasis is on what the child gains in the process of engaging with people, equipment, and materials, rather than on creating a product or a result.

Encouraging Prime Times with Activities That Are Learning Experiences

Teaching infants and toddlers must be fun. You rock them all day, and they look like they are having so much fun. You get to play all day with them?

In a good infant or toddler room, it all looks like play: children are busy exploring the world and testing their newly emerging ideas and skills. But the play that children experience is the result of their teacher's looking, listening, and learning in response to the children's abilities, needs, and interests, as well as her own good planning—in advance and on the spot. High-quality education is much more than a matter of doing; it is a product of careful observation, reflection, and teamwork.

The Importance of Authentic Experiences An exclusively child-oriented world peopled by children and women, filled with bright plastic things and pictures of animals and fairytale characters, is a very limited and artificial world in which to spend thirty to fifty hours a week. Instead, the best child care emphasizes authentic and natural experiences, ones that have meaning in the life of the program and in the ongoing lives of children. These real-life experiences do not rely on artificially contrived experiences, but instead include such activities as cleaning; food preparation; caring for other people, animals, and plants; and helping with laundry. There is an effort to bring the real world into the program as well as to get the children out into the community around them. Family child care has a wonderful natural advantage in providing authentic experiences if children are brought into the life of the home rather than relegated to a playroom that mimics a center's environment.

Planned Activities An emphasis on a rich learning environment, individualized learning, and children's own interests may sound as if teachers don't need to plan or do anything special. What about activities? Since we know how important the first three years of life are for learning, don't we need to offer babies and toddlers special educational activities—*don't we need to teach them?* Aren't we well past the days when you just put some stuff out for them to play with and let them play?

The answer is yes and no. In many programs in which activities have become the planned focus of the program, the term *activities* singles out those experiences that caregivers have thought about and planned for in advance and that have a purpose linked to children's interests, development, and learning. That's great, and infants and toddlers need experiences that come out of careful thought and planning. But *activities* also include all the important parts of a child's experience: eating is an activity, lunch is an activity, and separating from a parent is an activity. These activities are as important and powerful and just as much *learning* activities as are planned ones; unfortunately, in many settings, only planned activities are considered *important*.

Additionally, the term *activities* often carries with it the notion of being teacher-led, something done with a group, and perhaps with an end product and a fixed beginning and end. Often the pressure to be doing something educational with infants and toddlers leads teachers to attempt, with children under age three, watered-down versions of activities that are successful with children older than three years—usually with little success.

Because the term *activities* conjures these associations, some people prefer to avoid talking about what is offered to infants and toddlers as *activities* and to instead use terms such as *opportunities, possibilities,* or *experiences.* The words do not matter so much, and both *experiences* and *activities* are used in this book, but the principle is important. Infants and toddlers need lots of opportunities to explore, experiment, create, meet challenges, and learn about the world of objects and people within a rich environment with the help, interest, and encouragement of sensitive and sensible adults. They do not need to be taken away from such opportunities to be placed in a group that is doing something that may not be appropriate for their age or their interests, no matter what it's called.

Having a minimum of structured activities does not mean that infant and toddler teachers do not have to plan. They plan opportunities and experiences that flow from the learning centers and from their nurturing interactions, and their plans match the needs, interests, and abilities of the children. They plan individual activities for their primary care children and for small groups. Wonderful things do not happen in infant-toddler rooms unless there has been a lot of conscious reflection, critique, and planning, both ahead of time and as the day proceeds.

Initiating or Responding? Actually, Both

Responding to children's needs and interests is considered a keystone of good care and education. But this does not mean that teachers just sit back and respond—that they never try something completely new, that they never start something, that everything they do has to follow in a very literal way from something they have noticed through observation. How boring that would be for children and teachers alike! Clever, creative, sensitive teachers experiment all the time—*Let's try this, Let's change that, I have an idea, I wonder what would happen if. . . .*

The key is that when something new is offered or is placed in the environment, excellent teachers pay close attention to how children respond. Excellent care and education involve responding, initiating, and always paying close attention to what children are doing and saying.

Children learn best when the teacher works as their learning facilitator. Before planning any teacher-directed activity, first consider whether children could have the same experience on their own using a prop box or a learning center. Almost any teacher-planned and -directed activity, or at least part of it, can be developed as a prop box or learning center. (See discussions in chapters 7 and 17.)

A Not-So-Simple Cooking Experience

Simone, the teacher, believes that the older toddlers would enjoy a simple cooking experience. As she invites a small group of toddlers around her to participate, she realizes that this experience has many components that are likely to hold the children's attention and curiosity. The children enjoy the experience of making a cake, and all the items and materials it takes to do so, as much as they enjoy eating the end product. Any one of the steps below could be an appropriate stand-alone experience for the children.

- Bang the wooden spoons in the big metal bowls, pretend to stir, and stack the bowls. To extend opportunities like these, Simone could add wooden spoons and bowls to the dramatic-play learning center.

- Look at the containers of salt, flour, sugar, and other ingredients and pour out their contents. To extend this opportunity, Simone could place empty food containers in the dramatic play area for pretend cooking and pouring. Simone could also put these same food containers in the sand table for the children to fill and pour.

- Feel and taste the salt, flour, water, and other ingredients, and talk about how they taste. Simone could organize a tasting experience.

- Touch and shape the mixed dough. To extend the experience, Simone could give each child a small portion of the dough, plastic utensils and plates, and let them shape their own small cakes.

Group Activities—Few, Short, and Small Group life in an infant or toddler room is not about lots of planned group activities in which many or all the children are doing approximately the same thing. Instead, it focuses on learnable moments. Most group activities for infants and toddlers happen spontaneously when the children come together, not when the adults decide to pull together a group. Remember, for infants and toddlers, two or three children is a group, and four or more children is a large group. As toddlers develop, short, small-group activities can be enjoyable, and there is probably value in relatively brief (ten minutes or fewer) larger touch-base groups that develop children's sense of the whole group. These can include brief storytelling times, songs, good-morning circles, and walks. Children should be encouraged but never forced or required to participate in such experiences.

Short, teacher-directed circle times for older toddlers and for twos ready to make the transition to preschool rooms are appropriate to help children begin to learn the social skills needed for group activities. The burden is on the teacher to engage children so they don't tune out, rather than relying on coercive direction. Again, encouragement to participate is appropriate, but requiring children to sit in the group is not.

The best kinds of group activities, or for that matter, the best of any activities and experiences, are those that allow children to engage and participate in a variety of ways. These should include opportunities not just to watch and listen, but to engage in large- and small-motor activities, to vocalize and sing, or to engage the content in their own way. This allows a better match between children's interests and abilities and the opportunities offered—that is, open-ended materials and experiences that children are more likely to find enjoyable and enriching.

See Supplement: *Promoting Learning through Teacher-Guided Experiences: Planning for Success*

Five Key Parts to Planning Activities The most challenging times in group life usually occur during transitions from one activity to another, whether those activities are caring routines such as mealtimes, or planned activities for individuals or groups. It is important to think about the child's transition in and out of the activity as an integral part of the activity. Consider the following:

- Transitioning in: How is a child going to move into the activity without confusion and waiting?
- Entry: How is a child going to begin and to understand what to do?
- Activity: Will a child be able to do what is expected? Are there different ways that children with different interests and abilities can participate?
- Windup/cleanup: How does a child finish the activity and participate in cleanup?
- Transition out: How does a child move on to the next activity?

The more elaborate the activity, the more important it is to break it down and ensure that all the pieces are developmentally appropriate, given the time slot and space. Messy activities such as mealtime and fingerpainting obviously require more planning than reading a book or a flannelboard story or playing a quick game of Duck, Duck, Goose. But forethought is always important for any activity, because antisocial acts such as pushing or biting and overly directive or negative adult attention can occur during transitions in or out of an activity. Even the best-planned activities may not work well for a group or for individual children.

High/Scope's Key Experiences for Infants and Toddlers

Not all experiences are equal, and the learning environment is designed to promote experiences essential to development. The High/Scope Educational Research Foundation has developed a list of key experiences for the period from birth through age two and a half to help teachers plan for and guide children's experience in the program. Key experiences describe how infants and toddlers explore the environment, learn about themselves, and begin to interact with others in their world.

High/Scope's key experiences are organized into categories based on their cognitive-developmental approach to curriculum. Each experience is illustrated with an anecdote. Note that the anecdote may apply to other key experiences. For example, two babies playing peekaboo are having a social experience, a presentation experience of object permanence, and a movement experience.

Sense of Self

- Expressing initiative

  Tara turns her head to get her bottle.

- Distinguishing "me" from others (for example, recognizing one's own image in a mirror)

  Ali waves at his image in the mirror as he sits on the floor in front of it, touching first his face and then the reflection of his face in the mirror.

- Solving problems encountered in exploration and play

  After Keisha (a caregiver) asks Reem where his ball is, he proceeds to dig in the sand, find the ball, and hold it up while smiling.

- Doing things for themselves

  Leah eats her dry cereal out of a paper cup at snacktime, pouring the cereal into her mouth as if she were drinking it.

Social Relations

- Forming an attachment to a primary caregiver

  Daniel goes over to Mindy (his teacher) and sits down in her lap.

- Building relationships with other adults

  As they are getting ready to leave for the day, Laurel plays peekaboo with Yasir's mom.

- Building relationships with peers

  Henry and Sanjay, laughing, play a brief game of peekaboo around the basketball pole during outdoor time.

- Expressing emotions

  Matt goes over to Rebecca, who has just returned after a week's vacation, and gives her a kiss.

- Showing empathy toward the feelings and needs of others

  Mai hugs Christopher, who is crying because his mom left.

- Developing social play

  Tai chases Anna until they both fall on the ground giggling.

Creative Representation

- Imitating and pretending

  Elena (an adult) is folding diapers for the infants when Karlie comes over and starts folding diapers for her baby doll.

- Exploring building and art materials (for example, scribbling, using blobs of paint, using clay, attempting to make a circle)

  Nick colors with chalk on a chalkboard that lies flat on the floor. He makes long, curved scribble lines at one edge, and leaves the center of the board blank.

- Responding to and identifying pictures and photographs

  Carlos sees a picture of a duck in his book and excitedly says, "Quack, quack, quack."

Movement

- Moving parts of the body (head turning, grasping, kicking)

  Lying on his stomach, Mischa reaches for and bats at a beach ball.

- Moving one's whole body (rolling, crawling, cruising, walking, running, balancing)

  During outdoor time, Kemal and three other children jump up and down in the empty plastic wading pool.

- Moving with objects

  Gina pushes a car on the floor and crawls after it.

- Feeling and expressing steady beat

  Tia rocks back and forth to the steady beat as her teacher sings a lullaby.

Music

- Listening to music

  Robin turns his head toward the music.

- Responding to music

  Steven bobs up and down to "Wheels on the Bus."

- Exploring and imitating sounds

  Hakim rides around on a toy train, making the choo-choo sound over and over.

- Exploring vocal pitch

  When Zach's book falls on the floor, he says, "Uh-oh," making his voice go from high to low.

Communication and Language

- Listening and responding (to sounds, voices, words, sensations, and facial expressions)

  Nguyen looks at Tracy (an adult) when Tracy speaks to her, and smiles at the sound of Tracy's voice.

- Communicating nonverbally

  Lorenzo tugs on Toni's (a caregiver's) pant leg, then points to the box of Cheerios.

- Participating in communication give-and-take

  Shawna (an adult) is rocking Austin while looking into his face and singing to him. She begins singing the sounds "La, la, la" instead of the regular words to the song. Austin looks up at her and says, "La, la, ma, ma. . . ."

- Communicating verbally

  Lyle says, "Help me," as he brings his shoes over to an adult after naptime.

- Exploring picture books and magazines

  Darius looks through a familiar storybook, saying some words quietly to himself.

- Enjoying stories, rhymes, and songs

  At a circle time, Julia chimes in as the group sings a rhyming song:
  Marta (adult): One, two . . .
  Julia: Buckle my shoe.
  Marta: Three, four . . .
  Julia: Shut the door.

Exploring Objects

- Exploring objects with the hands, feet, mouth, eyes, ears, and nose

  Sophie takes her pacifier out of her mouth, looks at it, changes her position, and puts back it back in her mouth.

- Discovering object permanence (the awareness that objects continue to exist even when they are no longer visible, which usually develops by the age of eight months)

  Leandro continues to crawl toward a cup, even after his teacher has put it behind a chair, out of his sight.

- Exploring and noticing how things are the same or different

  Jenny tries to take a blanket another child is using. Dee (an adult) offers Jenny a different blanket that is almost identical except that it has a hole in it. Jenny refuses this blanket, saying, "No, Dee, it's broken."

Early Quantity and Number

- Experiencing "more"

  While playing with playdough during small-group time, Kati observes, "Hey, there's some more," upon discovering some playdough left in the container.

- Experiencing one-to-one correspondence

  Mee takes three play people out of a basket and puts each one inside its own little car.

- Exploring the number of things

  Tanya finds a shoe in a box of clothes and continues to search for another one.

Space

- Exploring and noticing the location of objects

  Jake has finished his snack (which the class ate outdoors). When Amber (an adult) asks him to throw away his napkin, Jake walks over to the trash can and puts his napkin in it.

- Observing people and things from various perspectives

  Juan looks at Jan (an adult) through his legs as he bends over with his hands touching the floor. Jan says, "Upside down!" and Juan responds, "Down!"

- Filling and emptying, putting in and taking out

  Taylor fills up her purse with small blocks and carries the purse around the room with her.

- Taking things apart and fitting them together

  Yoshi fits the small pegs into the pegboard, one at a time.

Time

- Anticipating familiar events

  Sam brings his chair across the room to the lunch table and sits down, an hour before lunch occurs.

- Noticing the beginning and ending of a time interval

  Raoul is taking turns jumping on the mini-trampoline with Carter. Raoul jumps several more times, says, "One more minute," then immediately gets off the trampoline and says to Carter, "Your turn." They alternate turns for several minutes.

- Experiencing "fast" and "slow"

  Andy is pushing another child on the swing during outdoor time. Andy says to David (an adult), "I pushin' Henry fast!"

- Repeating an action to make something happen again, experiencing cause and effect

  Bryan plays with a pop-up toy as he sits on his teacher's lap. He pushes the button four times to make the animal pop up.

(Post 1996, 239–44)

Using Key Experiences

Key experiences are useful to keep in mind as you organize the environment, plan activities, plan for individuals, and interact with children, because they cut across curriculum content and focus on the child's development. Key experiences are also valuable for structuring observations and analyzing and interpreting the behavior of children. Watching children is easy—figuring out what to observe amidst all that is happening is hard. Key experiences provide the structure.

- Exploring and noticing the location of objects; discovering object permanence

  Seven-month-old Sebastian is moving toward Emma's bottle. He stops when it disappears from his sight because it has been blocked by another child. He resumes when the child blocking the bottle moves on.

- Filling and emptying; imitating and pretending (using one object to stand for another); communicating verbally

  Two-year-old Lilly carefully pours her milk into her cup, takes a sip, and then gets up and dumps it out in the garbage. She sits down again, pours more, and dumps it out, this time watching the milk splash in the garbage can. "Rain," she shouts, before her teacher catches on and ends the waste of the milk.

Using key experiences helps caregivers stay focused on why children do things and "what children can do rather than what they cannot yet do or are not doing because they are not interested. Observation makes us more aware of the child's needs and interests at the moment; this in turn leads us to support the child more appropriately" (Post 1995, 3).

Helping Children Learn through Play and Exploration

Children's most effective learning occurs during play and exploration alongside sensitive adults in rich, prepared learning environments. The major kinds of learning are described below.

Cognitive Learning

Each time a teacher encourages motor or perceptual exploration or asks children questions or listens seriously to children's questions, she is promoting thinking skills (cognitive learning): supporting children's efforts to make sense of the world, to discover and develop all their bodily powers, to understand how everything works, and to learn how to fully communicate.

The better tailored a teacher's questions are to children's interests and current understanding, the more learning children are likely to do. Asking toddlers to clarify and expand on their responses is important. Some one-to-one experiences to consider:

- Object-permanence activities: Peekaboo; "Where is the _____?" "Where did the _____ go?"
- Anticipation games: Objects in space; "Where will my hand/the ball/the truck go?" "What happens next?" "What am I going to do next?"
- Cause-and-effect games: "What happens if we _____?"
- Recognition games: "What is that?" "What does that do?" "What am I doing?"

Perceptual Learning

Teachers can best facilitate children's perceptual development by recognizing their explorations, providing ways to extend and enhance newfound discoveries, and providing words for what they are experiencing. Children learn from an increasingly sophisticated continuum of experiences. For example, light to dark, sour to sweet, soft to hard, and quiet to loud become differentiated as children develop. Spontaneous and planned comparison games and stories such as "Goldilocks and the Three Bears" are increasingly interesting to children as their sensory capabilities develop.

Language Learning

Teachers can give infants and toddlers words for their increasingly sophisticated actions, feelings, and understanding: "You are trying so hard to hold that rattle." Alice Honig calls this parallel talk (1982). Also important is self-talk—talking about what you are doing with and for the baby (for example, saying "I'm rubbing your tummy now").

The key to successful communications is finding one-to-one opportunities for talking with the child. Talking *with*, not *at*, is important. It's the difference between real conversation with children and noisy, often annoying prattle. Look for cues and respond to their communication. Respect a child's need for quiet and for solitary observation.

There are lots of simple language games and one-to-one activities to enjoy spontaneously with infants and toddlers while being sensitive to their cues:

- Sentence completion games: "Let's go to the _____." "I just waved to _____."

- Word-sound games (rhyming, chanting): "The cat in the hat with a bat." "The truck and the train and the track and the tree." "The diaper and the wiper and the dryer."
- Counting games: "One, two, three spoons—one, two, three cups."
- Location games: "Where is the truck? Under the chair."
- Time and sequence games: "First we come in the door, then we put away our coats, then we give Molly a big hug."
- Who games: "Who is that in the rocking chair?"

See Supplement: *Twenty Ways to Encourage Children's Language Development*

Appreciating Books and Stories An early step to becoming a reader takes place when a baby is read to and learns to love and respect books through handling them (including smelling and mouthing them) and through trying to understand the images on the page. Even young infants enjoy being held and looking at a book with an enthusiastic teacher. What do you read to a baby in the first few months of life? Anything you enjoy that is rich in rhythmic language: rhymes, chants, songs, and lots of repetition. It is the togetherness, the eye contact, and the sounds that begin the child's love affair with language and books. It's the same with older babies, except now they can interact more with you and begin to recognize familiar images: people, household objects, animals, shapes. Babies enjoy point-and-say books ("See the baby"), books with questions ("Who said moo?"), and, as they get older, books they can hold and chew on as they ponder this wonderful world.

The world begins to open up to toddlers, and books about children, families, and challenges that toddlers can understand (often represented by animal surrogates) are valuable. Challenges of separation, friendship, hunger, desire to have or do things, and recognition of things they see and use in daily life appeal to young children, as do books that create moods or feelings.

Sharing books should occur frequently, and almost always works better individually or in small groups of two or three. When sharing a book with a larger group of five or six, it is important to always stay in tune with the children: from where they sit, what are they seeing and hearing? When children become restless, use questions, act out a role, and let them anticipate a word ("And the duck began to _____? *Quack!*") to sustain interest, but don't force completion of a story or require all children to participate.

Books that children can use by themselves should be durable and clearly displayed. Teachers should encourage respectful use of books. Occasionally reading a book yourself while they are reading their own is good modeling.

Storytelling is hugely valuable to language and cognitive development, particularly when the storyteller enjoys the language as much as the story content. Use your voice dramatically, play with the sound of words, and, for toddlers, occasionally use props, puppets, or flannelboards. Infants enjoy listening and watching small groups of toddlers. Of course, stories that call for physical responses or that can be acted out appeal to children and can promote development across several dimensions.

Large-Motor Skills and Development

With foam forms, pillows, planks, large blocks, crates, and cubes, teachers can offer infants and toddlers an endless variety of locomotor and nonlocomotor challenges. (The term *locomotor* refers to moving through space.) Nonlocomotor skills such as stretching, bending, balancing, falling, and rising develop in tandem with locomotor skills. The key to helping children learn is recognizing that slight variations are significant—the power of small changes, which we mention in chapter 17. Creating a slightly steeper incline to crawl or walk up, a bumpier surface to roll on, or a larger beach ball to carry may have the same effect on infants and toddlers as if teachers had asked the children to balance on a plank rather than on a path or to climb into a hammock instead of a cot. Walking up is easier than walking down. Pushing is easier than pulling. Moving and holding are a challenge. Stepping, jumping, and running are all challenges that follow becoming confident about being upright.

Teaching motor skills means providing support for practice and mastery, and providing challenging opportunities that lie beyond present ones. It is not necessary or appropriate to instruct children in these skills or to try to accelerate or push their motor development. Good teachers are attuned to an individual infant's effort to reach, grasp, hold, let go, and kick and to a toddler's mastery of pulling, carrying, walking, walking down an incline, and throwing, and all the other new skills that being upright and mobile entail.

Movement and Music Play Understanding that music can occur any time is not the same thing as playing a radio or CD arbitrarily or bursting spontaneously into song. Too much auditory stimulation is usually more of a problem than too little. Music is a wonderful tool for setting a mood. It can calm children down or inject a sense of whimsy or new energy. Take your cues from the children when using background music and spontaneous singing.

There are activity books filled with songs and fingerplays for infants and toddlers, but most children's music and movement can be improvised. Living each day as an opera and singing while you work are characteristics of a good infant or toddler room.

Young infants are aware of sounds and soon respond to the emotional content of music. As infants gain control over their bodies, they move in response to rhythms. Toddlers love songs that require physical responses, such as "Hokey Pokey" and "Ring around the Rosy"; songs about families; and songs that reflect moods (happy, sad, angry, or busy, for example). Waving scarves, banging spoons, and playing instruments should not have to wait for a designated music time.

Small-Motor Skills and Development

It is an amazing developmental journey that an infant takes from learning to grasp, to let go, to using the pincer grip, to becoming a confident toddler who can manipulate, put together and take apart toys, and string, pound, and scribble. Teachers encourage small-motor and perceptual motor learning by getting to know individual children and trying to provide the right range and number of material choices for each child. Having rattles, stackers, noisy squeakers, spoons, blocks, beanbags, and other infant toys available and selectively displayed is important. Observe and show interest in children's efforts, and occasionally change their experiences to find the right moderately novel experience to challenge them: put the rattle just out of reach, play catch, or substitute a more complicated puzzle or pull toy.

Construction/Block Play Having available a variety of blocks—large and small, soft and hard, multicolored—provides teachers with endless opportunities for facilitating learning. Big foam and cardboard blocks can be crawled around, sat on, knocked down, or pushed aside; they can be stacked in the form of a tower, made into a house, placed in falling domino rows, or used with a plank to form a bench or ramp. Blocks can be covered with blankets or other surfaces to form a bumpy terrain. Small blocks are great unstructured manipulatives, useful for building and for representing many objects.

Sand, Water, and Other "Messy" Sensory Exploration Children respond differently to messy materials: some seem to need to explore one finger at a time; others jump right in. Help children explore in the manner that fits their style.

Sensory exploration occurs naturally during bathing, hand washing, mealtimes, and puddle exploration—any time sensory materials are available. Offer an abundance of alternatives to off-limits exploration of toilets, sinks, and the lunch table.

Older infants and toddlers enjoy exploring sensory materials in water tables and tubs. An arrangement where they can play individually near, but not with, other children is often best—for example, back-to-back tubs or tubs separated by a few feet. Giving children the power to alter sensory materials (for example, soap or food coloring to change the water; water to add to sand), props, and tools adds to their play. They can help prepare an activity by putting down a tarp or by assisting in cleanup with towels and sponges, as long as you don't expect them to accomplish much.

Outdoors, of course, is a natural site for sensory exploration.

Play with Art Materials Infants and toddlers are definitely more in tune with the sensory qualities of art materials than with any artistic outcomes. Art for toddlers is not just a watered-down preschool activity. Developmentally appropriate art is usually a sensory exploration of materials and media and should always be more process-oriented than product-producing. Emphasizing product is inappropriate, because toddlers don't set out to make anything worth preserving. Teachers should not pressure them to think that way. Art for infants is only a matter of making sense of the world.

Visual explorations of form and color can include smearing, poking holes, and pounding. Teachers can help children by using open-ended questions ("What do you see?"), by giving words to the child's visual or tactile exploration ("It's really bright [soft, bumpy, etc.], isn't it?"), and by providing media to experiment with. Art is not just pictures and painting; it is also sculpture, light, and motion.

Infants can explore art materials on a lap, in a high chair, or on the floor. Toddlers (and preschoolers) often prefer to kneel or stand rather than sit.

Toddlers enjoy paint and clay, gluing and pasting. The sound of crinkly and tearing paper and the residual movement of balled-up newspaper are also part of experiencing art, as are pounding and kneading clay. Remember that tearing as well as using scissors works for making collages.

Diane Trister Dodge and Laura J. Colker (1996, 181) offer the following ideas for teachers when they talk to children about their artwork:

- Describe what you see: "I see you used a lot of colors."
- Talk about actions: "You made the lines go up and down."
- Ask about process: "Did you like smearing the gooey paint?"
- Use words to encourage and support: "You made a lot of pictures today. Which one do you want to hang up?"

It is not particularly meaningful to children to have the results of their art and craft projects displayed, but some children may enjoy seeing evidence of their work, especially in photos and when they are hung at eye-level. However, too much emphasis on the product teaches children to want to finish up and display their projects. Photographs are valuable because they can document the entire experience.

While the process, not the product, is the point, examples of children's art are valued by parents, who want to display these efforts in their home, and many teachers want to create portfolios or bulletin-board displays. The absence of any examples may be taken by parents as an indication that their child isn't doing much.

The way to resolve this dilemma is to recognize and articulate the distinction between artifact (the visual evidence of the effort) and art. *Artifact* is a better term than *product* because it conjures up a by-product of the experience rather than an end product. First, help parents understand what is developmentally appropriate. Second, satisfy parents' need for artifacts by using photographs of children's activities and pieces of what has resulted from children's process-oriented efforts; for example, snippets from fingerpainting, gluing, or scribbling.

Art experiences can be good opportunities to encourage group efforts. A large piece of paper attached to a fence and some paint and brushes can result in a great group mural. If teachers keep in mind that the main aim of offering art materials to children under three years old is to give them a chance to explore and experiment, new possibilities for wonderful experiences open up.

Play with Science

Infants and toddlers literally embody the scientific method. First they observe, followed by endless trial and error and experimentation with everything in their world; they use their mouth and entire body, and they begin to look closely rather than to simply see. Soon their scientific exploration becomes more sophisticated, and toddlers conduct fabulous experiments with whatever happens to be at hand in the kitchen, bathroom, indoors, or outdoors.

The best thing that a teacher can do is to enjoy the world and how it works and share that pleasure with children by noticing the infinite variety in nature, machines, humans, and animals, and by engaging children with open-ended questions and naming, cataloging, and marveling. The smoothness of a stone, the bumpiness of bark, the golden leaf with red veins, the boiling, whistling kettle, and the mist on the window are daily encounters with science, as are dropping a spoon, sliding down an inclined surface, filling up a bucket, or pushing a table.

Beyond engineering the rich world at their fingertips, teachers facilitate early childhood learning by encouraging exploration and by keeping materials and tools at hand that enhance children's experiences. Containers, magnifiers, string, and tape create physics experiments in gravity and resistance; other materials such as fabric, plastic, and prisms transform light. Growing plants, caring for animals and birds, and cooking offer other explorations of the physical world.

Cooking

Cooking is a wonderful activity that involves all the senses as well as small-motor skills. Young infants like to watch cooking, and toddlers can begin to participate in it. For example, they can snap beans, tear lettuce, pour milk, cut a banana, stir a pot, knead bread dough, and dish out pudding. Small, quick tasks such as popping toast in a

toaster, pouring pancake batter, using cookie cutters, or pouring salad dressing are easy to do. Such tasks empower children and become exercises in cause and effect. Children enjoy imitating the sounds as well as acting out the actions.

Play That Promotes Social Learning and Emotional Development

Teachers help children learn social skills as they go about their lives in a group setting. As articulate role models, teachers present children with pictures of social behavior. By noticing and encouraging children's attempts at social play (their acts of joining, cooperating, and caring) and by explaining to children the whys and implications of behavior, teachers promote social literacy. Teachers can provide words to help toddlers solve problems and to encourage them to help each other—for example, "Will you hold Moira's mittens while she puts on her coat?" (Do not, however, go beyond Moira's ability to even momentarily give up possession of them.)

Teachers can help children learn to cope with and control their developing emotions. The struggle for self-control begins in infancy when babies learn self-calming mechanisms: thumb sucking, rocking, and cooing. Adult support helps children learn they can manage the rockier aspects of life. Individual children require different levels and kinds of facilitation. Remember, children are born with fundamentally different personalities.

Jeremy is so enthusiastic that he sometimes overwhelms others and needs help with more relaxed overtures. Sally and Albert both hold back and need encouragement. Leah has trouble when children are too close, and does better when helped to carve out a more separate territory.

The job of the teacher is to help children develop prosocial behaviors, not to change their personality.

Dramatic Play Dramatic play does not have to be confined to a dramatic-play area or to the use of realistic props. Dramatic play is simply the representation of objects, events, or people that children are familiar with. Imitating adults, flapping arms like a bird, acting out eating a meal, popping up like a toaster, and holding your arms like Mommy are all examples of dramatic play.

Infants and toddlers enjoy watching and participating in the dramatic-play activities of older children, often while sitting on a lap at the edge of the activity. Older toddlers enjoy directing and narrating the dramatic play of a teacher who is acting out a familiar scene, such as rocking a baby, going out the door, or cooking. Always have on hand an array of props such as hats, scarves, purses, tools, and household items.

Adding play people, animals, cars, and trucks can enhance children's play, but it is important not to overwhelm children with props. Remember that for toddlers, taking out and putting away blocks is in itself play and a learning opportunity.

See Supplement: *One-to-One Learning and Fun: Ideas for Teachers of Infants and Toddlers*

A Final Word: Joyous and Exuberant Child Care

Children can learn from everything. Observe them, respond to their interests and explorations, play with them, support them, and enjoy them. When teachers have fun and take delight in reciprocal play, children experience the joy of being human.

Exercises

1. Pair up with another teacher and observe each other's interactions with children. Assess your interactions in terms of sensitivity and response to children's cues.

2. Record yourself for forty-five minutes while interacting with children (first in an infant room, and then in a toddler room). Assess your language according to the guidelines on page 58.

3. Select two areas of play that you are usually least likely to engage in (for example, blocks and music) and develop a list of experiences you could offer to or engage in individually with a nine-month-old, a fifteen-month-old, and a twenty-four-month-old.

References

Bruner, J. S. 1973. "Organization of Early Skilled Action." *Child Development* 44:1–111.

Dodge, D. T., and L. J. Colker. 1996. *The Creative Curriculum for Early Childhood.* Washington, DC: Teaching Strategies.

Post, J. 1995. "High/Scope's Key Experiences for Infants and Toddlers." *Extensions* 9 (4): 1–4.

Post, J. 1996. "The Infant and Toddler Key Experiences—Anecdotal Examples." In *Supporting Young Learners 2: Ideas for Child Care Providers and Teachers,* ed. Nancy Brickman. Ypsilanti, Mich.: High/Scope Press.

Chapter 17

The Indoor Learning Environment

εxcellence *A planned environment is organized for active, hands-on, developmentally appropriate, individualized learning for each child. A world at their fingertips maximizes sensory and motor opportunities, built-in learning, and independent access by children; it offers a full range of appropriate experiences; it allows staff to concentrate on prime times for caring and learning. Staff are sensitive to the learning experiences that naturally occur during day-to-day living, and provide a variety of toys, equipment, and household and natural materials.*

Chapter 7 offered guidance about setting up room environments to promote excellence in a program for infants and toddlers. Chapter 16 focused on curriculum: the learning experiences that infants and toddlers need. This chapter focuses on creating learning centers for infants and toddlers and on providing equipment and materials to optimize their learning.

Learning Centers

As we discussed earlier, learning centers help teachers organize materials and equipment sensibly and encourage children to spread out, to more easily see possibilities for play, and to explore and play more constructively and with more focus. They also help parents recognize the infant and toddler rooms as educational sites.

Choose learning centers based on your space, the age range and interests of the children, and staff expertise. If there is limited space, learning centers may be combined—

for example, the sensory and art areas, or the books area and a cozy space. Also create learning centers that are easy to transform: for example, a small table can change function with the change of a tablecloth (green felt for puzzles, and red vinyl for playdough). More space allows for more specialized learning centers. And remember, a learning center may be the size of a tub, a small table, a rug, a window, the space between the couch and the wall, or a small shelf that becomes a take-out learning center.

Learning centers
- have size, shape, and height
- have different surfaces
- can be sensoryscapes with personality and ambience
- can communicate and signal behavior
- can have understood rules and expectations of behavior

Keys to effective learning centers:
- the right size and scale
- open storage
- accessible adult storage
- good boundaries
- appropriate degree of seclusion
- clear expectations for children's and staff's behavior
- careful placement through zoning
- sufficient number of areas and choices
- occasional thoughtful rotation

The Power of Small Changes

In planning for infants' and toddlers' learning, our assumptions can get in the way. It is easy to forget that real learning is not always the result of huge efforts by a teacher. We sometimes underestimate how new the world is to young children and how delighted they are to do their job with the humblest of materials.

Small variations or adaptations in the learning environment can create, expand, and elaborate learning experiences. A couch pulled away from the wall to create an angular space, then covered with a blanket or made windy by a fan, provides a new spatial experience. Providing bigger and bigger balls for rolling, or larger and larger buckets creates different learning opportunities. If young children are crawling or walking on a plank that is level on the floor, and you then slightly elevate one end to create an incline, children often respond with delight, as if you have shifted the universe. The same thing happens if the crate they were crawling on is tipped over on its side or end to climb in, or if you alter a smell or sound, or create a breeze with a fan.

But is this really teaching—just moving a plank or a couch or adding larger buckets? Yes, because it creates learning about the world and its properties. Through such shifts, teachers also learn about infants' or toddlers' skill levels. And your interactions with the children as they explore certainly constitute teaching if you build on their play with responsive language and encouragement.

When we focus on how children sense the world, small changes to an experience can create lots of opportunities for engagement and learning.

Activity Areas as Learning Centers

The range of activity areas that serve as learning centers depends on the actual space and equipment available. As you develop centers, other possibilities should become evident: a home corner can become a bedroom; a please-touch area can become a please-shake or make-a-sound area. Remember that an adult label for an area should not restrict what children are allowed to do in it—for example, sensory exploration can occur in all areas. Adults should follow children's lead. Remember that it is important to build in lots of opportunity to haul, dump, and rearrange, because toddlers are obsessed with carrying and transporting.

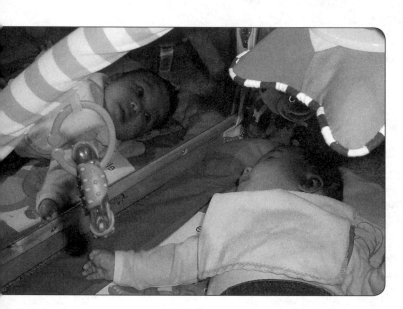

Note: As we discussed in chapter 13, staff should always be aware of the hazards that some materials present to small scientists who use their mouths to explore. For example, infants and toddlers could choke on small pieces or ingest toxic finishes, so keep a choke-testing tube handy in the room.

Following are some of the many possible learning centers or activity areas appropriate for infant and toddler rooms.

- *Infant reaching/grasping/kicking area:* various materials hanging on string, rope, elastic, or fabric.
- *Infant peekaboo/object permanence area:* divider with holes in it, large-appliance box with holes cut in it; curtained area; objects on a string that swing in and out of sight.
- *Infant swing area:* swing, cradle, or swinging platform.
- *Infant nest, play pit, playpen, or plastic wading pool:* a protected, contained space with materials placed in it.
- *Individual infant seat with tray:* an individual play space—for example, a low chair or high chair—for activities such as picking up and manipulating small objects.
- *Climbing, pulling-up areas:* couch, futons, easy chairs, planks and blocks, low cubes and rectangles, risers, one or two stairs.
- *Mirror areas:* various mirrors attached to walls or attached to divider backs.
- *Infant blocks:* large cardboard or milk cartons, or foam blocks or sturdy boxes.
- *Toddler block and construction area:* large cardboard or milk boxes, cardboard blocks, large plastic or foam blocks, unit blocks; small unit blocks, Duplo building block; props—wheelbarrows, trucks, wagons, dolls, and vehicles.
- *Vehicle center:* infants—smooth wooden and plastic vehicles; toddlers—trucks, cars, trains, props such as little plastic people, houses, trees, small rocks and bits of wood, blocks, ramps, and stuffed animals and dolls for passengers.
- *Hauling/transporting/push-pull area and collection points* (contents to be used throughout the room): pull toys, wagons, shopping carts, baskets, bins, buckets, cardboard boxes, toy boxes, mail slots, tubes.
- *Soft-toy area:* all sorts of stuffed animals (large and small) and soft toys.

- *Dramatic play:* prop boxes, cubbies, small tables and chairs, appliance boxes, flashlights, old baby equipment such as car seats and changing pads, Ace bandages, paintbrushes, bowls and buckets, household items, found or salvaged junk that is safe.
- *Language and book area:* pictures of objects that have meaning for children, sturdy board books, special picture books that may be used with adult supervision, pillows, couch, chairs, futon, stuffed animals, CD player (used with adults).
- *Home-corner area:* child-sized stove, table, and chairs; refrigerator; beds for dolls (it is important that doll beds be big and sturdy enough for children to lie in as well); strollers and buggies; props—dolls with pieces of cloth to wrap around them (wrapping cloth is easier than taking off and putting on doll clothes); blankets; play dishes, saucepans, and other cooking implements; real objects from homes.
- *Costume area* (materials to be used throughout the space): hats, helmets, carpenter's aprons, goggles, belts, shoes, scarves, mitts, animal noses, wigs, Ace bandages, nets, all sorts of dress-up clothes, handbags.
- *Art and expressive materials area:* whiteboard, chalkboard (can be used on the floor), easel, crayons, pencils (chunky, for ease of use), newsprint or other large pieces of paper for whole-arm scribbling, Etch-a-Sketch taped to wall or table, thick paints, collage materials, paste, cardboard, wood, tape, tables.
- *Messy area:* sand table, texture/water table, dish/garden tubs, sinks, smearing surfaces such as tabletops or linoleum tiles, sponges, brushes, dish towels.
- *Manipulative materials:* a nest made from a wading pool, pit, table with rim, small rugs for surfaces; unstructured materials (that meet the choking tube test) such as juice lids, pipe pieces, knobs, small pieces of wood, stones, poker chips, large washers, shoelaces, straws; manipulative materials from catalogs; large beads to string; any sort of container such as cans, cups, buckets, baskets, pans, boxes, tennis-ball cans.
- *Action center:* busy boxes, switches, zippers, Velcro fasteners, locks and latches, doors, pounding benches, ramps, tubes, containers to drop or roll materials into, things to take apart.
- *Sound area:* chimes, whistles, instruments, strings to pluck and plunk, shakers, CD player, listening center with headsets.
- *Animal area:* rubber or wooden animals, pictures, animal masks or noses, puppets, places for animals to live, props to create fences.
- *Cozy areas, places to pause:* all sorts of cushions and pillows, couch, bed, beanbag; inner tubes, throw rugs, bolsters, futons, blankets, parachutes, sheets, canopies, boxes, plastic wading pools. *Note:* A room should have more than one cozy area.
- *Body image space:* area that responds to the child's whole body movement— a space filled with beach balls, paper, hanging fabric.
- *Surprise area* (a place where surprises and new experiences occur): new materials or toys, mysterious music from a hidden source, hidden treasures. (Of course, this will not be the only place for surprises and new experiences.)

- *Please-smell area:* scent containers (film canisters or boxes), leaves, flowers, plants.
- *Please-touch area:* different textures—smooth metal, rough bark, ice, sandpaper, velvet, corrugated materials.
- *Please-look area:* mirrors, kaleidoscopes, colored plastic, smoked Plexiglas, paintings, videos, wave tubes, fish tanks.
- *Zoo area:* fish, birds (not from the parrot family), hamsters, bunnies, tadpoles/frogs.
- *Outdoor areas:* hills, paths, smooth low boulders, stumps under 18 inches, sprinklers and hoses, tunnels, shrubs, footpaths, wagons, push-along carts, ponchos, shade umbrellas. (See chapter 18.)

See Supplement: *A Quick Evaluation of Your Learning Centers: How Do You Rate?*

Treasure Baskets The treasure basket is a good way to organize experiences for infants and toddlers: it's a mobile variation of a learning center or an activity box, and a good source of unstructured materials and other loose parts. The treasure basket is a practical way to assemble different objects to engage and stimulate developing senses and understanding, particularly for infants who can sit independently but who cannot yet control moving to an activity or experience. What makes the concept come alive is putting thought into what the treasure basket contains, using natural and everyday household objects.

In their book *People under Three: Young Children in Day Care* (1994, 87–89), Elinor Goldschmied and Sonia Jackson discuss one concept of a treasure basket for younger babies:

This period of being able to sit up comfortably brings a new small piece of autonomy to a baby, but it also brings new vexations. We have all noticed a baby of this age alert and aware of what is going on around her and yet "grizzling" [whimpering]. The usual explanation is teething, which may sometimes be true, but it can also be that she is simply bored. Her close adults can't attend to her every moment and yet she is ready and waiting, it seems, for the next thing to happen. She is right to complain, and it was in response to the dissatisfaction which babies of this age clearly show with the often limited and not very interesting playthings offered to them that the "Treasure Basket" . . . was devised.

We know that babies' brains are growing fast, and that the brain develops as it responds to streams of input coming from the baby's surroundings, through the senses of touch, smell, taste, hearing, sight and bodily movement. The Treasure Basket gathers together and provides a focus for a rich variety of everyday objects chosen to offer stimulus to these different senses. The use of the Treasure Basket is one way that we can ensure a richness in the baby's experience when the brain is ready to receive, to make connections and so to make use of this information.

None of the objects in the Basket is a "bought toy," and many can be found in the home environment of young children. . . .

The concentration of a baby on the contents of a Treasure Basket is one thing that astonishes observers seeing it for the first time. Attention may last up to an hour or more. There are two factors which lie behind this and it is difficult to say which comes first, in fact they operate together. There is the infant's lively curiosity which the varied objects arouse, and her will to practice her growing skill in taking possession, under her own steam, of what is new, attractive and close at hand. Alongside this is the confidence which the attentive, but not active, presence of the grown up provides.

The fact that the adult is not active does not mean that we put down the Basket beside the baby and let her "get on with it." She needs the safety which our interested presence gives when she is faced with the challenge of objects, which she may be handling for the first time.

While the idea of treasure baskets goes back to the beginning of the twentieth century, Goldschmied and Jackson have pointed out its value for infants and toddlers in exploring objects. The teacher simply observes and ensures that children remain free from harm or interference, deliberately not guiding or reinforcing them through direction or praise. A teacher can casually introduce a treasure basket at moments when she is able to sit and become engaged with an individual child, use descriptive and reflective language with the child as he explores the properties of the objects, or quietly lean back and appreciate the learning that she is facilitating. This is also a perfect opportunity to record an observation or create an entry for the child's portfolio.

The best treasures are unstructured materials that are natural or household objects and objects that maximize interest through

- touch: texture, shape, weight
- smell: variety of scents
- taste: more limited scope, but possible
- sound: ringing, tinkling, banging, scrunching
- sight: color, form, length, shininess.

Play Materials

There are a huge number of commercial play materials available from early childhood supply companies. Many of them are great for infants and toddlers, but some, while initially attractive to adults and children, in the long run may not be valuable to infant and toddler programs. When you are considering the purchase of toys, think about the skills and interests of children in the program now, as well as what the needs of children might be in the future. Consider whether or not everyday household or natural materials could serve the same purpose. Could the real thing be substituted for the toy version? For example, a real picnic set of plastic dishes is superior on all counts to a toy tea set. The use of real objects and safe salvage or discards—for example, wooden knobs, jars, and lids—provides a good example for parents, demonstrating that staff believe there is considerable merit in play materials that do not cost a lot.

Infant-Toddler Equipment for Learning

Large Motor

mats/pillows
beach balls
push/pull toys
small wagon
foam rolls
tunnels
carts/strollers
variety of balls
planks
Note: no walkers, exersaucers,
   or jump-ups

Additional Equipment for Toddlers

stairs/slide
rocking boat
barrels
wheelbarrows
no-pedal trikes
simple climber

Dramatic Play

baby dolls
stuffed animals
rubber animals
rubber people
hats
Plexiglas mirrors
real pots and pans
blankets/tents

Additional Equipment for Toddlers

large doll furniture
dress-up clothes
children's furniture
suitcases

Blocks/Construction

fiberboard blocks
foam blocks
buckets/small blocks

Additional Blocks/Construction Equipment for Toddlers

more blocks
large trucks
large trains
snap blocks
waffle blocks

Creative/Art

fingerpaints
block crayons
markers

Additional Equipment for Toddlers

chalk
large brushes
chalkboard
playdough
ink stamps
paste

Sensory/Sand/Water/Science

dish/garden tubs
tub toys
sponges
plants
aquariums
bird feeders

animals
wind chimes
electric fans
texture/smell boxes

Additional Equipment for Toddlers

buckets/jars
funnels
sifters
measuring cups
pitchers
magnifiers
large magnets
flashlights

Books/Language/Musical Equipment

board books
cloth books
photos
posters
CDs
music boxes
musical mobiles

Additional Equipment for Toddlers

picture books
instruments
read-to books
telephones
listening centers

Perceptual/Motor/Games/Manipulative Equipment

cradle gyms
busy boxes
rattles
prisms
pop beads
poker chips
sorting boxes
simple puzzles

Additional Equipment for Toddlers

stacking/nesting toys
large pegboard
lock boards
pounding bench
jars and lids

General Guidelines for Toys

Good play materials should

- stimulate children to respond or act (Poor play materials encourage children to sit back and be entertained by something a toy or an adult has set in motion.)
- respond naturally rather than in a gimmicky way (for example, a bell that rings is more valuable than an electronic busy-box buzzer)
- encourage social interaction as well as solitary play
- give infants and toddlers choices while encouraging them to use their emerging skills
- be versatile and lend themselves to a variety of uses rather than a single one
- engage more than one of the senses
- complement the overall aesthetic and quality of the learning environment through color and substance (for example, wood, metal, plastic, cloth)
- appeal to the full range of developmental skills and interests of children in the room
- fit the fine-motor skills of the age group in mind
- be durable (remember, center use is much more wearing than home use)
- be provided in duplicate or triplicate (rather than having variety) in order to minimize the need for sharing and to support parallel play.

Purchasing with a Child's Sense and Sensibility

Often toys are selected and purchased to suit adults. The idea that infants and toddlers need variety more than they need duplicates reflects an adult appetite for novelty. The rapid development of young children has the effect of transforming familiar objects. After a few weeks pass in a child's life, it is almost a new child who returns to an object, exploring different dimensions and uses of it.

Adults firmly believe that children love primary colors. They do, and all toy makers have that fact embedded in their brains. Yet an abundance of primary colors creates a kaleidoscopic chaos that diminishes the attraction of all colors. With our greater cognitive and perceptual skills, adults see only a brightly colored truck. Children see yet another brightly colored plastic object amidst a sea of bright plastic.

Nicholson's Theory of Loose Parts

Simon Nicholson's theory of loose parts is powerful in its simplicity:

In any environment, both the degree of inventiveness and creativity, and the possibility of discovery, are directly proportional to the number and kinds of variables in it.

Creativity—the playing around with the components and variables of the world in order to make experiments and discover new things and form new concepts—has been explicitly stated as the domain of the creative few. . . . This is particularly true of young children, who find the world where they cannot play with building and making things, or play with fluid, water, fire, or living objects, and all the things that give us the pleasure that results from discovery and invention. . . . The simple facts are these:

There is no evidence, except in some special cases of mental disability, that some young babies are born creative and inventive and others are not.

There is evidence that all children love to interact with variables, such as materials and shapes; smells and other physical phenomena, such as electricity, magnetism, and gravity; media, such as gases and fluids; sounds, music, motion; chemical interactions, cooking, and fire; and other humans, and animals, plants, words, concepts, and ideas. With all these things children love to play, experiment, discover, and invent, and have fun.

One can quickly assess the creative potential of a setting by seeing if it contains loose parts and materials that transform themselves, such as water or sand. A television has no loose parts. A field, forest, or alley has thousands. As Robin Moore points out in support of Nicholson (speaking specifically about outdoor settings), "Kids

continued on next page

Nicholson's Theory of Loose Parts, *continued*

really get to know the environment if they can dig it, beat it, swat it, lift it, push it, join it, combine different things with it. This is what adults call creative activity; it is what artists do . . . a process of imagination and environment working together" (Coates 1974).

What are loose parts in an environment for children under age three? All things that can be combined, used together, or taken apart: blocks of all kinds, containers, such as margarine tubs or tennis ball cans, juice can lids, plastic curler rolls, pinecones, and wooden knobs; playground materials, such as balls and tires to roll, brushes and sponges, wagons and wheelbarrows.

Teachers also need loose parts and autonomy to turn their creativity free and to create wonderful learning experiences. Teacher-proofing with prescribed curricula and materials makes teachers' jobs mindless and teachers themselves poor role models.

When you purchase materials, buy wood as well as plastic, pastel as well as bright colors. Display materials with the aim of clearly presenting a manageable number of choices.

Unstructured Materials

These are materials you won't find in a catalog: found, homemade, household, and low-cost purchased objects the uses of which are not predetermined by adults and which are limited only by children's skills and imaginations. These objects may be simple and look like junk to adult eyes, but children immediately recognize their potential. Look for objects that can be grasped or squeezed and those with texture or with potential for action (such as rolling).

What do young children do with these kinds of materials? They hold, rub, squeeze, sort, put together, line up, drop, fill, stack, and on and on. They combine the materials in ways adults would not think of. In fact, the best way to approach junk (providing an item is safe—and that means safe to explore with the mouth) is to give it to infants and toddlers and see what they do with it.

Put these materials into a treasure basket or combine them in a variety of small containers, and store them in containers that require different motor skills to use. Carrying a container without a handle requires different skills from carrying one with a handle. There are many variations of handles for children to learn to use: for example, jug handles, wire, cane, and fixed. Possible containers include

- cups
- margarine tubs
- boxes
- buckets
- baskets, bowls
- utility trays
- tennis ball cans
- bags.

When using unstructured materials, keep the following in mind.

Always be aware of the hazards. These materials can present hazards for small scientists who use their mouths to explore: children can choke on small pieces that have broken off of larger objects, or can ingest toxic finishes. Keep a choke-testing tube handy when you equip learning centers. Watch for sharp edges, particularly when objects break.

Examples of Unstructured Materials

Natural Objects

pinecones (differing sizes)
large stones, pumice stone
shells
dried gourds
large chestnuts
big feathers
fruit (apple, orange, lemon)
corks (large sizes)
avocado pits and large walnuts
piece of loofah and natural sponge

Objects Made of Natural Materials

woolen ball
little baskets
bamboo whistle
small wicker mats
yarn

Brushes

toothbrush
shaving brush
shoe-shine brush
broad paintbrush
cosmetic brush

Wooden Objects

cylinders (bobbins, thread spools)
wooden rings
spoon/spatula
wooden dowels/knobs
castanets
clothes pegs
colored beads on string
cubes/short lengths of wood
egg cup
small turned bowl

Metal Objects

linked key rings
bells
triangle
closed tins containing rice, beans, gravel, salt,
    and other noisy materials
tea strainer
tin lids (all types)
lengths of chain
spoons (various sizes)
small egg whisk
canning-jar rings

Objects in Leather, Cloth, Paper, Rubber, and Other Materials

scarves, gloves
small cloth bags containing lavender, rosemary,
    thyme, cloves
small leather bag with zipper
velvet powder puff
rag doll
leather case for glasses
small spiral-bound notebook
wax paper
aluminum foil
cardboard
colored marble eggs
rubber tubing

Balls

baseball, tennis, golf balls
whiffle, nerf
high bouncer ball

Plastic Objects

film canisters
tubing
hair curlers
funnels
cylinders

Close supervision is important. Especially when children of mixed ages are present, monitoring play is critical. Older children have the strength to lift objects that are too heavy for babies, and in their hands a large stone or a small spoon that might otherwise be safe for infants to play with can unintentionally become dangerous.

Rotate materials in different combinations. Facilitate play by putting out different materials every week or so. For example, some jar lids on a plate next to a teddy sitting in a chair may suggest crackers for morning snack.

Play with the materials yourself. Every so often, casually plop down and try these materials out, but not with the aim of getting children to do what you do.

Use the materials inside a bounded area. The most efficient way to do this is to incorporate them into learning centers. This also reduces pickup.

Building Learning into the Environment

The more that learning is built into the environment, the less time staff need to spend setting up and taking down, and the less chance there is that everything will end up in one great pile.

Learning materials can be attached to almost every surface: walls, floors, benches, tables, backs of storage units, railings, doors, fences, rugs, ceilings, windows, the inside of cabinets, and pillars. The advantage of attaching them permanently with screws or bolts or temporarily but securely with duct tape is, of course, that they will stay put and not become part of the toddler hauling universe.

Some of the many items that can be attached are:

- busy boxes, cot gyms, music boxes
- rattles, squeeze toys, music makers
- toy steering wheels, other wheels
- beads on wire or string
- pegboard
- puzzles
- lazy Susans (for display, size, rotation)
- pounding benches and mallets
- doors with latches, locks, hinges, and handles
- fabric with zippers, hook-and-loop fasteners
- cardboard or plastic tubes to look through, make noises with, put, drop, or slide things through
- metal surface for magnets
- easel or whiteboard
- real or play telephones
- mirrors (polished, smoked, or colored Perspex), prisms, colored cellophane
- clear, opaque, wire, or woven containers for drop boxes and collection points
- poke-through and peekaboo boards
- pulleys and levers
- textured surfaces
- different-sized cans.

Alike and Different: Valuing Diversity in the Learning Environment
Helping children learn to value the uniqueness and diversity all around them is a significant challenge for everyone who lives with and teaches children. Very young children need opportunities to feel good about themselves, learn about others, and experience and value the ways they are alike and different.

The most personal and powerful way to teach diversity and inclusiveness is to model them in our lives, homes, programs, and communities. When diversity is obviously lacking in the program's staff and children, you can carefully select materials, stories, and pictures that expand the children's universe. Seeing people like themselves in print is a powerful affirmation: "I must be okay; there are pictures in this book of people who look like me, doing the things I like to do." Seeing people who look different affirms that people come in different colors and live in different ways. When we share pictures of children from many differenet cultures doing what children all over the world do, we validate the similarities as well as the ways in which each culture is unique.

Representing the richness of cultural diversity involves more than providing visual images. Multicultural experience is also multisensory: it has specific smells, textures, sounds, and tastes. Objects and fabrics to touch; music and dance; and food to taste bring cultural diversity to life.

A Final Word: Between Order and Chaos

It is not difficult or very expensive to create learning environments for young children. Their restless urge to discover and master will make a laboratory out of any setting that offers enough loose parts and motor opportunities. But it takes a lot of observation and reflection to design an environment that provides a *safe* laboratory for groups of children and a manageable workplace for staff. Striking a balance between too-stifling order and too-flexible chaos is a real challenge.

Exercises

1. Observe three children for fifteen minutes each: one under six months old, one around ten months old, and one around fifteen months old. Jot down what each of them is interested in and what skills they seem to be working on.

2. Develop three new prop boxes for the drama area of a toddler learning center.

3. Program twenty different indoor learning experiences that can occur in a nest or plastic wading pool.

4. Create three new built-in learning experiences.

5. Develop separate treasure baskets for a child who is four, eight, or fifteen months old.

6. Outline a project for children interested in bells.

   See Supplement: *Beyond the Familiar Learning Center: Creating More Centers in Your Environment*

References

Goldschmied E., and S. Jackson. 1994. *People Under Three: Young Children in Day Care*. London: Routledge.

Nicholson, S., 1974. "The Theory of Loose Parts" in *Alternative Learning Environments*, edited by G. Coates. Stroudsburg, PA: Dowden, Hutchinson and Ross.

Chapter 18

Infants and Toddlers Outdoors

εxcellence *The outdoors is a great place to be in general, and particularly with a very young child. On a daily basis, infants and toddlers safely experience all that the outdoors has to offer:*

- *a place for motor and sensory exploration*
- *a place for environmental experience*
- *a place for nurturing interaction and adult-child conversation.*

Why do infants and toddlers need a playground? Why do they need to go out at all? After all, what can they do besides fall down, get trampled, eat the flora and fauna, and get scrapes, bug bites, wet, or sunburned? Not only that, children's noses run, they poop, and it takes forever to get snowsuits on or off. And they get dirty!

What does the outdoors potentially offer that the indoor setting cannot? Fresh air essential to good health, new worlds to explore, and a broader range of opportunities that creates sensory and motor learning that human beings have needed since the dawn of time:

- *Climate.* The outdoors has weather—wind, sun, rain, fog, clouds, snow, warmth, and chills.
- *Landscape.* The outdoors has hills and knolls, hedges, ruts, holes, streams, surfaces of different textures, descriptions, and levels. It also has vegetation of varying color, smell, texture, and growth characteristics.
- *Openness.* Outside there is vastness and a sense of infinite boundaries (even if only in one direction—up). Openness creates a sense of freedom (although imposing fences can heighten children's feelings of confinement).

- *Messiness*. Outdoors, children can be much freer to be messy (or perhaps more appropriately, more earthy).
- *Wildlife*. The world of uncaged birds, squirrels, bugs, worms, and other life forms lies outside our windows.
- *People*. Outdoors, there are people in their natural habitats, working, living, playing, traveling.
- *Sensory richness*. The outdoors is a sensoryscape appealing to all senses, and it changes hour to hour and day to day.

For teachers, the outdoors offers a change of scenery and a different stage for being with babies. Child care can be mind-numbing in its routine and in its confined sense of place. While adults vary quite widely in their appreciation of the outdoors, going outdoors is necessary to add variety to an adult's as well as a child's day.

Single-minded attention to convenience and the appearance of safety can leave us with a pretty sterile experience. It is important when planning the outdoor experience to keep in mind the unique values of being outdoors.

The Importance of Nature

Each year, children lose ground in their relationship with nature. Beginning as babies at home and in child care, children are losing time, space, and the variety of outdoor experiences that have been integral to the development of humankind. *They are losing habitat.* They are losing necessary experience—and gaining weight. Direct, unfiltered, unmanaged, sustained experience with nature is shrinking. The loss is enormous for a number of reasons (adapted from Greenman 2005, 284–86):

- *Nature is universal and timeless.* No matter where you are on the globe, nature is there, connecting all life. Nature is an integral part of our history, stories, myths, and dreams.
- *Nature is unpredictable.* It is the uneven, the changing and evolving, the glorious untidiness of it all that provides such contrast with life indoors. The ground under our feet may slope or buckle. The air may be heavy and weigh us down, or be so light that time has fallen asleep in the sunshine. Indoors, nothing falls from the sky —but outdoors, there are leaves and snowflakes, rain and hail. Indoors, nothing flies (except flies) or burrows or leaps from tree to tree. Many of us age and forget the joy of small, unstaged natural events: the sudden dark cloud, the bird at the feeder, and the toad in the garden.
- *Nature is bountiful.* There are shapes and sizes, colors and textures, smells and tastes—an enormous variety of substances. In a world of catalogs and consumable objects, designed spaces and programmed areas, sometimes it helps to remember that the natural world is full of multidimensional, educational experiences for children. Nature is hard, soft, fragile, heavy, light, smooth, and rough. Armed with our senses, we explore the world and call the adventure *science;* or, if you prefer, *cognitive development, classification, sensory development,* or *perceptual-motor learning.*

- *Nature is beautiful.* There is art in the ant hills, in the rainbow in the oily water or the rainbow in the sky, and in the dandelion or the apple blossom. There is so much loveliness that we grow indifferent and leave the awe to artists. But *look* at those towering cliffs of clouds and the light streaking through the pine needles! *See* the silvery birch leaves and the swirls in the bark, the rain dripping from the roof, and the delicate, lacelike etchings in the leaf!
- *Nature is alive with sounds.* There are melodies in the waves and poetry in the wind that blows the leaves off trees. Thoughts are nourished by stillness and solitude. The wind and rain, and, of course, the birds, crickets, and dogs make music. The world is full of natural and manmade rhythms that children experience and imitate.
- *Nature creates a multitude of places.* Lie out in the open on that hill, or lie under that willow. Sit on that rock or sit in that high grass. Squeeze under the hedge or march through that puddle. A small stand of trees makes a forest if you are little.
- *Nature is real.* Everything dies—the ant, the baby bird that fell from the nest, the flower, and the leaf. Thistles have stickers, and roots trip unsuspecting feet.
- *Nature nourishes and heals.* Human beings evolved outdoors. Our bodies need sunlight and fresh air. Our minds need the experience and challenges that nature presents. Our souls need the day-to-day appreciation of the miracle of the world and all its complexity. Without a deep sense of awe at the vastness and majesty of the natural world, and a simultaneous ennobling sense that we are intrinsically a part of that world, we are diminished.

Designing Infant and Toddler Outdoor Areas

Imagine a playground for infants and toddlers. A what? You may not be able to conjure a lot of images. Playgrounds are typically rough-and-tumble places where running, jumping, climbing, throwing, the traffic of miniature speeding vehicles, and general wild abandon flourish. Life in the fast lane is no place for a baby, right?

Okay, then—what about an infant/toddler *park?* Again, it probably seems strange to think of an outdoor place for children under three years old.

Let's start over. Imagine outdoor places where it would be wonderful to be a baby and to be with a baby, that would enable everyone to enjoy the world outside the walls of the center or home while taking pleasure in the growing power and competence of a child. What comes to mind now? Probably images of parks with sun and shade, flowers, gentle breezes, grassy hills, winding pathways, and places to relax, talk, and appreciate the sounds of birds, water, crickets, and babies.

Now return to the idea of a playground for babies and toddlers. Imagine an outdoor arena for play: a setting that encourages the visual exploration of a four-month-old; the reaching and grasping, the rolling and leaning of a nine-month-old; and the stepping and toddling, pulling and pushing, hauling and dumping, and exuberant motor and sensory exploration of older babies and toddlers. If we begin with the idea of somehow adapting a playground built for older children, we may get nowhere. If instead we begin thinking about what we want babies to experience and what we want to do with them, we are likely to end up with something entirely different.

Centers will vary in their potential for providing outdoor play areas. It is important to make the best use of what you have, remembering that even small spaces such as planter boxes, patches of ground, and sidewalks can be sites for quality outdoor experiences.

Design Considerations

Good playgrounds are designed to fit children's, teachers', and parents' beliefs and values. They are also designed to accommodate individual sites. Because the amount of space is often less than desirable, good playgrounds are usually versatile and flexible. Experiences change as new props are added, including parachutes, waterproof blankets, tubs, planks, pillows, boxes, balls, blocks, and toys. Changes in the sensory characteristics of the playground can alter with the seasons.

The Nature of Infants and Toddlers Outdoor design has to take into account the nature of infants and toddlers: little scientists investigating with their eyes, mouth, hands, other senses, and entire body. Their curiosity is not tempered by much experience with the world, so we need to protect them.

Toddlers are newly mobile, and their body rarely is as capable as they imagine it to be. While older children are pretty good at protecting themselves, toddlers don't have the experience to judge what they can and can't do. And remember, toddlers are oblivious to the safety of others.

The challenge is creating an outdoor world that doesn't make infants and toddlers ill, frightened, or injured. All too often, playground supervision is viewed as mere surveillance because good equipment and activities that allow children to engage in safe play were not thought out ahead of time. Good design and thoughtful adults can meet the challenge.

The Nature of Infant and Toddler Teachers Teachers are only human. If there is no shade or windbreak, if access to the outdoors and to storage is inconvenient, if keeping the children safe and healthy appears to require considerable effort, if there is no comfortable place to sit or lie down with a baby—in short, if it feels like a hassle to get out and is an unpleasant experience to be outside—teachers' use of the outdoors will be minimal.

Caring for infants and toddlers outdoors is a difficult job and is very different than it is with older children. Going out with infants and toddlers requires more forethought when there is no direct indoor/outdoor access: *How will I change diapers? Which bottles should I bring? Which sunscreen? Whose naptime is coming up?* Preparation may be extensive: stuffing children into snowsuits, filling diaper bags, finding strollers. Being outdoors requires a level of groundskeeping found elsewhere only on putting greens—a watchfulness associated with the Secret Service, and a tolerance for periodic inactivity like that of Ferdinand the Bull (just smelling the flowers). Appreciating a six-month-old's grooving to the sounds and sight of water dripping from the gutter can last only so long.

The Nature of Parents Active outdoors learning for babies is a new concept for most parents, particularly first-time parents, whose image of a very young child is typically

Things to Do Outdoors

What can infants do outdoors?	What can toddlers do outdoors?
• Be fed	• Eat
• Be diapered	• Be held and sung to
• Sleep	• Read
• Be held and sung to	• Be rocked
• Be rocked	• Explore with each sense
• Relate to a sibling	• Watch
• Crawl, creep	• Look for
• Roll	• Inspect
• Crawl over, under, through	• Go in and out
• Pull up, stand	• Walk up/down
• Explore people	• Go over, under, around
• Listen, explore sounds	• Climb in, up, over, on top
• Look, explore color and form	• Stretch, hang
• Touch, explore texture and form	• Tumble
• Smell	• Jump off
• Explore water	• Slide
• Paint	• Swing
• Mouth, ingest	• Take apart/put together
• Reach/hold/drop	• Stack/pile/knock over
• Kick	• Collect, gather
	• Fill/dump/empty
	• Read symbols; sort/match
	• Carry, transport
	• Put in/take out
	• Hide, discover
	• Imitate adult behavior, pretend
	• Engage in doll play
	• Mix/separate
	• Pour/sift
	• Splash
	• Paint, smear
	• Draw, sculpt
	• Play alone
	• Play together

that of a relatively fragile creature. Much like teachers, they may need to be sold on the value of outdoor play. The idea of their child mucking about in sand, mud, and water, watching a bee pollinate a flower, or scaling the heights of a miniature climber may take some time to get used to. However, when you guide parents to observe their children as the persistent little scientists they are and they understand the safety precautions you have taken, many parents will come to understand the value of outdoor play.

Playground Health and Safety

Most accidents are the result of falls, bumps, blows, cuts, burns from metal equipment, or ingestion of toxic substances or materials that cause choking. The cause of most accidents is not equipment failure so much as poor playground design, equipment and surface selection, use, or maintenance. Developmentally inappropriate equipment and unsafe structures—wood structures that splinter, low-quality equipment that becomes increasingly dangerous as it wears out, or metal equipment that freezes and/or becomes dangerously hot—are all too common. Important considerations include:

- *Sufficient square footage.* Too-small spaces result in too few play experiences and crowding.
- *Drainage.* Good drainage is essential on playgrounds for young children.
- *Nontoxic landscape.* All vegetation should be checked by a poison control agency; teachers should be alert to the growth of mushrooms; soil should be tested for any chemical residues, and air quality should be monitored.
- *Resilient surfacing.* The ground beneath any surface higher than 18 inches that children are able to climb on without adults present should have a resilient surface that meets ASTM International and Consumer Product Safety Commission (CPSC) playground guidelines.
- *Use zones.* Active equipment should be surrounded by a 48-inch use-free zone, clear of equipment from every point of access or egress.
- *No crowding.* When crowding occurs among active toddlers, any equipment becomes dangerous and accidents follow, as well as toddler-on-toddler harm.
- *Good layout and zoning.* Define active play areas, clear pathways, and place challenging areas and equipment such as swings and bike paths on the perimeter; areas into which children might accidentally wander and get hurt should be on the perimeter or fenced; young infants must be out of the traffic flow.
- *Safe equipment and design.* It is essential that equipment meet all CPSC regulations for exposed surfaces, spacing (this should not allow head entrapment or strangulation), materials, design, and location.
- *Developmentally appropriate equipment.* Equipment should be scaled to the size and skills of babies and provide sufficient challenge to toddlers, because when children are bored, they seek challenge and stimulation and end up using people and things inappropriately. The result is unsafe motor play, biting, and other aggressive acts.
- *Maintenance and monitoring.* Accidents happen when equipment is not constantly monitored for signs of wear (for example, worn chains and loose fasteners), exposed hazards (for example, concrete pilings, bolts, splinters), and hazardous materials (for example, chokable, toxic, or sharp material; buried objects in sand; animal feces).

Balancing Health and Safety with Play

What concerns are important enough to be inflexible about? When is it necessary to accommodate real life? After all, children will ultimately be exposed to germs, and they will get bumps and scratches. Every center has to decide what matters most to the teachers and families, in concert with health officials and regulatory agencies. Two concerns that come up regularly are standing water and toxic shrubs.

Children need water play, but standing water can transmit germs, breed mosquitoes, and present a threat of drowning. Water that children can sit in is much less sanitary than the water in center tubs, in which they only place their hands. Individual tubs transmit the fewest germs, and changing the water often reduces exposure to germs. Circulating the water in a wading pool reduces transmission of germs, but serious health concerns still exist. Sprinklers and sidewalk puddles offer good infant and toddler play possibilities.

Many attractive shrubs are mildly toxic; nevertheless, a child would have to eat a lot of unpleasant-tasting leaves or berries to get sick. Should you plant these shrubs? Probably not, because even though the chance of harm is minimal, the attractiveness of the shrub is not worth the "No"s and the need to frequently explain to anxious parents and teachers that they are not harmful. There are other shrubs that present fewer problems.

Special Needs and the Americans with Disability Act (ADA)

Infant and toddler playgrounds need to be accessible to children and adults with special needs. Circulation routes should be accessible to wheelchair-bound adults, which also enables these areas to be used by buggies and carts.

Play for all requires thinking through how play areas can provide safe challenges to children with different experiences and different development of their senses and body without exposing them to unnecessary hazards. To serve all children, there needs to be a wide range of experiences that create equivalent, not identical, challenges and explorations. For infants and toddlers, the major issue may be conceptual. Seeing a child with different abilities as capable and not fragile, and making the effort to provide equivalent experience may require a leap of faith. As with indoor environments, clarity, multisensory clues, flexibility, and loose parts are necessary to make sure that children with sight, hearing, or physical disabilities are able to play outdoors.

How Do You Partition a Playground?

With limited space and/or a limited budget, how do you partition a playground? State regulations usually dictate who plays with whom and which areas are fenced off: infants separated from toddlers or not; toddlers with or separated from twos; twos and preschoolers together; or some other arrangement. Budget may determine and limit who gets a playhouse, swings, climbers, or water play.

A separate, fenced (or otherwise divided) area for children under age two or two and a half years makes good developmental sense and leaves a separate safe area for crawling infants. There should be ample large-motor challenge for toddlers. Two-year-olds should also have frequent use of any preschool play areas for older children, so that they can have challenging experiences. Teachers should be prepared to supervise and restrict the use of developmentally inappropriate equipment.

If there is a separate area for infants and toddlers, there should be platform climbing equipment scaled to toddlers.

Designing the Landscape

When designing the outdoor landscape, you need to keep health and safety features foremost in mind. The basic dilemma: the infant/toddler landscape has to be safe to eat. Shrubs, flowers, and trees can be toxic in all stages of growth, and should be checked with the local poison control office. Sand areas that attract cats, wooden objects that grow moss and mushrooms, and gravel present problems that need to be thought through. And on and on. Even with all the challenges, there are still a lot of options for creating a landscape with a rich palette of stimuli, using an array of structures and equipment for play.

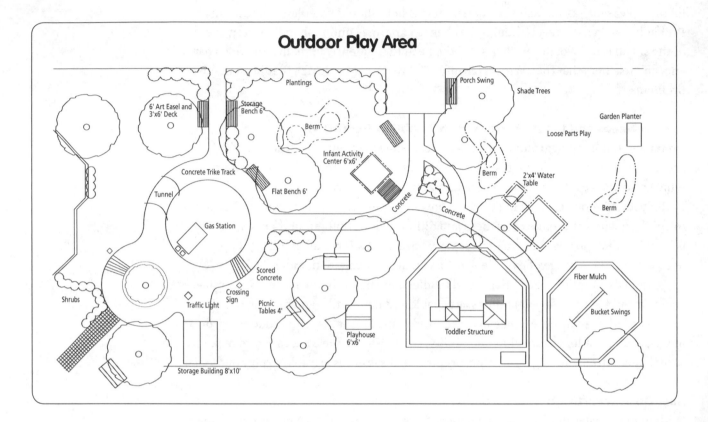

A Variety of Stimuli

Ideally, outdoor spaces for young children offer a variety of stimuli, some of which are listed below.

- *Surfaces.* Grass, sand, poured synthetic surface, wood, concrete, or asphalt (not pea gravel, which inevitably collects in toddlers' bodily orifices). There should be gentle inclines to roll down and toddle up, grassy knolls to feel secluded in, and flat surfaces to strut and wobble on. Wooden platforms and decks are desirable because they drain quickly and allow outdoor play even when the ground is wet. Resilient, quality synthetic surfaces also drain well when properly installed. Using concrete or asphalt can be controversial, but on sidewalks and paths, toddlers appreciate their flat, hard surfaces, and sidewalks are a fact of life they must learn to live with.
- *Textures.* Smooth, round boulders; coarse bark; smooth, sensual wood; soft and not-so-soft pine needles; and other vegetation that feels good to touch and rub up against.
- *Color and scent.* Trees and shrubs complement each other and are transformed when seasons change by falling leaves (make sure they're nontoxic), cones and blossoms, and peeling bark.

- *Places to be.* Round boulders and shrubs create miniature grottoes and secluded, baby-sized groves to go in and out, over, and around; shady spots and sunny spots; open areas and tight hideaways.
- *Pathways.* Pathways with destinations and loops not only structure traffic patterns but can become central sites for learning and exploration. Distinguish between footpaths that are used as garden paths and major circulation paths that require accessibility and are used as emergency escape routes accommodating emergency cribs and buggies. Toddlers love to endlessly go and come, come and go. Pathways provide motor challenges and sensory exploration for babies as they crawl, toddle, push, or haul. Foot pathways may be as simple and inexpensive as a stone dust footpath demarcated by stone borders or a simple railing; a gardenlike path using wood rounds, pavers, aggregate concrete rounds or squares; or a multisurface system with a mixture of resilient and hard surfaces, including planks, logs, rubber surfaces, and brick. Pathway railings create additional play—do you remember trailing your hand along a picket fence? A railing may be made from rope, two-by-fours, timber, pickets, or other materials.
- *Barriers.* Like pathways, barriers direct traffic flow and enclose activity areas. A creative use of barriers that restricts children to developmentally appropriate areas by requiring certain skills to surmount them creates self-regulation. Shrubs, planters, slatted wooden surfaces, and other surface changes can regulate the whereabouts of crawlers and freewheeling toddlers. Tiny retaining walls of rock or wood offer babies things they can lean against, scale, or explore with fingers and bellies; gates that open and close combine learning and crowd control.

Structures on the Landscape

- *Roofs, canopies, gazebos, umbrella mounts, pop-up beach shade structures.* Shade is essential. If there are not enough mature trees, then canopies, lawn umbrellas, and awnings become prime alternatives.
- *Decks or platforms.* Wooden or recycled plastic flooring offers a flat surface that drains easily and is thus a good site for water play or outdoor play when the ground is wet. A raised platform offers babies chances to get high up and explore new vantage points.
- *Swings.* Opportunities to move in space, alone or with a trusted adult, are provided through the use of swings with baby seats, porch swings, glider benches for swinging on adult laps, hammocks, and cradles. Soft rubber and plastic swings are much safer than ones made of wood or hard plastic. Fully enclosed surround swings are appropriate for infants, and bucket swings are appropriate for toddlers. *Note:* Swings can be overused and become restraints if used without adult supervision.
- *Skeletal structures.* These can be installations of natural wood logs or driftwood, ladderlike or benchlike structures. These are also motor structures for climbing on, over, and under. They can become much more: skeletons that change by adding planks, ladders, or fabric to create many more experiences.
- *Vistas.* Framing structures allow children to perceive the world from different angles, under different lighting conditions, and from different perspectives; use open frames or frames with Plexiglas or fabric.

- *Fabric and flapping things.* Banners, parachutes, wind chimes, and branches make wind visible and audible and create interesting light patterns.
- *Slides.* Slides that descend from platforms or that are set into hills eliminate most of the risk and leave the thrills and spills.
- *Half-buried tires.* Tires provide mini-tunnels, places to sit or lean on, and pathway railings. They can be painted to reduce surface heat.
- *Playhouses, lean-tos, crates, pop-up tents.* Anything with a roof becomes a playhouse.
- *Tunnels, overhanging trees, and shrubs.* Anything to be in or under or go through works.
- *Young infant area.* An enclosed area that encourages reaching, grasping, and kicking as well as a variety of visual, auditory, and other sensory experiences, perhaps with fabric, branches, or falling water is perfect.
- *Sound structures.* Make miniature shrines with chimes, fabric, or gongs that react with sound and motion to wind or touch.
- *Sandboxes.* Children love to play with sand, so use sandboxes with covers to reduce unsafe play with sand.
- *Sprinklers, water tables, tubs, or elevated waterways.* Elevated wooden, metal, or stone troughs provide water in motion, as do sprinklers. *Note:* Wading pools are unsanitary and unsafe and should not be used outdoors.
- *Diaper-changing areas.* In warm climates, outdoor diapering will maximize outdoor play.
- *Platform climbers.* Multilevel platform climbers allow the experience of being up high and can be designed with ladders, stairs, and ramps.
- *Dead trees and stumps, or smooth, rounded boulders.* Anything to pull up on, straddle, and climb safely, up to 18 inches off the ground is fine.
- *Wobbly structures.* Try boards on springs or tires, logs, and planks barely off the ground, fastened to frames with chains; anything with a slight wobble.
- *Logs, benches.* Have places for adults to sit on or up against while observing or nurturing infants or toddlers.
- *Stored equipment and materials.* These can include planks, ladders, parachutes and other fabric; wagons, wheel toys, wheelbarrows, pillows, balls, sand/water toys, and creative "junk."

Equipment for Play

Outdoor space can be transformed by equipment for a variety of purposes:

- *Just being.* Adults will be outside with infants and toddlers more often if the environment is convenient and comfortable (with shade, protection from wind, places to sit)—pillows, hammocks, waterproof pads and blankets, infant carriers, and, if possible, portable changing areas will increase outdoor time.
- *Transporting.* Toddlers love to transport themselves, toys, equipment, anything at all. Sacks, backpacks, utility trays, and buckets are all valuable loose parts to have on a toddler playground for children to haul around. Riding toys, wagons, wheelbarrows, shopping carts, and carriages are all good vehicles for toddler transport and fulfill toddlers' primal needs to collect and dump.

- *Pushing/pulling.* Play lawn mowers and pull toys (remember that beginning walkers push more readily than pull because it's hard to both walk and look behind you when walking is a new skill).
- *Riding.* Pedal-less riding toys and small trikes.
- *Rolling, kicking, and throwing.* Different-sized balls and wheeled toys.
- *Dramatic play.* Dolls, hats, purses, and small tables.
- *Sand play.* Buckets, funnels, tabletop surfaces, kitchen utensils.
- *Construction play.* Blocks of wood and plastic.
- *Art play.* Brushes, sponges, chalk, dirt, and clay.
- *Water play.* Hoses, sprinklers, water tubs. Do not use wading pools or other containers of standing water that children can climb into together because the water can spread germs.

- *Projecting.* Toddlers project themselves into space with their lunging, lurching bodies; they throw and kick objects ahead of themselves. Provide beach balls and other large balls, anything they can push, and small balls to kick and throw.
- *Place making.* Use tarps and parachutes to wrap climbers and playhouses, à la the artist Christo, and to create interesting places to be in. This not only adds interest but also teaches toddlers that they have the power to change their environment. Toddlers love working out the physics of places with their bodies.

- *Loose parts, and more loose parts.* Materials that can be used together, combined, collected, sorted, separated, pulled apart, stacked, lined up, and dumped including: natural materials (rocks, stones, driftwood, wood rounds, leaves, sand, water); toys; vehicles (wagons, wheelbarrows, carts); and fabric, backpacks, rope, chain, containers, blocks, dolls, brushes, sponges, ladders, PVC pipe, and plastic gutters. Loose parts are almost anything safe and not fixed in place; they allow children the freedom to use them in inventive ways. They can be stored in stuff sacks, backpacks, utility carts, or duffel bags for easy use.

"Get That Out of Here!" (What Does Not Work with Infants and Toddlers)

Some of the equipment besides wading pools that does not work well with infants and toddlers includes

- trampolines
- teeter-totters
- belt swings

- single-chain tire swings
- pedal trikes
- platforms that children can climb on but not climb down.

Being Outdoors with Infants and Toddlers: The Teacher's Role

The success of infant/toddler outdoor time ultimately depends on the adults in the setting: teachers who recognize and encourage the scientist and explorer in each child and who accept the ups and downs that ensue. At the same time, they must keep a watchful eye on and nurturing presence toward babies for long periods of relatively uneventful time.

What Do Teachers Do Outdoors?

Teachers watch, interact, and worry. Many infant and toddler caregivers have trouble allowing young children to explore. All their instincts tell them to keep young children clean, catch them before they stumble, and protect them from even the slightest scratch or risk of discomfort. Without the assurance that the children will be safe, teachers often severely restrict what their charges are allowed to do. To achieve confidence that children will be safe, teachers play the following roles:

Caregiver. Remember sunscreen, hats, towels, and other necessary supplies.

Safety monitor. Continually look for health and safety hazards.

Planner. Plan experiences and locations that avoid crowding and toddler swarming.

Enthusiast and participant. Encourage active engagement with the environment, and participate in the exploration.

Mentor and guide. Provoke conversation and questions, and help children make connections.

Provisioner. Provide the equipment and props that enhance the outdoor experience.

What Should Caregivers Not Do Outdoors? "It drives me crazy to go out on the playground and see the teachers just talking to each other," lamented the director. "It's not a break." Outdoor time should not be viewed as an opportunity to visit with other teachers. All too often, it offers the chance to see teachers from other rooms and to allow adults' needs to take precedence over children's play. Reasonable break times should replace playground breaks. Outdoor time is a time for great conversation—with children!

Walks, Rides, Field Trips, and Community Resources

Centers without playgrounds may have to develop other alternatives such as using sidewalks and available yards and parks. Centers can create a playground-in-a-box by filling a cart with planks, balls, crates, blankets, parachutes, pull toys, and other equipment.

Strollers, buggies, and carts are wonderful vehicles to use when taking children on walks. But remember: toddlers can walk, and infants can crawl. Don't substitute passive rides for active outdoor experiences. Combine the two, and get the children out of the carts.

Toddlers can enjoy field trips as long as the adults with them also enjoy themselves (and the trips meet all licensing and center requirements). Safe transportation in car seats in vans or parents' cars can add variety to daily life. Remember, field trips don't have to be to exotic locations such as a zoo. In fact, exotic locations are more likely to present problems. Trips to such places as parks, expansive open areas, and beaches provide more satisfying adult-child experiences. For safety's sake, stay away from crowded areas or places that you have never been before, and always have extra hands available.

A Final Word: Go Outdoors!

It is important to resist the trend toward indoor culture and help children develop an appreciation for the outdoors. They will inherit the planet, after all. What will happen if they don't understand and come to love the outdoors?

See Supplements: *Is Your Outdoor Learning Space a Great Place to Be an Infant or Toddler?* and *Twenty-Five Ways to Improve Your Outdoor Space*

Exercises

1. On your bare feet or knees, explore the outdoor area at a center or home.

2. Pick an outdoor location, and then close your eyes. List all the sensory experiences you have (sounds, smells, touch). Go to one or two other outdoor locations and do the same.

3. Observe children at different ages trying to make sense of the world using all their emerging bodily powers and discovering how everything works.

4. List the play opportunities available at any one time in a program and evaluate them against possible experiences listed in question 2.

5. Watch a child younger than three explore a backyard, a deck, or a stoop with no play equipment. What constitutes playing in such places?

6. Make a list of safe loose parts for infants and toddlers: include household (for example, spoons, sponges, and buckets) and natural (for example, pinecones, maple leaves, and twigs) items.

Reference

Greenman, J. 2005. *Caring Spaces, Learning Places: Children's Environments That Work*. Redmond, WA: Exchange Press.

Chapter 19

Planning for Learning

εxcellence *Planning the learning environment and the child's experience takes an unbroken cycle of observation, analyzation and reflection, brainstorming, planning, and implementation based on knowledge of child development, children, and families. Staff pay attention to what is happening, get to know children deeply over time, document their experiences, listen to what parents are saying, and reflect on what works well and what can be improved. The culture of the program encourages ongoing informal planning and evaluation as a team, taking into account input from families. Learning and daily experience is made visible to children and adults through documentation and display.*

If children are learning all the time, then planning must address all aspects of children's experiences, not just specific times of the day, particular areas of the environment, or identified projects or learning activities. Earlier chapters emphasized planning the day to give priority to caring routines and nurturing interactions and to viewing them as prime times for learning.

There are lots of ways to plan curriculum, and teachers usually adapt whatever system is given to them. Whatever the approach taken and the forms used, it is important to get out of the mind-set of lesson plans. Infants and toddlers do not need lessons—they need opportunities for experiences they can make the most of as individuals.

Planning the Child's Experience

Teachers set the stage (a rich learning environment) and set in motion successful collaborative experiences among children and adults, including parents. Teachers do this successfully by exploring children's discoveries, expanding on children's ideas and hypotheses, asking open-ended questions, provoking experiences, thoughtfully designing and choosing materials for learning centers, and continually developing the entire learning environment. Topics may emerge from children's interests, teachers' interests, or parents' observations. Teachers base experiences for individual children on their interests, strengths, and needs. Supporting children's learning in these ways involves careful planning.

Foundations for Planning

All effective planning is based on a foundation of knowledge and expertise in the following areas:

General child development and individual differences. All planning should begin with a clear sense of purpose based on knowledge of children, including

- the developmentally important key experiences necessary for maximizing individual development, and
- the experiences necessary for each child to have relaxed and happy days.

The families, cultures, and communities served in the program. Consider what is appropriate, relevant, and meaningful to them. Knowing what families value in child rearing and what they want for their child are essential. Having accurate information about diversity and cultural differences is important, although care must be taken to avoid stereotyping and making assumptions about individual families based on general knowledge about cultures and family lifestyles. Knowing the community also contributes to experiences being relevant and authentic.

Good early childhood teaching and learning practices. There is a body of knowledge sometimes called *pedagogy* that addresses how best to support children's learning. Teachers learn what works well and what does not through formal study, reading, experience, professional development, and experimentation (sometimes successful, sometimes not!).

Monitoring and evaluating past and present experience. This involves knowing what has worked well in the past, what the areas of concern are, and where improvement is needed.

Planning the Learning Environment

There are four dimensions to planning a great learning environment:

1. Planning learning areas and centers
2. Planning activities and projects
3. Planning for individual children
4. Planning for review

Planning the Learning Environment on a Bimonthly or Monthly Basis

Environmental planning assumes a basic framework of learning areas, centers, and stations (see chapters 17 and 18 on indoor and outdoor learning environments). This framework changes from time to time as you answer these questions:

- What learning centers and treasure baskets are available?
- What toys, props, and loose parts are regularly available?
- What learning is built into the setting?

Learning areas available will vary based on availability of space and on children's interests and emerging skills. A review of the basic framework of learning areas should be conducted at least monthly. The learning environment includes consideration of routines and the flow of the day, which should also be a focus of attention for staff to ensure that they maximize opportunities for learning and for prime times.

Planning Weekly and Daily Experiences, Activities, and Projects

Daily planning should be done in advance as well as during the day whenever alterations are needed on the spot because of emerging interests and skills of children. Ask these questions:

- What experiences are offered each day through rotation of materials in the learning centers?
- What activities are tentatively planned for each day by teachers?

Planning should be based on observations of the children, using your understanding of the development of each child (the key experiences listed in chapter 16 will be helpful): their interests, their new skills, their reactions to new materials, equipment, and experiences offered, as well as general observations about the use of time and space.

Planning the Environment and Experiences

Infants and Toddlers

Planning week of: _____ Teacher(s): _____ Homebase: _____
Emerging skills and interests: _____

Choose learning centers/stations that will be highlighted for the week. List materials added to Environment. (A station accommodates 1–3 children.)	Learning Center/Station_____	Learning Center/Station_____	Learning Center/Station_____
Possible Learning Stations/Centers: Reaching/grasping/kicking area Infant peek-a-boo/object permanence Communication center Electronics Play, pit, plastic wading pool Vehicles Hauling/transporting Soft toys area Action center Sound area Animal area Cozy areas, places to pause Tiny areas Body-image space Surprise area Please-touch area Please-look area Outdoor areas Treasure baskets Climbing area Mirror area Costume area Manipulative area	Learning Center/Station_____	Learning Center/Station_____	Learning Center/Station_____
	Experiences and projects planned for the week		
	Language/books (Stories, books, vocabulary)	Large-motor (Rolling, pull-up, push-pull, climbing, crawling, picking up, dumping)	Small-motor (Squishing, squeezing, turning, poking, fitting together)
	Sensory/creative/science (Textures, water, sand, paint, malleable materials, visual stimulation)	Music/movement (Songs, fingerplays, instruments)	Outdoors (Collecting-dumping, pushing-pulling, loose parts, motor and sensory exploration, nurturing interaction, adult-child conversation)

Why Not Plan by Themes? While themes or units do give a central focus that may assist staff in planning, they can often lead to a reliance on activities for the generic child rather than for the individuals present. They can impose activities at the expense of responding to and building on children's natural interests.

Themes are a convenience for adults: a hook on which to base the program for a time, but the meanings of themes are often lost on infants and toddlers. Before using themes, staff should ask themselves what the purpose is, how the themes relate to the infants' or toddlers' interests, and whether themes are the best way to meet the needs of the children they care for. In any event, themes should never replace or diminish the central focus on planning learning centers for independent use.

Infant and Toddler Projects A project, like a theme, is a series of connected experiences around a particular idea that can extend children's learning in time and space beyond the confines of daily activities and a single learning center. When projects grow out of observing the children's *emerging* skills and interests and are based on exploring a question or challenge, they are of much greater value than themes and they allow children to become scientific thinkers, investigating questions, experimenting, and seeking answers. For instance, toddlers Ben and Becca find some grasshoppers, and this leads to a whole outdoor project on bugs—with collecting, close-up exploration with magnifying glasses, reading books, fingerplays, poetry, pictures, and imitative drama. The project lasts as long as the children are interested. The questions to be explored are toddlers' questions: Where are grasshoppers? What else lives in the grass? What do grasshoppers do, sound like, smell, and eat?

> One-year-old Selina and fourteen-month-old Brett investigate melting snow and, later, ice cubes and Popsicles. What else is cold? How fast will something freeze or thaw?

> Eight-month-old Li Li and six-month-old Ryan are fascinated by light beams, leading them to activities involving translucent mobiles, prisms, and flashlights.

Projects with infants and toddlers are important because they allow children to extend and continue experiences or activities that become richer and more complex over time, offering them opportunities to integrate new knowledge and practice, master, and enjoy experiences over and over again. Unlike projects with preschoolers, which focus on content and on how children interpret knowledge, projects with infants and toddlers should focus on repeating and extending successful experiences.

Generally, projects with infants recur over and over again, lasting from morning to afternoon and sometimes to many days or even weeks. A project may also consist of several experiences that can last a few days.

Planning for Individual Children

Individual planning ensures that the program works for every child. Ask these questions:

- Is the primary caregiver aware of the child's current interests, needs, and strengths?

- Does the teacher have a list of goals and desirable experiences that are based on observations of the child's development, experiences in the setting, and discussions with the child's parents?

Planning is an ongoing process that takes advantage of prime times—the children's experience with routines and their interactions with adults and other children and with indoor and outdoor learning environments. Planning considers how to increase the number, quality, and duration of warm, reciprocal interactions with the primary caregiver and other adults, and to ensure safe, pleasurable interactions with other children. Developmentally appropriate goals are established for each child to suit the child's and parents' needs and interests. *Note:* Diagnostic goals to speed development are not appropriate (for example, beginning to walk, knowing all the colors). Instead, use the key experiences discussed in chapter 16 to guide observations and planning.

Supervisors are responsible for ensuring that planning on all levels occurs and that staff have appropriate individual goals for children and are working toward them. The director and supervisors have discretion about the most effective planning structure to use in planning daily and weekly variations of experiences.

Observation and Experience Review

On an ongoing basis, teachers should use documentation to look back on what actually happened as a basis for planning changes in the experiences offered. Ask these questions:

- Are experiences developmentally appropriate for the entire range of children?
- Do experiences offer the right balance:
  - across curriculum areas (for example, motor, art, dramatic play, and construction)?
  - for individuals and groups?
  - between new challenges and practice/mastery?
  - between structured and open?
- Are the experiences actively nonsexist, and do they reflect the cultural diversity of the community in which the program operates?
- Is the great majority of time spent in child-directed play and exploration, either independently or with teachers' support and encouragement?
- Can children engage deeply in their play and exploration without interruption?

The review should be done by all the staff, if possible. Staff should all be encouraged to observe and evaluate the program continuously and to jot down notes or comments while they work. These observations are invaluable in planning for the group or for individual children.

In other chapters of this book, there are extensive discussions of routines, interactions, and organizing time and space. These should be part of the ongoing reflection and planning that take place in relation to children's experiences. Because these topics are discussed thoroughly elsewhere in the book, our remaining discussion of planning will focus mainly on what are traditionally known as the *learning environments* and *learning activities.*

Documentation: Making Learning Visible

Documentation is one of the most important of the new expectations for high-quality programs. Documenting and displaying the efforts of individual children and their groups are essential both for optimal learning and for establishing the credibility of the educational experience in the minds of parents. This is achieved through several means:

- Posting planning forms to make visible a planned learning environment, daily activities, and projects.
- Visibly highlighting the discoveries and accomplishments of individual children, and documenting group and individual learning in documentation panels and other displays and portfolios.
- Tracking the development of each child through child-observation documents and portfolios.

It should be possible to walk into a room and know immediately what is being learned (through photographs and children's work, occasionally enhanced by the ideas and reactions of parents). Parents and teachers can contribute to children's portfolios and share observations with each other in child-observation documents.

Documentation records children's experiences through a variety of media, and it is a basic tool for reflection, planning, and communication. Observing and reflecting on the experiences of children provide a window on learning, and documentation frames the window through

Daniel looks up with a smile as he mixes all the ingredients with his hands and feels the different textures.
Contributing and participating
Daniel is contributing his unique and individual thoughts, feelings, ideas and activities

- notes
- photographs
- stories
- pictures or sculptures
- CDs and DVDs
- children's dictation
- other media that represent or recreate the experience and the learning involved in children's experiences.

Using a variety of media, staff and parents come to understand the processes, behaviors, and choices children have made and they have made. Documentation not only provides children with a way of reflecting on and interpreting their experiences; it also provides staff with information for evaluating their work with children and it gives parents visible representations of what is happening in their child's homebase and how that pertains to learning.

Documentation is also a great vehicle for communicating *among* children, staff, and parents. Children learn that their ideas are respected and taken seriously. Through providing representations of children's progress and growth, parents and staff gain a better understanding of the learning that is emerging. Documentation creates archives, preserving the ideas and progress of individuals and the group, which can later be used for assessment, planning, and creating a history of the center.

Documentation is an integral part of the infant- or toddler-room experience; it is not an optional feature. Most teachers use documentation in one form or another—some systematically, others occasionally.

Capturing Children's Development

Systematic documentation allows programs to follow the progress of children's growth by providing concrete representations of children's strengths, skills, ideas, dispositions, and needs. Continually collecting examples of children's abilities provides a clear picture of their growth and learning over time, and captures each child's competence. Collections may include

- observations
- conversations
- audio samples
- photographs
- dictations
- work samples
- videos
- webbing concepts.

Examples of children's learning and progress are used in developing portfolios, in child observation records, in individual journals, and in other media that track an individual child's development.

Learning Made Visible

One should be able to enter a homebase and instantly recognize that it is a place rich with learning experiences. In addition to what is actually happening, evidence of the learning that is going on includes

- posted planning forms
- daily notes
- individual journals
- assessment tools (portfolios)
- project/experience displays
- art and science shows
- homebase books and journals.

Posting planning forms gives parents (as well as substitutes and directors) a glimpse into what is happening in the homebase. The *Highlights of the Day* form in the supplements provides highlights and an explanation for changes in plans, based on the emerging interests of children or situations.

See Supplement: *Highlights of the Day*

Daily Notes and Individual Journals Daily notes and individual journals communicate to parents what each child's day or week has been like. They relay important care information about feeding, sleeping, and diapering. These tools are helpful not only in giving parents a better understanding of their child's experiences but also in communicating what staff are doing in order to get to know and appreciate each child.

Notes and journals are only as valuable as the thought that goes into them. The information should document the learning that the experiences have made possible. It is important to use the daily note or daily experience sheet to translate for parents the highlights of what has been happening and the learning experiences that have been generated: language, math, science, learning about diversity, emotional intelligence, and the arts. It is not enough to say that José loved his stroller walk. How does that walk relate to his growing language, sensory learning, and perceptual skills? Parents do not want to hear only that José had a good day. What learning is emerging? How does what we have observed help us develop a clearer picture of José, his strengths and his needs? This kind of documentation will also be useful for later assessments, because it gives a picture of the child across time and provides useful documentation for meetings or conferences with parents.

Panels and Displays Documentation provides staff with a visual record of their home-base experience—what they have done with children. Staff can look at what has happened in their homebase and see how it relates to teaching. By revisiting their experiences with children, staff can reflect on their interactions, behaviors, and skills. Staff can create their own portfolios to communicate their work and growth with children. This kind of self-reflection is important in evaluating their work with children, making decisions, and changing their behavior to enhance their teaching skills. By reflecting on their work, staff can continually move forward rather than become stagnant.

The process through which children explore and experiment with ideas during activities and projects can be documented visually, step-by-step, for infants and toddlers. These documents can then be used as a basis for discussion, staff reflection, and communication with parents. Such displays can become natural parts of the learning environment, sending messages that what happens in this environment is important and purposeful.

Documentary displays can represent the growth of each child and of the group. Parents, staff, and children can see the history of experiences and how these experiences affect children's development and learning. Adults value old photo albums, home movies, and reminiscing about past experiences; all the memories of those experiences come back, even things that they didn't remember before—feelings, ideas, smells, sounds, and tastes. The same is true for children.

Displays in the homebase communicate the message that the ideas of children and families are valuable and important. Displays should consist primarily of the words and photographs that document children's experiences and work. Photographs of families and the use of parent observations send a message of respect for the children's culture and home life. Display is not for decoration but rather for communicating the life, learning, and history of the homebase.

Commercial or cute displays are not as valuable or as meaningful as documentation of homebase experiences. Children are drawn to commercial images, but such images have far less value than the representations of their experience and emerging ideas.

Of course, staff's time is limited, and it is not possible to document every experience that occurs in the room. Thoughtful decisions about what to document and how to display children's work are important. Keep in mind what message you want to communicate through the display and what experiences best communicate that message.

Samples of children's activities can also include an explanation of the process and the learning involved. When parents or visitors see the documentation, they can develop an understanding of how that experience came about and what the children learned from it. Explanations might include

- how the materials were chosen
- how the children used the materials
- what learning took place
- what the children said
- how long the activity lasted.

In choosing work to display, a representation from each child should be visible in the room, but each child's work need not be used for every display. Children choose experiences and learn differently. Displays should be the best samples of a child's experiences in relation to personal growth and learning.

Samples for display can include much more than artwork. Photos of the process and examples of children's conversations, dictations, and three-dimensional work are also part of documentation and communicate the life of the homebase.

The composition of the documentation is also important. Activity samples should be displayed in a thoughtful manner. Artwork crammed together, haphazardly put up, or offering little explanation does not send the message that children's ideas are respected or valued. All chosen samples of children's learning should be treated as museum pieces, and displayed as such.

Documenting Projects A project is a series of connected experiences about a particular idea, extended over a period of time. Projects involving infants and toddlers are important because they allow children to extend and continue experiences or activities that become more complex over time, integrating new knowledge with the opportunity to practice, perfect, and enjoy experiences over and over again. Unlike preschoolers' projects, which tend to focus on content and on how children interpret knowledge, infants' and toddlers' projects should focus on repeating and extending successful experiences.

As we noted earlier, projects with infants usually get repeated over and over again, from morning to afternoon, across many days or even weeks. A project may consist of several experiences that last for a few days. Project work is a vital part of the learning experience. It assists children in building on ideas and developing problem-solving and critical-thinking skills and it makes meaningful connections between actions, events, objects, and ideas in their world.

Documentation is an essential aspect of the project process because it connects experiences. Documenting and displaying the steps of a project communicate its purpose and how ideas emerge and change based on the interests and direction of the children.

Displays should illustrate the history of the project from beginning to end, and usually contain a variety of media:

- samples of children's work
- children's words/conversations
- photographs of the process
- a description of the process
- an explanation of the learning involved
- narratives
- a list of books used
- three-dimensional items.

Displays can take shape on bulletin boards, on panels, in books, in big portfolio books (wallpaper sample–sized), and on shelf tops. Order is important. A display that is cluttered or unorganized will have much less impact in communicating what is happening. A display may be simple or complex, but it should always be professional.

Getting Started

Documentation is a never ending process. The best first step is to just do it. Like children, most adults learn by doing. The more that documentation is made a part of everyday teaching, the more documentation skills teachers will grow. Start out small and simple, but start. Start by using the planning cycle. As teaching teams create and implement systems for documenting, the documentation will become more complex and sophisticated.

Basic materials needed to help you get started include

- planning cycle forms
- observation forms
- digital cameras
- audio recorders
- bulletin boards
- posterboard
- shelf-top displays
- album books.

This list will increase dramatically as the process of creating documentary displays becomes more familiar.

The Planning Cycle

Planning is a cycle. Once in motion, there is no beginning or end. Planning sets the stage by developing a rich and responsive learning environment that engages children and at the same time encourages them to explore, discover, and play independently. High-quality planning recognizes that plans, environment, experiences, and projects reflect the *individuals* in the group and are not based on the average child or a generic child. In an environment organized for independent use, each child will be able to share in the delight of discovery with a focused adult during prime times.

See Supplements: *The Five Phases of Planning for Infants, Toddlers and Twos; Planning the Environment and Experiences: Infants* and *Toddlers;* and *Planning the Environment and Experiences: Twos*

The Five Phases of Planning

The five phases of planning are

1. Observing
2. Analyzing and Reflecting
3. Brainstorming
4. Planning
5. Implementing

Phase 1: Observing Observing is the way teachers get to know children and gather information to make thoughtful decisions for planning, communicating with parents, and tracking individual development.

How? On an observation form, jot down phrases and key words to help you remember what you have seen and heard. There is no need to write down paragraphs or sentences.

When? Observations can take place anywhere, any time, and can encompass as few as two to five minutes. When you are interacting with children during your busy day (not sitting back, watching from afar), and you notice something you want to remember about a child or a small group (such as a newly emerging skill or interest), document what you see. Focus on all areas of development.

Tips. Keep observation forms, Post-it notes, and a pen on a clipboard in every learning center for easy access. Jot down thoughts when the form is not accessible and transfer them to an observation form later.

Phase 2: Analyzing and Reflecting Thinking about what you observed is important. What happened and why? What does it mean in relation to the child or the environment? Reflections are preparations for appropriately tracking children's development, developing next steps for possible planning, writing concise daily notes, and communicating with parents.

Without this step, the valuable information you document will become useless.

How? From what you have documented, ask yourself: "What does this tell me?" You may have observed a certain skill or skills. This will be good information for the child's portfolio. You may have noticed a skill or skills that need to be developed. This will be helpful in planning future activities or experiences that will foster the development of that skill. Your observation may provide insights about what a child may be interested in. This will be important information for planning as well. You may learn something new about your environment or activities. You may notice that the room arrangement or environment planning was working really well, or that it was not, or you may learn about the ways the children were using the materials. This will be a good time to note changes and enhancements to make. Based on your reflection, jot down your possible next steps and whether each step is a planned experience, an environmental change, or further observation.

When? Reflect after the observation, while it is fresh in your mind.

Tips. Use "telegraphic" language—jot down words or phrases, not sentences.

Phase 3: Brainstorming Brainstorming helps organize ideas for planning by outlining what staff should be thinking about: topics, skills, resources, and challenges and questions for children.

How? Jot down thoughts, such as skills that could be developed, possible activities and projects, environmental changes, and resources. Also jot down ideas as you go about your day, and develop a process for five-to-ten-minute touch-base meetings with your team.

When? For teachers who have planning time, brainstorming is a great tool to use when meeting as a team to discuss the development of experiences for the room. This should be done weekly, if possible. When you can't meet to brainstorm, you can post a Web form so team members can add their brainstorming ideas throughout the day.

Tips. Have a brainstorming Web form accessible in a room so all staff can contribute to it and communicate ideas when there is no time to meet. When there is time for meeting as a team, use this form to organize thoughts based on your observations. This form will help keep the meeting on track, focusing on key areas to think about as you plan.

See Supplement: *Brainstorming Web*

Phase 4: Planning Planning puts into action the observations and ideas and is essential for thoughtful preparation and organization of the program and communication with families.

How? When planning for the environment and experiences (activities, projects, and individual experiences), consider the selection and presentation of materials and/or alterations of the materials in each learning center or treasure basket. Some environmental changes may be carried over from one week to the next, depending on goals and projects. Plan for individual experiences in selected learning centers. These can be self-directed or teacher-facilitated. You should also plan experiences for individual children in the course of routines and nurturing interactions, and during play. Finally, plan some group activities, projects, and enrichment experiences for toddlers. Consider the project and its goals, skills to focus on, and materials needed.

When? Use an environment and experiences planning form and post it weekly. Use an individual child objective form when meeting with parents at enrollment, when a child transitions to your room, and every three months thereafter. Review an individual child objectives form to develop new objectives during conferences. Use this form whenever you are documenting concerns or issues about development or behavior.

See Supplements: *Planning the Environment and Experiences: Infants and Toddlers; Planning the Environment and Experiences: Twos;* and *Individual Personal-Care Plan for Infants and Toddlers*

Tips. On an environment and experiences form, list only materials or props that you are highlighting or focusing on for that particular week. In other words, you don't need to list materials that are constants in a learning center. On the individual child objectives form, list general goals that you and the parent together have decided on. In between meeting times with parents, you can make additions or changes.

Phase 5: Implementing Planning always involves predicting the overall day, the group dynamics, and each child's mood and interests. Implementation should take into account what the children actually do with our plans. They often surprise us and take what is planned in an entirely different direction. It is important to let go of preconceived ideas and follow children's emerging interests, taking cues from them even though it may mean changing plans.

How? At the end of the day, document the selected experiences you would like to highlight in your room and post the notes (or documentation) in a place that is highly visible to parents, such as by an entry or exit door. Use notes on a daily experience sheet or journal to summarize and communicate individual learning. Communicate the learning by posting planning forms, displaying children's work, and using documentation panels with explanations of children's learning during the experiences. You can use room newsletters to report and reflect on the group's activities.

When? A highlights-of-the-day form should be posted daily. Children's experiences are recorded on a daily experience sheet or in a journal. Visible documentation should be displayed on an ongoing basis and changed at least monthly. Homebase newsletters can be done daily, weekly, or monthly. Journals (which complement daily experience sheets) are best when you have at least two or three entries per week per child.

See Supplement: *Highlights of the Day*

Tips. Journal entries and daily notes are for reporting and reflecting on individual experiences. Document what is happening in children's lives in child care: who they play with, what they're learning, and what their emerging skills and interests are. You only need to highlight two to four major experiences you want parents to know about on the daily highlights form. Over time, these records chart children's progress and become invaluable sources of information when preparing for family-staff conferences.

A Final Note

Planning for learning is all about preparation and possibilities: preparing the routines and the environment to create the possibility of wonderful prime times and preparing for the learning opportunities that children need. Planning is the process during which teachers use all they know, based on observation, reflection, and brainstorming. Teachers don't plan lessons or what to do; they plan for opportunities to explore, discover, and learn.

Exercises

1. Observe an infant group for a morning.
   a. Document a child's morning using the observation forms.
   b. Write a note to the child's parents based on your observations.

2. Observe a toddler group for a morning.
   a. Document a child's morning. Use a digital camera to create a display that reflects the child's morning.
   b. Identify and plan a project based on your observation of the emerging skills and interests of the child. Use a supplement *Brainstorming Web* form to generate ideas.

Staying Good: Evaluation and Quality Control

Chapter 20

Ongoing Program Evaluation and Change

εxcellence *The program is characterized by active intelligence—a culture and systems in which there is ongoing monitoring of program outcomes experienced by children and parents and evaluation of the program's purpose, philosophy, goals, and objectives.*

Good programs employ a range of formal and informal monitoring and evaluation strategies. There is a program culture that encourages continual critical appraisal with an eye toward improving, and a "Why not?" approach that welcomes ideas, suggestions, and constructive criticism from staff and parents, as well as celebrations of achievements. "What's happening?" "How are we doing?" and "Should we be changing?" are not only heard during periods of crisis but are continuously asked and represent a state of mind shared by staff and parents. Mistakes are viewed as something to be learned from, not occasions for blame. Much of the monitoring and evaluation takes place informally when staff and parents observe and discuss the program, children, and staff actions. Time is set aside to meet and discuss approaches and issues, resources available to read and to watch, professional development opportunities that spur growth, and opportunities for parents to discuss issues and concerns.

Note: It is important to distinguish between monitoring the outcomes experienced by children and child assessment efforts that monitor child development. Child assessment focuses on the child development and achievement: children's behavior and abilities. This is desirable in programs with staff trained in child development and assessment, but it is different from program evaluation and evaluating the child and family *experience*. Program evaluation looks at program policies and practices: what is actually occurring in the program and what is experienced by children, parents, and staff. Is the program that exists on paper (the policies and stated practices in brochures and handbooks) a reality? Are the program goals being achieved?

Assessing Quality

Achieving high quality requires a more systematic approach to monitoring and evaluation.

Monitoring is the process of identifying what is really happening: What is the actual experience of children, parents, and staff? Wait a minute—don't we know what is happening anyway? After all, we are right there ourselves. Yes and no. We know what we see, hear, and feel; we know what we pay attention to. But what about all the things we don't pay attention to—for example, the perspectives of others? We naturally see from our own vantage point and filter our perceptions through our values and beliefs. Good programs systematically monitor the outcomes experienced by *all* people involved, thereby ensuring a more complete picture. Monitoring involves directing attention and collecting perceptions from children and adults alike.

> *I realized that I went home and told my husband that it was a good or bad day entirely based on my perspective: "The day went really well, really smoothly, no problems, we all had a good time." On good days, nobody ate the paste and threw up, no biting, the activities seemed to go well, my assistant teacher showed up on time, and there was less chaos and crying. I didn't sum up the experiences of the kids and their days: Ali was calm and much more secure in his second week, Sophia was energetic exploring new things and enjoyed her dad visiting, we managed to have lots of one-to-one with Jake, Mimi, Tonia, and Hector, and so on.*
> —Toddler Teacher

Evaluation is the process of valuing what is happening: deciding what we think about what has been uncovered through monitoring and deciding whether change is necessary. For example, monitoring tells us that two-year-olds spend a lot more time in their room on indoor art than on outdoor sand and water. In an evaluation process, we determine whether we think this is a problem and, if so, what might be done about it. The bases for evaluation are the goals and objectives that underlie the program and the assumption about what constitutes good practice as spelled out in our handbook and other program materials. Evaluation requires knowledge and perspective: knowledge of child development, families, and the cultures represented, and understanding of the perspectives of parents in the program.

A Culture of Responsibility, Not of Blame

Evaluation can be threatening. It's hard not to be nervous if you or your room is the subject of scrutiny. What runs through your mind? "First, let me explain," "You are just focusing on what's wrong," and "It's not my fault." Establishing a culture of responsibility for outcomes, not blame ("It's your fault!"), can eliminate much of the threat. Child care is difficult and complex. The teacher's actions take place in a context. Responsibility for outcomes should be shared.

Why the Yelling

In the Bluebell room, it was not uncommon to find staff yelling at children from across the room. While they were not being particularly harsh, their actions set a loud, bossy, negative tone. "No," "Stop that," "Please come over here" rang out frequently, and even positive redirection came across as negative because it was done loudly at a distance. Obviously, it was a staff performance issue and the staff needed to change—they needed to stop yelling.

Staff performance was the issue, but not necessarily staff wrongdoing, ignorance, or indifference. In fact, for the most part, they were not aware of how much yelling was happening. Why were they yelling? There were a number of possible reasons:

- It was a loud room with lousy acoustics.
- The room had fourteen active toddlers and two staff.
- It was not a "Yes" space, no one had helped teachers with the room environment, and the teachers had little training.
- Staff were valiantly trying to create more individualized, small-group learning centers and activities and to spread out and use the whole room.

Efforts to correct the problem illustrate the shortsightedness of blaming individual staff and putting all the responsibility on them. The director approached the yelling as a room issue, not as a staff-in-the-room performance problem. She became as responsible for change as the staff were. Staff were made aware of the yelling and worked together to break the habit. They got some training and some help planning a "Yes" environment, and they were promised a long-range plan to reduce the ratio and group size as well as the installation of an acoustic ceiling.

Monitoring and evaluation are positive when they are part of a process of improvement that everyone has responsibility for.

Monitoring

There are a number of ways to systematically monitor what is going on: for example, through observation and polling—that is, asking parents, staff, and children about their experience.

Directed Observations

You can see a lot by watching.
—Yogi Berra

Yogi was right. If you watch, you will see what's happening with children and adults. One of the best ways to evaluate the daily program is to encourage staff to observe children as they work with them: their experiences in the environment, skills, strengths, interests, and also what they do not do—the experiences, parts of the environment, or people they avoid. This seems obvious. Observing happens all the time, of course, but much of the time we are only seeing a limited amount. Often we focus more on the event (our actions—the caring or learning activity or mishaps) than on the outcome (the children's experience—the care or learning experienced).

Directed observations are used most often when we are struggling with a child's behavior, such as biting, or a difficult time of the day when chaos periodically erupts, such as a transition time. Directed observations structure our looking; we focus on specific children, activities, interactions, aspects of the environment, or time periods. Recording those observations provides the raw material for discussion as a team. Teachers can help each other to see a fuller, less egocentric picture by intentionally observing from different perspectives (for example, the perspective of a particular child or parent) and sharing those perceptions.

For staff to remain motivated to frequently use directed observations as tools, information has to be used effectively; there must be mechanisms for sharing the information and translating it into eventual practice. Homebase meetings are a good time for this. But not having enough time to talk about the children is a common lament when meetings become taken up by announcements, planning, and staff issues.

When meeting time is short, touch-base times, mini-meetings, and short staff conferences between primary caregivers become invaluable.

Sampling Sampling is a useful way to structure observations. *Event sampling* involves recording behaviors of the child or children being observed during a particular period of time. If Anne is having difficulty separating, recording all her behaviors during the period of arrival (the "event") until she is engaged in the program should reveal a lot. Recording the behaviors of her parents, staff, and even other children would add to the picture. *Time sampling* records behavior observed at regularly timed intervals—for instance, recording a child's behavior every five minutes or recording the behavior observed at a particular location (for example, in the book area) every ten minutes.

Both methods of sampling force us to see in a more rigorous and complete manner. We may notice patterns of behavior and events we weren't aware of; for example, a lack of activity choices that engage Anne in particular situations.

Snapshots Snapshots are another way to structure observation and are particularly useful in observing how children use the environment. The goal is to capture what is happening at a given moment in time. This can be done literally with a camera, or simply by charting using a room map. A snapshot may reveal adults or children bunching up, incomplete use of the room, or problems with supervision. Used with time sampling, snapshots may focus teachers' attention on the flow of children or the actions of particular children.

Anecdotal Records Typically, this involves staff writing down what they feel is significant interactions, events, behavior—in a journal or log. It is important to record the information as soon as possible in order to capture details and ensure accuracy. Also important is distinguishing between a description of the behavior, which should be objective and detailed ("Joey threw the blocks"), and your feelings or conclusions about the behavior ("Joey disrupted the block area and ruined the morning"). Discussing the anecdotes may lead others to different interpretations of the behavior.

Checklists When something happens, we check it off. Behavioral checklists can be devised for individuals or groups of children around any behavior the staff is concerned with; for example, language use, exploration, distress, aggression, or withdrawal. A primary caregiver may devise a checklist in cooperation with a worried parent in order to track a child's emerging motor skills.

Polling Polling is just another name for systematically asking someone to tell you what he or she is thinking or feeling, either via interview or questionnaire. In the supplements we provide examples of questionnaires for new parents and examples of surveys for staff.

Polling can be long and comprehensive, such as an annual parent survey, or it can be a single question. It can be done on a computer at the front desk, with Post-it notes, or the old-fashioned way with a photocopied questionnaire. Almost anything to do with the experience of child care can be a topic for parents and staff. There is one important consideration, however. People tire of being asked their views if they don't

---

The Two-Minute Poll of the Week

Please take a moment to answer these three questions:
1. What was the best thing you noticed this week that happened at the center?
2. What did you see or experience that you would change if you could?
3. Did you get a chance to check out the documentation panel on "learning to wash our hands"?

Name _____ (optional)

---

see any results. Polling has to be followed by dissemination of the results, by discussion, and, if called for, by publicized records of change that has occured as a result of the poll or survey.

Assessing Child Outcomes?

As school-like expectations extend downward toward the earliest childhood care, there is a growing movement to assess developmental and achievement outcomes during the preschool years, an outgrowth of the "kindergarten readiness" pressure (a phenomenon that the authors believe is very unfortunate). This assessment, not to be confused with screening for developmental concerns, is promoted to ensure kindergarten readiness and to hold programs accountable for kindergarten preparation. Ideally, developmental screening of infants and toddlers by trained child development specialists would be available to every family through their health insurance or through other means. We hope it is unnecessary to even have to state this, but any movement to test the learning outcomes of toddlers and twos is an unnecessary and unfortunate mistake. The caring and learning *experience* of infants and the experience of their families in group care are what need to be monitored and evaluated: the quality of experiences and relationships.

Program Evaluations

Evaluation should extend beyond the homebase to periodic consideration of all aspects of the center: mission, philosophy, administrative and programming policies, and procedures. There should be regular opportunities for staff and parents to see if practice matches policy, if old policies need revising, and if new policies need developing.

Many centers are subject to outside evaluations or audits by funding sources, external administrators or owners, or regulatory agencies. These often identify problems and propel changes, but they may not be comprehensive and may not provide the information that center staff need to grow and change.

NAEYC Accreditation Accreditation by the National Association for the Education of Young Children (www.naeyc.org) is an excellent means of program evaluation because it forces you to look into nearly every nook and cranny of your center's operation. It is a voluntary process that includes extensive self-study and on-site assessment. It determines whether or not the program meets a superior national standard for early childhood education and care. Standards cover a comprehensive range of program issues around caring, learning, parents, and staff, as well as administrative procedures. The process involves staff and parents in monitoring the program. Accreditation is for a five-year period, with programs subject to random visits.

NAEYC accreditation has been in existence only since 1985, and it is now widely recognized as the most significant standard of quality available. Accreditation standards and processes are designed to be challenging yet achievable and to apply to any early care and education program serving children under the age of six. Developing a national standard that applies to a wide range of early childhood programs will inevitably result in compromises as well as some controversy. Some criteria may be too vague or too precise. Those programs that become accredited may represent a wide continuum of quality, and the low end may raise questions about the level of the standard. But accreditation is critically important for the child care industry, and all good programs should seek to be accredited. Without an established quality standard, the widespread public perception that meeting minimal licensing standards is the equivalent of quality will continue to plague child care and devalue real quality.

> ### Accreditation Is Like Flossing—A Bother, but Worth It. You Clear Out Some Stuff You Didn't Realize Was There.
>
> "You know, doing accreditation was a lot harder and a lot more rewarding than I thought it would be," said a director whose center had just been accredited. "We were surprised both by some things we thought were happening that weren't, and by some things that were happening that were just sloppy. We were good, but accreditation made us get better and stay good.
>
> "One of the best outcomes was that it made us proud of ourselves and really educated the parents. It sets us apart, and parents now understand better what they are getting (and we raised our fees without that much of an outcry)."

Statewide Quality Rating Systems Many states are considering either voluntary or required quality rating systems or "star systems." These systems define a continuum of quality, often from one star for basic quality to four stars for high quality. Licensing regulations have historically represented one level of standards: the basic floor that protected children from harm. These new systems are instead designed to help parents identify the quality of child care programs, and to indicate for child care programs the ingredients necessary for higher quality, creating a ladder of improvement that can form the basis for quality-improvement funding. In essence, a center that is defining its star status undergoes a thorough program evaluation. To assess quality in a quality rating system, some states may opt to use the environmental rating scales (see below).

The Environmental Rating Scales: ITERS, ECERS, FDCERS, and SACERS The Infant Toddler Environmental Rating Scale (ITERS) and companion scales, the Early Childhood Environmental Rating Scale (ECERS), the Family Day Care Environmental Rating Scale (FDCERS), and the School-Age Care Environmental Rating Scale (SACERS), are widely used instruments for quality evaluation, research, self-evaluation, and, in some states, quality rating systems (www.fpg.unc.edu/~ecers). They were developed by Thelma Harms, Richard Clifford, and Debby Cryer at the Frank Porter Graham Center at the University of North Carolina at Chapel Hill. The term *environment* is used in the broadest sense to include the physical environment and caring, learning, and organizational practices, including interactions, supervision, promoting diversity, and other dimensions. Because they attempt to be one-size-fits-all, it is easy to quibble with some items on their scales, but the clear and concrete criteria and continual efforts to refine and improve the scales make them valuable tools for programs to use in self-evaluation.

Develop Your Own Program Evaluation Centers or homes can develop their own program evaluation systems, perhaps in conjunction with a board of directors or an advisory board. One effective method of structuring regular program evaluation is to develop a three-year calendar for reviewing center materials: personnel policies and staff handbook, center brochure and parent handbook, program handbook and environmental and program checklists, and administrative operations materials. As each document is reviewed, policies and practices should be subjected to scrutiny by staff and parents, and revised as necessary.

A Final Word: Quality Takes Commitment and Time

The process of becoming a high-quality program is demanding, slow, and often frustrating—and maintaining excellence is equally demanding. Usually our recognition of what quality is and our desire to attain it outpace our efforts to produce it. Evaluation can easily become a source of frustration: we identify more concerns, more blemishes, and more things to do. It doesn't have to be that way. Evaluations can and should uncover all that is right with the program: all those positive interactions, satisfied parents, engaged children, and hard-working staff.

It goes back to the program culture. When evaluation is seen as a natural process, improvement as an ongoing need, and responsibility shared by a staff working together, programs will achieve the highest quality their resources allow.

Exercises

1. Observe one child during three different transition times during the day. Record as many of the child's behaviors as you can. What can you say about the child or the transition?

2. Observe a learning center for three days during the same thirty-minute period. Describe who used the center, how materials were used, how children engaged and disengaged from the center, language used, and social interactions. What similarities and differences did you observe among children in their use of materials, entry and exit, and social behavior?

3. Develop a checklist based on daily goals for a primary-care child and parents.

References

Harms, T., and R. Clifford. 2007. *Family Child Care Environment Rating Scale*. Rev. ed. New York: Teachers College Press.

Harms, T., R. Clifford, and D. Cryer. 2005. *Early Childhood Environment Rating Scale*. Rev. ed. New York: Teachers College Press.

Harms, T., D. Cryer, and R. Clifford. 2006. *Infant/Toddler Environment Rating Scale*. Rev. ed. New York: Teachers College Press.

Harms, T., E. Jacobs, and D. Romano. 1995. *School-Age Care Environment Rating Scale*. New York: Teachers College Press.

Resources

Publications

American Academy of Pediatrics, American Public Health Association, and National Resource Center for Health and Safety in Child Care and Early Education. 2002. *Caring for Our Children: National Health and Safety Performance Standards: Guidelines for Out-of-Home Child Care Programs*. 2nd ed. Elk Grove Village, IL: American Academy of Pediatrics and Washington, DC: American Public Health Association. Also available at http://nrc.uchsc.edu.

Albrecht, K., and L. Miller. 2000. *Innovations: The Comprehensive Infant Curriculum*. Beltsville, MD: Gryphon House.

————. 2000. *Innovations: The Comprehensive Toddler Curriculum*. Beltsville, MD: Gryphon House.

Aronson, S. 2002. *Healthy Young Children: A Manual for Programs*. Washington, DC: NAEYC.

Baker, A., and L. Manfredi-Pettit. 2006. *Relationships, the Heart of Quality Care: Creating Community among Adults in Early Care Settings*. Washington, DC: NAEYC.

Berk, L., and A. Winsler. 1995. *Scaffolding Children's Learning: Vygotsky and Early Childhood Education*. Washington, DC: NAEYC.

Bettelheim, B. 1969. *The Children of the Dream*. New York: Avon.

Bloom, P. J. 1997. *A Great Place to Work: Improving Conditions for Staff in Young Children's Programs*. Washington, DC: NAEYC.

————. 1982. *Avoiding Burn Out: Strategies for Managing Time, Space, and People in Early Childhood Education*. Lake Forest, IL: New Horizon.

Bloom, P. J., M. Sheerer, and J. Britz. 2005. *Blueprint for Action: Achieving Center-Based Change through Staff Development*. Lake Forest, IL: New Horizons.

Brazelton, T. B. 1989. *Infants and Mothers*. New York: Dell.

Brazelton, T. B., and S. I. Greenspan. 2001. *The Irreducible Needs of Children: What Every Child Must Have to Grow, Learn, and Flourish*. New York: Perseus.

Brazelton, T. B., and J. D. Sparrow. 2006. *Touchpoints: Birth to Three: Your Child's Emotional and Behavioral Development*. New York: Da Capo Press.

Bredekamp, S., and C. Copple, eds. 1997. *Developmentally Appropriate Practice in Early Childhood Programs Serving Children Birth through Age 8*. Washington, DC: NAEYC.

Bruner, J. S. 1973. "Organization of Early Skilled Action." *Child Development* 44:1-111.

Ceppi, G., and M. Zini. 1998. *Children, Spaces, Relations: Metaproject for an Environment for Young Children*. Reggio Emilia, Italy: Reggio Children.

Chess, S., and A. Thomas. 1987. *Know Your Child: An Authoritative Guide for Today's Parents*. New York: Basic Books.

Coates, G. 1974. *Alternative Learning Environments*. Stroudsburg, PA: Dowden, Hutchinson and Ross.

Coles, R. 1998. *The Moral Intelligence of Children: How to Raise a Moral Child*. New York: Plume.

Consumer Product Safety Commission. 1997. *Handbook for Public Playground Safety*. Washington, DC: Consumer Product Safety Commission.

Curtis, D., and M. Carter. 2003. *Designs for Living and Learning: Transforming Early Childhood Environments*. St. Paul, MN: Redleaf Press.

Dannenmaier, M. 1998. *A Child's Garden: Enchanting Outdoor Spaces for Children and Parents*. New York: Simon and Schuster.

Dodge, D. T., and C. Heroman. 2006. *Building Your Baby's Brain*. Washington, DC: Teaching Strategies.

Dodge, D. T., A. Dombro, and L. Colker. 2006. *A Parent's Guide to Infant/Toddler Programs*. Washington, DC: Teaching Strategies.

Dodge, D. T., S. Rudnick, and K. L. Berke. 2006. *The Creative Curriculum® for Infants, Toddlers, & Twos*. Rev. ed. Washington, DC: Teaching Strategies.

Elkind, D. 1998. *Reinventing Childhood: Raising and Educating Children in a Changing World*. New York: Modern Language Press.

Erikson, E. 1950. *Childhood and Society*. New York: Norton.

Gallagher, W. 1993. *The Power of Place*. New York: HarperCollins.

Gandini, L., and C. P. Edwards, eds. 2001. *Bambini: The Italian Approach to Infant/Toddler Care*. New York: Teachers College Press.

Gonzalez-Mena, J. 2007. *Fifty Early Childhood Strategies for Working and Communicating with Diverse Families*. Upper Saddler River, NJ: Pearson.

———. 2004. *The Caregiver's Companion*. New York: McGraw Hill.

———. 2004. *Diversity in Early Care and Education: Honoring Differences*. 4th ed. New York: McGraw-Hill.

Gonzalez-Mena, J., and D. Widmeyer Eyer. [1980] 1993. *Infancy and Caregiving*. Mountain View, CA: Mayfield.

———. 1992. *Infants, Toddlers, and Caregivers*. New York: McGraw-Hill.

Gopnick, A., A. Metzoff, and P. Kuhl. 1999. *The Scientist in the Crib: What Early Learning Tells Us about the Mind*. New York: Perennial.

Greenman, J. 2005. *Caring Spaces, Learning Places: Children's Environments That Work*. Redmond, WA: Exchange Press.

_____. 1998. *Places for Childhood: Making Quality Happen in the Real World.* Redmond, WA: Exchange Press.

Greenspan, S. 2000. *Building Healthy Minds.* New York: Perseus.

Harms, T., and D. Cryer. 1991. *Infant/Toddler Environment Rating Scale: Video Observations.* New York: Teachers College Press.

Hart, B., and T. Risley. 1995. *Meaningful Differences in the Everyday Experience of Young American Children.* Baltimore: Paul H. Brooke.

Hast, F., and A. Hollyfield. 2001. *More Infant and Toddler Experiences.* St. Paul, MN: Redleaf Press.

_____. 1999. *Infant and Toddler Experiences,* St. Paul, MN: Redleaf Press.

Herr, J., and T. Swim. 2002. *Creative Resources for Infants and Toddlers.* Clifton Park, NY: Delmar.

Hohman, M., and D. Weikart. 2002. *Educating Young Children: Active Learning Practices for Preschool and Child Care Programs.* Ypsilanti, MI: High/Scope Press.

Honig, A. 2002. *Secure Relationships: Nurturing Infant/Toddler Attachment in Early Care Settings.* Washington, DC: NAEYC.

_____. 1982. *Playtime Learning Games for Young Children.* Syracuse: Syracuse University Press.

Isaacs, S. 1968. *The Nursery Years: The Mind of the Child from Birth to Six Years.* New York: Schocken.

Isbell, R. 2002. *The Complete Learning Spaces Book for Infants and Toddlers.* Beltsville, MD: Gryphon House.

Keister, M. E. 1970. *The "Good Life" for Infants and Toddlers.* Washington, DC: NAEYC.

Keyser, J. 2006. *From Parents to Partners: Building a Family-Centered Early Childhood Program.* St. Paul, MN: Redleaf Press.

Kinney, M. L., and P. Ahrens. 2001. *Beginning with Babies.* St. Paul, MN: Redleaf Press.

Kohl, M. 2002. *First Art: Art Experiences for Toddlers and Twos.* Beltsville, MD: Gryphon House.

Konner, M. 1991. *Childhood.* New York: Little Brown and Company.

Lally, R. J., Y. L. Torres, and P. Phelps. 2003. *Caring for Infants and Toddlers in Groups: Developmentally Appropriate Practices.* Washington, DC: Zero to Three Press.

Leinfelder, J., and M. Segal. 2005. *Coaching for Quality In Infant-Toddler Care: A Field Guide for Directors, Consultants, and Trainers.* Washington, DC: Zero to Three Press.

_____. 2003. *Making Connections: A Field Guide to Infant & Toddler Care.* Fort Lauderdale: Mailman Segal Institute for Early Childhood Studies / Nova Southwestern University.

Maurer, D., and C. Maurer. 1988. *The World of the Newborn*. New York: Basic Books.

McCall, R. 1980. *Infants*. New York: Vintage.

Miller, K. 2004. *Simple Transitions for Infants and Toddlers*. Beltsville, MD: Gryphon House.

———. 2002. *Things to Do with Toddlers and Twos*. Beltsville, MD: Gryphon House.

———. 2000. *More Things to Do with Toddlers and Twos*. Beltsville, MD: Gryphon House.

Miller, L., and K. Albrecht. 2000. *The Comprehensive Infant and Toddler Curriculum Trainers Guide*. Beltsville, MD: Gryphon House.

Moore, R. 1993. *Plants for Play*. Berkeley: MIG Communication.

Moore, R., S. Goltsman, and D. Iafacono. 1992. *Play for All Children: Planning, Design, and Management of Outdoor Settings for All Children*. Berkeley: MIG Communication.

NAEYC Academy for Early Childhood Programs. 2006. NAEYC *Early Childhood Program Standards and Accreditation Criteria*. Washington, D.C: NAEYC.

Olds, A. 2001. *Child Care Design Guide*. New York: McGraw Hill.

Osborn, H. 1994. *Room for Loving, Room for Learning*. St. Paul, MN: Redleaf Press.

Pennsylvania Chapter of the American Academy of Pediatrics. 2002. *Model Child Care Health Policies*. Washington, DC: NAEYC.

Raines, S., K. Miller, and L. Curry Rood. 2000. *Story Stretchers for Infants, Toddlers and Twos: Experiences, Activities, and Games for Popular Children's Books*. Beltsville, MD: Gryphon House.

Rivkin, M. 1995. *The Great Outdoors*. Washington, DC: NAEYC.

Rogoff, B. 2003. *The Cultural Nature of Human Development*. New York: Oxford University Press.

Sandoval, M., and M. De La Roza. 1986. "A Cultural Perspective for Serving the Hispanic Client." In *Cross Cultural Training for Mental Health Professionals,* ed. H. P. Lefley and P. B. Pedersen. Springfield, IL: Charles C. Thomas.

Schiller, P. 2005. *The Complete Resource Book for Infants*. Beltsville, MD: Gryphon House.

Shore, R. 1997. *Rethinking the Brain: New Insights into Early Development*. New York: Families and Work Institute.

Silberg, J. 2000. *Brain Games for Babies*. Beltsville, MD: Gryphon House.

Snowden, L. 1984. "Toward Evaluation of Black Psycho-Social Competence." In *The Pluralistic Society: A Community Mental Health Perspective,* ed. S. Sue and T. Moore. New York: Human Sciences Press.

Stern, D. 1992. *Diary of a Baby.* New York: Basic Books.

Stine, S. 1997. *Landscapes for Learning: Creating Outdoor Environments for Children.* New York: John Wiley.

Stonehouse, A. 2007. *How Does It Feel? Childcare from a Parent's Perspective.* 2nd ed. Redmond, WA: Child Care Information Exchange.

Stonehouse, A., and J. Gonzalez-Mena. 2004. *Making Links: A Collaborative Approach to Planning and Practice in Early Childhood Services.* Sydney, Australia: Pademon Press.

Talbot, M. 2006. "The Baby Lab." *New Yorker,* September 4.

Tobin, J., D. Wu, and D. Davidson. 1989. *Preschool in Three Cultures.* New Haven, CT: Yale University Press.

Warshaw, S. 2006. *Help . . . at Home: Developmental Support and Information Handouts for Families with Infants and Toddlers—Birth to Three.* Palo Alto: Vort Corporation.

Videos

The Program for Infant/Toddler Caregivers. A series of training videos produced in three languages (English, Spanish, Chinese) on infant/toddler policies, environments, play and learning, and interaction. Available from WestEd, 415-565-3000. http://www.wested.org/cs/we/print/docs/we/home.htm.

Carter, M. *Time with Toddlers.* Available from Redleaf Press, 800-423-8309. http://www.redleafpress.org.

Greenman, J., and M. Lindstrom. *Great Places for Childhood.* Available from Kaplan Company, 800-334-2014. http://www.kaplanco.com.

Modigliani, K., and E. Moore. *Many Right Ways: Designing Your Home Child Care Environment.* Available from Redleaf Press, 800-423-8309. http://www.redleafpress.org.

Organizations/Web Sites

Early Care and Education

Bright Horizons Family Solutions
200 Talcott Ave. S.
Watertown, MA 02472
617-673-8000
www.brighthorizons.com

Child Care Exchange
PO Box 3249
Redmond, WA 98073-3249
800-221-2864
www.childcareexchange.com

Child Care Law Center
221 Pine Street, Third Floor
San Francisco, CA 94104
415-394-7144
www.childcarelaw.org

Clearinghouse on Early Education and Parenting
University of Illinois at Urbana–Champaign
Children's Research Center
51 Gerty Drive
Champaign, IL 61820-7469
877-275-3227
ceep.crc.uiuc.edu

Early Head Start National Resource Center @ ZERO
TO THREE
2000 M Street NW
Washington, DC 20036-3307
202-638-1144
202-638-0851 (fax)
www.ehsnrc.org

National Association for the Education
of Young Children (NAEYC)
1313 L Street NW, Suite 500
Washington, DC 20005
800-424-2460
www.naeyc.org

National Association of Child Care Resource &
Referral Agencies (NACCRRA)
3101 Wilson Boulevard
Suite 350
Arlington, VA 22201
703-341-4100
www.naccrra.net

National Association for Family Child Care
5202 Pinemont Drive
Salt Lake City, UT 84123
800-359-3817
www.nafcc.org

National Child Care Information Center
10530 Rosehaven St., Suite 400
Fairfax, VA 22030
800-616-2242
nccic.acf.hhs.gov

National Resource Center for Health and Safety in
Child Care and Early Education
Anschultz Medical Campus
Campus Mail Stop F541
P.O. Box 6508
Aurora, CO 80045-0508
800-598-5437
nrc.uchsc.edu

Zero to Three
National Center for Infants, Toddlers, and Families
2000 M Street NW, Suite 200
Washington, DC 20036
202-638-1144
www.zerotothree.org/

Environments

Natural Learning Initiative
College of Design
200 Pullen Road
North Carolina State University
Raleigh, NC 27695-7701
919-515-8344/5
www.naturalearning.org

Planet Earth Playscapes
182 Hart Road
Spencer, NY 14883
607-589-7887
mail@earthplay.net
www.planetearthplayscapes.com

SafeSpace Concepts, Inc
1424 North Post Oak
Houston, TX 77055
800-622-4289
www.safespaceconcepts.com

Nursery Maid
P.O. Box 922
Dinuba, CA 93618
800-443-8773
www.nurserymaid.com

Families

Family Communications: Mr. Rogers' Neighborhood
Family Communications, Inc.
4802 Fifth Avenue
Pittsburgh, PA 15213
412-687-2990
www.fci.org/

Families and Work Institute (*Publication: Rethinking the Brain*)
267 Fifth Avenue, Floor Two
New York, NY 10016
212-465-2044
www.familiesandwork.org

Special Needs and At-Risk Children

Clearinghouse on Disability Information
U.S. Department of Education
550 12th Street SW, Room 5133
Washington, DC 20202-2250
202-245-7307
www.ed.gov/about/offices/list/osers/codi.html

First Signs, Inc.
P.O. Box 358
Merrimac, MA 01860
978-346-4380
info@firstsigns.org
www.firstsigns.org

Child Welfare Information Gateway
Children's Bureau/ACYF
1220 Maryland Avenue SW, Eighth Floor
Washington, DC 20034
703-385-7565
800-394-3366
www.childwelfare.gov

National Center for Children in Poverty
Columbia University Mailman School of
Public Health
215 W. 125th Street, Third Floor
New York, NY 10027
646-284-9600
www.nccp.org

The National Center for Learning Disabilities
381 Park Avenue South, Suite 1401
New York, NY 10016
212-545-7510
888-575-7373
www.ncld.org

The National Dissemination Center for Children
with Disabilities
PO Box 1492
Washington, DC 20013
800-695-0285
www.nichcy.org

National Child Welfare Resource Center for Adoption
Spaulding for Children
16250 Northland Drive, Suite 100
Southfield, MI 48075
248-443-7080
248-443-7099 (fax)
www.spaulding.org

Health and Safety

American Academy of Pediatrics
141 Northwest Point Boulevard
Elk Grove Village, IL 60007-1098
847-434-4000
847-434-8000 (fax)
www.aap.org

American Association of Poison Control Centers
3201 New Mexico Avenue, Suite 330
Washington, DC 20016
202-362-7217
800-222-1222 (information)
info@aapcc.org
www.aapcc.org

National Resource Center for Health and Safety
in Child Care and Early Education
Anschutz Medical Campus
Campus Mail Stop F541
P.O. Box 6508
Aurora, CO 80045-0508
800-598-5437
nrc.uchsc.edu

National SIDS/Infant Death Resource Center
8280 Greensboro Drive, Suite 300
McLean, VA 22101
866-866-7437
www.sidscenter.org

Ounce of Prevention Fund
33 W. Monroe St., Suite 2400
Chicago, IL 60603-5400
312-922-3863
www.ounceofprevention.org

Standards

U.S. Consumer Product Safety Commission
4330 East West Highway
Bethesda, MD 20814
800-638-2772
800-638-8270 (Hearing Impaired)
www.cpsc.gov

United States Access Board
1331 F Street NW, Suite 1000
Washington, DC 20004-1111
800-872-2253
www.access-board.gov

Prime Times CD Supplements

Parent Partnership
    Exercises
        Aligning Program Practices with Parent Wishes
        Conducting a Successful Parent Conference
        How to Conduct Parent-Teacher Conferences
        Making Separation and Reunion Prime Times for Children and Their Parents
        Note to Parents: How Our Feelings about Transition Can Affect Our Children
        Note to Staff: Helping Parents with Separation
        Parent Partnership: A Continuum of Quality
        Parent's Handbook: Sample Table of Contents
        Successful Tours for Prospective Parents
        Twenty Steps to a Full Partnership with Parents
        Twenty Steps to Partnership with Parents: Child/Family Checklist in Child's File
    Handouts
        Insider's Guide to Quality Child Care
        Note to Parents: Children Who Bite
        Note to Parents: Daily Separation
        Note to Parents: Disciplining an Infant—Are You Kidding?
        Note to Parents: End-of-the-Day Reunions: They Do Love You Best!
        Note to Parents: Good-bye Diapers, Hello Underwear—Ideas for Successful Toilet Training
        Note to Parents: Living with Diversity
        Note to Parents: Moving On Up to the Twos
        Note to Parents: Primary Caregiving
        Note to Parents: Temper Tantrums
        Note to Parents: Toilet-Training Accidents: Successful Ways to Cope
        Preschool Partnership Agreement for Success in School and Life
    Questionnaires
        Family Room Departure Questionnaire
        Individual Personal-Care Plan for Infants and Toddlers
        New Family Homebase Satisfaction Questionnaire
        Parent-Staff Conference: Report Form
    Sample Forms
        Sample Director's Third-Week Note to New Family
        Sample First-Day Congratulations Note or E-mail
        Sample First-Day E-mail and Photo

Policies and Procedures
    Handouts
        Employee Counseling Procedure
        Recruiting and Hiring Tips
    Postings
        Teacher Reactions to Children's Distress: Performance Guidelines
        Toddlers' Rules of Property
    Questionnaires
        Tips for Supervisors: Questions for Poorly Performing Employees
    Sample Forms
        Individual Personal-Care Plan for Infants and Toddlers
        Observation Slip (long form)

Observation Slip (short form)

Orientation Checklist for New Staff

Ouch Report

Parent's Handbook: Sample Table of Contents

Parent-Staff Conference: Report Form

Planning the Environment and Experiences: Infants and Toddlers

Planning the Environment and Experiences: Twos

Rate Yourself as a Supervisor

Staff Handbook: Sample Table of Contents

Staff Resignation/Termination of Employment

Teacher Evaluation

Program Assessment

Exercises

Beyond the Familiar Learning Center: Creating More Centers in Your Environment

Brainstorming Web

Continuum of Quality: Infant/Toddler Program Continuums

Five Phases of Planning for Infants, Toddlers, and Twos

How to Improve Your Indoor Space for Infants and Toddlers

Infant and Toddler Learning Centers

Parent Partnership: A Continuum of Quality

Planning the Environment and Experiences: Infants and Toddlers

Planning the Environment and Experiences: Twos

Observation Slip (long form)

Observation Slip (short form)

Twenty-five Ways to Improve Your Outdoor Space

Questionnaires

Aesthetically Pleasing Environments for Infants and Toddlers

Aligning Program Practices with Parent Wishes

Are You a Place for a Childhood?

Is Your Outdoor Learning Space a Great Place to Be an Infant or Toddler?

Making Prime Times of Toddler and Twos Mealtimes: A Quick Assessment

Quick Evaluation of Your Learning Centers: How Do You Rate?

Twenty Steps to Partnership with Parents: Child/Family Checklist in Child's File

Sample Forms

Highlights of the Day

Infant Daily Experience Sheet

Objectives for Individual Children

Toddler Daily Experience Sheet

Staff Assessment

Exercises

Do I Maximize Learning Experiences for Infants and Toddlers?

Employee Counseling Procedure

Recruiting and Hiring Tips

Tips for Supervisors: Constructive Criticism

Tips for Supervisors: Questions for Poorly Performing Employees

Questionnaires

Basic Knowledge for Primary Caregivers: Ten Things Primary Caregivers Should Know about Children and Families

Basic Responsibilities for Primary Caregivers: Ten Things Primary Caregivers Should Do

Index